REVUE AFRICAINE DES SCIENCES JURIDIQUES

AFRICAN JOURNAL OF LAW

N° 1/2016

UNE PUBLICATION DE L'UNIVERSITÉ DE YAOUNDÉ II

Faculté des Sciences Juridiques et Politiques

RASJ

L'Harmattan

UNIVERSITÉ DE YAOUNDÉ II

UNIVERSITY OF YAOUNDF II

FACULTÉ DES SCIENCES JURIDIQUES FT POLITIQUES

FACULTY OF LAWS AND POLITICAL SCIENCES

ORGANISATION DE LA REVUE AFRICAINE DE SCIENCES JURIDIQUES

5-7, rue de l'Ecole-Polytechnique, 75005 Paris

http://www.harmattan.fr
diffusion.harmattan@wanadoo.fr
harmattan1@wanadoo.fr

ISBN : 978-2-343-10411-9
EAN : 9782343104119

SOMMAIRE

I.

DROIT PRIVÉ

UNVEILING LOCAL CONTENT PROVISIONS IN EXTRACTIVE SECTOR LAWS IN CAMEROON: PERSPECTIVES FOR SUSTAINABILITY OF NATIONAL LIVELIHOODS

Christopher F. TAMASANG[1]

Abstract : This paper sets out to recognize and acknowledge the emergence, within the extractive sector, of the all-important concept of local content now *en vogue* in current literature on the extractive sector and to investigate how useful the law can be in the development of the concept in resources-rich countries that have, unfortunately, become 'resource curse' countries. Picking examples of legal provisions of the extractive sector laws in Cameroon, the study unveils Mining, Oil and Gas legislations with specific attention to local content development considering the fact that a veritable local content development law and policy can, without doubts, contribute enormously to economic growth and enhance the sustainability of national livelihoods. It emerges from the statutory interpretation and analysis that the extractive sector laws are not only dispersed and superfluous but are also fraught with lots of gaps rendering local content compliance and observance by multinational corporations, and enforcement by the State machinery a difficult task. The study then recommends a separate, comprehensive and more viable legislation entirely devoted to address local content questions in order to better enhance sustainable economic growth and development and improve on the livelihoods of Cameroonians.

---

[1] PhD (Natural Resources Law), Senior Lecturer, Faculty of Laws and Political Science, University of Yaounde II, Soa. I must seize this opportunity to acknowledge Mr Nkumbe Ebong Mekede, a PhD Student and a Graduate Teaching Assistant in the Faculty of Laws and Political Science of the University of Yaounde II who assisted me in gathering data for the research.

Key words: extractive sector, laws, legislation, local content, national livelihoods, sovereignty, sustainable economic development, value addition.

1. Introduction

1.1. Context and rationale to the study

Africa is a top producer of several non-renewable natural resources in the world. Unfortunately, most of such extractives are exported without significant value-addition on the continent. The exploitation of extractives has created an "*enclaved*" sector that is poorly linked to the rest of the economy. It has failed to foster upstream, downstream and perhaps side stream and lateral investments that should promote a broad-based economic transformation, create opportunities and industries that add value to the primary commodities.[2] The adoption by African Heads of State of the African Mining Vision (AMV) in 2009 is seen as an important milestone in this direction. Indeed, the AMV as an African initiative is a clear demonstration of Africa's desire to enhance the development of non-renewable natural resources and forge the continent's development pathway. Hence, the initiative advocates for a transparent, equitable and optimal exploitation of mineral resources to underpin development and promote local processing and value addition of raw materials to build human, financial, and institutional capital that can outlast the exhaustible resources.[3] It calls for an improvement of the value chain and diversification of economies to reduce dependence on natural resources and in particular, resources from the extractive sector.

---

[2] The result is less diversified and commodity-dependent economies. According to the World Bank (2012), poverty rates in resource-rich African countries have generally fallen at a slower pace than those in countries without resources. Many countries in Africa suffer from this resource curse paradox widely documented in literature, where countries with abundant natural resources tend to register lower economic growth than those without these natural resources. Recently, the African Union, in its Common African Position (CAP) on the post-2015 Development Agenda3, reechoed these concerns "... that the benefits of Africa's resources have been concentrated in a few enclave sectors and limited to narrow segments of society, thus exacerbating poverty, inequality and fragility".

[3] Available at (www.worldminighistory.com) last consulted on December 12th, 2015.

Prompted by the boom in the mineral and oil commodity prices in the mid-2000s and by the sharp rise in the profits of resource companies while resource-rich countries remained poor, governments in countries such as Nigeria and Brazil began to set up local content requirements in laws and policies. Since then, local content policies have spread rapidly, often broadened to include value addition, and have now entered the agendas of most resource-rich countries.[4] According to Mercedes E. Milam[5], what was once a "*gentlemen's agreement,*" is now increasingly a binding constraint on resource companies. He has further underscored the evolutionary nature of local content policies and the role of knowledge with other countries in shaping what local content means, what works and what does not work and why.[6]

It is estimated that 90 percent of resource-driven countries now have legal provisions on local content[7] although in different legal architectures. It is therefore interesting to note that local content and value addition strategy are some of the methods which resource-rich countries are adopting to increase the benefits to their economies from resource extraction, beyond securing optimal rents (royalties, taxes, shares, and other revenues). Consequently, delivering local benefits in the communities where extractives companies operate is no longer a choice. It is a necessity and one that is increasingly mandated by law. In the new competitive landscape of waning supply and increasing demand for mineral resources, companies in the extractive industries face rising expectations to do more than simply mitigate negative impacts, serve as sources of tax/royalty revenue, and act as good neighbours. Today, business success depends upon the ability of

---

[4] Available at (http: // www.acetforafrica.org) last consulted on January 10th, 2016.

[5] Mercedes E. Milam is one of the Authorities in the Ministry of Mines, Industry and Energy of Equatorial Guinea. He made this statement during a conference in Vienna, Austria on Local Content Policies in Oil, Gas and Mining Sectors. The conference ran from the September 30 to October 1 2013. Attended that meeting were top global and regional institutional representatives from the World Bank's Oil, Gas and Mining Policy Unit, Sustainable Development Network, The African Petroleum Producers' Association and Exxon Mobil Corporation.

[6] Ibid

[7] McKinsey Global Institute (2013), "Reversing the curse: Maximizing the potential of Resource-driven Economies," A report published in Washington, D.C. p 3.

companies to develop local talent, build a competitive local supplier base, and deliver lasting socio-economic benefits to the areas where they operate. The growing number of reported cases of project interruptions due to non-technical risks including stakeholder pressures, socio-economic conditions and national politics is a testament to this.[8]

Some companies have responded to non-technical risks through isolated investments in community development. Increasingly, however, companies are finding that they can drive more sustainable and commercial value with integrated investment approaches to community engagement by leveraging company resources (from the asset to corporate level), third-party expertise, civil society and multi-lateral partnerships, and proactively developing local capabilities with strategic planning.[9] Although increasingly required by law in the mining, oil and gas industries, local content represents the most strategic contribution a company can make to securing its social license[10] to operate and leaving a positive legacy in countries.[11] If designed and implemented effectively, local content offers an opportunity to unlock mutual benefit from resource extraction by focusing on companies' core competencies and supporting long-term economic growth prospects. It is particularly relevant to large-scale projects in the mining, oil and gas industries, yet the drivers, approaches, and tools for implementation can vary between these industries.[12]

As the demand for scarce resources grows, companies are operating in areas that have yet to see widespread benefits from oil and mineral extraction and have experienced what many perceive to be significant negative environmental and social impacts. In response, both communities

---

[8] Analysis by Environmental Resources Management of delays associated with a sample of 190 of the world's largest oil and gas projects (as ranked by Goldman Sachs) found that 73 percent of project delays were due to "above-ground" or non-technical risk, including stakeholder resistance, compared to 21 percent due to technical risk.

[9] Hackenbruch, D and Pluess, J (2O11), *Commercial value from Local Benefits in the Extractive Industries: Local Conten*t, 1st edition, Boston Press, p.5.

[10] See Dashaco, J.T. and Bande G. M.T. (2015), 'Social Licence and its Bearing in Cameroon, in: African Journal of Law, Numero Special, l'Harmattan, Paris, pp 75 -118 for a more detailed understanding of the concept of social licence,

[11]Ibid, p.15.

[12] Ibid.

and governments are seeking ways to capture more value from their resource wealth, leading to a more competitive landscape and higher expectations on international companies. Local content provision measures aim to create backward linkages such as reliance on inputs from the local economy and local job creation, and increasing local participation through ownership and management; forward linkages such as processing sector output before exporting through the establishment of refineries, processing plants, petrochemical industries, and fertilizer production; and lateral linkages through transportation, communications, and financial services. From Angola to Indonesia, Nigeria to Timor-Leste, Trinidad and Tobago to Zimbabwe, the theory behind this paradigm shift in resource development is simple and laudable; the challenge is in the practice, so is the point of view of some authors.[13]

In Cameroon, within the mining, oil and gas sectors, the range of government actions to promote local content through existing pieces of legislation in force has been less satisfactory. As a matter of fact, there is need for a legislative review. Cameroon may be doing well in employment of local workers to some extent, but less so with service contracts, procurement of local goods, and local equity and management and is definitely falling short in technology transfer. The problem lies in the limited capacity and high costs of local companies, insufficient financial support, inadequate standards of certification, and inability of contractors to meet high industry standards. The prospects depend on how the industry, local businesses, and state institutions work together to overcome the obstacles facing local content opportunities.

Despite the strong contribution of oil in the State budget, development indicators continue to decline in Cameroon. Cameroon's growth rate fell to 3.5% between 2001 and 2007, and poverty and unemployment have increased. In addition, Cameroon ranks poorly in World Bank ratings on service delivery and Transparency International's Corruption Perceptions index. Although a marginal oil producer in Sub Saharan Africa, Cameroon's natural resource revenues are significant. Unfortunately, these revenues have failed to deliver poverty alleviation and improve national livelihoods.

[13] Available at (www.acetforafrica.org) last consulted on December 16th, 2015.

A recurring argument explaining the failure of oil to contribute to national development and poverty reduction in Cameroon is that decision-making in the oil sector is reserved for a selected group of authorities and political elites. For a long time, revenues were initially not even included in the government's national budget, but placed in an offshore account.[14] This practice continued until the late 1990s when oil revenues began to appear in the state budget under pressure from development partners and multilateral development institutions like the World Bank and IMF.[15] But the problem of translating such income into tangible benefits for local communities persists.[16] While companies face increasing competition in accessing resources, there are also more demands from stakeholders, particularly communities, to remedy the legacy of missed opportunities in translating resource wealth into widespread benefits for communities.[17] Mismanaged revenues by governments and entrenched corruption, combined with inefficiencies and poorly designed development projects, have limited opportunities for communities to reap direct local economic benefit of large-scale projects and have left many communities living in poverty[18] and other social degraded conditions. This has contributed to rising tensions among communities, resource companies, and governments. This is an important driver for rising expectations of companies, particularly in the mining industry, in which there are increasingly vocal communities backed by international NGOs, which have elevated community concerns to a global level and engaged media and end users in demands for more local benefits from resource extraction.[19] In sum, behind the above picture lies the real problem and it is that the extractive sector which can clearly make significant contributions to improving national livelihoods outside taxes, rents and royalties, has for a considerably long time been the exclusive business of the government and extractive companies not guided by clear

---

[14]Gauthier, B. and Zeufack, A. (2009), Governances and oil revenues in Cameroon, Oxcarre http://resources.revenuewatch.org/en/official-document/governance-and-oil-revenues-cameroon.

[15] Ibid.

[16] Ibid.

[17]Hackenbruch, D. and Pluess, J., op. cit, p. 34.

[18] Ibid.

[19] Ibid.

and comprehensive laws and policies to define and ensure effective implementation of local contents requirements, an imperative for the sustainability of national livelihoods. The objective of this paper is therefore to find out how the rich extractive sector in Cameroon, through legislative development, can be made to provide more than just taxes, royalties and rents to government but cross sector benefits by way of local content development and value addition.

1.2. Conceptual framework, relevant development related theories and methodology

A good number of countries from the developing world have discovered and are developing mining, oil and gas reserves. Stakeholders in such countries are anxious to obtain the highest benefits for their economies from the extraction of these exhaustible resources by elaborating comprehensive legal policies and options to achieve desired goals. One important theme of such policies is the so-called local content created by the sector; the extent to which the output of the extractive industry generates further benefits to the economy beyond the direct contribution of its value-added, as through links to other sectors.[20] Increasing local content is becoming a policy priority in many resource-rich developing countries, among both mature and recent entrants to the industry.[21] In this part of the paper, concern shall be had mainly on the real understanding of the concept of local content and value chain/addition in the mining, oil and gas sectors. We shall also attempt a discourse on sovereignty and sustainable economic development as relevant development related theories and finally unravel the methodology utilized in this piece of research endeavour.

1.2.1. Conceptual framework

1.2.1.1. Local Content Explained

The term local content is polysemy in nature. It is for this reason that within the extractive sector, it needs to be situated appropriately. Local content can refer to jobs or value-added that is created anywhere in the domestic economy as a result of the actions of an oil and gas company, or it

---

[20] Tardo, S. and Yahya, A. (2011), *"Local content policies in the Oil and Gas Sector": A World Bank study,* Greenleaf Publishing, Washington, DC, p.1

[21] Ibid.

can narrowly refer to jobs that are created in the neighbourhood of the mining, oil and gas production plant.[22] Local content may even refer to the provision, by the extractive companies, of infrastructure (schools, medical facilities) that is not an input into its own production but intended for the benefit of the local population (either of the nation generally or the neighbourhood of the installations). The term "*local content*" typically refers to the added value brought to a host country through the procurement of goods and services and local workforce development. Some companies expand this definition to include strategic community investments.[23] The World Bank defines local content broadly in terms of employment and procurement of inputs, as well as the basis of domestic ownership of firms.[24] The African Development Bank goes a step further to define "*local firm*" based on the place of registration, a majority of board members being nationals, and the proportion of shares held by nationals.[25] Generally, local content refers to the extent to which the exploitation of a natural resource benefits the economy beyond the revenue (rents, taxes and royalties) paid to the government, through upstream, downstream, side stream and lateral linkages.

Within Cameroon's extractive sector laws including systematically the Petroleum, Mining and Gas laws, the concept of local content has not been explicitly provided for especially in the Petroleum and Mining legislation. As far as the Mining and Petroleum legislation are concerned, local content development issues can only be tacitly inferred from them but this is dangerous because even express articulation and respect of local content provisions is still seriously problematic. It therefore becomes even more difficult where, as in the existing legislation on Petroleum and Mining, express local content provisions are clearly absent and if there exist any, it is only one of inference. However, some treatment of local content can be traced in the Gas legislation[26]. By way of definition, the Gas Code provides

---

[22] Ibid.

[23] Hackenbruch, D. and Pluess, J., op. cit, at p.3.

[24] Available at (www.aceforafrica.org), last consulted on December 4, 2015.

[25] Ibid.

[26] Law no 2012/6 OF April 19th, 2012 to institute the Gas Code and its enabling Instrument Decree No 2014/3438/PM du 16 fevrier 2014.

that local content refers to 'all activities relating to local capacity building, use of local industrial and service companies and the creation of measurable value added for the local economy'.[27] To prove the importance of this concept, the Enabling legislation to the application of the Gas Code retakes the definition of local content.[28]

With regard to the foregoing attempt at understanding the local content concept, one can state that Cameroon's extractive sector laws lacks comprehensiveness as far as the understanding of this concept is concerned in terms of the fact that clear definitional understanding is limited only to the Gas law and markedly absent in the Petroleum and Mining laws. In addition, it seems difficult to decipher effective enforcement mechanisms.

1.2.1.2. Local Content and the Value Chain

The extractive sector is spread along a value chain of recognizably different stages, some of which may even act as separate subsectors.[29] At each stage of the value chain, different technologies and inputs are utilized, so that the potential for local content enhancement is likely to be different along the value chain.[30] Over time, as the oil industry develops from its initial stages, the nature and extent of local content is likely to vary; some stages lend themselves more to the use of local inputs while others tend to rely more on imported inputs.[31] The ability of the local economy to supply these various inputs also depends on its level of development and industrialization. In the Cameroonian experience, it is noted that value chain or value addition in the development of local content in the extractive sector and in particular the Mining and Petroleum sub-sectors, is significantly minimal especially given the weak regulatory role of the law in such sub-sectors. For the Gas sub-sector, there is provision for local content which is expected to enhance value addition but again, it seems to us immature to draw conclusions on the effective application of the law in this

---

[27] S. 3, paragraph 9.

[28] Art 2(i) of Decree No 2014 du 16 Fevrier 2016 for the implementation of the Gas Code 2012.

[29] Hackenbruch, D. and Pluess, J. (2O11), *Commercial value from Local Benefits in the Extractive Industries: Local Conten*t, BSR Press, op. cit, at p.10.

[30] Ibid.

[31] Ibid.

direction for the simple reason that it is only a year and half that the law actually entered into force.

1.2.2. Relevant Development Related Theories

For obvious reasons, this paper has as a primary theoretical foundation, the theory of sovereignty which has been posited by renowned writers in International Law several centuries ago[32] and more recently[33] too and which is also enshrined in many international legal instruments of differing strength.[34] States therefore have the sovereign right to exploit their natural resources pursuant to their own environmental policies but should be careful that this does not cause harm to another state and the whole idea behind this is the enhancement of sustainable development and improvement of the livelihoods of nationals. The study equally builds on sustainable economic development theory propounded by leading natural resources experts.[35] The study relies on the fact that a well thought out local content policy and legal framework can enhance sustainable economic growth and hence improve on the livelihoods of Cameroonian population.

1.2.3. Methodology

The methodology utilized in this write-up consists in data collection and in the treatment of such data. Data collection consisted essentially in the reading of records relating to natural resources generally and the extractive sector in particular. Over and above the reading of records, we endeavoured to identify statutory instruments from the extractive sector. This constituted our main primary source of data. The paper attempts, in the treatment of secondary data collected, to review existing literature on the subject in order to determine the thinking and contribution of others on local content

---

[32] In Grotius, H. (1609), The Freedom of the Seas, N.Y.

[33] Notably, Winston, P., Nagan, A. and Haddad, M. (2012), Sovereignty in Theory and Practice, 13 San Diego Int'l LJ

[34] For instance, the Stockholm Declaration, Principle 21; The Rio Declaration, Principle 2, and the Convention on Biodiversity, Article 3

[35] See notably Esteves, A., Coyne B. and Moreno A. (2013), Local Content Initiatives: Enhancing the Subnational Benefits of the Oil, Gas, and Mining Sector, Natural Resource Governance Institute; Ovadia D.S. (2015), The Role of Local Content in Natural Resource-based Development, Osterreichische Entwicklungpolitik, Rohstoffe Und Entwicklung,

matters and from these, to make our own modest contribution to the understanding and advancement of the subject. In dealing with primary source of data, we basically utilized the statutory interpretation approach of the provisions of the extractive sector laws. This enabled us to unveil in each case, the intent of the legislator in the legal provision and to find out how feasibly applicable can such provisions be on the ground. The Institutional Strategic Approach consisted in analyzing the strategy and action plans of institutions whose work impact on the extractive sector, for instance the State, extractive companies and business and community organizations. In our thinking, such analysis could inform decision-makers on how local content issues could be properly addressed if sustainability of national livelihoods is anything to go by in Cameroon's extractive sector laws.

2. Local content provisions/stipulations in extractive sector laws and policies

As highlighted earlier, Cameroon's extractive sector has segregated laws and policies but such segregation is justified by the fact that there exist three different sub-sectors, to wit, the Petroleum, Gas, and Hard Mineral sub-sectors, each with its own specificities; and equally because the sector is truly broad but also undoubtedly sensitive. Albeit broad and sub-sector specific, there are however, certain matters that run across the board. One of such matters is, in our view, local content. What this means is that the extractive sector in Cameroon as elsewhere can only make its significant contribution to the national economy and sustain national livelihoods if local content considerations are given the widest imaginable and practical attention in the development of extractive laws and why not even treat it as a transversal issue. Now, to demonstrate that there is insufficient legislative attention to local content, where this has been manifested, we shall proceed to unveil the legislative initiatives in each of the sub-sectors in terms of what may qualify as local content requirements.

2.1. Provisions on Employment, Professional Training and other Social Infrastructural Development

The first and most salient aspect of local content development is undoubtedly employment, professional training and development of social infrastructure. In all economies of developing countries in general and

Cameroon in particular, employment, professional training and the development of social infrastructure is seriously problematic. This ought not to be the case at least with resources-rich countries such as Cameroon. Unfortunately, this has remained a critical issue in such countries. Current thinking is that the extractive sector can provide a milestone in the direction of addressing such problems. It is probably for this reason that some provisions can be discerned in the Petroleum, Mining and Gas legislations.

Beginning with the Petroleum Code of 1999[36] for instance, local content requirements with respect to the employment and professional training of Cameroonians are found in Section 77. That section provides that *the holder of a petroleum contract and its sub-contractors employ in priority qualified personnel of Cameroonian nationality for purposes of their petroleum operations.* Pertaining to professional or vocational training, the same section of the Code further provides that "*as soon as the petroleum operations start, the holder must set up and finance a training programme for Cameroonian personnel of all qualifications, according to the terms and conditions specified in the Petroleum Contract*". With regard to the Mining Code,[37] issues pertaining to the employment of locals or nationals,[38] professional training[39]

---

[36] Cameroonian Petroleum Code is referred to as Law N° 99/013 of December 22, 1999 to institute the Petroleum Code.

[37] Law no 2010/011 of 29 July 2010 modifying and completing certain provisions of law no 2001/ 01 of April 16, 2001 to institute the Mining Code.

[38] Mining companies are called upon to employ the local population in the unfolding of some of their operations. But this particular obligation is not fully respected. For instance, the manpower of C&K Mining Inc. is divided into a local, national and foreign staff. Regarding the national workforce, in contrast to the 57 national workers the company employed in 2011, in 2013 it is composed of 60-63 contractual employees, including temporary and seasonal workers. Positions of responsibility are primarily entrusted to staff with the required skills and a mastery of the English language. It is important to note that no Baka, who are the indigenous people of the project area, is employed by C&K despite the agreement signed in April 2013 between C&K Mining Inc. and the Ministry of Employment and Vocational Training (MINEFOP) through the National Employment Fund (FNE), whose objective is to ensure a fair recruitment nationwide.

[39] Capacity building (knowledge transfer and/or training) is an essential element of local participation. Indeed, a project can only be beneficial to a community if it can continue the said activity or those related to it. The Korea Mining Incorporation trains its employees on certain working techniques specific to the mining industry and the driving of their heavy

and social activities are dealt with in Section 16 (g).[40] Within the province of local content development laws in the extractive sector in Cameroon, we do inferred provisions relating to employment, professional training and the development of social infrastructures. In fact, section 62 of the Cameroon Gas Code[41] states that the development of national gas resources must be accompanied by a "*local content*" component that specifies the benefits of gas projects for Cameroon's economic, social, industrial and technological development. Local content referred to in section 62 above must normally comprise a human resources development aspect and a local enterprises and industries development aspect.

Still within the framework of employment and professional training, section 63(2) of the Gas Code of 2012 provides that local content include notably a vocational and technical training programme for Cameroonians nationals in order to upgrade their skills in gas trade and a programme of recruitment of Cameroonians nationals at all duty positions and at all levels in gas companies signing the gas agreement, or any other structure involved in the gas sector. Section 65 of the Cameroon Gas Code on its part states that gas companies must as a matter of priority employ staff of Cameroonian nationality with the required competence.

From the foregoing prescriptions of the Petroleum, Mining and Gas laws, the following analysis could be helpful in attempting to unveil the meaning that lies behind the provisions of the law in respect to employment, professional training and perhaps other social infrastructure. *Primo*, it is interesting to know that all the extractive laws allude to employment, professional training and social infrastructure and as highlighted earlier, these are disturbing issues in economies intending to be emergent in the next decades and consequently such legislative efforts can only be lauded. But it is equally interesting to note very quickly that but for

---

engine vehicles. However, the question of choice of individuals to train, the nature of the training and sustainability of acquired skills after training remains.

[40] It is clearly stated that an agreement may be concluded between the holder of an exploration permit and the State in order to develop and mine or finance the mining of a discovered mineral. This agreement may include among others provisions relating to obligations concerning employment, vocational training and social activities.

[41] Law no 2012/6 of April 19, 2012 to institute the Gas Code.

the Gas legislation, the Petroleum and Mining laws are very peripheral on issues of employment, professional training and other social infrastructures let alone mention of such matters as local content requirements. This view is glaring from the fact that these matters are dealt with in the extractive sector laws proper and no mention is made of same in the enabling instruments. Of course, we are conversant with the fact that in proper legislative crafting process, while the law alludes to these issues, the details for its understanding and effective implementation are addressed in the enabling instruments. In the case of the Petroleum and Mining legislations, this is markedly absent. The Gas legislation is more comforting than the other two just mentioned. It actually articulates not only on the local content requirement but has really devoted a whole section on local content meanwhile in the Petroleum and Mining legislations, local content requirements are not only inferential but also scantily dotted. A careful perusal of the Gas legislation reveals that the law does not just delve into prescribing expressly employment, vocational training and other social infrastructural matters to be undertaken by the gas companies intending to operate in Cameroon but actually opens up by stating first what local content is, in the context of gas exploitation.

Secundo, local content, as indicated earlier, means the recruitment and use of local manpower and the development of their skills. Unfortunately, while extractive sector legislations prescribe employment, professional training and development of social infrastructures to accommodate them, they leave a vacuum in terms of the percentage of persons to be recruited and trained, the training programmes and timetables in each case. By the tenors of article 77 of the Petroleum Code for instance, mention is made of the establishment of training programme and the consequent finance of all Cameroonian personnel of all qualifications under conditions fixed by the Petroleum Contract. Although, this provision of the Code must be lauded, one must not hesitate to state that these being pertinent issues, they ought generally to be addressed by the enabling provisions at least by indicating the percentage of manpower to be recruited and trained before allowing the individual petroleum contracts to determine the specific training programmes and timeframes. The average Cameroonian is interested in seeing this at least in the enabling legislation and all the more so as the contracts signed between the state and the multinationals especially petroleum contracts are usually not accessible to the public by way of publication for the citizens to be informed about this fact. Furthermore, even if the public is allowed to access the contracts, this should be a condition precedent to signing the contract and not subsequent to it as this will create no impact for an already negotiated and signed contract. Indeed, the justification for insisting on this percentage issue is that in the case of industrial mining for example, the needs became critically important.

However, in the light of the Information Technology Age, the above arguments on employment and professional training in connection with local content provisions may actually be difficult to implement with the advent of machine automation[42] where jobs and wages are seriously threatened. Most of the work in industry today is performed by machines designed with intent to replace man and its efficiency has been proved in many cases. The danger is therefore that very little recourse is made to services hitherto performed by man. This being the case, the whole idea of extractive sector laws insisting on the recruitment and training of local manpower and our suggestion that the percentage of such manpower be mentioned at least in the enabling instrument to the law and also the contract, is altogether frustrated. What must then be the way forward for the Cameroonian extractive sector legislator? It seems to us safe to say that the legislator must reconcile, in the context of local content laws, recruitment, training and social infrastructural development with technology transfer provisions in such a way that technology, which is inevitable here, does not completely replace manpower as is increasingly the case in the developed world.

Another challenge in relation to the provision on employment and training in particular for local content development is the misalignment between objectives and instruments. If a policy maker thinks that there is an

---

[42] For a more detailed understanding of machine automation and its impact on jobs and wages, see generally, Feng, A. and Graetz, G. (2011), Rise of the Machine: The effects on Labor –Saving Innovations on Jobs and Wages, Discussion Paper No. 8836, Bonn; Acemoglu, D. and Restrepo P. (2015), The race between Man and Machine: Implication of Technology for growth, factor shares and Employment, Michigan; Miller, B. and Atkinson, D.R. (2013), Are Robeots taking over Jobs or Making them?, ITIF, USA.

externality or a failure, he should actually ensure that there is indeed an externality and that the instrument chosen corrects the externality.[43] For example, if the labour force is not adequately trained to satisfy the requirements of the extractive sector, the policy maker should first establish whether training would be sufficient or if the situation demands rather structural changes to the country's educational system. If training would overcome the shortfall, imposing minimum local employment targets on extractive companies may not provide the optimal outcome.[44]

2.2. Provisions/Stipulations on the development of Local Entreprises/Industries and Local transformation of Products

2.2.1. Stipulations on the Development of Local Entreprises/Industries

An important trend in local content development in recent times is the assurance that local enterprises/industries expand as a result of the rush by multinationals to exploit natural resources in resources-rich countries of the developing world. Of course, this should make sense as the sustainability of national livelihoods depends largely on local industry growth and not on multinationals that come for a purpose and leave as soon as such a purpose has been achieved. So therefore, the extractive sector legislator in particular must ensure, by inserting provisions in extractive sector laws, on the obligation of multinationals to partner with local enterprises/industries. The present extractive sector laws in Cameroon are to an extent, emphatic on this albeit evasively. The Petroleum Code for instance, conditions the award of contracts for construction and the supply of goods and services to

---

[43] See generally, Local content in the Oil and Gas Sector, World Bank Studies, Washington DC, 2013

[44] Policies to support the training of nationals would be more closely related to the externality in question. Furthermore, as argued by Weitzman (1974), when there is uncertainty about costs and benefits, price interventions tend to produce results closer to the optimal result than quantity regulations. In our example, incentives and/or subsidies for training may produce better results than mandatory requirements. A similar case can be made about market failures. Consider MNCs' superior market power. The imposition of minimum local content targets may not produce the optimal outcome. The problem may be a lack of adequate competition regulation and/or market supervision. Therefore, regulations that try to ensure full, fair, and reasonable access to procurement opportunities for domestic suppliers might generate outcomes that are closer to the optimal solution.

Cameroonian companies safe where the terms are competitive with regard to quality, price, quantities, delivery, conditions for payment and after-sale-service.[45] The Mining Code on its part provides that the Mining Agreement may be concluded between the holder of an exploration permit and the State for the development and working of a new mine or financing thereof. The said agreement must in particular provide for: …relations with supplier and sub-contractors…[46] Although one cannot deny the intention of the legislator to enhance the growth of local enterprises/industries from the consequence of foreign investors in the Petroleum and Mining sectors, one must be quick to state that such intent is so skeletally expressed in the Mining Code and may tempt one to wonder whether effective enforcement can truly follow. This wonder is even stronger as the scope and content of such relations is not defined by an enabling instrument but may, according to the wordings of the Mining Code, be done by the so-called Mining Agreement which, as earlier stated, is a closed arrangement. On the part of the Petroleum Code provisions, a reading of it could suggest that where the Cameroonian companies are not competitive in terms of the quality and quantity of services required by the petroleum companies and the subcontractors, the latter could get those services from companies situated out of Cameroon. In fact, it does not suffice for the law to insist on holders and subcontractors to grant contracts for the construction and supply of goods and services when the terms are competitive, but it is more important for the State of Cameroon to create an enabling environment to make the local enterprises and industries more competitive so that the development of local enterprises and industries be more holistic and make local content to be more properly felt.

However, on this subject, the Gas Code appears to have made more realistic though incomplete in-roots as it provides that "local content must include notably; a programme and conditions for giving priority to local enterprises with the required capacities for the supply of goods, products, materials, tools, equipment and service delivery"[47]. It further states that,

[45] See s. 76 of the Petroleum Code

[46] See s. 16(new)(1) paragraph 8 of Law No 2010/011 of 29 July 2010 to amend and supplement certain provision of Law No 2001/1 of April 2001:Mining Code.

[47] See s. 63(1)

conditions for the periodic assessment of the capacities of local enterprises that can take part in the construction operation and the maintenance of specific gas installations and, as the case may be, a plan for the development and upgrading of enterprises lacking such capacities.[48] It does not end there. The Code continues to provide that: in awarding contracts, gas companies and their subcontractors are bound to give preference to companies under Cameroonian Law that meet international standards for constructions, service delivery of materials, equipment and products relating to gas activities.[49]

A reading of the above provision of the Gas Code in connection with the development of local enterprises and industries clearly indicates that there is some sort of a will to develop the local enterprises and industries but, a profound examination of the said dispensation gives the impression that for those gas companies and their sub-contractors to ever give preference to Cameroonian local enterprises and industries, the latter must indeed meet the standards set by the gas companies. Otherwise, the so-called preferential treatment to be granted to them is merely a farfetched requirement on the part of the Gas Code. By the way, the main activities observed falling within the ambit of enhancing the development of local enterprises by sub-contracting is so far limited to the completion of the environmental and social impact assessment (ESIA) by Soft Business Management Consulting Group which is a Cameroonian consulting firm based in Yaoundé.[50] The Korea Mining Incorporation also affirms that they use dynamite supplied by a local subcontractor.[51] The question however, is whether sub-contracting with local enterprises is a choice on the part of the multinational once the latter are qualified? The answer is obviously negative. One can therefore logically question the non-involvement of local suppliers in the construction of the base camp of the Korea Mining company and on the origin of the materials used to build them. Grounded on such analysis, it may be safe to state that the local participation requirements for partnership by way of sub-

[48] See s. 63 paragraph d

[49] See s. 66(1)

[50] Nguiffo, S. and Bamenjo, J. (2013), The Monitoring of Social Obligations of Mining Companies in Cameroon, op cit, at p.20

[51] Ibid.

contracting for instance are insufficient and may not as such help to create local wealth.

2.2.2. Stipulations on Local Transformation of Products

The whole philosophy behind local transformation of products is relatively recent. The trend has from time immemorial generally been for multinationals to come in, extract natural resources and proceed to transform them to finished goods outside the resource-rich country. Today, local transformation is founded on the fact that when imposed, local entreprises benefit in terms of services, the state equally benefits as taxes on such transformation processes are paid, and nationals benefit as jobs are created, lending more credence to the legislator's insistence on employment and others just discussed above. The result of all of these is contribution to economic growth of the country and consequently improved and sustained national livelihoods. The first time the Cameroonian legislator considered local transformation of exploited natural resources as one instrument of economic development was in 1994. That was in the so-called Forestry Law.[52] The extractive sector legislator has borrowed this spirit so much so that the extractive sector laws equally make allowance for local transformation of products. In this respect, section 16 (paragraph 11) (new) of the Mining Code for instance, focuses on local transformation. That provision actually places a floor of at least 15% of the minerals extracted by mining companies in Cameroon to be transformed locally. But it must be stated that the transformation can only take place where there exist the required facilities, equipment and technical knowhow to unfold with it.[53]

---

[52] Law No. 94/001 of 20 January 1994 to lay down Regulations on Forestry, Wildlife and Fisheries Resources, s. 71(1) and (2) and Decree No 95-531-PM of 23 August 1995 to determine conditions of implementation of forestry regulations, s. 116(1) and (2).

[53] It is therefore incumbent on the competent authorities to set forth the needed human and material resources to ensure the proper transformation of at least 15% of the minerals extracted by the mining companies as the law requires. Perhaps, it is for this reason that Assistance for Artisanal Mining (CAPAM) was created and given the needed resources to processed gold and other minerals. But this can only be effective and efficient where the extractive companies do declare all their extractions so that the 15% required by the law for local transformation actually takes place. Local transformation shall equally be land marking as already mentioned with the existence of adaptive tools to this end. In the

However, the experience in the forestry sector has demonstrated that the beginning was not easy but with the passage of time, the process has taken roots and it is hoped that this will be more facilitated in the mining sector.

2.3. Stipulations on Technology Transfer

Technology transfer has been en vogue in many international discourses since the Rio encounter of 1992. During discussions in that meeting, it emerged that technology transfer to developing countries is critical in any efforts to foster sustainable development including the exploitation of natural resources of a country. Hence, the Convention on Biological Diversity signed in 1992 obliges contracting parties to take legislative, administrative or policy measures, as appropriate with the aim that the private sector facilitates access to, joint development and transfer of technology referred to in paragraph 1 of the Convention for the benefit of both governmental institutions and private sector of developing countries.[54] This provision of the Convention actually fits into the situation under study in the sense that Cameroon, which is a contracting party to the convention, has taken legislative, policy or administrative measures through its extractive sector laws, and the aim is to have the private sector (extractive multinationals for instance) facilitate access to technology transfer for the benefit of both governmental institutions (the ministries, public and para-public) and the local enterprises as private sector. Whether the legislative and policy initiative regarding such technology is sufficiently wide enough to cover meaningful local content development is a question that will be answered in the next paragraph. But just before that, it is probably important to answer a preliminary question. What really is technology transfer? It is the process of transferring skills, knowledge, technologies, methods of manufacturing, and samples of manufacturing among institutions to ensure that scientific and technological developments are accessible to a wider range of users who can then further develop and exploit the technology into new products, processes, applications, materials or services.[55]

---

absence of the needed material resources and technical knowhow, transformation shall merely be an illusion.

[54] See article 16(1) and (4) of that convention

[55] Available at www.aceforafrica.org, last consulted on December 4, 2015

In the light of the foregoing analysis, it becomes plausible to investigate the appropriateness of the legislative and policy measures taken by the Cameroonian extractive sector legislator in answer to the convention's prescriptions and realities in the exploitation of mineral resources. In the Mining Code for example, one can infer technological and knowledge transfer. It is therein provided that the application for a mining permit...must be submitted in triplicate... alongside with...a statement giving details of the applicant's technical and financial resources[56]. This means that the Mining Code places as a condition *sine qua non* for an applicant for a mining permit, prove of the existence of sound and adapted technology which of course, shall be transferred to the country once the mining permit has been signed by the President of the Republic.

A number of concerns have not been addressed by the Mining legislation. One, what kind of technology transfer does the legislator envisage for a proper local content development for the improvement of national livelihoods? Is it the vertical or horizontal[57] technology transfer? It appears from the scanty provision of the code that this is to be determined by the multinational exploiter of the extractive resource because even the enabling legislation to the Mining Code which ought to have clarified such an issue is, unfortunately, completely silent on the point. But we are of the opinion that the law should integrate horizontal technology transfer, details of which should be carved out in the enabling instrument to the Mining Code if local content development must only be addressed in each of the extractive legislation. In any case, capacity building is at the centre of this

---

[56] See s. 45 paragraph 4 of the Code

[57] Vertical technology transfer refers to that technology transfer where the multinational brings in technology, direct nationals to and around the use and not training them on how to acquire and use the skills after their departure. Those who brought the technology use same to achieve their objectives and thereafter they go away with their skills and the nationals remain as blank as they were before the so called technology transfer. Horizontal technology transfer on the other hand refers to transfer of technology where the multinationals bring in the latter, train nationals and equip them with the necessary skill on how to use the technology in such a way that after their departure, nationals remain with the knowledge and skills and can be able use this for national development and improvement of national livelihoods.

kind of technology transfer.[58] Technological and knowledge transfer can involve licensing agreements or setting up joint ventures and partnerships to share both risks and rewards of bringing new technologies.[59] Two, even with the scanty provision on technology transfer, one is at lost as to who determines the appropriateness of the technology to be transferred, who monitors the effective transfer of such technology and who and how is reporting done at the level of improvement on national livelihoods. These are all pertinent concerns which in our humble view, would have be taken care of by the enabling legislation to the Mining Code. Unfortunately again, this is not the case.

It is interesting to note that the Petroleum Code does not allude to transfer of technology especially in the upstream sector. As indicated above, the only allusion made in the Code from which one can infer local content is that relating to sub-contracting construction and supply of local materials to local enterprises.[60] Technology transfer was not envisaged at all in this Code. Meanwhile, at the time of drafting the Code, technology transfer matters were already hotly debated in the international[61] and national circles. So, whatever the reason that may ground such an oversight, we cannot hesitate to hold that it is serious enough in the light of present day developments in that domain of the subsector. Then of course, it is consensus thinking that these sloppy provisions unrelated to technology

---

[58] Indeed, capacity building ensures that a project remains beneficial to a community if it can continue the said activity or those related to it . The Korea Mining Incorporation trains its employees on certain working techniques specific to the mining industry and the driving of their heavy engine vehicles. However, the question of choice of individuals to train, the nature of the training and sustainability of acquired skills after training remains.

[59]When we talk of technology transfer, it can either be horizontal transfer or vertical transfer. Horizontal transfer is the movement of technologies from one area to another. Vertical transfer on its part occurs when technologies are moved from applied research center to research and development departments.

[60] See for details article 76 and 77 of the Code

[61] See Hunter, D., James Salzman, and Durwood Zaelke (1998), International Environmental Law and Policy, Foundation Press, N.Y. p 884. Although discussed with specific focus on transfer of technology for the handling and treatment of waste, it must be understood that in the domain of petroleum exploration and exploitation, a lot of pollution occur by way of waste.

transfer may not enhance veritable local content development in Cameroon and consequently frustrate the improvement of national livelihoods.

Still on the technology transfer front, the Gas Code on its part seems to have been more ambitious than the Petroleum and Mining Codes. In this respect, Section 67 of the Gas Code is to the effect that gas companies are bound to submit to the State and execute, according to their priorities, a technological and knowledge transfer programme related to their activities in a bid to encourage, facilitate and enable the gradual replacement of expatriate personnel of gas companies by local personnel. In fact, the code is more ambitious in the sense that this provision envisages the entire dimension of technology transfer on the part of the gas companies including technological and knowledge programme and facilitate gradual replacement of expatriate of gas companies by local personnel. However, the provision is obscure in that it refers to 'gradual replacement of expatriate personnel of gas companies by local personnel' and one has reason to question what amounts to gradual. This question is pertinent because one would have expected the enabling law to the Gas code to spell out clearly when replacement may be due and how and who determines this.

In any case, whether it is the Petroleum, Mining or Gas Code and their enabling instruments, the intent of the legislator regarding local content must be the same and this is the more reason why one can rightly question the essence of addressing local content related issues in different but related codes of the extractive sector.

3. Some foreign good practices with respect to local content development

Local content development is fast becoming indispensable in resources-rich countries across the world. Such countries have realized fairly recently that for a considerable long time their non renewable resources of the extractive sector have been tapped by multinationals almost totally for their own gains and that after the exploitation exercise, the resource-rich countries have lamented for being unable to record any legacy. Consequent upon this state of affairs, there is an awakened spirit to develop local content policies in the extractive sector in most resource-rich countries and the aim has generally been, as indicated above, to encourage the participation and development of national labour, goods and services, technology, and capital. The objectives and guiding principles of these policies are sometimes outlined in overall or specific policy statements or plans.[62] Often principles and objectives are further detailed in primary or secondary legislation, as well as in negotiated contracts, licensing agreements, or concession agreements. These are referred to as 'channels of policy implementation'.[63] Implementation itself may rely on a variety of policy tools, including petroleum rights allocation systems, taxes, tariffs, incentives, penalties, procurement rules, and training arrangements.[64] In this section, we briefly describe the policy statements, channels, and legal tools used by some resource-rich countries in connection with the design and implementation of local content policies and show how they have up-graded their local content developments in the extractive sector laws and how the practice has been of immense benefits to the countries in general.

The manner in which local content policy is codified under law varies considerably from one country to another. Local content provisions may be embedded within the wider primary legislation governing petroleum exploration and development, or they may be the object of a separate law. Article 50 of the Law on Sub Soil and Subsoil Users in Kazakhstan, for instance, mandates that bids for new sub surface mineral rights include commitments to minimum levels of local content in goods, works and services, and the training of Kazakh personnel.[65] Article 1 of the same law establishes a minimum requirement for 95 percent of employees to be Kazakhstani citizens, and Article 78 requires that, for the purpose of contractor selection, procuring entities reduce the price of bids from Kazakhstani producers by 20 percent.[66]

In fact, in some countries, local content laws have been very comprehensive to embody principles, implementation flexibilities and enforcement mechanism. In Nigeria for example, the 2010 Oil and Gas Content Industry Development Act provides for, among other items: a local

---

[62] World Bank (2013), op cit, p.37

[63] Ibid.

[64] Ibid.

[65] Ibid.

[66] World Bank (2013), op cit, p.38

content monitoring regime integrated with the process of contracting suppliers and service providers; penalties for noncompliance with the local content legislation; ministerial waivers for certain requirements of the legislation for a temporary period, including, where targets established by law cannot be complied with due to limited local market capabilities; and the establishment of a Nigerian content development fund to support the development of national suppliers. Inherent in some of the legal and regulatory requirements for local recruitment, training, and promotion of nationals is the intent to preference nationals over foreign workers. In Nigeria, targets and preferences for national recruitment, training, and promotion are mandated by a combination of primary legislation and intervention by the regulator.[67] There equally exist provisions relating to the domestic sourcing of goods and services within the 2010 Oil and Gas Content Industry Development Act.

The 2010 Nigerian Oil and Gas Industry Content Development Act goes further, stipulating not only local sourcing targets for a wide range of goods and services but also, under Article 41(b), requiring that international companies operating as Nigerian-registered companies "shall demonstrate that a minimum of 50 percent of the equipment deployed in the execution of work be owned by Nigerian subsidiaries". This means that international companies that wish to be eligible to tender for work in Nigeria have to place into Nigerian ownership (that is, local companies with greater than 51 percent Nigerian equity) at least 50 percent of their equipment and technologies to be used in the contract.[68]

[67] Article 35 of the 2010 Nigerian Content Development Act requires that only Nigerians be employed "in junior and intermediate cadre [positions]." It is then left to the regulator—the Nigerian Content Development Monitoring Board—to agree with oil and gas companies on the minimum percentage of Nigerian labor in different job grades. This is mandated under Article 24 of the Nigerian Content Development Act, which requires a "Labor Clause" to be inserted in project agreements (or similar contracts) mandating the use of a minimum percentage of Nigerian labor in specified job levels.

[68] The advantage of this particular policy for technology transfer to the Nigerian economy is clear. But the policy is also not without challenges. These obligations may challenge the ability of equipment producers and service suppliers to protect propriety technologies. Meanwhile, not finding solutions to this challenge may prevent these companies from accessing local markets.

In Brazil, the strong local content policy framework and regulations have driven an increasing share of local employment, goods and services, and are contributing to reestablish Brazil as an extractive nation.[69] Brazilian regulations mandate targets for goods and services of domestic origin. In this sense, they encourage the emergence of a competitive local supply industry by incentivizing inward investment by international suppliers and service contractors that strive to meet these targets. If set too high compared to existing and short-term local supply capability, policy targets might reward less than competitive suppliers.[70]

Another leading practice in Africa is that of Ghana. In fact, Ghana has put forth an attractive local content regulation in the continent. Since 2010, Ghana has been working on local content policies in both the solid minerals and then hydrocarbon sectors. The passage of the Minerals and Mining General Regulations, 2012-LI 2173, marked the beginning of the implementation of local content policies in the mining sector. In the oil and gas and the petroleum sectors, the Local Content and Local Participation Regulations, 2013-Ll 2204, defined Ghana's expectations of local content.[71] The Minerals and Mining Law, 2006 (Act 703) sought to promote a localization policy and facilitate production linkages. Clause 50(3) of Act 703 calls for eventual "*localization*" of mining staff. However, the frameworks provided in the legislation were too generic and left the Ghana Minerals Commission (MC) with considerable discretion in enforcement. The passage of the Minerals and Mining (General) Regulations, 2012-LI 2173, was expected to be a game changer. The LI 2173 provides a clear

[69] Prior to 2002 there was no minimum local content requirement in Brazil. However, through the various bid rounds, local content rules have become more tangible and specific to different fields according to on/offshore and the depth of water involved. The primary objective of the Brazilian local content policy is to "maximize goods and services national industry content, within competitive and sustainable basis, in the implantation of oil and gas projects in Brazil and abroad." Petrobras' strategic investment plan calls for 65 percent of equipment and services to be sourced from domestic suppliers

[70] Some industry observers have voiced concerns over the extent to which the industrial base that is being constructed through the current mandatory local content targets is competitive and sustainable, when compared to similar industries in China, South Korea, Singapore, and Norway.

[71] See Columbia Center for Sustainable Development, 2014

interpretation of Act 703 and focuses on three areas, namely: (i) the employment and promotion of a local workforce, (ii) the procurement of locally produced goods and services, and (iii) additional licensing and reporting requirements. The regulation requires holders of mineral rights to hire a minimum of local staff in various employment categories, with the mineral commission working with mining companies to identify staff positions that can be filled by Ghanaians, local candidates that can be trained to replace foreign staff, a training programme and timing for local staff to replace foreign staff.[72] In capacity development, the law provides that the government and petroleum companies should support local training and technical institutions to develop capacity of international standards to train Ghanaians.

With regard to the provision of goods and services by Ghanaian companies, the extractive sector law provides that all operators must as far as possible use goods and services produced or provided in Ghana by Ghanaian companies, even if their prices are higher by up to 10%. It further provides that foreign companies that supply goods and services must have local participation of at least 10% initially and increase by 10% per year. Within the framework of technology transfer, the law provides that Oil companies must prepare and implement plans for the transfer of technology which plans should be monitored by specific institutions mandated to do so.

Outside the developing world, some good practices are insightful from some fairly recent discovery of resources in the developed world. With

[72] This provision requires existing license holders to present for approval a program for the recruitment and training of Ghanaians, including plans for the replacement of expatriates with Ghanaians. The regulation aims to promote local knowledge and to minimize the number of expatriates assigned to less complex jobs for which local capacity exists. The regulation specifically imposes a ceiling on the number of expatriate staffers a mining lease holder can have. It requires that the proportion of expatriate staff should not exceed 10 percent of the total of senior staff within the first three years, and 6 percent after three years. In other words, after six years of the passage of the LI, mining lease holders' maximum expatriate staff numbers should not exceed 6 percent of the total senior and management staff of the holder. Unskilled labor and clerical positions are generally to be reserved for Ghanaians. In addition, a comprehensive five-year plan to replace expatriates with Ghanaians, including training programs, is to be submitted to the MC for review and approval.

respect to Australia, for example, local content policy is designed to promote the development of a sustainable local industry, while abiding closely to international obligations on trade and competition law.[73] Thus, incentives, rather than mandated obligations, are the crucial policy tool.[74] One of the most notable incentives is the exemption from import tariff on equipment related to petroleum operations where such equipment is proved not to be available in Australia granted to oil companies and service companies in exchange for the formulation and execution of an Australian Industry Participation (AIP) plan.[75] Furthermore, companies bidding for large Commonwealth procurement contracts (over $20 million) may be required to prepare and implement an AIP plan. The process provides a mechanism for potential suppliers to familiarize themselves with the capabilities of small and medium-sized enterprises and to identify qualified suppliers. The international or foreign good practices x-rayed above may be helpful to resource rich countries of the developing world, Cameroon for example, in crafting more comprehensive, practical, reliable, sustainable and enforceable local content laws in their extractive sectors.

4. Highlights on some challenges to local content development and implementation in Cameroonian Law

To start with, a pertinent issue connected to local content development in the extractive sector laws is national compliance with international regulations on the subject. Both global and regional negotiated agreements regulate trade between nations.[76] The World Trade Organization (WTO) for instance, oversees compliance with such rules. The most relevant agreements among WTO members with implications on local content

---

[73]World Bank (2013), op cit, p.59

[74] Ibid.

[75] The criteria adopted by the federal government to assess Australian Industry Participation plans include the anticipated impact of the investments on employment of nationals and participation of Australian suppliers, and take into account whether the project will: Introduce new or enhanced skills into the Australian workforce; Encourage efforts to develop strategic alliances with Australian suppliers; Promote regional development; Support Australian research and development activities; Create innovative products and/or processes a

nd Integrate Australian industry into global supply chains.

[76] Local content in the oil and gas sector, a World Bank study, (2013) op cit, at p, 28.

policies and laws include the General Agreement on Tariffs and Trade (GATT), the agreement on Trade-Related Investment Measures (TRIMs), the General Agreement on Trade in Services (GATS), and the agreement on Government Procurement (GPA). The agreement on TRIMs is based on the "*national treatment*" principle of Article III of the GATT, and pertains to trade in goods. TRIMs apply to all WTO members, Cameroon inclusive and prohibit local content requirements that mandate particular levels of local purchases by an enterprise. The rules also prohibit trade balancing requirements that restrict the volume or value of imports that an enterprise can purchase to an amount related to the level of products it exports.[77] The rules may equally impose restrictions on the design of local content policies and laws. For example, the imposition of minimum targets for the participation of domestic subcontractors/suppliers may be contrary to a country's WTO undertakings.[78] Like many other international agreements, Cameroon sometimes do not respect these trade regulations either by failing to comply with or where there is compliance, effective implementation may not be ensured and consequently the veritable development of local content becomes a huge challenge.

---

[77] In essence, the rules require a host country to extend to foreign investors a treatment that is at least as favorable—insofar as the purchase of products is concerned—as the treatment it accords to national investors in like circumstances. The TRIMs agreement allows for transitional arrangements to maintain certain (protectionist) measures for a limited time following a country's entry into the WTO. The grace period is two years in the case of developed countries, five years for developing countries, and seven years for least-developed countries. In this regard, with the exception of Vietnam, all developing countries that produce oil and/or gas acceded to the WTO prior to 2006, which would suggest that their eligibility for transitional arrangements under GATT has expired.

[78] Part III of the GATS contains provisions on access to WTO members' markets by foreign suppliers, and the treatment of national suppliers. In the case of market access, all WTO members should accord services and service providers from other WTO member countries and show them treatment no less favorable than that provided for under the common terms, limitations, and conditions mutually agreed among WTO members. Furthermore, Article XIII of GATS extends to government procurement. As with TRIMs, GATS has provisions for the "special and differential treatment" (SDT) of developing countries, which allow for certain exceptions from the general rule. In addition, there are provisions that allow flexibility to encourage foreign suppliers to assist in technology transfers and training through offsets of particularly relevance to the design of LCPs.

Secondly, the improvement of national livelihoods/welfare depends, to a large extent on the development of local content policies and laws. What this means is that local content development should be clearly focused to achieve among others, the above objective. Consequently, there is need, within any sector of the economy, to cluster objectives and goals and synergize institutional plans and strategies to achieve the same. Unfortunately, we have observed in our research, that in the case of Cameroon, the legislator seems to have different objectives and goals for the same sector – the extractive sector with its mining, oil and gas subsectors as far as local content development is concerned. This is evident from the dispersed and unnecessary duplication of local content stipulations in the mining, oil and gas sub-sectors by the legislator although addressing or alluding to local content in similar articulations in these sub-sectors. The extractive sector legislator is challenged to think across all the subsectors that make up the sector since the objective is or ought to be one – contribution to sustainable economic growth and development and by extension the improvement of national livelihoods or welfare through a thoroughly thought out industrial investment policy that passes the Mill and Bastable tests.[79]

Another setback to local content development in the extractive sector laws in Cameroon is a shallow coverage of matters. For example, we have argued above that the provision on employment and professional training is shallow enough as it does not stipulate the percentage of nationals to be employed, the period within which nationals must be employed, the quality/level of training that must be afforded to the nationals by the multinational investors, and who attests whether or not these matters have been addressed. In addition, most of the provisions on local content are tacit and not express and these gives room for multiple interpretations. These and other gaps are challenging to the effective implementation of the extractive local content provisions.

---

[79] The Mill test requires the protected sector to eventually survive international competition without protection; the Bastable test is more stringent and calls for the present value of future benefits arising from the policy to compensate the present costs of protection. To be viable, Local Content Policies in the extractive sector would need to pass both tests.

A related challenge is that the extractive sector laws do not prescribe clear monitoring and development institutions let alone the monitoring mechanisms. This is critically important as most multinationals will not be honest enough to implement their obligations either arising from the legislative stipulations or from their contractual arrangements for exploitation of extractive resources. To bring them to book, there must be an effective monitoring organ with clearly defined mandates whose report can then serve as evidence of respect or not of the local content clauses and give reason for pressure to be brought to bear on the almighty multinationals to keep its legal commitments or be prosecuted in accordance with existing legislation. It is therefore our considered opinion that, institutional development and clear mandatory prescriptions for monitoring will play the role of watch-dog in the development, compliance and effective implementation of local content provisions.

5. Conclusion and projections

The discussions above lead one to come to a number of conclusions. Firstly, that a majority of resource-rich countries of the developing world and Cameroon specifically have to date, not recorded significant legacy from the exploitation by multinationals of their natural resources in general and their non-renewable natural resources in particular. Secondly, and flowing from the first, local contents developments initiatives are not yet widespread in resources-rich countries of the developing world meanwhile a true development of the local content policies are a cornerstone for sustainable economic development and poverty reduction. Thirdly, that the rich extractive sector in Cameroon can be made to provide more than just taxes, rents, and royalties to government but cross sector benefits by way of local content development and value addition which require at least an elaborate coverage of the extractive sector laws. Fourthly, that in Cameroon, as in many other developing economies, local content laws and policies which ought to guide and guarantee sustainability of national livelihoods are, unfortunately, dispersed and superfluous with the result that implementation of such policies and laws is haphazard and uncoordinated.

With the foregoing shortfalls therefore, there is need to review local content provisions in the extractive sector laws so that omissions, tacit inferences, obscurity, dispersion and duplication of important local content hallmarks such as employment, professional training and other social infrastructure; development of local entreprises and local transformation of products; and technology transfer are properly handled. In this regard, we suggest and strongly too that the Cameroonian legislator should adopt an all-embracing or comprehensive and viable legislation addressing only local content matters for the extractive sector – Mining, Oil, and Gas subsectors. Such a law which must be crafted together with its enabling instruments should address among the hallmarks just outlined above, such other issues as a local content monitoring and evaluation institution; a National Content Development Fund to support the development of national suppliers; strong, dissuasive but also feasible sanctions for non-compliance or violation of local content laws and why not incentives for compliance with local content provisions. In fact, all these issues should be addressed by the laws so that contractual arrangements may only be inspired by the Law since, as we know, most of the extractive contracts are not usually open negotiations where the public could make valuable inputs in view of ensuring the sustainability of their livelihoods.

EVALUATING THE EFFECTIVE IMPLEMENTATION OF ENVIRONMENTAL AND SOCIAL IMPACT ASSESSMENT UNDER CAMEROONIAN LAW: THE CASE OF HYDROPOWER PROJECTS

Dashaco John TAMBUTOH[1]
And
Bande Gulbert MBAH TARH[2]

SUMMARY

This Article provides a systematic and periscopic view of environmental and social impact assessment (ESIA) with special focus on hydropower projects in Cameroon. This approach is based on national legislation and the soft-law which are essential when considering the constraints and impacts of ESIA to hydropower projects. The paper envisages that the ESIA practice in Cameroon is plagued with many constraints especially from the infrastructure and ESIA resource perspective. The present legal and procedural disposition vis-à-vis ESIA in Cameroon is monumental and manifest some clarity of exposition with regard to the practical and fundamental steps for ESIA practice in Cameroon. However, a number of impediments still prevail that deter the full efficiency of national legislation. In search for explanations for this trend, the paper provides an overview of the current framework governing the ESIA in Cameroon. Moreover, content analysis and interviews with appropriate stakeholders on the ESIA process identify the key barriers associated with ESIA practice in Cameroon. The Article thus maintains that the inadequate baseline data, procedural flaws in scoping, exorbitant administrative fees, absence of an appeal procedure, unclear proviso, incompetent personnel and the over-centralization of the ESIA powers are crucial barriers that appear to impede

[1] Associate Professor, The University of Bamenda
[2] Dr., University of Yaounde II

the healthy ESIA practice in Cameroon. The paper also submits that for a robust ESIA practice in hydropower projects to prevail in Cameroon, there is the need for focus on the recommendations made in this Article.

INTRODUCTION

Environmental Impact Assessment (ESIA) is the formal process used to predict the environmental consequences (positive or negative) of a plan, policy, program, or project prior to the decision to move forward with the proposed action. Indeed, ESIA has been a tool for safeguarding the environment since the late 1960's. Therefore, the first ESIA were developed in response to requirements set out in the National Environmental Policy Act (NEPA) of the United States. The NEPA requires federal agencies to integrate environmental values into their decision making processes by considering the environmental impacts of their proposed actions and reasonable alternatives to those actions.[3] Thus, the roots of ESIA are in policy and programme level decisions called the strategic environmental assessment (SEA). From this initial basis as a policy and programme-focused tool, ESIA evolved in the 1980's onwards to become increasingly applied to project level decisions.[4] The passing of the European Union Directive on SEA[5] in 2001 marked a re-orientation of impact assessment towards the progamme and policy level of decision making.[6] In the context of the energy sector, ESIAs have been widely applied to large scale energy infrastructure projects such as those associated with oil and gas exploration and development, coal mining and large-scale hydropower generation. Thus, the strategic assessments are increasingly important as a means of addressing the potential cumulative effects of renewable projects, as well as a higher-order approach for identifying alternative technologies and systems designs.

---

[3] Pub. L. 91-190, 42 U.S.C. 4321-4347 January 1, 1970, as amended by Pub. L. 94-52, July 3, 1975, Pub. L. 94-83, August 9, 1975, & 97-258, § 4(b), Sept. 13 (1982) *The National Environmental Policy Act of 1969*.

[4] Wathern, P. (editor) (1988)., *Environmental Impact Assessment: Theory and Practice*, Unwin Hyman Ltd., Winchester, Mass, USA.

[5] EU SEA Directive (2001/42/EC)

[6] Ends Legal Compliance Manager (2008), *Strategic Environmental Assessment,* August, http://www.endscompliance.com/ENDSDoc/PB/SEA.pdf.

Hence, through literature review, interviews with experts and analysis of the world Bank renewable Energy Project database, the authors posit that although a good deal of experience and expertise is available in Cameroon for conducting ESIAs of hydropower projects, there is a more limited body of practice available for renewable energy technologies. So, they readily consider the general notion of ESIA in context and then examine its scope and constraints in theory and practice in Cameroon by considering its application in the hydropower sector.

I. THE NOTION OF ENVIRONMENTAL IMPACT ASSESSMENT

The International Association for Impact Assessment (IAIA) defines the ESIA as the process of identifying, predicting, evaluating and mitigating the biophysical, social, and other relevant effects of development proposals prior to major decisions being taken and commitments made.[7] Thus, the purpose of the ESIA is to ensure that decision makers consider the environmental impacts when deciding whether or not to proceed with a project. Therefore, ESIAs are unique in that they do not require adherence to a predetermined environmental outcome, but rather they require decision makers to account for environmental values in their decisions and to justify those decisions the in light of detailed environmental studies and public comments on the potential environmental impacts.[8] However, there is a trend towards strategic levels of assessments which focus on policies, plans and programmes rather than projects. This growing interest in SEA stems, in part, from the recognition that project level impact assessments are limited in the scope of mitigation measures which can be established for potential impacts, and that there are more potential opportunities for avoiding, reducing, and minimising impacts through good decision making at the policy, programme and planning stages of development. Altogether, the awareness of climate change impacts, concerns about security of supplies, an

---

[7] "Principle of Environmental Impact Assessment Best Practice". (1999)., International Association for Impact Assessment.

[8] Holder, J., (2004)., Environmental Assessment: The Regulation of Decision Making, Oxford University Press, New York; For a comparative discussion of the elements of various domestic ESIA systems, see Christopher Wood Environmental Impact Assessment: A Comparative Review (2nd edition, Prentice Hall, Harlow, 2002).

urgent need to improve access for millions of households, and ageing infrastructures are some of the key factors driving changes in energy systems around the world. The changes that are afoot will have implications for ecosystems and livelihoods.[9] For policies, plans and programmes around renewable energy investments, SEA needs to be applied. Such assessments will increasingly need to consider the changing nature of supporting ecosystem services and the need for climate adaptation. Financing institutions are also promoting the appropriate safeguards, supported by capacity building activities from international organizations, in order to unleash the full sustainable potential of hydropower projects. The hydropower sector has seen a significant increase in investment in recent years and a corresponding increase in strategic planning and assessments; as realized in the initiatives and endeavours of the international organization involved in the sustainability of hydropower projects.

A. THE WORLD BANK INITIATIVES ON ENVIRONMENTAL IMPACT ASSESSMENT

Apparently interesting, in the context of the World Bank database[10] of renewable energy projects, there is little evidence of strategic assessments framing project-level investment opportunities coming through the World Bank pipeline. The World Bank does, however, appear to recognise the importance of strategic planning and assessment for hydropower investments, and has produced[11] a working note outlining the World Bank Group's role in scaling up hydropower. Included among five priority engagements for the Bank Group are efforts to promote good practice including environmental management and contributions to support governments in strategic planning though it is not clear if strategic assessments are part of the pre-feasibility studies referenced in this section.[12] The issue of insufficient information may be the case more generally for

---

[9] Boyle, G., Everett, B., Ramage, J. (2003)., *Energy for a Sustainable Future*. Oxford University Press.

[10] Kingdom of Cambodia (January 2010). Environmental and Social Management Framework (ESMF) for the Rural Electrification and Transmission Project (RETP).

[11] International Bank for Reconstruction and Development/The World Bank (2009). *Directions in Hydropower: Scaling up for development*. Note No. 21, June 2009.

[12] *Ibid*

strategic assessments for the renewable energy sector, as there appears to be a gap between the policies and the practice when it comes to SEA. A recent Opinion issued by the Committee of the Regions on the European Union's ESIA and SEA directives[13] concluded that there is "a vital need to develop capacity in the Member States so as to ensure effective implementation of the SEA Directive". Evidence from the environmental and social impact assessments reviewed from the World Bank renewable energy project database indicates that project level assessments are, when applied, effective tools for identifying potential environmental and social impacts of renewable projects and outlining management strategies for addressing those impacts, but that strategic issues are more difficult to address at the project ESIA level. Additionally, single projects in the renewable sector may not trigger environmental assessment procedures, but there is some movement towards grouping several renewable projects together and developing frameworks for managing the environmental impacts of the collective projects.[14] The increased use of strategic assessments for renewable energy policies, especially in hydropower plans and programmes should be further encouraged, and supported with better information particularly when it comes to biodiversity and ecosystems and community participation in decision-making.

According to the World Bank's project database[15], there were 195 renewable energy projects listed as of June 2010 that are active or in the pipeline for investment. Of these, 22 are graded environmental category "A", meaning they are likely to have significant adverse environmental impacts that are sensitive, diverse, or unprecedented and thus require an environmental assessment which examines the project's potential negative and positive environmental impacts, compares them with those of feasible alternatives (including the "without project" scenario), and recommends any measures needed to prevent, minimize, mitigate or compensate for adverse

---

[13] Committee of the Regions (2010) 84th plenary session 14 and 15 April, 2010. Opinion of the committee of the Regions on Improving the ESIA and SEA Directives.

[14] *Ibid*

[15] Kingdom of Cambodia (January 2010). Environmental and Social Management Framework (ESMF) for the Rural Electrification and Transmission Project (RETP).

impacts and improve environmental performance.[16] A further 121 were graded environmental category "B" meaning that they are considered to have potential adverse environmental impacts on human populations or environmentally important areas – including wetlands, forests, grasslands, and other natural habitats. The impacts of Category "B" projects are considered to be site-specific, few if any of them are irreversible and in most cases mitigatory measures can be designed more readily than for Category "A" projects.[17] The environmental assessment for these projects is similar to, but narrower in focus than that of Category "A" assessment. 21 of the renewable energy projects in the database are classified as environmental category "C" meaning they are not considered to have a risk to the environment, and 17 are categorised as "E" meaning they are investments in financial intermediaries. The remaining 14 projects are not classified according to any environmental category.

However, of the Category "C" projects listed in the World Bank database, nearly two thirds had clearly been screened for their potential environmental impacts and determined to be of low or no environmental risk.[18] The level of information in the screening reports varies considerably, with several of the reports just providing a check-list of "yes-no" responses to the list of safeguard policies which may apply without further justification or analysis to substantiate the responses. Those with integrated safeguards data sheets have the most consistent and thorough approaches to screening for environmental risks. Also, of the Category "B" projects in the database, nearly 80% of the projects have demonstrated evidence that they have been screened for environmental impacts. A review of a sampling of the environmental assessments prepared for Category "B" listed projects reveal that the impact assessment process is helpful in identifying potential impacts of the project on the surrounding environment, but less attention is paid to the changing conditions of the surrounding environment and potential implications for the project. This could be significant in, for instance, the case of biofuels projects which rely on reliable and steady

---

[16] World Bank (2010) Environmental Categories descriptor on the Advanced Search tool. web.worldbank.org/WBSITE/EXTERNAL/PROJECTS

[17] *Ibid*

[18] *Ibid*

sources of feedstock from the surrounding landscapes. Climate change is factored into energy projects in terms of the project's potential contributions to or reductions of greenhouse gas emissions, but climate change impacts on the project models and assumptions are not evident in the assessments reviewed.[19] Leading on from this omission, climate change adaptation strategies for the projects are not evident in the assessments. Moreover, of the Category "A" projects in the database, nearly 85% have environmental information available about the project, and have clearly gone through a screening exercise but only three have environmental assessments available online.[20] Over 80% projects in this category are hydroelectric power projects which total nearly 3 billion USD, thus accounting for over 75% of the Category "A" renewable energy project portfolio when calculated by size of project. While environmental assessment documents are available for some of the Category "A" projects, most (nearly 90%) of the hydroelectric projects do not have environmental assessment available on the World Bank website. Further searches do not reveal either ESIA or SEA documentation for the projects without documents available on the website.

Furthermore, one project in the Category "A" list has an SEA available on the website. From analysis, it appears to be a strategic assessment which was triggered by the ESIA of the project. This type of SEA, known in the impact assessment community as an "ESIA inspired SEA"[21], is often used when projects are contentious or politicized and the ESIA has not been able to resolve the tension around the project. SEAs can help to engage stakeholders in a higher-order discussion which may provide routes for resolving disputes not otherwise available at the project level. Such ESIA inspired SEAs may lead to solutions, but can be costly and time consuming when compared to a process which starts with strategic levels of engagement and then works through to project design and development and impact assessment. Thus, projects which have environmental assessments available

---

[19] *Ibid*

[20] *Ibid*

[21] Rajvanshi, A. And Mathur, V. (2009)., *Integrating Biodiversity into Strategic Environmental Assessment: case studies from India.* http://oldwww.wii.gov.in/ESIAnew/ESIA/globalcasestudies/sea%20netherland/sea.htm

include a geothermal expansion, a hydropower project, and a rural electrification project. The triggers for the environmental assessments include the size and scale of the project as well as the sensitivity of the location of the project. The impact assessments focus on impacts from the project on the receiving environment and communities, and follow a standard ESIA approach, that is, summarizing the project and its justification; reviewing legal, regulatory and management frameworks; describing the project (receiving) environment; describing the project components and activities; identifying potential impacts (positive and negative) on the receiving environment from the project components and activities; outlining management plans for the potential significant impacts; and drawing conclusions about the project. Therefore, the environmental assessment of the project which is a compilation of projects is interesting in that it outlines a simplified approach to identifying, measuring and managing the potential impacts of small-scale renewable energy options such as small scale biomass, solar home systems and mini and micro hydropower projects. As with Category "B" assessments, the impacts of possible changes in the environments in which projects are being placed are not raised or addressed in the assessment. These include potential changes to water availability in the case of the geothermal project, where the water modeling clearly indicates that there is a historical trend of significant fluctuations in the water levels at the source for the project, for cooling and drilling activities. While the assessment identifies the potential off-take of the project on the water source, there is no consideration of the potential impact on the project of a fluctuation of the water availability on the project. Such a scenario may emerge not just because of the potential for local climatic change, but also because of competing demands for water from the source. SEA may have identified and addressed this issue, particularly if the scope of the strategic assessment crossed sectorial boundaries and included other industrial and non-industrial sectors in the region.

B. THE WORLD COMMISSION OF DAMS' INITIATIVE ON ENVIRONMENTAL IMPACT ASSESSMENT

The World Commission of Dams (WCD) constitutes a reference point for all actors to understand the controversies and what is at stake in decisions around dam policies and projects.[22] So, even if the WCD report is no longer at the forefront of policy innovation, the WCD Strategic Priorities set the standards which all projects should still attain. The broadly held perception is that the WCD Strategic Priorities are more common currency than the WCD Guidelines of which there was, from the outset, little mention in debate. As to whether the WCD Strategic Priorities and Guidelines were meant to be advisory or mandatory, the debate continues. It has been stated that the role of the Commission was *"strictly advisory"*. Meanwhile, Chapter 9 setting out the 'Criteria and Guidelines' is *"heavily normative"* and repeatedly uses the word *'compliance'*.[23] The UN-funded Dams and Development Project led the process of absorption of the WCD. The key test of the WCD and the other policies is in the follow-up: the challenge of translating principles and guidelines developed at the global level to practice that could be implemented at the national and project level.[24] As earlier alluded, the publication by the WCD of its guidelines did not result in the adoption by the industry of the environmental and social safeguards which the WCD was promoting. Whatever the rights and wrongs of that lack of *'buy-in'*, a consequence of the WCD raising the bar to the height which the WCD Commissioners chose to set as a standard was that the WCD did not bring industry along with its agenda, to use one person's expression, *"pushing for the gold standard"* is not always useful and, interpreting the response of this constituency, it was not useful in this case[25]. As shall be discussed below with respect to its applicability in the Lom Pangar hydropower project (LPHP), there is a gap which the Hydropower Sustainability Assessment Protocol[26] is designed to fill, to provide a *"platform for engagement"* with dam developers/operators, to promote improved practice. The Protocol offers an assessment tool which can be adopted and applied by the actors involved in the hydropower projects and

---

[22] Smith (2010), *op cit.* p.438

[23] Briscoe (2010), *op cit.* p.404

[24] Smith (2010), *op cit.* p.438

[25] *Loc. cit.*

[26] International Hydropower Association (August 2009) *Draft Hydropower Sustainability Assessment Protocol.*
www.hydropower.org/sustainable_hydropower/HSAF_Hydropower_Sustainability_Assessment_Protocol.html

it does not seek to specify a standard[27]. The idea is that the performance under each project component works towards the 'basic good practice' as described at each of the stages[28], and thereafter up to the higher levels. The Protocol is the product of the collaborative process of over 2 years.[29] A feature of this dialogue was the participation of the Chinese research institute and the engineering consulting group. The value of this approach is in the inclusion on the *'radar'* of project promoters and developers of the environmental and social aspects, alongside the economic/financial and technical ones. Therefore, this cannot be considered as an advancement of the WCD and as some NGOs are concerned that the Protocol will *"dilute"* the standards of the WCD. But the publication by the WCD of its guidelines did not result in the adoption by the industry of the environmental and social safeguards which the WCD was promoting as the Protocol is not intended to replace the WCD. The score-card against each of the 'sustainability topics' allows a project to see where it is placed in terms of performance and the project leaders can monitor or move performance to a higher score.

However, the World Bank Safeguard Policies considered above prescribe one standard with which the developers and other project participants are required to comply. The key function of the Protocol is to clarify the industry attitudes to the facets of the projects[30] which go beyond the technical and financial aspects. The advantage of the Protocol is that it is a "*platform for engagement*", and, for this, the sliding scale is an advantage because it allows for flexibility. Moreover, it should be noted that the Protocol has offered a tool which is "complementary" to the procedures conducted under national laws and regulations. Therefore, the adoption of the Protocol may also be complementary to the application of the guidelines set by the financing institutions[31]. Thus, the finance sector representation

---

[27] Components of projects called 'sustainability topics' are assessed individually to draw up a 'sustainability profile' of the project, without scoring the project as a whole.

[28] 'Preparation', Implementation' and 'Operation'

[29] Namely the Hydropower Sustainability Assessment Forum in which representatives of "developing countries, developed countries, the hydropower sector, the finance sector and NGOs (both environmental and social aspects)" participated.

[30] Environmental and social aspects.

[31] For instance, the World Bank Safeguard Principles and the Equator Principles etc.

on the International Hydropower sustainability Forum and the International Hydropower Association, has kept the World Bank and the Equator Principles Institutions informed of the evolution of the Protocol including the detailed wording of what constitutes basic good practice.

Furthermore, one question addressed by these researchers in this write-up is whether confronted with the scale under the terms of the Protocol and the different possible levels of standards in relation to the environmental and social goals, the developers can readily resolve to maintain the appropriate level of achievement. Under the Safeguard Policies of the World Bank, as well as the IFC Performance Standards and the Equator Principles, the standard is specified by the third party bank and financier, whose position is: "*Accept our offer of finance, and you must fulfil this standard which we have set thus*"[32]. Then, during the implementation and operation phases, the bank/lender watches over any fluctuations in the developer's resolve. Thus, under the Protocol, the issue that arises is whether there are risks that, in practice, the environmental and social performance will slide back down, from Level 3 to Level 2 and finally to Level 1. The counter-argument, as noted above, is that the Protocol has an advantage in terms of flexibility. The leverage which the banks exert on the developers, operators and the governments arguably reduce after the preparatory stage of the projects, once the boards of the banks have approved the loans as was the case of the LPHP. Therefore, the key test of all the five international policies reviewed in this study is in the follow-up that is, translating principles developed at the global level into practice through national and project level implementation as envisaged in the LPHP context in Cameroon.

II. THE SCOPE AND CONSTRAINTS OF ENVIRONMENTAL IMPACT ASSESSMENT IN CAMEROON

For a rigorous and vigorous ESIA practice to prevail in Cameroon, there is need that focus should be to enhance the viability and sustainability of the hydropower investments. However, following the 1972 declarations of the United Nations Conference on the Human Environment, the importance of environmental protection has become predominant in global policies and plans towards development. Moreover, according to the United Nations

[32] World Bank (2010), op. cit.

International Strategy for Disaster Reduction, an ESIA is intended to assess the effects on a specified environment of the introduction of any new factor, which may upset the current ecological balance. It further establishes that ESIA is a policy making tool that serves to provide evidence and analysis of environmental impacts of activities from conception to decision-making. It is utilized extensively in national programming and for international development assistance projects. Thus, the ESIA has been recognized all over the world as a fundamental tool to achieve sustainability especially within the development arena and Cameroon is not an exception. As *Bitondo*[33] puts it, the directives of nearly all donors as well as legislation of nearly all countries require that before funding is made available, projects likely to be detrimental to the environment should undergo a sound and thorough ESIA prior to their commencement.

According to *Appiah*[34], many African countries including Cameroon are making efforts to establish ESIA procedures. The implementation of the ESIA legislative framework in Cameroon although belated, portrays the government's commitment towards regulating and advocating sustainable development. This commitment is further reflected by the fact that environmental management laws although not fully regulated had been inherent in relevant Cameroonian legislation. After the Rio de Janeiro summit in 1992, the Cameroonian government created a Permanent Secretariat for the Environment in October 1996. This governmental agency had the authority to regulate ESIA nationwide. It was however not clear how this would be achievable since the legal framework for ESIA in Cameroon had not yet been enacted, although some good practices of ESIA had already existed in Cameroon in the public works and forestry sectors. In February 2005, the Decree for the process and procedural framework governing the ESIA in Cameroon was finally enacted.[35] It is our intention therefore in this part of this study to unveil the constraints to ESIA practice

---

[33] Bitondo, D. (2000)., Environmental assessment in Cameroon: State of the Art. Impact Assessment and Project Appraisal, 18(10), pp. 33-42. [Online] http://dx.doi.org

[34] Appiah-Opoku, S. (2001)., Environmental impact assessment in developing countries, the case of Ghana. *Environmental Impact Assessment Review, 21*, pp. 59-71. http://dx.doi.org/10.1016/S0195-9255(00)00063-9

[35] See Decree No. 2005/0577/PM of the Prime Minister of the Republic of Cameroon enacting the process and procedural framework governing ESIA in Cameroon.

in Cameroon in the post ESIA new law era. We shall also tender a plethora of pragmatic views to show that some aspects that govern the ESIA framework in Cameroon are untenable and also make some recommendations for its improvement. In this regard, we shall examine the genesis and evolution of ESIA, and identify the constraints of the same.

A. ENVIRONMENTAL IMPACT ASSESSMENT UNDER CAMEROONIAN LAW

As discussed above, Cameroon has a comprehensive legislation on the environment. The legislation provides for the establishment of a National Environmental Management Plan (NEMP) adopted in 1996. Law No. 96/12 of 5 August 1996[36]. The basic principles for the formulation of the framework legislation on the environment include: precaution in view of the limits of current knowledge; polluter pays principle; prevention and corrective action principle; principle of participation; principle of liability and mutual decision; and the principle of substitution It should be noted that Section 9 (f) of Cameroon's Framework Law on the Environment provides for substitution where certain rules are omitted or missing in the said law. This Section stipulates that where a general or specific rule relating the environment is not provided for in the Framework Law, a rule derived from other regulations or a rule from another context that will be more efficient with regard to the protection of the environment, may be used. Regarding ESIA, Section 17 of the Law stipulates that:

"(1) The promoter or owner of any development, project, labour or equipment, which is likely to endanger the environment, owing to its dimension, nature or the impact of its activities on the natural environment shall carry out an environmental impact assessment. This assessment shall determine the direct or indirect incidence of the said project on the ecological balance of the zone where the plant is located or any other region, the physical environment and quality of life of populations and the impact on the environment in general.

(2) The environment impact assessment shall be included in the file submitted for public investigation where such a procedure is provided for.

[36] Here inafter referredvto as the 1996 Law

(3) The impact assessment shall be carried out at the expense of the promoter".

According to Section 19 (2) the impact assessment shall of necessity comprise: an analysis of the initial state of the site and its environment; reasons for choosing the site; evaluation of the anticipated consequences of the implementation of the project on the site and its natural and human environment; outline of the measures envisaged by the promoter or owner to eliminate, reduce and, if possible, compensate for the harmful consequences of the project on the environment and estimates of the ensuing cost; presentation of other possible solutions and reasons for selecting the project from the perspective of environmental protection. According to section 20 (2) of the 1996 law, where the impact assessment is not known or the impact assessment procedure is totally or partially disrespected, the competent Administration, or where necessary, the Administration in charge of the environment shall demand the implementation of appropriate emergency procedures to suspend the work envisaged or already initiated. These emergency procedures shall be initiated without prejudice to the sanctions provided for by this law. The ESIA is therefore the proper process used to predict the environmental result of a plan, policy, program, or project prior to the decision to move forward with the proposed action. In fact, despite the current sustainable development dogma, there remains an antagonistic relationship between economic development and environmental protection as decision-makers still face significant challenges when trying to create a balance between natural processes and human aspirations and between the costs of environmental management versus the provision of basic services to ensure quality of life.[37] If well implemented, ESIA is a fundamental tool that can help in the integration of the environment into developmental projects. Since the publication of the ESIA procedural framework legislation in Cameroon, few studies have attempted to examine the effectiveness of the law especially within the context of the existing constraints. This extant literature runs counter to the prevailing trend in other African countries. The gap may

[37] Petts, J., Herd, A., Gerrard, S. & Horne, C. (1999)., 'The Climate and Culture of Environmental Compliance within SMEs', Business Strategy and the Environment, vol. 8(1), pp.14-30.

however be bridged through the exposure of the fundamental constraints that still impede the efficiency of the law as the rhetoric of environmental protection after the 1972 Conference on Human Environment led to the formation of sectoral laws in Cameroon.

1. The Development of Environmental Impact Assessment in Cameroon

The Decree regulating the establishment of ESIA classifies as dangerous, unhygienic and obnoxious and prescribes that a fundamental prerequisite for the opening of a classified factory should be the presentation of a global plan of the project by the proponent.[38] This plan is to be used to appreciate whether the materials and the dispositions of the project in question sufficiently take care of its impacts on safety, health and environment. According to this decree, risk assessment and prevention was to be achieved within the framework of the so-called *"commodo and in-commodo"* inquiry which take into account such aspects like water supply, waste disposal and treatment, odours, all of which are pertinent to the safety and health of the neighbourhood. Three categories of classified factories are described in the Decree - those that must be located far from housing areas, those that do not need to be established rigorously away from housing areas but for which authorization is required to ensure the provision of clearly defined adequate preventive measures, and finally those that do not present any serious foreseeable inconvenience to the neighbourhood and the public but are however required to submit general provisions that safeguard the neighbourhood and the public interest. This illustrates the simple use of the concept of proximity to the receptors and magnitude of the impact in ESIA. This is complemented by a Ministerial Notice relating to the collection, transportation and treatment of industrial waste, domestic waste treatment plants and sanitary sewage matters which is instrumental to the enhancement of sustainability.[39]

In addition to the above, a Ministry of Environment and Forest was created in 1992. This Ministry, as *Bitondo* explains, had the mandate to elaborate and implement the National EMP, a plan that clearly

---

[38] See Article 2 of Decree No. 76-372 of 2 September 1976

[39] See Notice No. D69/NC/MSP/DMPH/SHPA of August 1980,

recommended an ESIA for projects that were likely to affect the environment from a negative perspective.[40] Indeed, the participation of Cameroon in the Rio de Janeiro Conference in 1992 further boosted its positive philosophy in the arena of environmental protection. This was evident in the constitution[41] that recognized the right of the Cameroonians to a sound environment and considers environmental protection a collective responsibility. In the subsequent law of 20 January 1994 to lay down the forestry, wildlife and fisheries regulations for projects with a potential impact on forestry or the aquatic environment in Cameroon, the ESIA was included[42].

Moreover, the environmental management law provides the main legislative bedrock or foundation for environmental management in Cameroon. It contains provisions relating to the ESIA, prescribing it for all projects which had a propensity to degrade the environment.[43] Shortly after its enactment, and specifically in October 1996, a decree reorganizing the Ministry of Environment and Forest created a Permanent Secretariat for the Environment at the Ministry of Environment and Forest. This Secretariat, as *Bitondo* asserts, had a Department of Sustainable Development that had as one of its fundamental duties the responsibility of ensuring that ESIA is practised effectively and efficiently on a national scale.[44] Later on, this ministry was split into two separate ministries, that is, the Ministry of Forest and Wildlife (MINFOF) and the Ministry of Environment and Nature Protection (MINEP) with the Department of Sustainable Development attached under MINEP. Thus, it was not until February 2005, that is, nine years later, that a Prime Ministerial Decree No. 2005/0577/PM formally launched the ESIA procedure. This was consolidated by the publication and enactment of Order No. 0069/MINEP of March 2005 by MINEP prescribing the different categories of projects that would necessitate an ESIA.

---

[40] Bitondo (2000)., *op cit.*

[41] See Law No. 2008/1 of 14 April 2008 to amend and supplement some provisions of Law No. 96/6 of 18 January 1996 amending the Constitution of 2 June 1972.

[42] The ESIA is prescribed in Article 16 of this legislative enactment.

[43] See Article 17 of Law No. 96/12 of 5th August 1996 of Environmental Management

[44] Bitondo (2000)., *op cit.*

2. The Features and Procedure of the Environmental Impact Assessment in Cameroon

The principal regulatory framework that lays down the different categories of projects requiring an ESIA is Order No. 0069/MINEP of March 2005. The Order classifies projects requiring an ESIA into two categories. Category 1 projects are those projects requiring a simple ESIA while Category 2 projects are those projects requiring a detailed ESIA study. Article 2 of the Order prescribes the requisite contents for reports emanating from a simple and a detailed ESIA study. According to this Order, a report originating from a '*simple ESIA study*' must comprise: the summary of the study in a simple language and in English and French, the description of the current environment where the project is envisaged, a description of the project, a report of the field work, an inventory and the description of the impacts of the project on the environment including envisaged mitigating measures together with an estimate of the corresponding cost, the approved terms of reference of the study and the bibliographic references.

The contents of a report emanating from a '*detailed ESIA study*' as prescribed by this regulation must include; the summary of the study in a simple language, and in English and French: a description and analysis of the initial state of the site and its physical, biological, human, and socio-economic environment; a description and analysis of all the components as well as natural and socio-cultural resources likely to be affected by the project, including reasons for choosing the site; a description of the project; the presentation and analysis of the different alternatives; the reason for choosing the project amongst other possible solution; the identification and evaluation of the possible effects of implementing the project on the natural and human environment; an indication of the envisaged measures for avoiding, reducing, eliminating or compensating the detrimental effects of the project on the environment together with an estimate of the corresponding cost; a program for the sensitization and information including minutes of meetings held with the public, NGOs, syndicates and other organized groups affected by the project; an EMP comprising surveillance mechanisms and the environmental follow up of the project and, where necessary, a compensation plan; and the terms of reference of the study including the bibliographic references.

The 2005 Decree detailing the process and procedural framework governing ESIA in Cameroon was finally promulgated in March 2005, nine years after the 1996 Environmental Management Law. As *Alemagi et al.,*[45] postulate, the Decree is monumental because it represents the first attempt made by the GoC to incorporate the legal and procedural framework governing ESIA into a comprehensive legal document. Indeed, the ESIA procedure laid down in the ESIA framework included the various steps which a project requiring an ESIA undergoes from proposal to endorsement implementation leading to the issuing of a Certificate of Environmental Conformity (CEC). These include the: screening and scoping, ESIA study leading to the compilation of the Environmental Impact Statement (EIS), review and public participation, decision making, monitoring and evaluation, auditing for operating industries and establishments of existing pre-ESIA. Moreover, under the prevailing or current ESIA procedure in Cameroon, the proponent is mandated to initiate an ESIA study by submitting a project's file to the Competent Administration (CA) and the MINEP. The law prescribes that the project file must constitute the following: a project's general file; an application for the implementation of the environmental impact study comprising the name, share capital, sector of activity and the number of jobs provided for in the project; terms of reference of the study, along with a report describing and justifying the project with emphasis on the protection of the environment and grounds for choosing the site and a receipt justifying the payment of the file processing fee as provided for in Article 9.

After receiving or obtaining the project's file for the implementation of the environmental impact study, the CA has a deadline of ten days to forward the said file including its comments and opinion to the Minister in Charge of the Environment. From the date of submission, the Administration in Charge of the Environment or Ministry has twenty days for internal screening. Screening is a fundamental prerequisite as it enables

[45] Alemagi, D; Sondo, A; Ertel, J. (2006)., Constraints to Environmental Impact Assessment Practice: A Case Study of Cameroon. *Journal of Environmental Impact Assessment Review*

the Ministry to opine and determine the category of the project as submitted within the context of terms of reference by the proponent. It also gives the authorities the opportunity to comment on the scoping of potential impacts resulting from the implementation of the project. Should this Ministry not respond after thirty days from the date of submission of the application, the proponent can consider the terms of reference admissible. Otherwise, a screening report with specifications on the contents of the impact study according to the category of the project, the level of analysis required as well as the responsibilities and the obligations of the proponent, is sent to the proponent for a full-scale environmental impact study to be commissioned. The proponent is obliged to carry out the environmental impact study using a consultant. The proponent must conduct the environmental impact study with the population concerned, through consultations and public meetings, with the purpose of sampling the opinion of the population on the project. At least thirty days before the date of the first meeting, the proponent must send to the representatives of the population concerned, the program of public consultations comprising the date and venue of meetings, the descriptive and explanatory report of the project and the purpose of consultation.

After the ESIA study, two and twenty copies of the Environmental Impact Statement (EIS) are submitted or handed over to the CA and the Administration in Charge of the Environment respectively. As soon as the CA receives the EIS, an evaluation and advice is then made and transmitted to the administration or Ministry in Charge of the Environment. It is at this stage that the afore-mentioned administration puts in place a mixed team to conduct field trips for the purpose of checking or verifying qualitatively as well as quantitatively, information contained in the EIS and collecting the views of the population concerned in a public meeting. This public meeting enables the team to correlate the information in the EIS with the views of the public. The mixed team has fifteen days within which to forward its findings to the Inter-Ministerial Committee for the Environment for simple ESIA studies and twenty days for detailed studies.

Within twenty days of the receipt of the EIS, the Administration in Charge of the Environment concludes the evaluation of the EIS and rules on the admissibility of the impact study. If this Ministry rules in favour of the study, the proponent is contacted to this effect. Otherwise, review comments necessary for the admissibility of the study are furnished to the proponent. The Inter-Ministerial Committee for the Environment gives a final opinion with regard to the impact study. Therefore, it is the responsibility of the Administration in Charge of the Environment to forward to the Inter-Ministerial Committee for the Environment files it adjudged admissible or satisfactory, comprising the following documents: (1) the EIS declared admissible, (2) the evaluation reports of the impact study, and (3) the evaluation reports of public audiences and consultation. Moreover, within twenty days of the receipt of the aforementioned documentation, the Inter-Ministerial Committee for the Environment opines on the EIS and forwards its opinion to the Ministry in Charge of the Environment. The Minister in Charge of the Environment has twenty days within which to make a final ruling on the environment impact study following the advice or opinion of the Inter-Ministerial Committee for the Environment. Should the Minister rule in favour of the study, a CEC is issued by its Ministry before the project is allowed to commence. Otherwise, a conditional ruling is accompanied by measures to be taken by the promoter in order to fulfil all the requirements needed to secure a certificate of environmental conformity. Alternatively, an unfavourable decision is tantamount to a prohibition of the execution of the project. The CEC is valid for three years from the date it is issued. In case the project is not commissioned within the validity period stipulated on the certificate, the certificate becomes void. In this vein, a revised and updated EIS becomes mandatory or obligatory for revalidation. It is important to recognize that the 2005 Decree also has provisions for monitoring and evaluation. The Decree requires relevant government services to undertake administrative and technical compliance monitoring, evaluation and enforcement. This is indeed carried out to ensure that there is effective and efficient implementation of the Environmental Management Plans (EMP) included in the EIS.

Finally, units that have never been subjected to an ESIA and are under operation are given thirty-six months from the date of signature of the decree[46] within which to conduct an environmental audit of their

[46] That is from the 23rd February 2005

installation. The audit, the law stipulates, must be accompanied by an EMP approved by the Administration in charge of the Environment and must comprise the following items; (1) the introductory summary which comprises the context, activity of installation studied; (2) the site which comprises of the location, environmental and historical context, land status; (3) the environmental management plan which comprises the facilities for the management of the environment, air emissions, effluents, management of waste, storage of chemical products, noise, emergency plan, maintenance of installations, underground water and contaminated soils, etc; (4) the investigation on the compliance with the laws, regulations and policies; and (5) the conclusions and recommendations for additional studies. This auditing was intended to proactively facilitate the integration of the ESIA within all already operating development sectors of Cameroon considering the fact that the environmental audit process was is still at an embryonic stage unlike the formal ESIA.

2. The International Commitments of Cameroon to Environmental Impact Assessment

Much efforts have been made by the Cameroonian government in the direction of ESIA. Cameroon is a signatory to a number of international conventions relating to environmental management. The most important ones include the Convention on International Trade in Endangered Species of Wild Fauna and Flora[47], which is an international agreement between governments drafted after a resolution adopted in 1963 at a meeting of members of the International Union for Conservation of Nature (IUCN). The text of the convention was agreed upon in 1973, and it entered into force on the 1st of July 1975. Its aim is to ensure that international trade in species of wild animals and plants does not threaten their survival. It accords varying degrees of protection to more than 33 000 plant and animal species. Other conventions include: the Convention for Co-operation in the Protection and Development of the Marine and Coastal Environment of the West and Central African Region[48] which covers the marine environment,

---

[47] Cameroon's Accession date is the 5th of June 1981 and it entered into force on the 3rd of September 1981.

[48] The Resolution adopted on 23 March 1981 in Abidjan and it came into force in Cameroon on 5th of August 1984.

coastal zones and related inland waters that fall within the jurisdiction of West and Central African States, including Mauritania and Namibia, which have become Contracting Parties to this Convention; the Convention on the Conservation of Nature and Natural Resources which has as objectives to enhance environmental protection; foster the conservation and sustainable use of natural resources, and harmonize and coordinate policies in these fields with a view to achieving ecologically rational, economically sound and socially acceptable development policies and programs; the Central African Forests Commission (COMIFAC) which was established in 2005, at a summit of the Central Africa Heads of State in Brazzaville, act as a regional forum for the conservation and sustainable joint management of the forest ecosystems in Central Africa[49]. It is the primary authority for decision-making and coordination of sub-regional actions and initiatives on conservation and sustainable management of the Congo Basin forests.

Moreover, the Vienna Convention for the Protection of the Ozone Layer signed in 1985, is a Multilateral Environmental Agreement which was agreed upon at the Vienna Conference of 1985 and entered into force in 1988. It acts as a framework for international efforts to protect the ozone layer. It includes the Montreal Protocol on Substances that Deplete the Ozone Layer which was signed in Montreal in 1987. The Montreal Protocol[50] is an international treaty designed to protect the ozone layer by phasing out the production of a number of substances believed to be responsible for ozone depletion. It is believed that adherence to the international agreement will lead to the recovery of the ozone layer by 2050. Also, the Convention on Biological Diversity (CBD)[51] is an international legally binding treaty adopted in Rio de Janeiro in June 1992. Its three main

[49] The countries include Cameroon, Central African Republic, Democratic Republic of Congo, Equatorial Guinea, Gabon, Chad, Burundi, Sao Tomé and Rwanda.

[50] The treaty was opened for signature on 16 September 1987, and entered into force on 1 January 1989, followed by a first meeting in Helsinki in May 1989. Since then, it has been revised seven times, in 1990 (London), 1991 (Nairobi), 1992 (Copenhagen), 1993 (Bangkok), 1995 (Vienna), 1997 (Montreal), and 1999 (Beijing).

[51] The Convention was opened for signature at the Earth Summit in Rio de Janeiro on 5 June 1992 and entered into force on 29 December 1993. The convention came into force in Cameroon on 17 January 1995. Law No. 94/1 and its implementing instruments reflect its application at the national level.

goals are conservation of bio-diversity; sustainable use of its components; and fair and equitable sharing of benefits arising from the exploitation of genetic resources. However, its objective is to develop national strategies for the conservation and sustainable use of biological diversity. Therefore, it is often considered as the key document regarding sustainable development. Also, the Global Strategy for Plant Conservation came to light in April 2002, when the parties of the UN CBD adopted the recommendations of the Grand Canarias Declaration Calling for a Global Plant Conservation Strategy, and adopted a sixteen-point plan aimed at reducing the rate of plant extinction around the world by 2010. Apparently, the United Nations Framework Convention on Climate Change[52] as an international environmental treaty drafted at the United Nations Conference on Environment and Development (the Earth Summit), held in Rio de Janeiro from 3 to 14 June 1992, has as objective to stabilize greenhouse gas concentrations in the atmosphere at a level that would prevent dangerous anthropogenic interference with the climate system. The UNFCCC was opened for signature on 9 May 1992, after an Intergovernmental Negotiating Committee produced the text of the Framework Convention as a report following its meeting in New York from 30 April to 9 May 1992. Also, the Kyoto Protocol[53] is the protocol to the United Nations Framework Convention on Climate Change (UNFCCC) aimed at fighting global warming. The Protocol was initially adopted in December 1997 in Kyoto, Japan, and entered into force on the 16th February 2005.

Furthermore, the United Nations Convention to combat desertification in those countries experiencing serious drought and/or desertification, particularly in Africa, is a Convention aimed at combating desertification and mitigating the effects of drought through national action programmes that incorporate long-term strategies supported by international cooperation and partnership arrangements. The Convention, the only one stemming from the direct recommendation of the Conference's Agenda 21, was adopted in Paris on 17 June 1994 and entered into force in December

---

52 It came into force on 21st of March 1994 and as of December 2009, the UNFCCC had 192 parties. Cameroon ratified the UNFCCC on the 19th of October 1994.

53 As of November 2009, 187 States had signed and ratified the protocol. Cameroon is also signatory to the Kyoto Protocol which entered into force in February 2005.

1996. It is the first and only internationally legally binding framework set up to address the problem of desertification. The Convention is based on the principles of participation, partnership and decentralization - the linchpin of good governance and sustainable development. It now has 193 country Parties to the Convention, giving it truly global scope. The Stockholm Convention on Persistent Organic Pollutants[54] is an international environmental treaty that aims to eliminate or restrict the production and use of persistent organic pollutants. Negotiations for the Convention were completed on 23 May 2001 in Stockholm. Co-signatories agreed to outlaw nine of the dozen dirty chemicals, limit the use of DDT to malaria control, and curtail inadvertent production of dioxins and furans. Also, the Rotterdam Convention on the Prior Informed Consent Procedure for Certain Hazardous Chemicals and Pesticides in International Trade is a multilateral treaty to promote shared responsibilities in relation to the importation of hazardous chemicals. It promotes the sharing of information and calls on exporters of hazardous chemicals to use proper labeling, include directions on safe handling, and inform purchasers of any known restrictions or bans. Parties can decide whether to allow or ban the importation of chemicals listed in the treaty, and exporting countries are obliged to ensure compliance by producers within their jurisdiction. Thus, the Ramsar Convention called the Convention on Wetlands of International Importance, is an international treaty for the conservation and sustainable utilization of wetlands, i.e. to stem the progressive encroachment on and loss of wetlands now and in the future, recognizing the fundamental ecological functions of wetlands and their economic, cultural, scientific, and recreational value. Also, the International Maritime Organization's International Convention on Civil Liability for Oil Pollution Damage[55] signed in 1969 to ensure adequate compensation for oil pollution damage resulting from maritime casualties involving oil tankers. It also places the liability for such damage on the owner of the ship from which the polluting oil escaped or was discharged.

[54] The convention came into force on 17 May 2004 with ratification by an initial 128 parties and 151 signatories.

[55] It was ratified on 17 May 1984 and came into force on 12 August 1984. It is covered by Law No. 83/16 of 21 July 1983.

B. CONSTRAINTS OF "ESIA" IN HYDROPOWER PROJECTS IN CAMEROON

The requirement of a state to conduct an ESIA in respect of activities with the potential to significantly affect the environment is reflected in Principle 17 of the UN Conference on Environment and Development (UNCED).[56] The UNCED recognized ESIA as a key tool for environmental protection and sustainable development. By implication, unless sustainable development criteria are included specifically among those used in environmental assessments, the ESIA may not contribute to sustainable development. This is crucial if developing countries are to integrate environmental concerns into their hydropower development plans.

1. Factors Limiting the implementation of Environmental Impact Assessment in Cameroon

- **Inadequate Scientific and Baseline Data**

The ESIA law of Cameroon fully dictates the administrative procedures that need to be followed in order to obtain planning permission. The use of baseline information ensures that identified and evaluated impacts are traced within the ESIA process, thus providing an efficient method of predicting the significance of impacts through existing environmental conditions. The insufficient or inadequate scientific and baseline data on the environment in most sectors in Cameroon undermine the efficiency and quality of EIS and the whole ESIA process.

- **Incompetent Personnel and Over Centralization**

A Prime Ministerial Decree[57] designating the Inter-Ministerial Advisory Committee for Environmental Impact Study was found to be inappropriate. In fact, in a series of personal communication with a senior specialist in the environmental management of highway projects in the Ministry of Public Works, a senior policy officer with a local NGO and a Director at the MINEP, it was revealed that the committee is composed of incompetent people. A committee of this sort is supposed to include scientists and a

---

[56] United Nations. (1992). *Report of the United Nations Conference on Environment and Development* (Rio De Janeiro, 3-14 June 1992). Original Report A/CONF.151/26 (Vol. I).
[57] See Article 15 paragraph 2 of Decree No. 2005/0577/PM

multidisciplinary technical staff with the requisite knowledge of ESIA and its applicability in their respective sectors. The problem probably stems from the fact that the ESIA review and approval is centralized in Yaounde and the officials lack a robust mastery of the ecological, physical, chemical, socio-economic and cultural environment of communities where ESIA projects are envisaged. The result of filling this committee with novices and incompetent personnel is poor performance, schism and approval of EIS that are fundamentally flawed, resulting to a detrimental impact on the substratum of CSR.

- **Constraints to Effective Public Participation**

Indeed, public participation is a fundamental component of the ESIA process. As *Wood*[58] explains, ESIA is not ESIA without consultation and participation. The European Commission strongly advocates public participation arguing that it increases the accountability and transparency of the decision – making process. The role and importance of public participation in environmental decision-making cannot be overlooked. The European Commission further established that effective public participation in the taking of decisions enables the public to express their views, and the decision maker has to take account of options and concerns which may be relevant to those decisions, thereby increasing the accountability and transparency of the decision-making process and contributing to public awareness of environmental issues and support for the decisions taken. However, looking at the current legal and procedural disposition regulating ESIA in Cameroon, it is glaring that public participation is not statutorily protected. Indeed, it is poorly represented in terms of timing and Communicational hurdles. Even though Article 17 of 2005 Decree states that the promoter or proponent shall send to the representatives of the population concerned at least thirty days before the date of the first meeting the program of public consultations comprising the date and venue of meetings, the descriptive and an explanatory report of the project and the purpose of consultations. But looking at the legal provision, it is not clear when this first meeting should be scheduled during the ESIA process and under what circumstances these consultations should be made. In fact it

[58] Wood (2002)., *op cit.*

would even seem that with regard to the first public participation is at the discretion of the proponent. This epitomises the fact that the public is treated with disdain in the current legal disposition. Indeed, the public should know exactly when the law mandates them to take part in public consultation within the framework of the ESIA procedure in Cameroon.

Although Article 11(1) of the 2005 Decree states that "the environmental impact study shall be carried out with the participation of the population concerned, through consultations and public meetings, for the purpose of sampling the opinion of the population on the project", paragraph 2 of the same article further stipulates that "public consultation shall refer to meetings held during the study in towns concerned by the project". As for public audience, it shall aim at advertising the study, recording possible oppositions to the project and enabling the population to give their say on the findings of the study. What impedes effective public participation with regard to the aforementioned provision is effective and efficient communication. Although Pidgin English and French are used to transmit fundamental knowledge about proposed ESIA projects to the illiterate Cameroon populace during public consultation, available information to enable the public participate effectively during public meetings is difficultly grasped by the lay person. The problem is accentuated by the lack of public knowledge on legal issues and the fact that most legal documents in Cameroon are in French and this presents a constraint to the English speaking population.

- **Inadequate Human Resources**

One of the factors that impede effective ESIA implementation in Cameroon is the inadequacy of scientists and technical staff or personnel. It would seem that so far only one institution[59] offers a post-graduate program in ESIA in Cameroon.

- **Lack of Indicators to Measure Progress towards Ecological Sustainability**

Article 21 of the 200r5 Decree provides that "units under exploitation and/or functioning shall within thirty six (36) months from the date of

[59] *"CRESA– Forêt-Bois"* – a regional centre affiliated to the University of Dschang

signature of the Decree carry out an environmental audit of their installations, accompanied by their EMP". However, as *Alemagi et al*[60] opine, this law fails to lay down any ecological threshold against which the provisions for a corporate environmental management plan can be evaluated. For example, the law does not prescribe a set of indicators that can be used to measure and evaluate the progress of the provisions provided in the corporate environmental management plan. It is our opinion, therefore, that evaluation will undoubtedly provide fundamental feedbacks that could be used to tackle arenas with deficiencies and shortcomings.

2. The "ESIA" Practice in Hydropower Projects in Cameroon

In Cameroon, the environmental assessment process is managed by the Office[61] of the Environmental Assessments in MINEP[62], created in 2004 by splitting it off from the MINFOF[63]. However, the budget allocated to MINEP is "not usually commensurate to its responsibilities".[64] In fact, the World Bank has noted that the Office of the Environmental Assessments within MINEP does not currently have the number of staff, with the necessary technical skills, or the resources to independently monitor and

[60] Alemagi, D; Sondo, A.V; Ertel, J. (2006)., *op cit.*

[61] The Office of the Environmental Assessments comprises of 3 units dealing with the Environmental Assessments, Environmental Audits & the Environmental Management Plans. The Office also serves as a secretariat to the Inter-ministerial Committee on the Environment, which formally reviews environmental assessments and environmental audits, as well as the EMPs

[62] As regards the environment, MINEP: the elaboration, coordination and follow up of the execution of the national politics of the environment; the coordination and follow up of regional and international cooperation in matters relating to the environment; the definition of measures regarding the rational management of natural resources in collaboration with other related ministries; informing the public to enable its participation in the management, protection and restoration of the environment; the elaboration of sectoral plans for protecting the environment in collaboration with other related ministries; negotiating international accord and conventions which are related to environmental protection.

[63] Given the importance of the forest industry in Cameroon's economy, MINFOF retained most of qualified staff

[64] World Bank (2008a)., 'Report no. 43880-CM, the Project Appraisal Document for the Environmental and Social Capacity Building for the Energy Sector Project –PreCesse', May 2008, p.15

control the implementation of the agreed EMPs. Furthermore, the Office is already struggling to keep pace with the increasing number of environmental assessments and audits. Therefore, under the 2005 Decree[65] on the conduction of the ESIA, all existing facilities are required to carry out environmental audits.[66] Indeed, without increase of capacity, the Office will not be capable of responding to the surge in the large infrastructure investments in the energy sector.[67] However, the PreCesse project was put in place with the aim to help MINEP restore its position as the national regulator of the environment by giving it a central coordination role in the ESIA and audits, resulting in the greater recognition and credibility vis-a-vis other governmental departments, civil society, the private sector, and the development partners.[68]

Altogether, the implementing agencies of the LPHP include MINEE, EDC[69], ARSEL[70] and AER[71]. However, experience has shown that the skills required for the preparation of a large hydro-energy sector generation investments are not readily available to governments in developing countries. For the preparatory activities of the LPHP, the project has a pragmatic solution of assisting the project unit which the EDC has put into place with a team of independent technical, environmental and social consultants, which are fully dedicated to project preparation and the bringing of international best practice experience.[72] Also, the LPHP[73]

---

[65] See Decree No. 2005/0577/PM of February 23, 2005; establishing the method for conducting environmental and social impact assessments (ESIA).

[66] According to the Decree, within 3 years after its adoption.

[67] *Ibid*

[68] *Ibid*

[69] Created by Decree No. 2006/406 of 29 November 2006

[70] Established by Law No. 98/ 022 of December 24, 1998 governing the Electricity sector in Cameroon and created by Decree No. 99/125 of June 15, 1998 as the hydro-electric sector regulator.

[71] Established under the Electricity Law of 1998 and Electricity Decree of 2000

[72] World Bank, (2008)., Project Appraisal Document for World Bank project P104456 on Energy Sector Development.

[73] The LPHP's environmental and social activities have been designed in a complex context, where challenges are numerous and opportunities multiple. These activities are monitored and evaluated at several levels by the various stakeholders according to the following design; EDC is LPHP's implementing agency, under the umbrella of both the MINEE and the

involves the activities of several ministries beyond the MINEE. At the centre, we have MINEP, MINFOF, MINFI, the Ministry of Social Affairs, the Ministry of Economy and Regional Planning, and the Ministry of Public Works, for the construction of access roads. At the peripherial level, EDC coordinates closely with these Ministries, either in a bilateral mode, or through the inter-ministerial coordination. At the field level, notably the implementation of the local development support activities, government activities have been coordinated in the framework of a Steering Committee - the 'Accompaniment, Facilitation and Monitoring Committee', placed under the leadership of the Governor of the Eastern Region with the EDC as the *'de jure'* vice-president, logistics provider and coordinator. The Independent Environmental and Social Panel made up of experts with proven international experience in Environmental and Social Assessments, is an independent entity set up by the EDC in agreement with the GoC and the donors to provide advice and recommendations on all environmental and social aspects of the LPHP.

Altogether, Coyne and Bellier/ISL group, that is, the dam engineer, has the overall mission to manage and ensure the control and supervision of the construction works of the LPHP. However, on the environmental and social aspects, the engineer must ensure compliance of the PTSs and the methods designed and prepared by the work contractors with the Construction of the ESMP as required in the call for bids by the EDC, check and control the implementation of the said PTSs and lastly, for all the associated infrastructure works, provide the EDC with the technical assistance required to guarantee compliance with the environmental and social standards

---

MINFI. The project has received close attention from the Cameroonian Presidency. A technical advisor to the Director General of EDC is dedicated to the environmental and social matters. The Project Director, placed under the authority of the Director General has overall responsibility for the design and implementation of all financial, technical, environmental and social issues related to the Lom Pangar dam and its associated infrastructure. The Sub-directorate of Safety Environment and Regional Development is under the Project Director and ensures the day-to-day steering and monitoring of all environmental and social aspects of the LPHP, notably the organization of environmental studies, monitoring of the environmental aspects of the construction works, the management of the compensation and resettlement-linked aspects, and the implementation of the ESMP.

defined in the 'Construction of the ESMP', provide the engineering services for the construction of the bridge and of the second phase of the EDC's workers camp. Also COTCO play a specific role in the construction of the pipeline before the reservoir was flooded. In doing so, COTCO complied with its own IFC/World Bank requirements and cooperated with the EDC under the conditions laid-out in the Interface Agreement that was finalized in February 2011.

- **The National Legal Framework of the Environmental and Social Management**

In fact, in the final draft report of the Environmental and Social Plan of July 2010, the GoC referred to the national laws, regulations and policies applicable to the LPHP before the Safeguard Policies of the World Bank.[74] In this light, the 1996 environmental management law[75] provides the general legal framework relying on six basic principles.[76] Moreover, the law was complemented by other national laws on environmental and social concerns. Indeed, the role of the environmental regulator in Cameroon was assigned to MINEP, since it was established in 2004, and had the mandate to design, coordinate and monitor Cameroon's environmental policy. The decree defining the modalities for conducting the environmental assessments was adopted in February 2005.[77] Thus, in the context of large infrastructure investments, MINEP is empowered to provide investors and promoters with regulatory services, including: (1) the review and clearance of terms of reference (ToRs) for the preparation of environmental assessments and audits, (2) the review of these assessments and audits, and (3) the monitoring and control of the environmental management plans arising from these assessments and audits.[78]

---

[74] GoC, (2010)., *op cit.* pp. 16-25

[75] See Law No. 96/12 of 5 August 1996 on environmental management

[76] See Title I Chapiter III, Article 9 of Law n° 96/12 of 5 August 1996 on Environmental Management on the Fundamental Principles (precautionary, preventive and corrective action, polluter pays, responsibility, participation and subsidiarity).

[77] See Decree No. 2005/0577/PM of February 23, 2005; establishing the method for conducting environmental and social impact assessments (ESIA).

[78] The monitoring and control of industrial plants is the responsibility of a corps of inspectors within the Ministry of Industry.

Thus, the Law[79] laying down the forestry, wildlife and fisheries regulations, seeks to protect and regulate the use of forests, wildlife and fishery resources. Moreover, the provisions of this Law are highly applicable in the management and conservation of the Deng Deng forest which is vital for the sustainability of the LPHP. Also, Law No. 85/09 of 4 July 1985, lays down the procedures governing the expropriation for public use and the conditions to compensate the affected population. However, this law falls short of the international standard, although it is still instrumental within the national arena as it provides some guidelines for the implementation of the ESIA. The law[80] relating to phytosanitary protection also provides that chemical treatments should be conducted with due respect for agricultural good practices so that human and animal health and the environment should be protected. Therefore, only the certified phytosanitary products and those benefitting from a temporary sale authorization should be used within the LPHP area. Also, the Law[81] on the gazetted and hazardous industrial units provides in its Article 3 that the hazards generated and/or the potential nuisances generated by the gazetted units shall be split into two classes. Thus, the LPHP can be categorized as Class 1 in accordance with this law. Equally, Law No. 98/005 of 14 April 1998 laying down the regulations governing water resources and provisions to safeguard the principles of the environmental management and the protection of public health is paramount to the enhancement of the sustainability of the LPHP. Also, Law No. 98/15 of 14 July 1998 on establishments classified as dangerous and unhealthy provides the legal framework for the control and check of their impact on environmental management and public health.

Moreover, space management and land tenure form the substratum for any hydropower engagement. In this regard, they are governed by thirty three (33) legal instruments. For land tenure, there is the Land Ordinance[82] which provides the modalities for the acquisition of land title, the State

---

[79] See Law No. 94/001 of 20 January 1994 lays down forestry, wildlife and fisheries regulations.

[80] See Law No. 2003/003 of 21st April, 2003 relating to phytosanitary protection.

[81] See Law No. 98/015 of 14th July, 1998 on the gazetted and hazardous industrial units.

[82] See Ordinance No. 74/001 of July 1974 fixing land regulation.

Land Ordinance[83] which provides the modalities for the recognition and demarcation state land, the 1974 Ordinance[84] which provides the modalities for expropriation for public use and the terms of and conditions for compensation and the law[85] laying down the terms and conditions for compensating owners of property destroyed. Indeed, the law[86] on civil society also regulates the functioning of NGOs and lays down the conditions for their creation which include effective participation in poverty reduction and the accomplishment of the public interest missions. However, the participation of civil society in the energy sector is very low as energy policies are formulated without consultations with the civil society. So, the adoption of a participatory approach and the dissemination of information are mandatory in the conduct of the impact assessments.[87] Furthermore, the validation of the impact assessments is subject to the opinion of the ICE, which is often not made public. This may explain the low participation of the public in the approval of ESIAs, which is an important step in the process although the situation has been alleviated by donors and other international NGOs. Also, two other instruments govern women's empowerment, and they include Decree No. 97/148/PM of 8th April 1997 to create a National Steering Committee for the Economic Empowerment of Rural Women and the Improvement of Women's Living Conditions and Decree No. 2000/001/PM of 4th January 2000 to organize and lay down the functioning of women's empowerment centers. Thus, the basic laws and decrees governing environmental and social management in Cameroon are inextricably linked to the LPHP.

There may always be a gap between what the government undertakes on paper to do and what it practically does. So stakeholders, including the project-affected populations, may also have doubts as to the extent to which the government will deliver its sustainability promises. This is because in

---

[83] See Ordinance No. 74/002 of July 1974 fixing State lands regulation.

[84] See Ordinance No. 74/003 of July 1974 fixing for the modalities for expropriation for public purposes and the terms and conditions of compensation.

[85] See Law No. 85/009 of July 4, 1985 laying down procedures governing expropriation for public purposes and the conditions for compensation

[86] See Law No. 99-14 of 22 December 1999 which regulates the functioning of NGOs

[87] See Part IV, Section 74 *et seq* of Law No. 96/12 of 5th August 1996, on provisions concerning the ESIA.

terms of compliance and enforcement, transparency is still in doubt. In some cases, the government approves long ESIA reports, without subsequently deploying sufficient energy and resources to ensure that the measures contained in the resettlement and development plans are implemented and enforced. This debility is mitigated in the LPHP through the putting in place of ESAMP in accordance with international Safeguard Policies

- **The International Policies on Environmental Management**

The policies applicable in hydropower projects in Cameroon are the Strategic Priorities of the World Commission on Dams[88], the Safeguard Policies of the World Bank, the Performance Standards of the IFC, the private financing arm of the World Bank, the 'Equator Principles' adopted by the EP Financing Institutions and the Hydropower Sustainability Assessment Protocol produced by the Hydropower Sustainability Assessment Forum as published by the IHA.[89] These are analyzed below with a view to bringing out the key features for the purposes of this write-up.

- **The World Bank Safeguard Policies Requirements:** The policies of the international organisations, such as the Safeguard Policies of the World Bank, readily complement national laws and regulations. Thus, the environmental and social management of the LPHP has made it more attractive to financiers, and thus has facilitated its funding under the best possible terms for the GoC. However, integrating the environmental and social issues upstream also increases the project's profitability by anticipating potential problems and avoiding *ex-post* mitigating measures, always more costly than prevention. Thus, the impact of the LPHP on the economic and

---

[88] World Commission on Dams (2000), 'Dams and Development: a New Framework for Decision-Making', Earthscan Publications, November 2000; Bosshard, P. (2010a), 'The Dam Industry, the World Commission on Dams and the HSAF Process', Water Alternatives 3 (2): 58-70 and Briscoe, J. (2010), 'Viewpoint-Overreach and response: the politics of the WCD and its aftermath', Water Alternatives 3 (2): 339-415; WWF (2005), 'To dam or not to dam? Five years on from the World Commission on Dams', report of the World Wide Fund For Nature, Dams Rights initiative

[89] IHA (2010), 'Hydropower Sustainability Assessment Protocol', recommended final draft, September 2010

social development in Cameroon is also enhanced by the proper management of the social and environmental issues and challenges. Beyond the obvious need for complying with the national rules and regulations on the environmental assessment as explained above, the GoC has decided to exert due social and environmental diligence on the LPHP according to the international good practices, notably the World Bank's safeguard policies. In this light, the other main donors have followed suit and considered that in the case of the LPHP funding, aligning on the World Bank's safeguard policies would fulfill their own requirements. In fact, the safeguard policies have been screened to assess which of them, if any, were triggered by LPHP. The triggered safeguard policies of the World Bank comprise the '*Environmental Policies*'[90] and the *'Social Policies*'[91], while its *'Legal Policies*'[92] are non-triggered. Therefore, for the environmental assessment (EA) purposes, the World Bank has placed projects in three categories[93] in order to determine the baseline on which to carry out the EAs. Beyond the screening[94], no further EA action is required for a Category "C" project. The Safeguard Policies stress that the environmental management plan is to be established within the project, 'integrated within its overall planning, design, budget and implementation'. From the particular perspective of the populations affected by the projects, the World Bank's Safeguard Policies provide some reassurance such as, for example, that the resettlement plan will form part of the project. It should also be noted that where the

---

[90] Which are 'environmental assessment', 'forests', 'critical natural habitats', 'pest management', 'safety of dams'

[91] Which are 'involuntary resettlement', 'indigenous peoples'(non-triggered), 'physical cultural resources'

[92] Which are 'international waterways', 'disputed areas'

[93] A proposed project is classified as *'Category A'* (if it is likely to have significant adverse environmental impacts that are sensitive, diverse or unprecedented); A proposed project is classified as *'Category B'* (if its potential adverse environmental impacts on human populations or environmentally important areas, including wetlands, forests, grasslands and other natural habitats, are less adverse than those of Category A projects; these impacts are 'site-specific'; few if any are irreversible; and in most cases mitigation measures can be designed more readily than for Category A projects) - The scope of the EA for a Category B project may vary from project to project, but it is narrower than for Category A projects; And a proposed project is classified *'Category C'* if it is likely to have minimal or no adverse environmental impacts.

[94] The initial process by which the need for an EA and its extent/type is determined.

domestic law does not meet the standard of compensation at replacement cost, compensation under the domestic law is supplemented by the additional measures necessary to meet the replacement cost standard[95]. Indeed, this situation was readily visible in the case of the compensation of the indigenous people affected by the LPHP where the national legal provisions applicable were found to be inadequate. In this regard, these provisions were complemented by the safeguard policies of the World Bank, in order to adequately compensate the indigenous people in accordance to international standard. Moreover, the World Bank Procedures[96] provide that the World Bank and the Borrower can review past borrower and implement the agency's experience with similar operations. Also, the Procedures[97] provide the key requirement to notify borrowers and prospective borrowers of the need to respond on time, if the impacts of the hydropower endeavours 'are irreversible', or raise issues under the Operational Policies, for example, the natural habitats, involuntary settlement or the indigenous peoples as appreciated in the case of LPHP with the preparation of the ESAMP.

The World Bank Triggered Environmental Policies: There are four in number. The first is environmental assessment. In relation to the LPHP, there was a hindrance as it was considered to have a significant and irreversible environmental impact. However, the government prepared an environmental assessment with the support of the AFD, to reduce or mitigate these impacts. Also, the ESIA and the ESMP were prepared, following the World Bank guidance[98] for LPHP as a category "A" project. Therefore, the draft environment assessment (EA) was publicly disclosed and discussed in 2006, to enhance its sustainability in Cameroon. The government also requested additional work before the EA was approved, in a decision by the Minister of Environment in May 2006. Also, an additional study was done in 2007 regarding the location of the workers camp and the access patterns to the dam site. This study was reviewed by the World Bank. Thus, the critical issue that was addressed was the flooding by the reservoir

[95] Operational Policy (OP 4.12), Annex 3-B, in the footnote defining 'replacement cost'
[96] World Bank Procedures (BP 4.12) on involuntary resettlement
[97] World Bank Procedures (BP 7.50) on the Projects on International Waterways
[98] *Ibid*

of the Chad-Cameroon pipeline. However, the management of change was prepared by the IFC and COTCO, including the preparation of the ESAP and the amendment to the Chad-Cameroon EMP to ensure that its implementation remained compliant. The cumulative impact assessment conducted on the basis of the ToRs was satisfactory to the World Bank. Also, a detailed forestry study regarding the recovery of wood in the reservoir and its induced impacts was commissioned on the basis of the ToRs satisfactory to the World Bank, in coordination with the AFD. A panel of experts had been functioning intermittently since 2005, supported through the World Bank.

The second environmental policy is recited to the natural habitats[99]. The LPHP. Project had significant impact on the natural habitats, both during the construction and the operation phases of the dam. The main impact was the flooding of about 540 km^2, including approximately 300 km^2 of natural forest. The EA indicated that none of the flooded terrestrial habitat was critical.[100] However, the dam site was located next to portions of the Deng Deng Forest that was critical habitats, particularly because of the presence of a viable population of gorillas, and a significant population of chimpanzees. The environmental significance of the Deng Deng forest was identified in the context of the Chad-Cameroon Pipeline Project and led to its realignment, and was also discussed with the government in the context of the Forestry and Environment Project. Moreover, the no project alternative was a gradual degradation of the Deng Deng forest that could lead to the extinction of its gorilla population. In the context of the LPHP, the government commissioned additional work by the World Conservative Society on the Deng Deng gorillas in the late 2008, including the immediate protection measures that led to the establishment of the National Park before the construction of the dam, which occurred in January 2010.[101]

The third environmental policy is related to forest issues.[102]. These include the recovery of wood from the reservoir, as well as the control of the

[99] World Bank Policies (OP/BP 4.04) on Natural Habitats

[100] *Ibid*

[101] See Decree No. 2010/0482 of 18 March 2010 on the creation of the Deng Deng National

[102] World Bank Policies (OP/BP 4.36) on the Forest Issues

induced impacts at the periphery of the reservoir. However, a supplementary study was commissioned on the basis of ToRs satisfactory to the World Bank and it proposed that the recovery of the wood followed the World Bank guidelines, including the benefit-sharing with the local population, and that any induced impact be limited. The study also disclosed that most of the biomass needed to be removed in order to reduce greenhouse gases after flooding.

The fourth environmental policy relates to the Management of Pest[103]. Given the limited, but potentially harmful quantities of pesticides and other biocide products utilized for the three major categories of works related to the LPHP, that is, the construction/tree removal works, the support to agricultural development and the public health management as a mitigating measure, it was decided in the course of the ESA preparation, to prepare a PMP which was attached to the ESIA report.

The World Bank Triggered and Non-Triggered 'Social Policies': The social policy applicable to the LPHP, whether or not trigged by the World Bank, are three in number. The first has to do with the management if physical natural resources. This is a triggered policy since the Physical Cultural Resources were covered in the draft EA from 2005. Further work was in the application of the World Bank policies for the future flooded area as well as for the major linear infrastructure works. Thus, the need for capacity enhancement in the Ministry of Culture was identified and appropriate action recommended.[104] Moreover, the processes for building capacity in the construction teams as well as to ensure the appropriate conservation of the archaeological artefacts found during the construction and maintenance of the main infrastructure works were built into a discrete sub-component of the environmental management plan.

The second social policy is related to Involuntary Resettlement[105]: This is also a triggered policy since the LPHP had direct and indirect social

---

[103] World Bank Policies (OP 4.09) on the Management of Pest

[104] Decree No. 2008/178 of 22 May 2008 on the ratification of the UNESCO Convention of 17 October 2003, for the Safeguarding of Intangible Cultural Heritage

[105] World Bank Policies (OP/BP 4.12) on Involuntary Resettlement

impacts[106] in the project area and beyond. Consistent with the World Bank Group safeguards policies, the Involuntary Resettlement was triggered and the social mitigation plans identified. The resettlement action plans by the broad categories of works, that is, the dam and reservoir, the power plant and the transmission line and the access roads, were done as well as the Deng Deng national park to mitigate, offset, reduce the negative impacts and strengthen the positive impacts on the communities in the project area. Indeed, the resettlement recommendations were packaged in a separate set of Resettlement Action Plans (RAPs).

The third social policy is related to the indigenous peoples[107]. This is a non-triggered policy since no pygmies and other indigenous peoples were found in the project area. The case of the Mbororos present in the project area, mostly through herding activities, was analysed and discussed and targeted measures were built into the RAPs. This case, in fact, proves the World Bank's failure to respect its own Guidelines on the indigenous peoples. As a bank which had to play a vital role in financing the LPHP, it should have adhered to its policy on indigenous people.[108] Moreover, the Bank's policy on indigenous peoples requires, among other things, that an

---

[106] Social impacts include changes in people's way of life, their culture, community, political systems, environment, health and wellbeing, their personal and property rights and their fears and aspirations. Examples of projects with significant social impacts include: landfill and hazardous waste disposal sites; power and industrial plants; dams and reservoirs; and roads and linear developments. The main types of social impacts that occur as a result of these project related changes can be grouped into five overlapping categories: *Lifestyle impacts* – on the way people behave and relate to family, friends and cohorts on a day-to-day basis; *Cultural impacts* – on shared customs, obligations, values, language, religious belief and other elements which make a social or ethnic group distinct; *Community impacts* – on infrastructure, services, voluntary organisations, activity networks and cohesion; *Quality of life impacts* – on sense of place, aesthetics and heritage, perception of belonging, security and livability, and aspirations for the future; *Health impacts* – on mental, physical and social well being, although these aspects are also the subject of health impact assessment

[107]World Bank Policies (OP/BP 4.10) on the Indigenous Peoples

[108] It should be noted that the World Bank is not a human rights organization. It is a financial institution with the main purpose of giving loan for development projects and making the assurance of its return unless in the case of concession agreements. However, recently the Bank has declared its concern for the human rights of the indigenous peoples with the adoption of OD 4.20.

impact assessment be made by the Bank where there is a legal gap concerning the recognition of the local communities' rights.[109] In this regard, the Bank had relied on the Indigenous Peoples Plan (IPP) which was meant to develop the indigenous community, but was criticized because the IPP was built on the assumption that the future commitments would be made by the GoC towards the protection of the indigenous communities affected by the project.[110] Yet these commitments were still not fully achieved and the IPP was not prepared in line with the Bank's Operational Directives which stressed the need for the informed participation of the local communities.[111]

The World Bank Triggered and Non-Triggered 'Legal Policies'

The legal policies of the World Bank, whether or not triggered, are two in number. The first is related to the safety of dams[112]. This is considered as a triggered policy because EDC had already appointed an independent dam safety panel during the project preparation. However, an instrumentation plan was elaborated as part of the revised engineering design. Also, a construction, supervision and quality assurance plan, including a provision for the continuation of the dam safety panel, and the draft operating and the maintenance plan were reviewed by the dam safety panel and submitted to the World Bank before the authorization to appraise the LPHP.

The second which relates to Non-Triggered Policies are projects on international waterways[113] and in disputed areas[114]. Moreover, any commonalities and differences between the requirements of the seven triggered safeguard policies and national laws and decrees were identified

---

[109] The directive provides policy guidance to (a) ensure that indigenous people benefit from development projects, and (b) avoid or mitigate potentially adverse effects on indigenous people caused by Bank-assisted activities. It also requires special action to be taken by the Bank where its investments affect indigenous peoples, tribes, ethnic minorities, or other groups whose social and economic status restricts their capacity to assert their interests and rights in land and other productive resources. See Operational Directives 4.20 on Indigenous Peoples. 1991.

[110] Horta., *op cit,* 2006, p. 11

[111] World Bank Policies (OD 4.20)., 1991. Parag. 6, 8 & 9

[112]World Bank Policies (OP/BP 4.37) on the Safety of Dams

[113] World Bank Policies (OP/BP 7.50)

[114] World Bank Policies (OP/BP 7.60)

and several safeguard policies requirements that are beyond the Cameroonian expectations, in particular for large and complex projects like the LPHP, were identified. Therefore, the safeguard policy compliance was a requirement to authorize project appraisal which is a key step in the World Bank project processing. Thus, based on its own internal review of the environmental and social assessment, the World Bank decided whether or not to appraise the LPHP. Once the decision was made, all environmental and social documentation needs were disclosed to the GoC and on the World Bank's external Web site, and a summary in English sent to its Board of Directors. The Board presentation of the project is generally at least four months after the decision to appraise; a delay fulfils the requirements of the US so-called *Pelosi* amendment. Should the environmental and social documentation be deemed unacceptable by the Bank, the Bank's comments on the compliance check need to be incorporated before a new appraisal decision process is started?

- The World Commission of Dams' Recommendations on "ESIA"

There is a difference between the WCD and the other four policies mentioned above as far as the LPHP is concerned. While the latter are directed at their own particular areas of activity, the World Bank and IFC are directed to projects funded by the World Bank group, the Equator Principles to the commercial bank financings and the Protocol to the developers/operators and other actors. The reality is that the WCD recommendations "were not embraced by all stakeholders".[115] The WCD recommendations did attract the approval of many NGOs and civil society groups, and some governments.[116] However, the hydropower sector felt that the weight of the group of WCD commissioners was tilted in favour of other actors and participants in the dams' debate. The then World Bank Senior Water Adviser has since recorded[117] that, the agreed-on process was

[115] Smith, (2010), *op cit,* p.438.

[116] International River 2010 points to five governments (Germany, Nepal, South Africa, Sweden and Vietnam) which organized processes of dialogue to discuss the WCD recommendations and national policies, and additionally comments that the member countries of the OECD and EU issued statements recognizing the value of the WCD Strategic Priorities.

[117] Briscoe (2010), *op cit.* p.406

for a draft of the WCD report to be circulated prior to finalisation in a manner inclusive of all stakeholders. This, he adds, was not done and the Report was not shared with stakeholders before its release[118]. One body of opinion has considered that the WCD commissioners had tried to push the dams and development agenda too far and too fast. In contrast, another body of opinion supported the setting of the demanding agenda with which, in accordance with the case argued by the WCD, all large dam and infrastructure projects should comply. So, for instance, the Strategic Priorities 1 of the WCD proposed the *'free, prior and informed consent'* of the indigenous people, which was both warmly applauded by some as being essential for the protection of the ways of life of the tribal peoples, but vigorously rejected by others, as a 'de facto' veto right on development. The WCD represented a benchmark.

CONCLUSION

Although the prevailing legal disposition regularizing ESIA from a process and procedural perspective is monumental, it is usually imperative to identify the constraints on its successful implementation in relation to hydropower projects. Since hydropower investments can play an important role in the Cameroonian economy by enhancing sustainable development. The reasons why hydropower projects encounter problems have been explained. However, by implementing the necessary reforms and learning from best practices, the GoC and its development partners took solid steps towards resolving the hydropower debility. Moreover, the improvement of incentives for private investors has had a key role for catalyzing investment in the sector. These initiatives have not only helped to close the demand-resources gap but they have equally improved the management of services in the hydropower sector as appreciated with respect to the development, operation and management of the LPHP. This has been done by taking into cognizance the viable legal mechanisms to mitigate the economic, social and environmental risks in the project. Thus, as the findings of this article suggest, if concrete improvements are to be secured, there is a need to focus more attention on the recommendations prescribed within the context of

---

[118] *Ibid*

this paper. Moreover, it is worth acknowledging that even though the GoC has undertaken the monumental step, by promulgating the ESIA law and its requisite procedural guidelines, there are still lots of barriers to the effective and efficient implementation of the current legislative framework. Altogether, in recognition of this, the following concrete strategies and recommendation could be used to obviate the existing impediments of ESIA: the need for indigenous knowledge in ESIA, the decentralization of powers in the ESIA process, the pro-active approach vis-à-vis communication and consultation with the public, and the need for capacity building and monitoring.

TENDANCE DES DISPOSITIONS PÉNALES DANS LA CONSTITUTION CAMEROUNAISE DE 1996

Hervé Magloire MONEBOULOU MINKADA[1]

Résumé

La Constitution est souvent définie comme la loi fondamentale d'un État. Cette définition permet de se faire une idée de la place qu'occupe la Constitution dans l'ordonnancement juridique interne. C'est la norme suprême à partir de laquelle les autres trouvent un fondement juridique. Dès lors, la loi pénale, à l'instar de toutes les autres lois internes, ne peut qu'avoir un fondement dans la Constitution. Toutefois, l'analyse ne se contente pas de cette évidence. Elle cherche à dégager les tendances observables après identification des dispositions constitutionnelles structurant le droit pénal. Et deux tendances se dégagent : l'objectivation d'une part et la subjectivation d'autre part des dispositions pénales dans la Constitution camerounaise du 18 janvier 1996.

Mots clés : Constitution– droit pénal- procédure pénale–droit objectif–droits subjectifs.

Abstract

We use to say that the Constitution is the fundamental law of the State. It means that the Constitution is the higher law amongst the laws of the State. For this reason, the penal law has a link with the Constitution. However, it is not the aim of this study to describe this statement. Our challenged is to identify the penal provisions of the cameroonian Constitution of 1996 and to discover the tendencies. The result of the analysis gives two tendencies. The first tendency deals with the provisions in

[1] *Agrégé des Facultés de Droit, Université de DOUALA (Cameroun), Tel : 679783741 ; BP : 4982, moneboulou@yahoo.fr*

favour the law as a general rule. The second tendency put together the provisions in favour of individuals.

Key words : Constitution–penal law–penal proceedings–positive law–subjective rights.

Introduction

Un pénaliste dans un banquet sur les 20 ans de la révision constitutionnelle du 18 janvier 1996[2], n'est-ce pas un cheveu dans une soupe ? L'étonnement peut être fondé pour ceux qui rattachent le Droit pénal[3] au droit privé et infondé pour ceux qui en font une discipline mixte ou rattachée au droit public. Toutes choses qui relancent la question de la distinction entre droit privé et droit public[4]. Loin de ce débat, l'intérêt de cette intervention est tributaire de la nature de la Constitution[5] et de sa place dans la hiérarchie des normes d'un État. La Constitution est une loi fondamentale et se trouve au sommet des normes à l'intérieur d'un État[6]. Elle est le chapitre introductif de tous les droits objectifs en vigueur dans un État. Au regard de cette position, il devient difficile au droit pénal de ne pas

---

[2] Loi n°96/06 du 18 janvier 1996 portant révision de la Constitution du 02 juin 1972 modifiée et complétée par la loi n° 2008/001 du 14 avril 2008.

[3]. De façon générale, le droit pénal pose les interdits fondamentaux qui sont la condition même de toute vie sociale. Voir, DESPORTES. F et LE GUNEHEC. F., *Droit pénal général*, Paris, 10e édition, Economica, 2003, p. 1.

[4] Montesquieu définissait le droit public (appelé par lui « droit politique ») comme « les lois dans le rapport qu'ont ceux qui gouvernent avec ceux qui sont gouvernés », et le droit privé (pour lui « droit civil »), comme « les lois dans le rapport que tous les citoyens ont entre eux ». V.GUILLIEN. R., « Droit public et droit privé », *Mélanges Brèthe de la Gressaye*, 1967, p. 311 s., ZOLLER.E., *Introduction au droit public*, 2006 ; *De l'intérêt de la summa divisio Droit public-Droit privé ?,* (dir.) BONNET et DEUMIER. P., 2010 ; TERRE. F., *Mélanges Gandolfi,* éd. Giuffre, 2004, t. 4, p. 1811 s.

[5] Ensemble des règles suprêmes fondant l'autorité étatique, organisant ses institutions, lui donnant ses pouvoirs, et souvent aussi lui imposant des limitations, en particulier en garantissant des libertés aux sujets ou citoyens. On distingue la constitution formelle (document écrit) et la constitution matérielle (règles ayant un objet constitutionnel, quelles que soient les formes qu'elles revêtent). CORNU. G., dir. *Vocabulaire juridique*, Paris, 10e édition, PUF, 2014, p.251.

[6]HAMON. F. et TROPER M., *Droit constitutionnel,* Paris, LGDJ, 2005, p. 45. Voir aussi COHENDET.M-A., *Droit constitutionnel*, Paris, Montchrestien, 2002, p. 71.

présenter un lien avec la Constitution. L'expression utilisée dans la thématique est : « les dispositions pénales ». Cependant, il convient d'éviter une scission avec la discipline normative qui les abrite, c'est-à-dire le Droit pénal[7]. Ce vocable mérite d'être approché largement en intégrant le droit pénal de fond et le droit pénal de forme. Le droit pénal de fond ou droit pénal général est une discipline qui étudie les composantes de l'infraction, le régime de la responsabilité et les sanctions applicables[8]. Et le droit pénal de forme ou procédure pénale est la discipline orientée vers les enquêtes et la poursuite des infractions, le jugement et les voies de recours[9]. Le droit pénal présente des liens avec la Constitution, parce qu'il peut être constitutionnalisé d'une part, ou parce qu'il peut contourner la Constitution[10] d'autre part. Mais tel n'est pas la grille d'analyse retenue. Plutôt, il importe de lire la Constitution du 18 janvier 1996 au Cameroun, de rechercher les dispositions relatives au Droit pénal et de dégager les tendances possibles. Les précisions terminologiques permettent d'éviter des équivoques sur le thème : « Tendance des dispositions pénales dans la Constitution du 18 janvier 1996 ». Il en ressort une question axiale

---

[7]La majuscule du terme « Droit pénal » est ici entendu au sens le plus large, couvrant non seulement le droit de fond (droit pénal général des éléments constitutifs de l'infraction, de la responsabilité et des peines et droit pénal spécial naturel des personnes et des biens), mais aussi l'organisation pénale en matière de police et de juridictions, mais encore la procédure pénale, de la constatation des faits au jugement et aux voies de recours. Voir, CEDRAS. J., *Le droit pénal américain*, Paris, PUF, Collection « Que sais-je ? », 1997, p. 3.

[8] Lire sur cette question : DESPORTES. F et LE GUNEHEC. F., *Droit pénal général*, op.cit., 1055 pages ; PRADEL. J., *Droit pénal général*, Paris, 18e édition, Cujas, 2010, 726 pages.

[9] Lire sur la question : PRADEL. J., *Procédure pénale*, Paris, 16e éditions, Éditions Cujas, 2011, p. 933 pages.

[10]On peut au regard des lois pénales en vigueur au Cameroun affirmer que les unes passent par la Constitution. Elle est le texte qui les introduit dans l'ordonnancement juridique. Les autres lois contournent la Constitution, c'est-à-dire n'entrent pas dans l'ordonnancement juridique camerounais par l'entremise de la Constitution. Il en est ainsi des normes pénales communautaires (droit pénal de la CEMAC et droit pénal CIMA), les normes pénales uniformes (droit pénal de l'Organisation Africaine de la Propriété Intellectuelle et droit pénal Organisation pour l'Harmonisation en Afrique du Droit des Affaires). Lire sur cette question : OUMAROU. A., *Code de lois pénales*, Yaoundé, PUA, 2006, 462 pages ; SOCKENG. R., *Droit pénal des affaires OHADA*, Douala, Presses MINSI, 2007, 242 pages.

permettant de guider l'analyse : **peut-on ressortir la tendance que prennent les dispositions pénales de la Constitution camerounaise de 1996 ?**

La question présente un intérêt aux plans théorique et pratique. Théoriquement, elle s'inscrit dans l'interdisciplinarité. Les dispositions de la Constitution prouvent que droit constitutionnel et droit pénal dialoguent, à côté du dialogue déjà illustré entre droit constitutionnel et science politique[11]. Et les réflexions sur la Constitution ne passionnent pas seulement les publicistes[12] et politologues[13], mais aussi les pénalistes[14]. Pratiquement, le sujet interpelle sur les techniques de constitutionnalisation du droit pénal. Pour ce qui est de la constitutionnalisation du droit[15] en

---

[11] MELONE S, MINKOA SHE. A, SINDJOUN L., (dir), *La réforme constitutionnelle du 18 janvier 1996 au Cameroun, Aspects juridiques et politiques*, Yaoundé, Fondation Friedrich Ebert-GRAP, 1996, 418 pages.

[12] OLINGA.A. D., *La constitution de la République du Cameroun*, Yaoundé, PUCAC, 2013, 272 pages, NGUELE ABADA. M, « Ruptures et continuités constitutionnelles en République du Cameroun : réflexion à propos de la réforme constitutionnelle du 18 janvier 1996 », RJPIC, 1996, n° 3, pp. 272-293. ; MELONE S, MINKOA SHE. A, SINDJOUN L., (dir), *La réforme constitutionnelle du 18 janvier 1996 au Cameroun, Aspects juridiques et politiques*, lire les auteurs suivants : DONFACK SOKENG. L., « Les ambiguïtés de la révision constitutionnelle du 18 Janvier 1996 au Cameroun », pp 34-53, MOUELLE KOMBI. N., « La loi camerounaise du 18 janvier 1996 et le droit international », pp. 126-145, GUIMDO. B., « La constitutionnalisation de la décentralisation », pp. 292-219. ; ONDOA. M., « Loi n° 96-06 du 18 janvier 1996 portant révision de la constitution du 02 juin 1972. Commentaire » in Juridis Périodique, n° 25, 1996, p. 11. ; KAMTO. M., « La révision constitutionnelle ou écriture d'une nouvelle Constitution ? », Lex Lata, n° s 023-024, 1996, pp. 17-20 ; OWONA. J., *Droits constitutionnels et institutions politiques du monde contemporain. Etude comparative*, Paris, L'Harmattan, 2010, 730 pages.

[13] SINDJOUN. L., « L'imagination constitutionnelle de la nation », in MELONE S, MINKOA SHE. A, SINDJOUN L., (dir), *La réforme constitutionnelle du 18 janvier 1996 au Cameroun, Aspects juridiques et politiques*, op.cit., pp. 78-103.

[14] Lire sur cette question : HOURQUEBIE. F. et PELTIER.V., (dir.), *Droit constitutionnel et grands principes du droit pénal*, Paris, Éditions Cujas, Actes du colloque, Novembre 2012, 186 pages ; MELONE S, « Constitution et droit pénal : piste de recherche après la loi N° 96/06 du 18 janvier 1996 », MELONE S, MINKOA SHE. A, SINDJOUN L., (dir), *La réforme constitutionnelle du 18 janvier 1996 au Cameroun, Aspects juridiques et politiques, op.cit.*, pp. 54-69.

[15] MINKOA SHE. A., « Quelques variations sur la portée de la réforme constitutionnelle du 18 janvier 1996 », in MELONE S, MINKOA SHE. A, SINDJOUN L., (dir), *La réforme constitutionnelle du 18 janvier 1996 au Cameroun, Aspects juridiques et politiques, op.cit.*, p. 76.

général, on distingue : la déclaration de principe, l'énumération exhaustive, l'insertion dans le préambule ou dans le corpus de la Constitution. La constitutionnalisation des dispositions pénales recourt à la déclaration de principe, l'insertion dans le préambule et dans le corpus[16]. Cependant, l'étude évitera la technique du renvoi, pour se contenter des dispositions pénales qu'on trouve limitativement déclinées dans la Constitution.

La réponse à la question centrale peut être unilatérale ou bilatérale. Le choix de cette notule est une réponse bilatérale. Elle postule l'ambivalence des dispositions pénales de la Constitution du 18 janvier 1996. On observe deux tendances. La première permet d'observer des dispositions à caractère général traitant du droit objectif[17]. C'est le sens de l'expression « objectivation » (I). Et la seconde se singularise par des dispositions à caractère personnel intéressant les sujets de droit. Elles leur confèrent des droits subjectifs[18]. C'est le sens à donner à la « subjectivation » (II).

I– UNE OBJECTIVATION DES DISPOSITIONS PÉNALES DE LA CONSTITUTION

Certaines dispositions pénales contenues dans la Constitution du 18 janvier 1996 rendent compte de manière objective du Droit pénal. On envisage le droit pénal et la procédure pénale comme deux branches du droit objectif. Il est question de scruter dans la Constitution des dispositions sur le droit pénal (A) et la procédure pénale (B).

A–Des dispositions objectives sur le droit pénal

Une lecture de la Constitution permet d'observer des dispositions rattachables au droit pénal. Ces dispositions peuvent être rangées dans deux rubriques : les principes directeurs (1) et les sources non législatives du droit pénal (2).

---

[16]MINKOA SHE. A., *Droits de l'homme et droit pénal au Cameroun,* Paris, Economica, collection La vie du Droit en Afrique, 1999, p. 19. KAMTO. M., « L'énoncé des droits dans les constitutions des Etats africains francophones », *R. J. A.*, 1991, n° 1-3, p. 15 et sq.

[17] Le système juridique apparaît comme un ensemble de règles qui gouvernent la vie sociale. Ce corps de règles, « corpus juris », s'appelle Droit objectif. Voir, CORNU. G., *Droit civil : Introduction au droit,* Paris, 13e édition, Montchrestien, 2007, p. 15.

[18] Le droit objectif aménage à chaque individu des prérogatives individuelles pour la satisfaction de ses propres intérêts. On les nomme droits subjectifs. Voir, CORNU. G., *op, cit.*, p. 15.

1–Les principes directeurs du droit pénal

Les principes directeurs du droit pénal déductibles de la Constitution du 18 janvier 1996 au Cameroun sont : la légalité criminelle et la non-rétroactivité. La légalité criminelle[19] est aménagée dans la Constitution de 1996 au regard des dispositions de l'article 26 (c) 6. Il dispose : « *La loi est votée par le Parlement. Sont du domaine de la loi : la détermination des crimes et délits et l'institution des peines de toute nature, …* ». Il ressort de cet article que les crimes et délits d'une part et les peines de toute nature d'autre part sont du domaine de compétence du pouvoir législatif. À l'inverse, les contraventions ne sont pas du domaine de la loi[20]. L'attribution de la compétence législative en matière pénale est une traduction de la séparation des pouvoirs[21]. Et en latin, le principe de la légalité criminelle prend la formulation suivante : « *nullum crimen nulla poena sine lege* ». Cela signifie : « *Pas de crime, pas de peine sans loi* ». La Constitution du 18 janvier 1996 légitime ainsi la pluralité des lois pénales en vigueur au Cameroun. Il en est ainsi du code pénal[22] en tant de droit commun et les textes pénaux particuliers[23]. Toutefois, certaines lois pénales échappent à la Constitution, mais demeurent conformes à la légalité criminelle[24]. Sur cette base, on

---

[19] Lire sur la question : BONNET. J., « Le principe de légalité criminelle : le point de vue du constitutionnaliste », in HOURQUEBIE. F. et PELTIER.V., (dir.), *Droit constitutionnel et grands principes du droit pénal*, Paris, Éditions Cujas, Actes du colloque, Novembre 2012, pp, 11-23. ; BOULOC. B., « Le principe de la légalité criminelle : le point de vue du pénaliste », in F. Hourquebie et V. Peltier, *op.cit.*, pp. 25-35.

[20] Les contraventions sont du domaine du pouvoir réglementaire. Dans le code pénal camerounais, les contraventions sont précédées de la lettre « R » ; qui signifie « Règlement ».

[21] Lire sur la question : Montesquieu, *L'Esprit des lois*, Paris, Éditions de Robert Derathé, 2011, 753 pages ; LOCKE. J., *Traité du gouvernement civil*, Québec, Les classiques des sciences sociales, 1690, 144 pages.

[22] Lois n° s 65/LF/24 du 12 Nov. 1965 et 67/LF/1 du 12 Juin 1967 et toutes leurs modifications subséquentes notamment les lois n° s 90/061 du 19 Déc. 1990, 91/007 du 30 Juillet 1991, 93/013 du 22 Déc 1993 et 97/009 du 10 Janvier 1997. Décret n°66/DF/157 du 12 Avril 1966 fixant la date d'entrée en vigueur de la loi n° 65/LF/24 du 12 Nov. 1965 portant institution d'un Code pénal.

[23] Lire le Prologue de l'ouvrage : OUMAROU. A., *Code de lois pénales*, *op.cit.*

[24] Le législateur pénal n'est pas seulement le pouvoir législatif de l'Etat ou le législateur national. Il arrive que le législateur international édicte des lois pénales, qui s'appliquent au sein de l'Etat.

constate une internationalisation ohadienne du droit pénal et une communautarisation du droit pénal.

La non-rétroactivité de la loi pénale est un principe structurant le droit pénal[25]. C'est un principe contenu dans le préambule de la Constitution du 18 janvier 1996. Il se décline dans la formulation suivante : « *La loi ne peut avoir d'effet rétroactif. Nul ne peut être jugé et puni qu'en vertu d'une loi promulguée et publiée antérieurement au fait punissable* ». En de termes simplifiés, une loi nouvelle s'applique aux faits commis après son entrée en vigueur et non avant. Il s'agit précisément de la non-rétroactivité de la loi pénale plus sévère[26]. C'est un principe fondamental en droit pénal au regard de l'application de la loi pénale dans le temps[27]. Le code pénal camerounais la réceptionne en son article 3. Il dispose : « *Ne sont pas soumis à la loi pénale, les faits commis antérieurement à son entrée en vigueur ou ceux qui n'ont pas été jugés avant son abrogation expresse ou tacite* ». Cependant, la non-rétroactivité n'est pas un principe absolu. Il arrive qu'on soit en présence d'une disposition pénale de fond rétroactive. On en veut pour preuve : le principe de la rétroactivité de la loi pénale plus douce[28]. Cette hypothèse n'a pas été envisagée par la Constitution du 18 janvier 1996. Outre les principes directeurs, les dispositions de la Constitution de 1996 abordent aussi les sources non parlementaires du droit pénal.

2–Les sources non parlementaires du droit pénal

Par source, il faut entendre l'origine de quelque chose[29] ou les lieux d'inscription de cette chose[30]. L'origine renvoie aux sources substantielles et

---

[25] Lire sur cette question : ROUBIER. P., *Les conflits de lois dans le temps (théorie dite de la non-rétroactivité)*, 1929-1933, ouvrage réédité en 1960 sous le titre *Droit transitoire*.

[26] MINKOA SHE. A., *op. cit.*, p. 47.

[27] MATHIEU. G., « L'application de la loi pénale dans le temps (dans la perspective du nouveau code pénal) », *R.S.C.*, 1995, pp. 257 et s. ; VITU. A., Des conflits de lois dans le temps en droit pénal, thèse, Nancy, 1945.

[28]DEKEUWER. A., « La rétroactivité in mitius en droit pénal. Un principe encore et toujours contesté », JCP, 1997, I., 4065.

[29] Le terme source renvoie, ici, aux forces créatrices du droit. On parle de sources réelles. Cf. PRADEL. J., *Droit pénal général*, Paris, Cujas, 2008/2009, p. 124. ; RIPERT. G., *Les forces créatrices du droit,* Paris, L.G.D.J., 1955.

[30] Le terme source désigne dans ce cas, les formes dans lesquelles s'exprime la règle de droit. On voit les sources formelles. Cf. PRADEL. J., *op. cit.* p. 124.

les lieux d'inscription désignent les sources formelles. De la sorte, les sources du droit désignent à la fois les sources substantielles et les sources formelles du droit[31]. Les sources du droit pénal peuvent dès lors renvoyer, soit à l'origine de la loi pénale d'une part, soit les lieux d'inscriptions de cette loi d'autre part. Les sources non parlementaires du droit pénal renvoient aux instances qui édictent la loi pénale en dehors du Parlement. On peut aussi appréhender ces sources à partir des supports formels de la loi pénale. Mais il convient de préciser que ces sources doivent être seulement dans la Constitution. Les dispositions de la Constitution du 18 janvier 1996 traitent aussi des sources non parlementaires du droit pénal. Ce sont des dispositions de la Constitution, qui aménagent le droit pénal en dehors du pouvoir législatif pris comme pouvoir parlementaire. Il convient d'y voir une légalité criminelle en matière pénale *lato sensu*. Entrent dans cette rubrique : les règlements, les ordonnances et les pouvoirs implicites.

Le règlement est un acte émanant du pouvoir exécutif pendant l'exercice du pouvoir réglementaire[32]. La Constitution camerounaise fait du pouvoir réglementaire une source du droit pénal. Pour y parfaire, elle recourt à la technique du renvoi. En effet, après avoir délimité le domaine de la loi à l'article 26, le constituant reconnaît au pouvoir réglementaire une compétence illimitée. On en veut pour preuve la teneur de l'article 27. En substance, « *Les matières autres que celles qui sont du domaine de la loi ressortissent au pouvoir réglementaire* ». Cette disposition, apparemment imprécise, redevient précise et claire, lorsque le législateur reconnaît dans le code pénal, l'incrimination des contraventions au pouvoir réglementaire. C'est pourquoi les contraventions du code pénal camerounais sont précédées de la lettre « R ». Dans l'exercice du pouvoir réglementaire, l'exécutif prend aussi des décrets, qui deviennent une source formelle du droit pénal. De même, l'article 26 de la Constitution limite le domaine de la loi parlementaire à l'incrimination des crimes et délits.

Le pouvoir exécutif n'a pas seulement une compétence législative en droit pénal par le biais du règlement, mais aussi par le truchement des

---

[31] Sur cette distinction, v° ROUBIER. P., « L'ordre juridique et la théorie des sources du droit », in *Le droit privé français au milieu du XXe siècle*, Etudes offertes à G. Ripert, éd. L.G.D.J., 1950, T.I. p. 9 et s.

[32]CHAPUS. R., *Droit administratif général*, tome 1, Paris, Montchrestien, 1993, p. 518.

ordonnances[33]. Le constituant de 1996, par le mécanisme des ordonnances, permet au président de la République d'édicter une loi. Ce mécanisme est assujetti à la condition de validation parlementaire. C'est l'économie de l'article 28 de la Constitution de 1996. Il dispose : « (...) *le Parlement peut autoriser le Président de la République pendant un délai limité et sur les objets déterminés, à prendre des ordonnances. Elles ont un caractère réglementaire tant qu'elles n'ont pas été ratifiées. Elles demeurent en vigueur tant que le Parlement n'a pas refusé de les ratifier* ». Les ordonnances fondent un pouvoir législatif distinct du Parlement. C'est un mécanisme utilisé aussi pour poser la loi pénale. La pratique des ordonnances est effective au Cameroun en matière pénale[34].

Il arrive enfin qu'en cas de circonstances exceptionnelles, le président de la République recoure à toute mesure qu'il juge nécessaire. L'hypothèse est établie en cas d'état d'exception prévu par les dispositions de l'article 9 (a) de la Constitution. La teneur de cette disposition est la suivante : « *Le président de la République peut, en cas de péril grave menaçant l'intégrité du territoire, la vie, l'indépendance ou les institutions de la République, proclamer, par décret, l'état d'exception et prendre toutes mesures qu'il juge nécessaires. Il en informe la Nation par voie de message* ». Le chef de l'État concentre tous les pouvoirs y compris celui de faire la loi pénale. En fait, il reste le seul pouvoir en activité au sein de l'État[35]. Les principes directeurs et les sources non législatives résument les dispositions objectives sur le droit pénal de la Constitution de 1996. En complément à celles-ci existent des dispositions objectives sur la procédure pénale.

---

[33] CHAPUS. R., *op.cit.*, p. 530.

[34] Ordonnance N° 73/17du 22 Mai 1973 portant organisation de la prévoyance sociale modifiée par la loi N°84/06 du 04 juillet 1984. Ordonnance N°72/18 du 17 octobre 1972 portant régime général des prix.

[35]BANKOUNDA – MPELE. F., « Repenser le Président Africain », *Congrès français de droit constitutionnel*, Paris, 25, 26, 27 septembre 2008, p. 10. Voir également ABIABAG. I., *Les droits de l'Homme et libertés publiques au Cameroun*, Yaoundé, Fass édition, Collection études et documents, 1998, p. 79.

B–Des dispositions objectives sur la procédure pénale

Une seconde lecture de la Constitution permet d'observer des dispositions rattachables à la procédure pénale[36]. Ces dispositions peuvent être organisées en deux rubriques : les principes directeurs d'une part (1) et la détermination des juridictions pénales (2).

1–Les principes directeurs de la procédure pénale

À la lecture de la Constitution du 18 janvier 1996, deux principes structurant la procédure pénale se dégagent : la légalité de la procédure pénale et la présomption d'innocence. La légalité de la procédure pénale voudrait que celle-ci soit prévue et organisée par la loi. La Constitution a aménagé la légalité de la procédure pénale par des dispositions aussi bien du préambule que du corpus. Au niveau préambule, la formule suivante en est la preuve : « *Nul ne peut être poursuivi, arrêté ou détenu que dans les cas et selon les formes déterminés par la loi* ». Et dans le corpus, l'article 26 (c) 6 dispose : « *La loi est votée par le Parlement. Sont du domaine de la loi (…) la procédure pénale* ». La procédure pénale doit être prévue par la loi, à l'instar du code procédure pénale[37]. Le préambule se veut plus tatillon dans la description des phases de la procédure pénale. Il vise la poursuite, l'arrestation et la détention. En effet, après la commission d'une infraction, le présumé délinquant fait l'objet d'enquête. Si les indices concordants et graves sont réunis ou les charges établies, il est arrêté pour jugement. Au terme du jugement, si sa culpabilité est avérée, il sera placé en détention au sein d'un établissement pénitentiaire. C'est ce processus que l'article 26 (c) 6 synthétise en visant la procédure pénale. La légalité de la procédure se réclame aussi comme une victoire des Classiques[38]. Beccaria, par exemple,

---

[36] La procédure pénale ou la mise en œuvre du droit pénal de fond suppose le déroulement d'un procès devant une juridiction répressive. La procédure pénale ou droit pénal de forme va s'attacher à l'organisation et à la compétence des juridictions pénales ainsi qu'aux phases successives du procès ; Voir PRADEL. J., *Droit pénal général*, Paris, Éditions Cujas, 17e éd., 2008/2009, p.55. ; Article 1er de la loi n°2005/007 du 27 juillet 2005 portant code de procédure pénale au Cameroun.

[37] Loi n°2005/007 du 27 juillet 2005 portant institution d'un Code de procédure pénale.

[38] À partir de MONTESQUIEU (*Esprit des lois*, 1789) et de BECCARIA (*Traité des délits et des peines*, 1764), s'ouvre une période qui s'achèvera en 1876 avec l'ouvrage révolutionnaire de Lombroso, *L'homme criminel*. Pendant cette période de cent vingt-quatre ans, vont se succéder des auteurs nombreux et souvent essentiels puisque leurs idées vont se

entend que les cas de détention avant jugement soient indiqués dans la loi[39]. Les Classiques ont milité pour soustraire les auteurs d'infraction de l'arbitraire, afin qu'ils soient punis selon une procédure préalablement définie par la loi. Cette victoire se matérialise au Cameroun par l'organisation de la procédure pénale par le législateur. Après le code d'instruction criminelle français de 1808 applicable au Cameroun oriental et les textes nigérians appliqués dans le Cameroun occidental, le Cameroun s'est doté d'un code de procédure pénale, produit d'une loi. Ce qui enracine la légalité de la procédure pénale.

Le second principe organisant la procédure pénale depuis la Constitution du 18 janvier 1996 est la présomption d'innocence[40]. C'est un principe prévu dans le préambule. Il est identifié par la formulation suivante : « *Tout prévenu est présumé innocent jusqu'à ce que sa culpabilité soit établie au cours d'un procès conduit dans le strict respect des droits de la défense*[41] ». La constitutionnalisation de la présomption d'innocence a été suivie de la

---

transmettre plus ou moins jusqu'à nous et imprégner notre législation. Tous ces penseurs peuvent être qualifiés de « classiques ». On peut citer : Beccaria, Bentham et Lardizabal. Cf. PRADEL. J., *Histoires des doctrines pénales*, Paris, PUF, Collection « Que sais-je ? », 1989, p. 40 et ss.

[39] PRADEL. J., *op.cit.*, p. 28.

[40] C'est le principe selon lequel en matière pénale, toute personne poursuivie est considérée comme innocente des faits qui lui sont reprochés, tant qu'elle n'a pas été déclarée coupable par la juridiction compétente. Cf. R. GUILLIEN. R. ET VINCENT. J., *Lexique des termes juridiques*, Paris, 22e édition, Dalloz, 2014-2015, pp. 769-770. Essaid, La présomption d'innocence, these, Paris, 1969. Cl. Lombois, « La présomption d'innocence », *Pouvoirs*, n° 55, 1990, pp. 81-94. JEAN DIDIER. W., « La présomption d'innocence ou le poids des mots », *R.S.C.*, 1991, p. 52 et sq. A. De Raulin, « La présomption d'innocence en droit interne et international : sur quelques évolutions récentes », in *La présomption d'innocence*, Revue de l'institut de criminologie de Paris, volume 4, 2003-2004, p.109. NGONO. S., « La présomption d'innocence », *Revue Africaine des Sciences Juridiques*, vol 2, N° 2, 2001, p. 152. LAZERGES. C., « La présomption d'innocence en Europe », Archives de politique criminelle, Éditions A. Pedone, 2004/1 n° 26, p.129-130. ; MGBA NJIE.M. S. J., « La présomption d'innocence à l'épreuve de la consécration de l'infraction d'enrichissement illicite (cas spécifique du Cameroun) », *Mision Juridica*, juin-décembre, 2015, pp. 29-47.

[41] Cette présomption d'innocence, dont bénéficie toute personne poursuivie pénalement, est une garantie fondamentale de la liberté individuelle ; voir, AMBASSA. L. C., « La présomption d'innocence en matière pénale », *Juridis Périodique*, n° 58, Avril–Mai–Juin, 2004, p. 43.

reprise du principe dans la loi portant code de procédure pénale[42]. La présomption d'innocence est le principe structurant la procédure pénale dans les États démocratiques et de 'droit de l'hommiste'[43]. Il met en avant la protection de l'individu au détriment de celle de la société. La preuve est que l'individu ne doit être inquiété que si les preuves sont établies à son encontre[44]. C'est donc un mécanisme qui endosse la charge de la preuve de la partie poursuivante[45]. En latin, la maxime est « *actori incumbit probatio* [46] ». C'est au demandeur au procès pénal, ministère public et partie civile, qu'il incombe d'établir le corps du délit et la participation de la personne poursuivie au délit : « *Actori incumbit probatio* » ou « *Onus probandi incumbit el qui dicit* »[47]. En pratique, la partie civile bénéficie des preuves fournies par le ministère public[48]. L'effet le plus clair de la présomption d'innocence est de faire du poursuivi un défendeur bénéficiaire

---

[42] Article 8 du Code de procédure pénale : « Toute personne suspectée d'avoir commis une infraction est présumée innocente jusqu'à ce que sa culpabilité ait été légalement établie au cours d'un procès où toutes les garanties nécessaires à sa défense lui seront assurées ».

[43] La présomption d'innocence se trouve au cœur même de la conception démocratique du procès pénal. Cf. HUET. A. ET KOERING-JOULIN. R., *Droit pénal international,* Paris, Dalloz, Collection Thémis, 1994, p. 28, n° 178.

[44]Lire sur la question : A. BERGEAUD-WETTERWALD. A., « Le respect de la présomption d'innocence : le point de vue du pénaliste », in HOURQUEBIE. F. ET PELTIER. V., *op. cit.*, pp.59-68.

[45] Affaire Ngami François contre Ministère Public et Nguem Eyango Jonas, C.S. du Cameroun, Arrêt n° 99/P du 16 avril 1998, le ministère public a accusé le prévenu pour corruption de la jeunesse, et lui a demandé d'apporter la preuve du contraire. L'avocat de la défense, Maître Ntsamo Etienne, Avocat à Nkongsamba, après l'instance et l'appel, s'est pourvu en cassation. Il a argué que le prévenu bénéficie de la présomption d'innocence et qu'il revient à l'accusation de prouver sa culpabilité. Le juge de la Cour Suprême a cassé et annulé l'Arrêt n° 256/co rendu le 9 décembre 1986 par la Cour d'Appel de Douala. Il a renvoyé l'affaire à la Cour d'Appel de Bafoussam ; voir, DIPANDA MOUELLE. A., *Droit pénal, Répertoire chronologique de la jurisprudence de la Cour Suprême du Cameroun,* tome1, deuxième partie, 1980–2000, p. 1231. En principe, cette affaire ne devrait pas donner lieu à un mandat d'arrêt, parce qu'on n'arrête pas un justiciable sans éléments compromettants pour lui demander de prouver les raisons de son arrestation.

[46] Article 307 du CPPC dispose : « *La charge de la preuve incombe à la partie qui a mis en mouvement l'action publique* ».

[47]MINKOA SHE. A., *op.cit.*, p.189.

[48]AMBASSA. L. C., « La théorie des preuves pénales », *Revue Africaine des Sciences Juridiques*, vol.7, n°, 2010, 105.

de tous les avantages stratégiques de la défense procédurale. La partie poursuivie va seulement se défendre.

Ce qui n'est pas le cas de la présomption de culpabilité[49]. Elle opère le renversement de la charge de la preuve au détriment de la partie poursuivie. Toutefois, la frontière entre les deux présomptions est souvent difficile à respecter. Il est des cas où l'on évoque la présomption d'innocence, alors que la personne poursuivie est traitée comme un présumé coupable. Toutes choses qui persuadent de la crise de la présomption d'innocence[50]. La protection de celle-ci passe par une meilleure circonscription. À côté des principes directeurs de la procédure pénale, la Constitution de 1996 détermine les dispositions pénales.

2–La détermination des juridictions pénales

La légalité en procédure pénale ne se limite pas à l'organisation de la phase d'enquête et des poursuites. Elle se poursuit avec la légalité des juridictions devant dire le droit. La Constitution du 18 janvier 1996 n'est pas étrangère à cette question. Elle détermine les juridictions compétentes en matière pénale. En latin, cette idée est formulée par la maxime suivante : « *Nullum judicium sine lege* ». Cela signifie « *Pas de juridiction sans loi* ». Le constituant de 1966 prévoit les juridictions susceptibles de se prononcer en matière pénale. Elles sont organisées dans le cadre du pouvoir judiciaire pour les juridictions de droit commun. À celles-ci, on peut ajouter les juridictions d'exception. Concernant les juridictions de droit commun, l'article 37 de la Constitution de 1996 dispose : « *(2) Le pouvoir judiciaire est exercé par la Cour suprême, les Cours d'appel, les Tribunaux...* » Il apparaît de cette disposition, une énumération hiérarchisée des juridictions composant le pouvoir judiciaire au Cameroun[51]. La base de la pyramide est composée

---

[49]SYR. J. H., « Présomption d'innocence et présomption de culpabilité (Analyse de sociologie juridique) », in *Problèmes actuels de Sciences criminelles* XIII, Marseille, PUAM, 2000, pp. 60-61.

[50]MONEBOULOU MINKADA. H. M., « La crise de la présomption d'innocence: regard croisé sur la procédure pénale camerounaise et de la Cour pénale internationale », *Juridical Tribune*, Volume 4, Issue 2, December 2014, pp. 68 – 102.

[51] SOCKENG.R., *Les institutions judiciaires au Cameroun*, Douala, 3eme édition, Groupe Saint-François, 1998, 242 pages. SOCKENG, R., *Les institutions judiciaires au Cameroun*, Douala, 4e édition, MACACOS, 2005, 233 pages.

des tribunaux. De manière extensive, sont visés les tribunaux de première instance et les tribunaux de grande instance. Ils constituent un premier degré de juridiction. Lorsque le justiciable ne trouve pas satisfaction devant l'une ou l'autre instance en fonction de la nature du litige, il interjette appel. Cette voie de recours s'exerce devant les cours d'appel. On dit qu'elle constitue un second degré de juridiction[52]. Si la décision de la cour d'appel ne donne pas satisfaction au justiciable, il dispose d'une autre voie de recours. Est visé, le pourvoi en cassation. Le justiciable doit concrètement saisir la Cour suprême en général et la chambre judiciaire en particulier. C'est le sens des articles 38[53] et 39[54] de la Constitution. Cependant, une question demeure relativement au pouvoir d'évocation[55]: la Cour suprême constitue-t-elle un troisième degré de juridiction ? La réponse est mitigée à la lecture des articles 39 de la Constitution[56] et 510 du Code procédure pénale[57]. En effet, lorsque les moyens du pourvoi sont fondés, la chambre judiciaire casse et annule l'arrêt attaqué. Ensuite, elle évoque et statue. Dans ce cas, elle constitue un troisième degré de juridiction. À l'inverse, lorsque les moyens du pourvoi ne sont pas fondés, la chambre judiciaire ne casse pas et n'annule pas l'arrêt attaqué. En conséquence, elle n'évoque pas et ne statue pas. Ce qui veut dire qu'elle ne constitue pas un troisième degré de juridiction dans cette hypothèse. La chambre judiciaire se prononcera pour

---

[52] Le principe du double degré de juridiction permet au justiciable d'obtenir que le litige soit jugé, en droit et en fait, une deuxième fois. Le recours en cassation lui offre la garantie qu'en toute hypothèse, il pourra obtenir que soit vérifiée la conformité aux règles de droit de la décision prononcée par les juges du fond. Cf. CADIET. L., *Découvrir la justice*, Paris, Dalloz, 1997, p. 108.

[53] « (1) La Cour suprême est la plus haute juridiction de l'Etat en matière judiciaire, … ».

[54] « La Chambre judiciaire statue souverainement sur les recours en cassation admis par la loi contre les décisions rendues en dernier ressort par les cours et les tribunaux de l'ordre judiciaire ».

[55]NJEUFACK TEMGWA. R., « Le droit d'évocation reconnu aux juridictions de cassation statuant en matière civile : le cas de la cour suprême du Cameroun », *Civil Procedure Review*, vol.1, n.3: 3-27, sep./dec., 2010, pp. 3–27.

[56] « La Chambre judiciaire statue souverainement sur les décisions des juridictions inférieures de l'ordre judiciaire devenues définitives dans les cas où l'application du droit est en cause ».

[57] « Lorsque les moyens de pourvoi sont soulevés, soit par les parties, soit d'office sont fondés, la Chambre judiciaire de la Cour suprême casse et annule l'arrêt attaqué. Dans ce cas, elle évoque et statue. ».

valider la décision de la cour d'appel. La validation d'une décision est-elle une nouvelle décision ? La réponse positive fera de la chambre judiciaire un troisième degré de juridiction, de pleine juridiction. Et la réponse négative en fera un troisième degré de juridiction à compétence partielle.

Pour ce qui est des juridictions d'exception à caractère pénal, les dispositions constitutionnelles sont de deux natures. Certaines sont explicites et d'autres implicites. De façon explicite, la Constitution de 1996 indique la Haute cour de justice. Elle est contenue dans l'article 53 de la Constitution du 18 janvier 1996. Quant aux autres juridictions d'exception[58], elles ne sont pas énumérées dans le texte constitutionnel ; cependant, la technique du renvoi permet de les identifier. C'est pourquoi on peut soutenir une constitutionnalisation implicite. En ce sens, l'article 9 (2) de la Constitution sur l'état d'exception fonde la compétence du tribunal militaire. De même l'article 53 (1) en évoquant le complot contre la sûreté de l'État donne un fondement à la Cour de sûreté de l'État[59].

En synthèse, un regard panoramique sur les dispositions pénales de la Constitution permet de constater une première tendance. Elle consiste en l'organisation des droits objectifs, d'où la tendance à l'objectivation des dispositions pénales de la Constitution. En seconde amorce, d'autres dispositions pénales profitent aux sujets de droit. C'est ce qui fonde la tendance à la subjectivation des dispositions pénales de la Constitution.

II– UNE SUBJECTIVATION DES DISPOSITIONS PÉNALES DE LA CONSTITUTION

La Constitution du 18 janvier 1996 comporte des dispositions pénales visant les sujets de droit directement. Ces dispositions leur confèrent des droits subjectifs[60]. Elles sont à la base de l'idée de « subjectivation ».

---

[53] SOCKENG R., Les institutions judiciaires au Cameroun, Douala, Saint-François, 1998, p. 49.

[59]Loi n° 90/060 du 19 décembre 1990 portant création et organisation de la Cour de sûreté de l'Etat.

[60] La définition du droit subjectif a opposé deux doctrines. La première est défendue par Savigny. Il affirme que le droit subjectif est « un pouvoir de la volonté ». Sur cette base, la volonté du titulaire est l'élément essentiel du droit subjectif. La seconde est défendue par Jhering. Il affirme que le droit subjectif est « un intérêt juridiquement protégé ». De cette définition, la volonté du droit objectif est l'élément essentiel du droit subjectif. La théorie

Toutefois, si certaines dispositions subjectives ont un caractère impersonnel (A), d'autres ont un caractère personnel (B).

A–Des dispositions subjectives à caractère impersonnel

Les dispositions subjectives à caractère impersonnel sont celles qui confèrent aux sujets de droit des privilèges sans discrimination. On peut les identifier en droit pénal (1) et en procédure pénale (2).

1–Les dispositions subjectives en droit pénal

La Constitution du 18 janvier 1966 comporte des dispositions pénales, qui confèrent des privilèges aux individus. Et ces dispositions peuvent être rangées dans le champ disciplinaire du droit pénal. On les trouve en majorité dans le préambule de la Constitution. Par la technique de l'énumération, le préambule de la Constitution de 1996 déclare : « *Nul ne peut être contraint de faire ce que la loi n'ordonne pas* », « *Toute personne a droit à la vie et à l'intégrité physique et morale* » et l'interdiction de la torture.

« *Nul ne peut être contraint de faire ce que la loi n'ordonne pas* ». Par une exégèse *a contrario*, « *on peut être contraint de faire ce que la loi ordonne* ». Cette déclaration de principe dans le préambule de la Constitution constitue une disposition subjective. Il en est ainsi parce qu'elle influence les libertés individuelles[61] du sujet de droit personne physique. La marge de manœuvre permise est dans l'ordre de la loi et la marge sanctionnée est dans l'acte interdit par la loi. Il apparaît une relation bijective entre le sujet de droit et la loi. Et cette disposition du préambule trouve un accueil dans le droit pénal au moyen d'une disposition du code pénal. C'est l'article 76 intitulé « Exécution de la loi ». En substance : « *Ne constitue aucune infraction le fait ordonné ou autorisé par la loi et accompli conformément à la loi* ». Il en ressort un privilège au profit du sujet de droit, qui pose un acte ordonné ou autorisé par la loi. C'est un obstacle à la mise en œuvre de sa responsabilité pénale. *A contrario*, le sujet de droit peut aussi se trouver dans une situation de contrainte ou d'obligation de faire ce que la loi ordonne. S'il ne le fait

---

de Jhering est la plus rapprochée du droit romain, tandis que celle de Savigny est la plus rapprochée du droit moderne. Cf. ROUBIER. P., *Droits subjectifs et situations juridiques*, Paris, Dalloz, 1963, p. 67.

[61] Lire sur cette question :ABIABAG. I., *Les droits de l'homme et libertés publiques au Cameroun*, Yaoundé, Éditions du FASST, 1998, 307 pages.

pas, il s'expose à des sanctions pénales. Les exemples sont dans la dimension normative du droit pénal. Les infractions déterminent ce qui est permis et interdit. Tout comportement qui n'est pas permis est sanctionné.

« *Toute personne a droit à la vie et à l'intégrité physique et morale* ». Cette disposition du préambule énonce trois droits subjectifs : le droit à la vie, le droit à l'intégrité physique et le droit à l'intégrité morale. « Le droit à la vie » énoncé dans le préambule de la Constitution a été traduit en droit pénal par l'érection de la vie en valeur protégée[62]. Dans le code pénal camerounais, il figure au titre des crimes et délits contre les particuliers en général et les atteintes à l'intégrité corporelle en particulier. Dans l'ensemble, la vie des personnes physiques est protégée par l'interdiction de tuer et la sanction pénale des auteurs d'infractions ayant pour conséquence la suppression de la vie. Sont mis en exergue : les homicides volontaires tels le meurtre de l'article 275[63], l'assassinat de l'article 276[64], les coups mortels de l'article 278 du code pénal[65] d'une part et les homicides involontaires d'autre part[66].

[62] Lire sur la question : ANGEVIN. H., « Atteintes volontaires à la vie », art. 221-1 à 221-5, C.pén., Jurisclasseur pénal ; PRADEL. J., « L'homicide volontaire en droit pénal comparé », R.I.D.P., 1997. 145.

[63] « Est puni d'un emprisonnement à vie celui qui cause la mort d'autrui ». C.S.C.O. Arrêt n° 186/P du 15 juin 1971 Bull n° 24, p. 2908. L'Arrêt qui énonce que la préméditation est établie non seulement par l'aveu de l'accusé, qui avait résolu froidement de tuer A…et O… et M…parce que celui –ci avait donné asile à A…, mais encore par le soin qu'il avait pris d'aiguiser la machette dont il devait se servir pour perpétrer ses forfaits, et que le guet-apens résulte du fait qu'il est allé s'embusquer à proximité d'une voie que devait emprunter A…, en précisant ainsi les circonstances aggravantes de la tentative de meurtre, a légalement justifié sa décision. C.S.C.O. Arrêt n° 15 du 12 Oct.1965.

[64] Par l'assassinat, l'article 276 vise le meurtre commis soit par préméditation, soit par empoisonnement, soit préparé autrement. Le guet-apens implique forcément la préméditation. C.S.C.O. Arrêt n° 213 du 24 mai 1961 Bull n° 4, p. 138.

[65] « (1) Est puni d'un emprisonnement de six à vingt ans celui qui, par des violences ou des voies de fait, cause involontairement la mort d'autrui. (2) La peine est l'emprisonnement à vie au cas où les violences ou les voies de fait sont exercées au cours d'une pratique de sorcellerie, magie ou divination ». Cet article n'exige pas que la mort soit la conséquence directe et immédiate des violences causées sur la personne de la victime. C.S.C.O. Arrêt n° 179/P du 25 avril 1972, Bull. n° 26, p. 3416

[66] Article 289 du code pénal : « (1) Est puni d'un emprisonnement de trois mois à cinq ans et d'une amende de 10 000 à 500 000 francs ou de l'une de ces deux peines seulement celui qui, par maladresse, négligence, imprudence ou inobservation des règlements, cause la mort

Quant au droit à l'intégrité physique, il assure la protection de la personne physique dans son enveloppe corporelle[67]. De la sorte, le corps humain apparaît comme une valeur protégée. En conséquence, le droit pénal punit toute personne qui porte atteinte à cette valeur. Plusieurs infractions du code pénal traduisent la pénalisation des atteintes au corps humain. Il n'est que de citer : les blessures graves[68], simples[69], légères[70], coups avec blessures graves[71] (…). Quant à l'intégrité morale, elle vise les atteintes à l'honneur d'une personne. On parle aussi d'atteintes à l'honorabilité[72]. Il en ressort que l'honneur d'un sujet de droit devient une valeur protégée par le droit pénal. On en veut pour preuve des infractions du code pénal protectrices de l'intégrité morale. Sont concernées : les injures[73], la diffamation[74], la dénonciation calomnieuse[75](…).

---

ou des blessures, maladies ou incapacités de travail telles que prévues aux articles 277 et 280 ».

[67]LEVASSEUR. G., « Le nouveau régime répressif des infractions contre l'intégrité corporelle d'autrui », J.C.P., 1959, I. 1515.

[68] Article 277 du code pénal : Blessures graves « *Est puni d'un emprisonnement de dix à vingt ans celui qui cause à autrui la privation permanente de l'usage de tout ou partie d'un membre, d'un organe ou d'un sens* ».

[69] Article 280 du code pénal : Blessures simples « *Est puni d'un emprisonnement de six mois à cinq ans et d'une amende de 5000 à 200 000 francs ou de l'une de ces deux peines seulement celui qui, par des violences ou des voies de fait, cause même involontairement à autrui une maladie ou une incapacité de travail supérieure à trente jours* ».

[70] Article 281 du code pénal : Blessures légères « *Est puni d'un emprisonnement de six jours à deux ans et d'une amende de 5000 à 50 000 francs ou de l'une de ces deux peines seulement celui qui, par des violences ou des voies de fait, cause même involontairement à autrui une maladie ou une incapacité de travail de plus de huit jours et jusqu'à trente jours* ».

[71] Article 279 du code pénal : coups avec blessures graves « *(1) Est puni d'un emprisonnement de cinq à dix ans et s'il y a lieu d'une amende de 5000 à 500 000 francs celui qui, par des violences ou des voies de fait, cause involontairement à autrui des blessures telles que prévues à l'article 277. (2) L'emprisonnement est de six à quinze ans lorsqu'il est fait usage d'une arme ou d'une substance explosive, corrosive ou toxique, ou d'un poison ou d'un procédé de sorcellerie, magie ou divination* ».

[72]ALVAREZ. N., « Les délits d'injure et de diffamation », Rev. prat. dr. soc., 1972. 185. ; B. Beignier, *L'honneur et le droit,* Paris, L.G.D.J., 1995.

[73] Article 307 du code pénal. C'est le fait d'utiliser à l'encontre d'une personne une expression outrageante, d'un geste, d'un terme de mépris ou d'une invective qui ne renferme l'imputation d'aucun fait.

[74]Article 305 du code pénal. La diffamation consiste en l'imputation d'un fait précis susceptible d'être reconnu effectif ou réel, dont on ne peut rapporter la preuve et portant

L'interdiction de la torture est un principe constitutionnel au regard de son insertion dans le préambule de la Constitution[76]. On en veut pour illustration cette formule du préambule : « *Elle doit être traitée en toute circonstance avec humanité. En aucun cas, elle ne peut être soumise à la torture, à des peines ou traitements cruels, inhumains ou dégradants* ». Le législateur a donné une réponse précise à cet appel général du constituant. C'est pourquoi on retrouve dans le code pénal une disposition relative à l'interdiction de la torture. Il s'agit de l'article 132 (bis) du code pénal[77]. Son contenu est le suivant : « *Est puni par l'emprisonnement à vie, celui qui par la torture cause involontairement la mort d'autrui* ». le terme torture désigne tout acte par lequel une douleur ou des souffrances aiguës, physiques, mentales ou morales, sont intentionnellement infligées à une personne, par un fonctionnaire agissant à titre officiel ou à son instigation ou avec son consentement exprès ou tacite, aux fins notamment d'obtenir d'elle ou d'une tierce personne des renseignements ou des aveux, de la punir d'un acte qu'elle ou une tierce personne a commis, ou est soupçonnée d'avoir commis, de l'intimider ou de faire pression sur elle ou d'intimider, de

---

atteinte à l'honneur ou à la considération d'une personne. Manque de base légale, la décision de justice qui retient le même fait comme étant constitutif à la fois de diffamation et d'injures publiques. C. S. Arrêt n° 185 / P du 22 sept 1977 Bull n° 37.

[75] Article 304 du code pénal. Dénonce calomnieusement, celui qui fait à une autorité publique ou privée une dénonciation fausse et susceptible d'entraîner des sanctions soit pénales, soit disciplinaires, à moins qu'il ne prouve qu'il avait de bonnes raisons de croire aux faits dénoncés. Ne peut être considéré comme dénonciation, le fait de déposer au cours de l'enquête officieuse ou devant une juridiction d'instruction. C.S.C.O. Arrêt n° 192/P du 15 juin 1971 Bull n° 24 p. 2914.

[76] La prohibition de la torture est affirmée en droit camerounais au niveau constitutionnel, par le biais de la ratification et donc de l'intégration dans le bloc de constitutionnalité de divers instruments internationaux protecteurs de droits de l'Homme : Déclaration universelle de 1948 (article 5) ; Pacte relatif aux droits civils et politiques de 1966 (article 7) ; Charte africaine des droits de l'homme et des peuples (article 5) ; et surtout : Convention de l'ONU du 10 décembre 1984 contre la torture et autres peines ou traitements cruels, inhumains ou dégradants (Ratifiée par le décret n° 97/079 du 25 avril 1997).

[77]KITIO. E., « Observations sur le nouvel article 132 bis du code pénal relatif à la torture », *Juridis Périodique,* n° 32, Oct-Déc 1997, Doctrine et Etudes, pp. 47-52. ; BEGONDE. J. P., « La loi du 10 janvier 1997 contre la torture, un pas en avant sur la protection des Droits de l'homme au Cameroun », *Juridis-Périodique,*n° 39, Aout-Sept, 1999, Doctrine et Etudes, pp. 77-88.

l'intimider ou de faire pression sur une tierce personne, ou pour tout autre motif fondé sur une forme de discrimination, quelle qu'elle soit[78]. Le terme torture ne s'applique pas, lorsqu'il résulte d'une sanction légitime[79]. La constitutionnalisation de l'interdiction de la torture par insertion au préambule est une disposition profitable au sujet de droit ou la personne physique. Les dispositions subjectives ne se limitent pas au droit pénal, mais s'étendent aussi à la procédure pénale.

2–Les dispositions subjectives en procédure pénale

On retrouve dans la Constitution camerounaise de 1996 des dispositions relatives à la procédure pénale en faveur de tout sujet de droit. Elles se résument dans l'inviolabilité du domicile et la présomption d'innocence. Dans le préambule de la Constitution de 1996, l'inviolabilité du domicile est formulée en des termes ci-après : « *Le domicile est inviolable. Nulle perquisition ne peut avoir lieu qu'en vertu de la loi* ». Il apparaît un principe : celui de l'inviolabilité du domicile. La notion de domicile n'est pas comprise au sens civil du terme. Ce n'est donc pas le lieu du principal établissement[80]. Il renvoie plutôt à la résidence, c'est-à-dire le lieu où une personne demeure effectivement[81]. Et sur cette base, toute personne physique a un domicile. Le domicile a été défini par la Cour suprême comme « *toute demeure permanente ou temporaire occupée par celui qui y a droit ou de son consentement par un tiers et qui comprend la maison et ses dépendances immédiates telles que magasins, hangars, cour, que protège l'ensemble des clôtures*[82] ».

Ce dernier ne doit pas être pénétré par quiconque sans autorisation. Ainsi, aucune introduction dans un domicile privé ne peut avoir lieu contre le gré de son occupant légitime sans autorisation de la loi[83]. À l'inverse, avec

---

[78] Article 132 bis (5) a du code pénal.

[79] Article 132 bis (5) b du code pénal.

[80] CARBONNIER. J., *Droit civil : les personnes*, Paris, PUF, Collection Thémis, 2000, p. 94. TEYSSIE. B., *Droit civil : les personnes*, Paris, 11e édition, Litec, 2010, p. 184 et s.

[81] CARBONNIER. J., *op.cit.*, p. 102.

[82] C.S.C.O., 27 août 1967.

[83] Ainsi, par exemple, un inspecteur de police avait été condamné pour violation de domicile à trois mois d'emprisonnement ferme pour s'être introduit de force chez un individu au prétexte qu'il avait soif et voulait se faire offrir un peu de boisson fraîche.

une autorisation de la loi, on peut pénétrer dans un domicile sans être convaincu de violation en temps normal[84] et en période de circonstances exceptionnelles[85]. À la vérité, le principe est assorti d'une restriction : la possibilité de violer le domicile en effectuant une perquisition autorisée par la loi. L'idée se traduit dans le code de procédure pénale par des dispositions relatives aux enquêtes de police : articles 92 (2)et 93[86] du code de procédure pénale. L'inviolabilité du domicile est un principe qui profite à tous les sujets de droit de manière générale et impersonnelle, tout comme la présomption d'innocence.

« *Tout prévenu est présumé innocent jusqu'à ce que sa culpabilité soit établie au cours d'un procès conduit dans le strict respect des droits de la défense* ». Ce principe a plusieurs fonctions. La régulation de la procédure pénale par la détermination de l'apporteur de la preuve a déjà été examinée. L'affirmation de ce principe dans la Constitution peut fonder une autre exégèse. Elle consiste à voir dans la présomption : un droit subjectif et le bénéfice du doute en faveur de la personne poursuivie. La présomption d'innocence est un droit subjectif. À ce titre, son titulaire ou la personne poursuivie des prérogatives : d'abord la liberté d'aller et venir, ensuite la préservation de sa réputation[87], enfin le droit de ne pas collaborer à la collecte des preuves. Le

---

L'inspecteur avait fait appel de cette décision en même temps que le ministère public. La Cour d'appel aggrava la condamnation en la portant à 6 mois d'emprisonnement et 10 000 francs d'amende en vertu de l'alinéa 2 de l'article 299 (Décision citée par MBOUYOM. F.X., « Les mécanismes juridiques de protection des droits de la personne au Cameroun », *R.J.P.J.C.,* n° 1, mars-janvier, 1982).

[84] En temps normal, la protection du domicile est garantie par l'exigence d'un mandat du juge ou du procureur pour effectuer une perquisition dans un domicile privé.

[85] En cas de proclamation de l'Etat d'urgence sur tout ou partie du territoire national, les chefs des unités administratives couvertes par cet état peuvent « autoriser, par tout officier de police judiciaire, civile ou militaire, des perquisitions à domicile de jour ou de nuit dans les formes légales ». Article 5 (6) de la loi n° 90/047 du 19 décembre 1990.

[86] « (1) Les perquisitions et les saisies sont effectuées par l'officier de police judiciaire muni d'un mandat de perquisition. Toutefois, il peut agir sans mandat en cas de crime ou délit flagrant ».

[87] Relativement à la protection de la réputation de l'individu, le présumé innocent devrait jouir des mêmes droits que l'innocent en principe. Sur cette base, toute atteinte à sa réputation doit être sévèrement sanctionnée. Le présumé innocent ne doit pas être diffamé, calomnié, faire l'objet d'une publicité, si les preuves de sa culpabilité ne sont pas rapportées. La présomption d'innocence doit être un moyen de défense contre l'arbitraire du tribunal

statut de présumé innocent signifie qu'on doute de l'innocence d'une personne, sans avoir en même temps des éléments pour établir sa culpabilité. En l'absence de ces éléments, il n'est pas possible de vouer aux gémonies la réputation du prévenu. Ce qui justifie le secret de l'enquête ou de l'instruction à l'égard du public. C'est dans la même lancée que s'explique le respect de sa liberté d'aller et venir. Toutefois, il arrive qu'on proclame la présomption d'innocence, tout en portant atteinte à la liberté et la réputation. On en veut pour illustration : la garde à vue et la détention provisoire. Il faut y voir une difficile adéquation avec les effets classiques de la présomption d'innocence. Le second privilège du sujet de droit attaché à la présomption d'innocence est le bénéfice du doute. Et le doute profite à l'accusé[88] : « *in dubio pro réo* ». Ce bénéfice du doute est considéré et consacré dans la loi pénale camerounaise[89]. À la fin du XVIIIe siècle, Jacob-Nicolas Moreau exprimait l'idée selon laquelle : « *il valait mieux qu'un coupable échappât au châtiment plutôt qu'un innocent fût condamné*[90] ». L'application du principe « *in dubio pro reo* » est effective en droit camerounais[91]. De même, la présomption d'innocence comme droit

---

de l'opinion publique. Cf. CLERO. J. P., « Une pensée utilitariste de la présomption d'innocence », in *La présomption d'innocence*, Revue de l'institut de criminologie de Paris, volume 4, 2003-2004, p.73.

[88] Dans l'Affaire Malam Abo, la Cour d'Appel de DOUALA affirme : « *Considérant (…) qu'un doute subsiste dans les accusations (…) doute dont il faille faire bénéficier à l'accusé (…) il importe donc de l'acquitter du chef de vol aggravé (…) au bénéfice du doute* » ; C.A. Douala, n° 34/Crim du 22 mars 1974, Affaire Malam Abo, inédit.

[89] L'article 395 (2) du CPPC dispose que ; « *En cas de doute, le prévenu est relaxé. Mention du bénéfice du doute doit être faite dans le jugement* ».

[90]MOREAU. J. N., *Les Devoirs du prince réduits à un seul principe, ou Discours sur la justice*, Versailles, 1775, Partie II, chap. X, p.435-436 : « *Il vaut mieux encore que la loi puisse être éludée par un coupable habile et audacieux, que d'être une arme meurtrière contre un innocent faible et timide* ».

[91]TGI du Mfoundi, chambre criminelle, jugement N°69/CRIM du 25 janvier 2013, Affaire Ministère public et Moukouri Ekeke Claude contre Tata Dominic Nditor : en l'espèce, Moukouri Ekeke Claude a déclaré que sa fille a subi les assauts sexuels de la part de son maître (Tata Dominic Nditor) et d'un de ses amis resté introuvable. L'accusé a nié les faits. Le certificat médico-légal fait état d'une tentative de viol, mais aucun élément ne permet d'établir que l'accusé en est l'auteur. La victime encore moins le plaignant ne s'est pas présenté pour éclairer le tribunal. Le juge a déclaré l'accusé Tata Dominic Nditor non coupable des faits mis à sa charge ; et l'acquitte au bénéfice du doute. On peut citer dans le

subjectif offre à la poursuivie le droit de ne pas collaborer à la collecte des preuves. En effet, la partie poursuivie jouit du droit de ne pas contribuer à sa propre accusation. Sur cette base, la personne poursuivie peut dissimuler toute information susceptible d'être utilisée contre elle. En d'autres termes, elle est dispensée de toute forme de collaboration forcée. Concrètement, le droit de ne pas contribuer à sa propre accusation se décline en un droit de se taire et en un droit de ne pas produire des éléments de preuve susceptibles d'établir la culpabilité[92]. En bref, la présomption d'innocence octroie des droits au sujet de droit au plan de son intégrité physique et morale. Si certaines dispositions subjectives à caractère impersonnel profitent à tous les sujets de droit, d'autres dispositions subjectives revêtent un caractère personnel.

B–Des dispositions subjectives à caractère personnel

Les dispositions subjectives à caractère personnel sont celles qui confèrent à un sujet de droit individualisé un privilège excluant les autres sujets de droit. C'est pour cette raison qu'on parle de personnalisation. Celle-ci concerne la juridiction (1) et l'immunité (2).

1–La personnalisation d'une juridiction

La Constitution du 18 janvier 1996 comporte des dispositions sur les juridictions à caractère personnel. L'idée est que les juridictions en cause sont personnalisées au regard de la compétence ratione personae. C'est dire que seule une catégorie de personnes limitativement énumérées et identifiables par leurs fonctions, est justiciable devant cette juridiction. Est visée la Haute cour de justice. L'article 53 (nouveau) de la Constitution de 1996 dispose : « *La Haute Cour de Justice est compétente pour juger les actes accomplis dans l'exercice de leurs fonctions par : le Président de la République en cas de haute trahison ; le Premier ministre, les autres membres du gouvernement et assimilés, les hauts responsables de l'administration ayant reçu délégation de pouvoir en application des articles 10 et 12 ci-dessus, en cas de complot contre la sûreté de l'État* ». Sont ainsi justiciables comme sujets de droit personne

---

même sens : TGI du Mfoundi, jugement N° 59/CRIM du 25 janvier 2013, Affaire Ministère public c/ Djoumatchoua Ekang David, nature du crime : vol aggravé.

[92]BERGEAUD-WETTERWALD. A., « Le respect de la présomption d'innocence », *op. cit.*, p. 64.

physique : le président de la République, les membres du gouvernement et assimilés. Il ressort de cette disposition une donnée sur la nature de la juridiction compétente. C'est une juridiction d'exception et non une juridiction de droit commun. Sa spécialité réside dans le fait qu'elle n'entre pas dans l'organisation judiciaire de droit commun. Un autre argument de la spécialité de la Haute cour de justice est dans sa compétence ratione materiae. Cette juridiction connaît des infractions suivantes : Haute trahison commise par le président de la République et complot contre la sûreté de l'État commis par les membres du gouvernement et assimilés. La notion « haute trahison » reste sans définition dans un texte précis. Ce qui en fait une infraction-vide. Toutes choses qui constituent une entrave à la légalité criminelle et à la qualification de cette infraction. La conséquence logique est l'impossibilité d'intenter une poursuite sur ce chef d'accusation. Quant au complot contre la sûreté de l'État, deux observations peuvent être effectuées. La première est un renvoi au code pénal. En effet, la notion « sûreté de l'État » existe déjà. On distingue les atteintes à la sûreté extérieure[93] et intérieure[94] de l'État. Ce qui confère une matérialité et une assise juridique à ces concepts. La seconde est une notion floue. Il est question du « complot ». Juridiquement, c'est une notion imprécise. On peut y voir un concept ouvert, permettant au juge de le qualifier souverainement. Il est à craindre une qualification à tête chercheuse. Dans l'ensemble, l'article 53 détermine une juridiction et une catégorie élitique de personnes susceptibles d'être justiciables. Ces dernières bénéficient d'un privilège de juridiction. Si ce privilège les met au même niveau, l'immunité démarque le président de la République.

2–La personnalisation de l'immunité

La Constitution du 18 janvier 1996 illustre une tendance à la personnalisation par la place réservée à l'immunité[95]. Ce qui suppose au

---

[93] Les articles 102 à 110 du code pénal.

[94] Les articles 111 à 117 du code pénal.

[95]Lire à ce sujet : ONDO T., *La responsabilité introuvable du chef d'Etat, analyse comparée de la contestation du pouvoir présidentiel en Afrique noir francophone,* Thèse de doctorat droit public, Université de Reims Champagne–Ardenne, Faculté de Droit et de Science politique, 2005, p. 531. Lire aussi ATANGANA (E. J.L.), La révision des Constitutions en

préalable l'éviction de la question de l'immunité du président de la République sur le plan international[96]. L'immunité que la Constitution de 1996 aménage en faveur du président de la République prend deux visages au regard des données *de jure* et *de facto*. L'immunité *de jure* est celle qui est prévue par un texte de droit. Elle met son titulaire à l'abri des poursuites judiciaires parce que le droit le prévoit. Dans la Constitution du 18 janvier 1996, l'immunité profite personnellement au président de la République aux termes de l'article 53 (3). La teneur est la suivante : « *Les actes accomplis par le Président de la République en application des articles 5, 8, 9 et 10 ci-dessus, sont couverts par l'immunité et ne sauraient engager sa responsabilité à l'issue de son mandat* ». Pour lesdits actes, le président de la République est couvert pendant et après la fonction. Cette couverture implique qu'il ne fera pas l'objet de poursuites devant une juridiction. Par extension, même s'il commet une infraction, si l'acte constitutif de l'élément matériel est pris pendant l'exercice de ses fonctions, l'action publique ne saurait être intentée. En fait, la particularité de l'immunité du président de la République est qu'elle ne peut être levée ; contrairement à celle des parlementaires. On peut y voir non pas une immunité suspensive de l'action publique comme l'immunité parlementaire[97], mais un véritable fait justificatif ou une cause d'irresponsabilité pénale.

---

droit camerounais, Thèse de Doctorat en droit public, Université de Douala, Faculté des Sciences Juridiques et Politiques, 2012, p. 254.

[96]ONDO. T., « Réflexion sur la responsabilité pénale internationale du chef d'Etat africain », *Rev. trim. dr. h.* n° 69, 2007, pp. 153-209. Cet article synthétise et actualise les éléments importants de notre thèse, La responsabilité introuvable du chef d'Etat africain. Analyse comparée de la contestation du pouvoir en Afrique noire francophone (Les exemples camerounais, gabonais, tchadien et togolais), Université de Reims, juillet 2005. Lire aussi : METILLE. S., L'immunité des chefs d'Etat au XXIe siècle Les conséquences de l'affaire du mandat d'arrêt du 11 avril 2000, Mémoire de Licence, Université de Neuchâtel, 2003, 53 pages.

[97]Lire sur la question : ISAR. H., « Immunités parlementaires ou impunité du parlementaire ? », *Revue Française de Droit Constitutionnel*, n° 20, 1994, p. 699 et s.; KEUTCHA TCHAPNGA.C., « Les immunités parlementaires en droit camerounais : réflexion sur une exception au principe de l'égalité des citoyens devant la loi », *Revue juridique et politique : indépendance et coopération*, Vol. 52, Issue 2, 1998, p. 177-193 ; ABIABAG.I.,« Réflexions sur le régime camerounais des immunités parlementaires », *Revue juridique et politique : indépendance et coopération*, Vol. 36, issue 3-4, 1982, p. 947-955. ;

Toutefois, l'immunité du président de la République n'est pas absolue. Elle est limitée à certains actes que la Constitution détermine. C'est dire que pour les autres actes n'entrant pas dans cette énumération, on peut le poursuivre. Il en est ainsi en cas de « haute trahison ». Le mécanisme de poursuite a été prévu par l'article 53(2) de la Constitution de 1996. En substance, « *Le Président de la République ne peut être mis en accusation que par l'Assemblée Nationale et le Sénat statuant par un vote identique au scrutin public et à la majorité des quatre cinquièmes des membres les composants* ». Un tel mécanisme est juridiquement appréciable, au regard du rôle de contre-pouvoir que joue le Parlement[98] d'une part et de la possibilité qui lui est donnée d'évincer le président de la République en cas de haute trahison. Néanmoins, en effectuant une lecture du jeu politique et de l'influence dont dispose l'actuel président de la République au sein du Parlement, on peut constater une véritable immunité *de facto*. En fait le président de la République bénéficie d'une majorité obèse à l'Assemblée nationale et au Sénat. Ce qui a pour conséquence la paralysie de toute mise en accusation à la faveur d'un vote. Dans ces conditions, la mise en accusation risque d'être un espoir vain. Un tel mécanisme ne pourra prospérer que si le rapport de force est défavorable au président de la République au Parlement et s'il y a une volonté politique d'en découdre avec le président de la République. Peut-être, c'est dans cette entreprise qu'on votera une loi définissant la procédure devant la Haute cour de justice et la notion de « haute trahison ». Pour l'instant, on n'y est pas depuis l'entrée en vigueur de la Constitution du 18 janvier 1996 jusqu'en 2016.

Conclusion

En dernière analyse, l'entreprise a consisté à dégager les tendances des dispositions pénales de la Constitution du 18 janvier 1996. C'est une œuvre qui passe par l'identification de ces dispositions, un regroupement par

---

« Le député et le droit pénal », *Revue trimestrielle de droit et des activités économiques*, n° 9, Janvier-Mars, 2009, pp. 3-18.

[98]OLINGA.A. D., *La constitution de la République du Cameroun*, op.cit., p. 107 ; BIDIAS à AMBASSA J. P. B., « La fonction de contrôle du Sénat », in *Le Sénat au Cameroun : regards croisés sur une nouvelle institution*, (dir.) Alain Didier OLINGA, Yaoundé, Éditions Clé, 2016, pp. 69-96.

affinité et une lecture panoramique. Le résultat d'une telle démarche a permis de dégager deux tendances. La première est à l'objectivation et la seconde est à la subjectivation des dispositions pénales de la Constitution 18 janvier 1996. Peut-on à partir de cette analyse postuler l'existence d'un droit pénal constitutionnel au Cameroun ? La réponse fera l'objet d'une autre réflexion dans l'espoir que toutes les institutions de la Constitution de 1996 seront définitivement mises en place.

REGARD SUR LE STATUT DU DIRIGEANT SOCIAL EN DROIT OHADA

Clotilde ETOULA ESSOH[1]

Résume

La fonction de dirigeant social, de par ses attributions, est très déterminante pour la croissance économique et sociale d'une entreprise. C'est sans doute pourquoi elle fait l'objet d'une réglementation épaisse, qui se caractérise par sa pluridisciplinarité et surtout sa rigueur. Mais l'importance de cette fonction pour l'existence d'une entreprise conduit de plus en plus le droit à l'assouplir pour permettre aux personnes qui s'y intéressent de minimiser les risques qui y sont attachés.

La question qui est posée dans cette étude est dès lors celle de savoir comment le législateur OHADA a aménagé cette fonction. Posant un regard général sur le statut de dirigeant social en droit OHADA, cette étude vise à montrer que, même si l'analyse des textes fait ressortir son caractère contraignant, on observe par ailleurs que le législateur, le juge et même la pratique convergent davantage vers la recherche d'une protection dudit statut.

---

[1] **Formation :**
- ✓ 2010 Diplôme d'études approfondies (D.E.A), Université de Yaoundé II Soa, Cameroun
- ✓ 2015 Doctorat en droit des affaires, Université de Yaoundé II Soa, Cameroun.

Emploi :
- ✓ 2009-2010 Attaché de recherche à l'Université de Yaoundé II Soa, Cameroun.
- ✓ Depuis 2011, Assistant Lecturer, Department of Law, Faculty of Social and Management Sciences (FSMS), University of Buea, BP 63, Buea, Cameroon.

Introduction

Le dirigeant de société est défini comme la personne qui assure effectivement la direction d'une entreprise en droit et parfois seulement en fait[2]. Toutefois, la question de qui assure effectivement ce rôle soulève parfois des problèmes de compréhension ou de légitimité. Est-ce le représentant légal de la société au sens de la loi, l'associé majoritaire qui en raison de sa situation de prééminence détient le pouvoir d'orienter la politique économique et sociale de l'entreprise, ou même le cadre supérieur chargé d'un secteur d'activité de la société[3]. La doctrine OHADA[4], dans une approche globale du concept, affirme qu'il s'agit aussi bien des représentants légaux de la société strictement définis par les lois sur les sociétés, c'est-à-dire, ceux qui bénéficient d'un contrat de mandat et qu'on qualifie de dirigeants de droit, que de ceux de la catégorie hétéroclite qualifiée de dirigeants exceptionnels[5]. Ces derniers renvoient aux dirigeants de fait et dirigeants de crise qui sont désignés à la tête des sociétés de façon ponctuelle pour résoudre des crises ou préparer une privatisation de ces sociétés[6]. Mais le dirigeant considéré dans cette étude est le dirigeant de droit, c'est-à-dire le représentant légal qui a reçu mandat de gérer la société suivant l'Acte

---

[2] G. CORNU, *Vocabulaire juridique*, Puf, 2015. p. 351.

[3] R. NEMEDEU, *Le contrôle des dirigeants de la société anonyme*, thèse Université de Strasbourg, 2000, p. 2. Il a été démontré que l'actionnaire majoritaire est très souvent un dirigeant qui s'impose. Dans un groupe de sociétés, c'est la société mère qui, en raison de sa situation de prééminence, détient le pouvoir d'orienter la politique économique et sociale de l'entreprise ; les dirigeants de filiales se chargent alors simplement d'exécuter ses ordres, puisqu'elle est le dirigeant effectif. Mais ce peut aussi être l'associé majoritaire personne physique qui impose ses orientations stratégiques et tactiques au dirigeant de droit qui devient alors l'exécutant servile des décisions prises par le « Boss », le maître de l'affaire, le véritable dirigeant. Voir, J. AYANGMA AYANGMA, *Le dirigeant sociétal*, thèse, Université de Douala, 2009-2010, p. 289.

[4] L'OHADA signifie l'Organisation pour l'harmonisation en Afrique du droit des affaires. C'est le fruit d'un traité signé à Port-Louis le 17 octobre 1993, entrée en vigueur le 18 septembre 1995 et révisé le 17 octobre 2008. L'organisation comporte 17 États: Bénin, Burkina Faso, Cameroun, Centrafrique, Côte d'Ivoire, Comores, Congo (Brazza), Congo (RDC), Gabon, Guinée, Guinée-Bissau, Guinée équatoriale, Mali, Niger, Sénégal, Tchad, Togo.

[5] B. NJOYA NKAMGA, « Dirigeants sociaux », in P.G.POUGOUE (sous la direction de), *Encyclopédie du droit OHADA*, LAMY, 2011, n° 4, p. 634.

[6] B. NJOYA NKAMGA, *Les dirigeants sociaux*, thèse, Université de Dschang, août 2007.

uniforme OHADA portant Sociétés commerciales et groupement d'intérêt économique (AUSCGIE)[7]. Il s'agit tout d'abord du gérant de la société en nom collectif (SNC), de la société en commandite simple (SCS) et de la société à responsabilité limitée (SARL). Ensuite, de l'administrateur général et l'administrateur général adjoint dans les sociétés anonymes (SA) avec administrateur général, ou le président du conseil d'administration, le président-directeur général, le directeur général et le directeur général adjoint dans la société anonyme avec conseil d'administration. Enfin du président de la société anonyme simplifiée (SAS).

Toutefois, peu importe la catégorie de dirigeants considérée, la compétence est un critère nécessaire pour pouvoir bien diriger une entreprise, car rassembler les moyens matériels et humains ne suffit pas, encore faudrait-il que l'entreprise ait un décideur capable d'opérer les choix nécessaires à une bonne utilisation de ces ressources. Pourtant, l'AUSCGIE, qui constitue le droit commun de la gestion des sociétés dans l'espace OHADA, ne requiert pas du dirigeant une quelconque aptitude à gérer. Dans presque toutes les formes de société, sans faire allusion au critère de la compétence, le législateur laisse simplement le soin aux associés à travers les statuts de désigner à leur guise les dirigeants de leur société[8]. Cependant,

[7] Cet Acte uniforme qui sera abrégé AUSCGIE dans la suite de ce travail fait partie des multiples textes adoptés dans le cadre du traité OHADA. Il a été adopté le 17 avril 1997 et a fait l'objet d'une réforme le 30 janvier 2014.

[8] Dans les sociétés en nom collectif, l'article 276 AUSCGIE prévoit que les statuts peuvent désigner un ou plusieurs gérants, associés ou non, personnes physiques ou morales. Dans la société en commandite simple, le principe est que tous les commandités gèrent la société, sauf si les statuts désignent un ou plusieurs gérants. Dans les SARL, l'article 323 AUSCGIE prévoit que la société est gérée par une ou plusieurs personnes physiques associées ou non, nommées par les associés dans les statuts. Pour la SA, le président-directeur général et le président du conseil d'administration étant à la base des administrateurs, les modalités de leur élection sont librement fixées par les statuts aux termes de l'article 424 AUSCGIE. Seuls le directeur général et le directeur général adjoint peuvent être ou pas des actionnaires, confer article 471 AUSCGIE. Pour la SA avec administrateur général, l'article 485 prévoit juste qu'il est choisi parmi les actionnaires ou en dehors d'eux. Pour les sociétés par actions simplifiées, l'article 853-7 prévoit également sans autre précision que les statuts fixent les conditions dans lesquelles la société est dirigée et que le président représentant légal est désigné dans les conditions prévues par les statuts (art 853 -8). La seule exigence qui ressort de la loi concernant le statut de ces dirigeants dans la SA est qu'ils doivent être des

cette compétence est clairement requise pour candidater à la gestion de certaines sociétés en raison de la délicatesse de leur objet. Il s'agit des sociétés d'assurance et des banques pour lesquelles le législateur insiste particulièrement sur la compétence technique des candidats au poste de dirigeant[9].

Diriger une société est un métier compliqué, car, en plus des connaissances techniques qu'impose l'activité sociale, il faudrait en outre avoir des connaissances précises dans le domaine de la gestion et du droit. En effet, la gestion d'entreprise recouvre de nombreuses disciplines (comptabilité, finance, marketing, gestion des ressources humaines gestion de production, stratégie...)[10] pour lesquelles le dirigeant doit pouvoir détenir un minimum de connaissances nécessaires à une bonne implémentation de la stratégie d'entreprise. Sur le plan juridique, le dirigeant doit avoir la maîtrise des disciplines qui encadrent la gestion de la société, telles que le droit des sociétés, le droit du travail, le droit de la consommation, le droit de l'environnement et bien d'autres. Le dirigeant est alors au carrefour de multiples législations qui édictent chacune des obligations qui peuvent être source de responsabilité à son endroit, surtout avec l'exigence croissante de la bonne gouvernance qu'a imposée le

---

personnes physiques. Au final, dans toutes ces formes de société, rien n'est dit à propos de la qualification du dirigeant.

[9] Pour les établissements bancaires, l'article 22 de l'annexe à la Convention du 17 janvier 1992 portant harmonisation de la réglementation bancaire dans les États de l'Afrique centrale prévoit que le candidat à la fonction de dirigeant soit titulaire d'au moins une licence en sciences économiques, bancaires ou financières, juridiques ou de gestion ou tout autre diplôme équivalent. En l'absence d'un diplôme de l'enseignement supérieur, il doit pouvoir justifier d'une expérience professionnelle de dix ans dans les fonctions d'encadrement de haut niveau. Quant aux sociétés d'assurance, l'article 329 alinéa 1 à 4 du Code CIMA (Conférence interafricaine des marchés d'assurance) exige que le directeur général soit titulaire d'un diplôme d'études supérieures en assurance ou en actuariat, soit d'un diplôme de l'enseignement supérieur et d'une expérience professionnelle dont la durée minimale varie selon qu'il s'agit d'un diplôme d'assurance, d'orientation économique, juridique ou alors d'autres spécialités.

[10] I. CALME, J. HAMELIN, J-P. LAFONTAINE, S. DUCROUX, F. GERBAUD, *Introduction à la gestion*, Dunod, Paris, 2003, voir Avant-propos, p. IX.

phénomène de la *Corporate governance*[11] dans la gestion des sociétés. La doctrine OHADA a d'ailleurs suffisamment épilogué sur les responsabilités du dirigeant pour mettre en exergue les nombreux risques juridiques que comporte cette fonction[12]. Elle n'a d'ailleurs pas manqué de relever que les personnes qui entendent s'engager comme dirigeants dans une société commerciale, qu'elles aient la qualité d'associé ou non, doivent se poser la question des risques juridiques qu'elles sont susceptibles d'encourir[13].

Mais, le tableau serait incomplet si le statut de dirigeant est analysé en s'arrêtant uniquement sur ces éléments qui ne présentent sa fonction que comme étant un risque, car de plus en plus, le droit tend vers une amélioration de son statut. La question qui se pose dans ce travail est donc celle de savoir comment le droit OHADA aménage le statut de dirigeant social. Posant un regard général sur cette fonction, cette réflexion vise à déterminer si compte tenu de l'importance de cette fonction, le législateur OHADA l'a suffisamment aménagée afin la rendre attractive. En ce qui concerne le cadre de l'étude, il est important de préciser que le recours au droit et à la jurisprudence française du droit des sociétés, permet juste d'avoir davantage d'éclairage dans la réflexion. Le droit des sociétés OHADA est un droit autonome depuis la rédaction des Actes uniformes OHADA, même si ceux-ci sont très souvent inspirés des textes français.

L'on constatera alors à l'occasion, que même si le statut de dirigeant s'avère contraignant au regard des diverses exigences légales attachées à sa

---

[11] La *corporate governance* née aux États-Unis à la fin des années 1890, en réaction aux scandales financiers perpétrés dans les grandes firmes américaines, est définie comme le système par lequel les entreprises sont dirigées et contrôlées. Voir R. NEMEDEU, *Le contrôle des dirigeants de la société anonyme*, Thèse, Université de Strasbourg 2000, p. 272. Sur l'adaptation de ce phénomène en droit OHADA, voir F. TAGOURLA, « Les pouvoirs des dirigeants sociaux dans l'espace OHADA à l'épreuve des principes de bonne gouvernance », *Rev. Penant*, avril/juin 2013, n° 883, p. 189 et s.

[12] En guise d'exemples, voir, sur la problématique de la responsabilité des dirigeants sociaux, W. J. NGOUE « La mise en œuvre de la responsabilité des dirigeants de sociétés anonymes en droit OHADA », *Ohadata D-05-52* ; A. AKAM AKAM, « La responsabilité civile des dirigeants sociaux en droit OHADA », *RIDE*, Vol 21, 2007 ; A. AFANI, *La responsabilité pénale des dirigeants de la société anonyme, étude de droit comparé : France-Allemagne- Espace OHADA*, Thèse, Perpignan Via Domitia, 2009.

[13] B. MEUKE, « Brèves observations sur le risque juridique du mandataire social dans l'OHADA », *Jurifis Info*, 2ème numéro, mars-avril 2009, p. 4.

fonction (I), l'on évolue tout de même vers une véritable protection dudit statut (II), dont le but vise à ne pas rendre précaire la fonction de direction de société qui est essentielle pour la prospérité d'une entreprise.

I. Le statut de dirigeant social : un statut contraignant

La contrainte dans la fonction de dirigeant social pourrait s'expliquer par deux observations majeures : l'extrême loyauté juridiquement attachée à ses fonctions (A), et la diversité des sanctions qui peuvent frapper ses actes de gestion (B).

A. Une contrainte due à l'extrême loyauté attachée à sa fonction

Même si la loi ou la jurisprudence OHADA[14], ne la consacre pas expressément, l'on constate qu'une obligation de loyauté existe envers le dirigeant social dans la mesure où la loyauté apparaît comme le dénominateur commun à l'ensemble de ses obligations légales. Cette obligation emprunte plusieurs visages dans le droit des sociétés, et tire son fondement aussi bien de la technique du mandat (1), que de sa fonction même d'organe social (2).

1. Une obligation de loyauté multi-facette tirée de la technique du mandat

Malgré les divergences doctrinales au sujet de la véritable qualification juridique du dirigeant social[15], il n'en demeure pas moins que sa qualité de

[14] La jurisprudence française a déjà consacré cette obligation de loyauté : voir Cass. com., 27 février 1996, Bull. civ. IV, n°65, p. 50.

[15] Les différentes positions doctrinales classiques sur la qualité du dirigeant partent en fait de leur perception de la nature juridique même de la société pour déduire le statut de ce dernier. Les défenseurs de la thèse contractuelle affirment plutôt que la société étant un contrat, le dirigeant social est un ''mandataire social''. Voir D. SCHMIDT, « De l'intérêt social », *Rev. Droit Bancaire et Bourse* 1995, p. 1130 (II), A. COURET, « Les apports de la théorie microéconomique à l'analyse du droit des sociétés », *Rev. sociétés* 1984, p. 14, A. COURET, « Le gouvernement d'entreprise », D. 1995, chron. Spéc. p. 165. Pour les tenants de la thèse institutionnelle de la société, parce que la société est une institution, le dirigeant social est un ''organe social'' et pas un mandataire. Voir Ph. MERLE, *Droit commercial sociétés commerciales*, 10ème éd. 2003, n° 94, pp. 126-127, citant Cl. J. BERR, *L'exercice du pouvoir dans les sociétés commerciales*, Sirey 1961, G. MARTIN, *La représentation des sociétés commerciales par leurs organes*, thèse Nancy, 1977…

mandataire est difficilement réfutable[16]. Une lecture synthétique de l'AUSCGIE, fait ressortir que plusieurs obligations attendues du dirigeant social ne sont que des variantes du devoir de loyauté exigé du mandataire ordinaire du code civil. Ceci se vérifie aussi bien dans la relation qui lie les associés aux dirigeants (a), que dans celle qui lie le dirigeant à la société (b).

a. Les variantes de l'obligation de loyauté du dirigeant à l'égard des associés

L'article 1993 du code civil camerounais[17] dispose en partie que tout mandataire est tenu de rendre compte de sa gestion. Cette obligation se trouve bien appliquée en droit des sociétés dans les rapports dirigeants/associés, où sans distinction du type de société, les dirigeants doivent rendre compte de leur gestion à travers au moins deux prescriptions que sont le rapport de gestion attendu du dirigeant et le devoir d'alerte de l'associé.

Dans les sociétés en nom collectif et en commandite simple, les articles 288 et 306 AUSCGIE prévoient qu'il est tenu chaque année, dans les six mois qui suivent la clôture de l'exercice, une assemblée générale annuelle au cours de laquelle le rapport de gestion, l'inventaire et les états financiers de synthèse établis par les gérants sont soumis à l'approbation de l'assemblée des associés. Dans les SARL, le même rapport de gestion est attendu du gérant les 15 jours précédant la tenue de l'assemblée générale aux termes de

---

[16] Un point de vue réaliste et constant dans la doctrine classique française soutient en effet que l'acte de société émanant d'un acte volontariste, le dirigeant reste avant toute chose un mandataire, voir Mémento Pratique F. LEFEBVRE, *Sociétés commerciales,* éd. F. LEFEBVRE 2009, n° 2003, p. 196, M. COZIAN, A. VIANDIER, Fl. DEBOISSY, *Droit des sociétés*, 27ème édition, LexisNexis 2014, p. 163. Dans la doctrine OHADA, la qualité de mandataire a été également réitérée (P. –G. POUGOUE, F. ANOUKAHA, J. NGEUBOU, *Le droit des sociétés commerciales et du GIE OHADA*, PUA Coll. « Droit uniforme », 1998, n°168, p. 73 ; voir aussi B. NJOYA NKAMGA, « Dirigeants sociaux », *Encyclopédie du droit OHADA*, LAMY, 2011, p. 630 et s., plus précisément, les n° 189 à 212). L'auteur de cette contribution a auparavant pris clairement position en qualifiant le dirigeant de "mandataire spécial". Son mandat se trouve particularisé par le fait que l'exercice de ses missions s'inscrit dans le cadre du mécanisme particulier de la technique sociétaire et au regard du caractère régulateur de l'intérêt social. B. NJOYA NKAMGA, *Les dirigeants sociaux*, thèse, Université de Dschang, n° 379 et s, p. 201 et s.

[17] Le code civil, qu'il soit camerounais ou même d'un autre État membre constituant le droit commun, le mandat social de l'AUSCGIE s'inspire des règles du mandat telles que prévues par le code civil.

l'article 345 AUSCGIE. Les documents visés ci-dessus doivent être impérativement communiqués aux associés 15 jours avant la tenue de l'assemblée à défaut de quoi toute délibération prise pourra être annulée[18]. Dans les sociétés anonymes, un rapport de gestion est également attendu du conseil d'administration, ou de l'administrateur général dans les mêmes conditions[19]. Lorsque la société est cotée, ce rapport devrait contenir des informations relatives au gouvernement d'entreprise de la société, ainsi qu'à la structure et au fonctionnement du conseil d'administration[20]. Si le but recherché en premier est d'assurer la transparence dans la gestion de la société, le rapport de gestion présenté par le dirigeant pour approbation des associés traduit en fait l'idée de rendre compte à ces derniers de la gestion de la société.

Le dirigeant peut en outre être amené à rendre compte de sa gestion, à l'initiative des associés lorsque ceux-ci exercent leur droit d'alerte. Il s'agit du droit dont dispose tout associé de poser par écrit des questions aux dirigeants sur tout fait de nature à compromettre la continuité de l'exploitation de la société. Ce droit est reconnu à l'associé dans tous types de sociétés commerciales[21] et le dirigeant doit répondre par écrit dans un délai de 15 jours aux questions qui lui ont été posées. En général, ce droit matérialise la relation d'agence qui existe entre dirigeants et associés et indique bien que le dirigeant est un mandataire, car il peut être amené, à la demande des associés inquiets qui l'ont désigné pour gérer la société, à en rendre compte. La jurisprudence OHADA réitère d'ailleurs cette obligation du dirigeant dans le cas d'une SARL en faisant injonction à l'ex-gérant d'une SARL, d'avoir à rendre compte de la gestion effectuée durant son mandat sous astreinte comminatoire[22].

---

[18] Voir respectivement les articles 288 alinéa 2, 306 alinéa 2 et 345 alinéa 5 AUSCGIE.

[19] Voir les articles 525 1°) et 2°), 547, 547-1 AUSCGIE.

[20] Confer article 831 -2 AUSCGIE.

[21] Voir les articles 157 à 158-1 AUSCGIE.

[22] Cour d'appel d'Abidjan, chambre civile et commerciale C, arrêt n° 226 du 19 mai 2011, *Ohadata J-13-54*.

b. Les variantes de l'obligation de loyauté du dirigeant à l'égard de la société

La société constitue une entité indépendante de la personne de ses associés. Voilà pourquoi les exigences de loyauté du dirigeant ne se traduisent pas en des termes identiques à l'égard des associés et de la société. La jurisprudence française permet de mieux comprendre cette différence à travers un arrêt rendu par la chambre commerciale de la Cour de cassation du 24 février 1998, qui met à la charge du dirigeant une obligation de loyauté non plus vis-à-vis des seuls associés, mais de « l'entreprise »[23]. Cette obligation se traduit fondamentalement par l'obligation d'exercer ses pouvoirs de direction dans le respect de l'intérêt social. Ce respect implique que le dirigeant devrait s'abstenir de poser tout acte de concurrence déloyale envers la société, indépendamment de l'exigence de loyauté qui pourrait peser sur lui lorsqu'il a par ailleurs le statut de salarié[24]. En cours de mandat social, le dirigeant est tenu, même en l'absence de prévision contractuelle d'une obligation de loyauté qui lui interdit de conclure des affaires, en qualité de dirigeant d'une autre société, dans le même domaine d'activité[25]. Par conséquent, si la loi n'interdit pas au dirigeant de cumuler des mandats dans plusieurs sociétés, il est cependant astreint d'agir de façon loyale et fidèle à l'égard de chacune de ces sociétés, même si elles font partie d'un groupe[26].

Cette obligation de loyauté ne se termine d'ailleurs pas avec la fin du mandat social, car après celui-ci, il reste soumis aux règles du droit commun de la concurrence, même s'il peut en principe travailler dans une société concurrente. Cependant, la concurrence déloyale réalisée par des moyens

---

[23] B. DAILLE-DUCLOS, « Le devoir de loyauté du dirigeant », JCP E, n°89, 24 septembre 1998, p. 1489.

[24] L'article 31 du code du travail camerounais dispose à cet effet que « *Le travailleur doit toute son activité professionnelle à l'entreprise, sauf dérogation stipulée au contrat. Toutefois, il lui est loisible, sauf convention contraire, d'exercer en dehors de son temps de travail une activité à caractère professionnel non susceptible de concurrencer l'entreprise ou de nuire à la bonne exécution des services convenus* ». Il en ressort alors l'obligation pour le travailleur de ne pas faire concurrence à l'entreprise qui l'emploie.

[25] Cass. com., 15 nov. 2011, n°10-15.049, *JCP E* 2011, 1893, note A. COURET et B. DONDERO.

[26] M. COZIAN, A. VIANDIER, Fl. DEBOISSY, *op. cit.*, p. 163.

frauduleux est sanctionnée. Elle est constatée si l'ancien dirigeant débauche les salariés de son ancienne société ou s'il détourne sa clientèle par des moyens visant à créer la confusion entre la nouvelle et l'ancienne société[27]. Il est également à noter que l'obligation de non concurrence peut résulter d'une clause entre l'ancien dirigeant et la société, même si elle est appréciée de façon stricte en ce qu'elle restreint le principe de la liberté du commerce et de l'industrie[28]. L'obligation de non concurrence du dirigeant peut alors être sanctionnée, soit en raison des règles générales de concurrence, soit sur le terrain de la responsabilité contractuelle, dès lors que cette obligation était d'origine contractuelle. Cependant, il faut constater qu'en tant qu'organe social, la fonction de dirigeant impose en elle-même une obligation de loyauté.

2. Une obligation de loyauté imposée par la fonction même d'organe social

Recherchant le fondement du devoir de loyauté du dirigeant, un auteur dans la doctrine française conclut logiquement que le devoir de loyauté du dirigeant apparaît comme un devoir « fonctionnel » ; en ce qu'il découle de la fonction de direction elle-même[29]. Ceci pourrait se vérifier aussi bien dans le droit des sociétés (a) que dans d'autres disciplines qui interfèrent dans la gestion de la société (b).

a. La fonction de direction comme fondement au devoir de loyauté du dirigeant dans le droit des sociétés

L'on peut induire un devoir de loyauté à l'endroit du dirigeant social à travers l'incrimination par l'AUSCGIE de certains comportements déloyaux, pouvant être commis par celui-ci dans la direction de la société. Cette incrimination est révélatrice de la présence sous-jacente d'un devoir de loyauté de la part du dirigeant social, alors attaché à sa fonction.

L'article 890 AUSCGIE dispose qu'« *encourent une sanction pénale, les dirigeants sociaux qui ont* ***sciemment****, même en l'absence de toute distribution*

---

[27] F. FRANCOIS, I.MAIGRET et A. MARLANGE, *Dirigeant de société, statut juridique, fiscal et social*, 1ère édition DELMAS 2003, n° 2505, p.250.

[28] Idem, n° 2507, p. 251.

[29] L. GORDON, « Précisions quant au fondement juridique du devoir de loyauté du dirigeant social envers les associés », *Rev. sociétés,* N° 1/2005, p. 148 et s.

de dividendes, publié ou présenté aux actionnaires et aux associés, en vue de dissimuler la véritable situation de la société, des états financiers de synthèse ne donnant pas, pour chaque exercice, une image fidèle des opérations de l'exercice, de la situation et celle du patrimoine de la société, à l'expiration de la même période ». L'article 889 dispose suivant la même logique, qu' « *encourent une sanction pénale les dirigeants sociaux qui, en l'absence d'inventaire ou au moyen d'inventaire frauduleux, ont* ***sciemment****, opéré entre les actionnaires ou les associés la répartition de dividendes fictifs* ». C'est encore dans la même lancée que dans les sociétés par actions et les SARL, l'article 891 AUSCGIE condamne les dirigeants qui « *...de* ***mauvaise foi****, font des biens ou du crédit de la société, un usage qu'ils savent contraire à l'intérêt de celle-ci, à des fins personnelles, matérielles ou morales, ou pour favoriser une autre personne dans laquelle ils sont intéressés, directement ou indirectement* ».

On remarque que ces infractions relatives à la direction de la société impliquent bien la présence d'une attitude déloyale de la part du dirigeant, par le fait qu'elles doivent avoir été commises « **sciemment** » dans les deux premiers cas ou de « **mauvaise foi** » dans le second. Leur répression vise alors à imposer un devoir de loyauté chez le dirigeant social, directement attaché aux fonctions de direction.

b. La fonction de direction comme fondement au devoir de loyauté du dirigeant dans d'autres disciplines

La fonction de direction se trouve également régentée par diverses autres disciplines en dehors du droit des sociétés. Il faut cependant préciser ici que lesdites disciplines, étant hors de la sphère des matières harmonisées en droit OHADA, elles seront invoquées ici en référence au droit camerounais que nous comprenons le mieux[30]. Il s'agit par exemple du droit fiscal et du droit de la prévoyance sociale. Ces disciplines imposent des obligations au dirigeant social à l'égard des tiers. Certaines de ces obligations sont empreintes de fortes considérations de loyauté, puisque leur inexécution est très souvent sanctionnée sur la base de la mauvaise foi.

[30] La présence d'un droit des affaires uniforme dans l'espace OHADA n'occulte pas le fait que bien d'autres disciplines relèvent du droit interne des États membres. Le Cameroun faisant partie de ces États, nos analyses se réfèrent alors au droit camerounais auquel nous sommes rattachés.

Dans le domaine du droit fiscal par exemple, le dirigeant doit déclarer l'activité sociale[31] et recouvrer les impôts dus par la société en sa qualité de représentant légal de cette dernière. À cet effet, l'article L 107 du livre des procédures fiscales camerounais punit d'un emprisonnement d'un (1) à cinq (5) ans et d'une amende de cinq cent mille (500 000) à cinq millions (5 000 000) de francs, ou de l'une des deux peines seulement, quiconque : « *Se soustrait frauduleusement ou tente de se soustraire frauduleusement à l'établissement, au paiement, au reversement total ou partiel des impôts, droits et taxes visés dans le Code général des impôts ; refuse expressément de faire sa déclaration dans les délais prescrits ; dissimule une part des sommes sujettes à l'impôt; organise son insolvabilité ou met obstacle au recouvrement de l'impôt et enfin, obtient par des manœuvres frauduleuses un remboursement de crédits de TVA* ». Ces pratiques incriminées à l'article L 107 ont toutes en commun d'être dictées par la mauvaise foi de l'auteur, et il faut souligner que si la sanction vise d'abord la société, elle s'applique également au dirigeant social sur le fondement de l'article L 109 du même livre[32].

Dans le domaine de la prévoyance sociale, l'ordonnance N° 73-17 du 22 mai 1973 portant organisation de la prévoyance sociale au Cameroun prévoit en ses articles 24 et 30 que l'employeur[33] a l'obligation d'affilier la société à la Caisse nationale de prévoyance sociale, déclarer les employés et cotiser pour leur compte. Il doit à cet effet couvrir les risques sociaux prévus à travers la convention n° 102 de l'Organisation internationale du travail (branches des pensions vieillesse, d'invalidité et de décès, des prestations familiales, des risques professionnels). Il s'expose à une sanction pénale, car la loi prévoit une peine d'emprisonnement de trois mois à deux ans, et une amende de vingt mille à deux cent mille francs ou de l'une des deux peines

[31] En effet, l'article L 1 du livre des procédures fiscales met à la charge de toute personne physique ou morale assujettie en sa qualité de redevable légal au paiement de l'impôt, l'obligation de déclarer l'activité de la société dans les 15 jours ouvrables qui suivent son début, en vue de son immatriculation.

[32] Il prévoit la solidarité dans le paiement de l'impôt en les termes suivants: « *Tous ceux qui font l'objet d'une condamnation définitive en application des dispositions de l'article L 107 du présent livre sont tenus avec le redevable de l'impôt compromis, au paiement de cet impôt, et des pénalités y afférentes* ».

[33] Suivant l'article 4 de ladite ordonnance, l'employeur renvoie à toute personne physique ou morale employant un ou plusieurs travailleurs relevant du code du travail.

seulement à l'endroit de quiconque organise par voie de fait, menaces ou manœuvres concertées le refus de se conformer aux prescriptions de la législation sur la prévoyance sociale et notamment de s'affilier à la Caisse nationale de la prévoyance sociale ou de payer les cotisations dues. L'employeur est frappé de majoration[34] dans le paiement desdites cotisations au cas où il n'accomplit pas son devoir dans le délai légal[35]. Mais en cas de force majeure ou de bonne foi dûment établie par décision du comité de la Caisse nationale de prévoyance sociale prise sur proposition du directeur général, ces majorations peuvent toutefois être réduites ou remises totalement[36].

On peut alors constater que l'exigence de loyauté, même loin du droit des sociétés, continue de s'imposer au dirigeant, dans la mesure où l'application des sanctions ci-dessus tient compte de l'intention qui a habité le dirigeant au moment de la commission des faits reprochés. À ces sanctions pénales qui imposent en réalité au dirigeant un devoir de loyauté, s'ajoutent d'autres sanctions qui résultent des fautes commises dans la gestion de la société et qui, par leur diversité, rendent davantage complexe la fonction de dirigeant social.

B. Une contrainte due aux diverses sanctions attachées au statut de dirigeant

L'étude du vaste régime de responsabilité du dirigeant aboutit à la classification des sanctions qui peuvent le frapper en deux catégories : les

---

[34] Cette majoration est de dix pour cent et est augmentée de trois pour cent des cotisations pour chaque trimestre ou fraction de trimestre écoulé après l'expiration d'un délai de trois à compter de la date. Voir article 32 du décret n° 74-26 du 11 janvier 1974 fixant les modalités d'application de certaines dispositions de l'ordonnance n° 73-17 du 22 mai 1973 portant organisation de la Prévoyance sociale, modifié par le décret n°99/223/PM du 30 septembre 1999.

[35] L'article 30 du décret n° 74-26 du 11 janvier 1974 fixant les modalités d'application de certaines dispositions de l'ordonnance n° 73-17 du 22 mai 1973 portant organisation de la prévoyance sociale, modifié par le décret n°99/223/PM du 30 septembre 1999, prévoit que les cotisations dues en raison des rémunérations et gains versés au cours d'un mois civil déterminé doivent être réglées par l'employeur dans les vingt premiers jours du mois suivant.

[36] Article 32. 3 du décret ci-dessus.

sanctions juridiques (1) et la sanction politique de la révocation qui pèse en permanence sur lui (2).

1. Les sanctions juridiques: la responsabilité civile et pénale dans la gestion de la société

La responsabilité pénale du dirigeant (a) sera envisagée avant sa responsabilité civile (b).

a. La responsabilité pénale du dirigeant

Le dirigeant social est susceptible de commettre des infractions diverses dans la gestion de la société. Ces infractions ne relèvent pas uniquement du droit des sociétés, car plusieurs autres disciplines réglementent des aspects qui touchent à la gestion de l'entreprise. Le dirigeant est alors exposé à la commission d'infractions dans des domaines spécifiques très différents relevant tant du droit du travail que du droit fiscal, du droit des transports, du droit boursier, ou encore du droit de l'environnement[37]. Ces matières, à l'exception de la réglementation boursière et du droit des transports de marchandises par route, font l'objet de législations diverses propres à chaque État dans l'espace OHADA.

Dans le contexte camerounais, on a déjà par exemple fait allusion à la fraude fiscale et au refus de se conformer aux prescriptions de la législation sur la prévoyance sociale qui peuvent entraîner la responsabilité du dirigeant. La responsabilité pénale du dirigeant peut aussi intervenir en droit de la consommation. L'article 32 de la loi-cadre N° 2011/012 du 6 mai 2011 portant protection du consommateur au Cameroun dispose par exemple qu'« (1) *Est puni d'un emprisonnement de 6 mois à deux ans et d'une amende de deux cent mille à un million de francs ou de l'une des deux peines seulement, celui qui fournit des informations erronées sur la qualité des technologies, biens ou services fournis à un consommateur.* (2) *Est puni des peines prévues à l'alinéa 1 ci-dessus, celui qui donne de fausses informations aux autorités compétentes, ou à toute structure, organisme ou association des consommateurs au cours d'une enquête menée dans cadre de la présente loi* ».

---

[37] F. FRANÇOIS, I. MAIGRET et A. MARLANGE, *Dirigeant de société, statut juridique, social et fiscal*, *op. cit.*, n° 2002, p. 203.

En matière sociale, il est important de mentionner qu'un avant-projet d'Acte uniforme relatif au droit du travail mis en place depuis 2006 par les États membres de l'OHADA, tarde encore à être adopté[38]. Nous allons donc nous tourner une fois de plus vers le droit camerounais où le code du travail dans son article 95 à 103 a, par exemple, pris des dispositions visant à assurer la santé et la sécurité des travailleurs dans l'entreprise, et dont le non-respect entraîne l'application de sanctions pécuniaires à l'endroit de l'employeur[39]. C'est ainsi que l'article 167 punit d'une amende de 100. 000 à 1.000.000 de francs l'employeur qui n'organise pas un service médical et sanitaire au profit des travailleurs malades.

Loin de ces quelques exemples de sanctions pénales que peut encourir le dirigeant dans d'autres disciplines, l'AUSCGIE prévoit une diversité d'infractions. Certaines sont relatives à la constitution de la société (émission d'actions avant l'immatriculation de la société, infractions relatives à la souscription des actions ou parts sociales et aux versements respectivement aux articles 886 et 887 AUSCGIE). D'autres sont attachées à la gérance de la société (distribution de dividendes fictifs, présentation de comptes infidèles, abus de biens sociaux (articles 889, 890, 891)... D'autres encore concernent les modifications du capital social (articles 893 et suivants), tandis que certaines sont relatives à la tenue des assemblées générales (articles 893-3 et 894), à la dissolution (article 901)... Il est important de préciser ici que la détermination des sanctions proprement dites aux infractions ci-dessus a été laissée à la portée des États, suivant les prescriptions de l'article 5 du traité OHADA. Par exemple le Cameroun et

[38] On peut se réjouir par anticipation de ce qu'il présente un riche tableau en matière d'infractions commises par l'employeur (article 260 à 274).

[39] Il faut dire que le droit social n'utilise pas le concept de dirigeant, mais plutôt d'employeur pour qualifier le détenteur des pouvoirs patronaux. Le droit social fait de l' « employeur » le dirigeant et fait fi de la notion de « dirigeant ». Mais si le dirigeant est censé être le représentant de l'employeur, les deux qualités (employeur et dirigeant) ne se recouvrent pas nécessairement. Voir B. NJOYA NKAMGA, « Dirigeants sociaux », *op. cit*, n° 149 p. 660. L'Avant-projet OHADA relatif au droit du travail semble plus précis pour sa part, en utilisant dans ses dispositions pénales les termes : « employeur ou le représentant de l'employeur » pour indexer le dirigeant social.

le Sénégal ont à cet effet adopté des textes qui visent la répression de certaines infractions contenues dans l'AUSCGIE[40].

Le dirigeant est ainsi soumis sur le plan pénal à des sanctions d'origines diverses. Il n'est d'ailleurs pas épargné de responsabilité sur le plan civil.

b. La responsabilité civile du dirigeant

L'étendue de la responsabilité civile encourue par le dirigeant est aussi grande que sur le plan pénal. En effet, le dirigeant est exposé à une responsabilité de triple origine : tout d'abord il peut commettre une faute contre la société, ensuite il peut commettre une faute contre les associés, enfin, il peut commettre une faute à l'égard des tiers. De façon globale, sans distinction du type de société, les règles générales sur la responsabilité des dirigeants sociaux sont prévues à partir de l'article 161 de l'AUSCGIE. Mais elles ont spécifiquement été reprises dans le cas des SARL et des sociétés par actions où le législateur apporte plus de précisions sur la typologie des fautes susceptibles d'engager la responsabilité des dirigeants[41].

Lorsque la faute du dirigeant a causé un tort à la société, on parle d'action sociale[42] dont le but visé est la reconstitution des fonds sociaux, dans la mesure où l'AUSCGIE précise désormais clairement qu'en cas de condamnation, les dommages et intérêts sont alloués à la société et non au(x) requérant(s)[43]. L'article 165 AUSCGIE dispose à cette fin que chaque dirigeant social est responsable individuellement envers la société, des fautes commises dans l'exercice de ses fonctions. L'action sociale est en principe exercée par les dirigeants sociaux[44]: on parle de l'action sociale *ut universi.*

---

[40] Il s'agit de la loi N° 98-22 du 26 mars 1998 au Sénégal et la loi N° 2003/008 du 10 juillet 2003 pour le Cameroun.

[41] Ces fautes sont de trois ordres : des infractions aux dispositions législatives ou réglementaires, des violations des clauses des statuts et des fautes de gestion. Pour la responsabilité des gérants de SARL, voir les articles 330 à 332 AUSCGIE, dans les SA, ce sont les articles 740, 741, 742 et 743 qui s'appliquent également aux sociétés par actions simplifiées (renvoi de l'article 853-10).

[42] Elle est définie à l'article 166 AUSCGIE comme l'action en réparation du dommage subi par la société du fait de la faute commise par le ou les dirigeants sociaux dans l'exercice de leurs fonctions.

[43] L'expression « et non au(x) requérant(s) » venait juste d'être ajouté à l'article 167 al 1.

[44] Art.166 al 2 AUSCGIE.

Mais les intéressés sont rarement enclins à tresser la corde qui servira à les pendre[45], car c'est une action dirigée contre eux-mêmes. Mais pour remédier à cet obstacle, le législateur a prévu dans l'article 167 AUSCGIE, la possibilité pour les actionnaires d'exercer cette action après une mise en demeure des organes compétents non suivie d'effet dans un délai de 30 jours[46]. On parle dans ce cas de l'action sociale *ut singuli*. Elle se prescrit par trois ans à compter du fait dommageable ou, s'il a été dissimulé, de sa révélation. Pour les crimes, son délai de prescription est plutôt de dix ans. Son efficacité a récemment été améliorée[47]. Cette amélioration introduite à l'article 167 alinéa 3 offre à la société ou à tout associé, la possibilité de demander la désignation d'un mandataire *ad hoc* pour représenter ladite société à l'instance lorsqu'il y a conflit d'intérêts entre elle et ses représentants légaux[48]. Ceci tend à éviter que le dirigeant défende ses intérêts au détriment de ceux de la société qu'il est appelé à représenter au procès.

Lorsque la faute du dirigeant a plutôt causé préjudice à un associé ou même à un tiers, on parle d'action individuelle. L'article 162 AUSCGIE l'a définie comme l'action en réparation du dommage souffert par un associé ou par un tiers lorsqu'il subit un dommage distinct de celui subi par la société, du fait de la faute commise individuellement ou collectivement par les dirigeants sociaux dans l'exercice de leurs fonctions. Les règles de prescription de cette action sont les mêmes que dans le cadre de l'action sociale. Une condition importante détermine le succès de cette action : que le dommage subi par l'associé ou le tiers soit différent de celui subi par la société. Il doit alors rapporter la preuve d'un dommage indépendant ou

---

[45] M. COZIAN, A. VIANDIER, Fl. DEBOISSY, *Droit des sociétés*, *op. cit.*, n°295 ; M.-A. MOUTHIEU NJANDEU, obs. sous CCJA, arrêt n°015/2005, 24 févr. 2005, Angoua Koffi Maurice c/ la société Win SARL, Les grandes décisions de la CCJA de l'OHADA, p. 162. Ce n'est qu'éventuellement en cas de changement de dirigeants sociaux que le successeur n'ayant aucune raison d'épargner son prédécesseur pourrait engager l'action sociale.

[46] Voir Cotonou, n°65/99, 29/4/99, Affaire M. Guy BARBARA c/ Société SIVAPT.

[47] Il faut signaler que l'AUSCGIE continue juste en effet d'améliorer le résultat de l'action sociale dans la mesure où certaines de ses dispositions allaient déjà dans ce sens. Voir à cet effet les articles 168, 169 et 171.

[48] Pour plus d'éclairage sur l'importance du rôle joué par ce mandataire, voir L. MONGIN-ARCHAMBEAUD, « Action sociale *ut singuli* formée contre le dirigeant, représentant légal de la société : le rôle fondamental du mandataire *ad hoc* », préc., p. 479.

« détachable » de celui souffert par la société[49]. Tel est par exemple le cas du détournement de dividendes revenant à un actionnaire[50], du défaut de convocation de l'actionnaire aux assemblées générales ou du défaut d'information des actionnaires sur la nécessité de présenter leur titre en vue d'une mise au nominatif[51]. Il n'est cependant pas parfois facile pour l'associé d'en rapporter la preuve lorsque le préjudice individuel s'avère en effet n'être qu'un corollaire du préjudice subi par la société[52]. Toutefois, les associés peuvent simplement décider de révoquer le dirigeant.

2. La sanction politique du dirigeant : la révocation

L'acte le plus redoutable des associés envers les dirigeants coupables de faute de gestion est la révocation. C'est le pouvoir suprême des associés sur les dirigeants, car face à une gestion déficitaire de la société, ils peuvent tout simplement décider de se débarrasser de ces derniers. L'AUSCGIE leur offre à cet effet le choix entre deux types de révocations : la révocation *ad nutum* et la révocation pour justes motifs.

Suivant le régime de la révocation pour justes motifs appliqué jusqu'ici dans l'AUSCGIE[53] aux dirigeants de SNC, de SCS et de SARL, les associés qui veulent se débarrasser du dirigeant social doivent présenter une cause ou

---

[49] A. AKAM AKAM, « La responsabilité civile des dirigeants sociaux en droit OHADA »,*op. cit*, p. 221; F. FRANÇOIS, I. MAIGRET, A. MARLANGE, *op. cit*, n° 1904, p 199.

[50] Paris, 2 mai 1935, Gaz. Pal. 1937, II, 113. Pour une conception plus extensive, Paris, 19 janv. 1996 et 15 déc. 1995, RTD com. 1997, p. 286, B. Petit et Y. Reinhard.

[51] Cass. com., 19 mai 1992, BJS, 1992, p. 775, note D. Lepeltier.

[52]La jurisprudence française décide par exemple que l'associé, qui invoque une dépréciation de la valeur de ses titres due à une mauvaise gestion des dirigeants, ne caractérise pas un préjudice individuel distinct du préjudice social, car le premier n'étant qu'un corollaire du second, la demande en réparation doit prendre la voie de l'action sociale : Cass. com., 1er avr. 1997, *BJS*, 1998, p. 650, note J. F. Barbieri. Dans le même sens, ne peut être accueillie, faute de rapporter la preuve d'un préjudice personnel, l'action individuelle intentée par un actionnaire contre le président-directeur général de la société qui avait dû procéder à un « coup d'accordéon », le dommage subi par le demandeur n'étant que le corollaire de celui supporté par la société en raison des fautes de gestion commises par le dirigeant : Com. 15 janv. 2002, *BJS*, 2002, p. 689, n° 155, S. Sylvestre.

[53]En revenant un peu plus tard sur la notion de « juste motif », l'on verra que le législateur OHADA étend désormais ce régime de révocation à certains dirigeants de SA : voir le point sur la notion de justes motifs de révocation.

un motif valable, à défaut de quoi, ils s'exposent au paiement de dommages-intérêts[54]. Mais il est important de préciser que l'absence de justes motifs ne prive pas les associés de la possibilité de révoquer le dirigeant, car la révocabilité du dirigeant est un droit d'ordre public. Il en résulte que, même en l'absence de juste motif, les associés peuvent révoquer le dirigeant sans que leur décision ne puisse faire l'objet d'annulation. L'absence de juste motif est seulement sanctionnée par l'allocation de dommages-intérêts en réparation du préjudice effectivement subi par le dirigeant en pareille hypothèse[55].

La révocation *ad nutum* quant à elle signifie littéralement « au moindre signe de tête ». Elle s'applique au président-directeur général et au président du conseil d'administration suivant les articles 469 et 484 AUSCGIE selon lesquels ils peuvent à tout moment être révoqués par le conseil d'administration[56]. Cette forme de révocation comporte trois conséquences : le dirigeant peut être démis de ses fonctions sans justes motifs, sans préavis et il n'a en principe droit à aucune indemnité[57]. Le dirigeant ainsi révoqué fût-ce sans justes motifs, ne pourra prétendre ni à sa réintégration ni même à des dommages-intérêts, toute convention contraire tendant notamment à l'allocation d'indemnité étant en principe nulle[58]. Mais, il apparaît que la puissance de cette forme de révocation connaît de plus en plus d'atténuations, et rentre de ce fait dans le vaste mouvement de sécurisation du statut du dirigeant social observé dans le droit des sociétés.

II. Le statut de dirigeant social : un statut protégé

La fonction de dirigeant social est une fonction à risque au regard des multiples obligations et responsabilités auxquelles elle l'expose. Mais l'on ne

---

[54] Voir dans l'AUSCGIE les articles 281 et 293-1 pour les dirigeants de SNC et de SCS, l'article 326 alinéa 2 pour les dirigeants de SARL.

[55] F. FRANÇOIS, I. MAIGRET, A. MARLANGE, *Le dirigeant de société, statut juridique, social et fiscal*, *op. cit*, n°2316, p. 240.

[56] Il est important de faire observer ici que l'AUSCGIE n'a rien prévu en ce qui concerne la révocation du président de la société par actions simplifiées. Mais s'il revient aux statuts de fixer les conditions dans lesquelles la société est dirigée aux termes de l'article 852-7, on en déduit que les questions relatives à la nomination et à la révocation des dirigeants y figurent.

[57] M. COZIAN, A. VIANDIER, Fl. DEBOISSY, *Droit des sociétés*, *op. cit*, n°574, p. 316.

[58] F. FRANÇOIS, I. MAIGRET, A. MARLANGE, *op. cit*, n°2321, p. 242.

saurait cependant affirmer que le dirigeant est un sacrifié dans l'entreprise, car le droit s'attelle de plus en plus à le protéger tantôt par des mécanismes juridiques visant à l'exonérer de sa responsabilité (A), tantôt à travers un contrôle renforcé de sa révocation (B).

A. La protection par les mécanismes juridiques exonérant de responsabilité

Ces mécanismes renvoient successivement à la construction prétorienne de la notion de faute détachable des fonctions qui trouve son explication dans la théorie de la représentation (1), et à la souscription d'une assurance par la société pour couvrir le dirigeant de la responsabilité qui découle de ses fautes de gestion (2).

1. L'effet exonératoire de la notion de faute détachable des fonctions

À titre de rappel, la responsabilité du dirigeant social peut être établie dans trois directions : à l'endroit de la société, à l'endroit des associés, à l'endroit des tiers. On parle d'action sociale dans le premier cas et d'action individuelle dans les deux autres cas. Quand il s'agit de sa responsabilité envers la société, le dirigeant ne dispose d'aucun mécanisme d'exonération. La loi s'assure bien au contraire que ni la société ni les associés n'exemptent le dirigeant de ses responsabilités en étouffant l'exercice de l'action sociale. C'est au sujet de l'action individuelle et particulièrement celle exercée par le tiers que la jurisprudence française, pour être plus précis, a introduit une condition qui vise en réalité à exonérer le dirigeant.

En principe, la responsabilité du dirigeant envers les tiers a un caractère exceptionnel, car la société seule doit être tenue responsable vis-à-vis des tiers des fautes commises dans la gestion. Lorsqu'un tiers souffre de l'inexécution ou de la mauvaise exécution d'un contrat conclu avec la société, par exemple le défaut de paiement d'une facture ou encore la mauvaise exécution d'une prestation convenue, le principe est qu'il appartient non pas au dirigeant, mais à la société de répondre du préjudice ainsi subi par le cocontractant[59]. C'est qu'en effet, une fois la société immatriculée et donc ayant acquis une personnalité juridique autonome, pour pouvoir réaliser l'objet social pour lequel elle s'est constituée, elle a

---

[59] *Idem*, n°1906, p. 199.

besoin de dirigeants qui la représentent. Sur la base de cette représentation, le dirigeant n'étant qu'un mandataire agissant pour le compte de la société, il revient à cette dernière d'assumer les fautes commises par son dirigeant en raison de l'autonomie de la personne morale. Ce qui l'exonère alors d'une responsabilité personnelle chaque fois qu'il a agi dans le cadre de ses fonctions. Voilà pourquoi pour le protéger de toute action en responsabilité intentée par les tiers, en partant sur le principe que la société entité autonome endosse la responsabilité des actes effectués pour son compte, la jurisprudence française a mis sur pied la théorie de la faute détachable des fonctions.

En effet, dans un arrêt du 22 janvier 1991, la chambre commerciale de la Cour de cassation en France décide que « *la responsabilité personnelle d'un dirigeant à l'égard des tiers ne peut être retenue que s'il a commis une faute séparable de ses fonctions et qui lui soit imputable personnellement* »[60]. C'est plus tard qu'elle apportera une définition de la faute détachable des fonctions[61]. « *Il en est ainsi lorsque le dirigeant commet intentionnellement une faute d'une gravité particulière incompatible avec l'exercice normal des fonctions sociales*[62] ». Les juges français ont ainsi transposé en droit des sociétés les solutions admises en droit administratif selon lesquelles l'agent ne répond que de sa faute personnelle détachable de ses fonctions et non de sa simple faute de service[63].

Cette évolution de la jurisprudence française n'étant pas encore connue du droit OHADA, l'on attend bien de voir quelle sera la position du juge OHADA sur cette question. Mais un auteur OHADA fait déjà observer que cette évolution de la jurisprudence affecte la fonction normative de la responsabilité civile en droit des sociétés dont l'objectif est de sanctionner et

---

[60] Com., 22 janv. 1991, *RJDA*, 1992, n°152.

[61] Il est important de noter que le juge français va plus tard exclure du champ de la faute non détachable des fonctions la commission d'une infraction. Cela signifie que le dirigeant social n'est pas exonéré de tout type de comportement fautif, car sa faute pénale intentionnelle lui reste imputable. Voir M. COZIAN, A.VIANDIER, Fl. DEBOISSY, *Droit des sociétés, op. cit*, n°307, p. 181.

[62] Cass. Com., 20 mai 2003, D. 2003, p.2627, note B. Dondero.

[63] M. COZIAN, A.VIANDIER, Fl. DEBOISSY, *Droit des sociétés, op. cit*, n°301, p. 178.

dissuader les comportements fautifs[64]. Dans ce schéma, elle reporte simplement la charge de la réparation sur la société, car le tiers n'aura pas à prouver que la faute du dirigeant est détachable de ses fonctions. C'est le dirigeant qui en tire profit, car la preuve par le tiers d'une faute détachable de ses fonctions n'étant pas aisée à établir, elle conduit forcément à une espèce d'irresponsabilité du dirigeant. Pour également parvenir au même résultat, la société peut simplement souscrire à une assurance pour le bénéfice de son dirigeant.

2. L'effet exonératoire de la souscription de l'assurance-responsabilité des dirigeants

Prenant appui sur des contrats nés dans les pays anglo-saxons, le contrat d'assurance de responsabilité civile est souscrit par la société pour le compte d'un ou de plusieurs dirigeants personnes physiques[65]. En fait, le métier de dirigeant est un métier à risque et le risque appelle l'assurance[66]. Les différentes responsabilités qui découlent de la fonction de direction sont potentiellement source de risques juridiques divers pour le dirigeant social, car il pourrait être amené à répondre sur son patrimoine des fautes commises dans l'exercice de ses fonctions. Le risque juridique se manifeste alors essentiellement par le danger pour le mandataire social de voir sa responsabilité engagée[67]. Face à l'importance du risque, il serait souhaitable pour les chefs d'entreprise de l'espace OHADA de se protéger en recourant à des assurances de responsabilité civile et professionnelle qui, même si elles ne permettent pas d'éviter la mise en œuvre de leur responsabilité, peuvent parer aux conséquences financières de celle-ci[68].

Toutefois, il est important de faire observer que dans la pratique, les entreprises OHADA ne sont pas totalement étrangères à la souscription

---

[64] La jurisprudence est plutôt attachée à la fonction réparatrice de la responsabilité en reportant la charge de la réparation sur la société. *Idem*, p.231.

[65]F. FRANÇOIS, I. MAIGRET, A. MARLANGE, *op. cit.*, n°1909, p. 201.

[66] M. COZIAN, A. VIANDIER, Fl. DEBOISSY, *Droit des sociétés, op. cit*, n°308, p. 182.

[67] Pour une étude détaillée de l'étendue du risque juridique encouru par les mandataires sociaux en général, voir B. MEUKE, « Brèves observations sur le risque juridique du mandataire social dans l'OHADA », *op. cit.*.

[68]A. AKAM AKAM, « La responsabilité civile des dirigeants sociaux en droit OHADA », *op. cit.*, p.229.

d'assurance pour le compte de la société. Une enquête personnellement menée auprès de quelques entreprises d'assurance[69] dans la ville de Douala au Cameroun a révélé qu'elles souscrivent à des polices d'assurance pour les risques professionnels et sociaux découlant de leurs activités. Mais il ressort des entretiens avec le personnel de ces sociétés que les chefs d'entreprise sont réfractaires à assurer les risques de fautes de gestion au regard du montant important de la prime à payer. Si la couverture de ce type de risque n'est pas encore monnaie courante dans le contexte, rien ne l'interdit cependant, car sur le plan légal, l'article 51 du code CIMA[70] fait allusion aux assurances de responsabilité civile sans limitation des domaines dans lesquels elles peuvent intervenir. L'assurance responsabilité des dirigeants couvre les fautes commises par ces derniers dans l'exercice de leurs fonctions, à la condition qu'elles n'aient pas été intentionnelles.

B. La protection à travers le souci de maîtrise de la révocation des dirigeants

On observe aussi bien sur le plan légal (1) que judiciaire (2), une tendance de plus en plus élevée à vouloir maîtriser le phénomène de la révocation des dirigeants sociaux dans l'espace OHADA.

1. Les indices légaux de la recherche de maîtrise de la révocation

Il s'agit d'une part de l'exigence croissante d'un juste motif de révocation (a) et de la possibilité du cumul de fonctions (b).

a. L'exigence croissante d'un juste motif de révocation

Jusqu'ici, l'exigence d'un juste motif de révocation ne s'est posée dans l'AUSCGIE que pour les dirigeants de sociétés de personnes et les SARL. On constate aujourd'hui à travers la réforme du droit des sociétés OHADA

[69] Cette enquête a été menée au mois de novembre 2015 auprès de trois sociétés d'assurance : AXA Assurance, ACTIVA Assurance et PRO ASSUR (compagnie d'Assurance et de Réassurance).

[70] Le code CIMA (Conférence interafricaine des marchés d'assurance) est le code des assurances que partagent plusieurs pays de l'espace OHADA (excepté la Guinée-Bissau et la Guinée Conakry) qui ont pris part au traité signé le 10 juillet 1992 à Yaoundé instituant une organisation intégrée de l'industrie des assurances dans les États africains. Ce code entré en vigueur depuis le 15 Janvier 1995, a été modifié à plusieurs reprises par le conseil des ministres, organe législatif de cette institution.

que l'une des préoccupations du législateur a été de défaire certains dirigeants de sociétés anonymes de leur statut précaire dû à la révocation *ad nutum* à laquelle ils pouvaient être sujet à tout moment. Désormais, à l'exception du président-directeur général, du président du conseil d'administration ainsi que des administrateurs qui restent révocables *ad nutum,* c'est-à-dire sans motifs ni préavis[71], tout autre dirigeant de la SA est révocable pour justes motifs[72]. Pour le cas du directeur général, il faut observer que lorsqu'il est administrateur, la révocation de son mandat n'entraîne pas pour autant la perte de son statut de directeur général, dans la mesure où l'article 485 AUSCGIE prévoit qu'il peut ou non être actionnaire. Le statut de directeur général en sort ainsi renforcé.

Il reviendra au juge OHADA de définir la notion de « justes motifs » au regard du silence de la loi. *La jurisprudence française établit qu'il y a juste motif de révocation dès lors que les fautes commises par le gérant présentent une certaine gravité, notamment, en cas de violation de la loi*[73]*, des statuts*[74] *ou même de faute de gestion*[75]*. Elle admet aussi qu'en dehors de toute faute, il y a juste motif de révocation dès lors que la mésentente compromet l'intérêt social ou le fonctionnement de la société*[76]*. Le juste motif s'apprécie alors, non seulement en fonction du comportement du dirigeant, mais aussi au regard de l'intérêt social.* L'exigence du juste motif apporte ainsi une garantie de stabilité très importante pour les dirigeants de SA. Ils ne peuvent plus être révoqués parce

[71]Les administrateurs sont révoqués par l'assemblée générale ordinaire et les autres par le conseil d'administration. Voir respectivement les articles 469, 484 et 433 alinéa 2 AUSCGIE.

[72] Sous l'empire de l'ancien AUSCGIE, le directeur général et le directeur général adjoint étaient révocables à tout moment et sans exigence de justes motifs par le conseil d'administration suivant les articles 492 et 475 AUSCGIE. La situation était aussi la même pour l'administrateur général qui pouvait être révoqué par l'assemblée générale dans les mêmes conditions suivant l'article 509.

[73] Poitiers, 29 août 2002, *Dr. sociétés*, 2002, n°220, J. Monnet (contrat de travail non soumis à la procédure des conventions réglementées).

[74] Bordeaux, 21 janv. 1988, *Rev. Droit bancaire*, 1988, p. 201, M. Jeantin et A. Viandier (violation d'une clause limitative de pouvoirs).

[75] Com. 21 oct. 1997, *BJS*, 1998, p. 27, n°6, B. Saintourens (concurrence déloyale).

[76] Com. 4 mai 1999, *BJS*, 1999, p. 914, n° 215, P. Le Cannu ; Paris, 5 nov. 2000, *BRDA*, févr. 2000, p. 5 (mésentente entre cogérants).

qu'ils ont cessé de plaire, sauf pour la société à en payer le prix[77]. Cette recherche de stabilité était déjà implicitement visée à travers l'institution du cumul de fonctions dans l'AUSCGIE.

b. La possibilité du cumul des fonctions d'administrateur et de salarié

Les administrateurs ont parfois la tentation de profiter de leur situation pour conclure avec la société des contrats qui leur confère des fonctions salariales à l'instar de celles de directeur technique, directeur commercial, financier, etc. Établissant d'un point de vue théorique les avantages que peuvent présenter le cumul pour les dirigeants sociaux, la doctrine française fait tout de même valoir que sa pratique risque d'entraîner la création d'emplois fictifs destinés à se prémunir indirectement contre la règle de la libre révocabilité[78]. Mais ceci n'a pas empêché le législateur OHADA de consacrer le cumul de fonctions à travers l'article 426 AUSCGIE qui dispose à cet effet qu'« *...un administrateur peut conclure un contrat de travail avec la société si ce contrat correspond à un emploi effectif* ». C'est alors que les articles 481, 489 et 499 AUSCGIE admettent sans équivoque la possibilité pour le président du conseil d'administration, le directeur général et l'administrateur général de conclure avec la société un contrat de travail dans le respect des conditions de l'article 426.

Le législateur soumet ce cumul à deux conditions précises pour éviter qu'il ne soit utilisé que comme un parapluie contre la révocation *ad nutum* : l'effectivité de l'emploi et l'autorisation préalable du conseil d'administration ou de l'assemblée générale. Cette deuxième condition n'appelle pas de commentaire particulier, puisque le contrat de travail passé par un administrateur avec la société est qualifié de convention réglementée aux termes de l'article 426 AUSCGIE, et est de ce fait soumis à la procédure

---

[77] Voir Ph. MERLE, *Droit commercial sociétés commerciales*, 10ème éd., Dalloz, 2005, n° 431, p. 507.

[78] Il assure la promotion des cadres de l'entreprise, facilite le fonctionnement des petites sociétés de caractère familial dans lesquelles les administrateurs sont chargés par nécessité des fonctions de direction technique... Voir G. RIPERT et R. ROBLOT, *Traité de droit commercial*, Tome 1, 15ème éd., par M. Germain et L. Vogel, LGDJ, 1993, n°1278, p. 964. Le cumul a également l'avantage de permettre la participation des salariés à la gestion de la société.

de contrôle des conventions réglementées[79]. Quant au caractère effectif de l'emploi, la doctrine établit qu'il découle de son caractère sérieux et sincère[80] qui devrait pouvoir s'analyser à l'aune de la définition même du contrat de travail. En effet, d'après l'article 23 du code de travail camerounais, « *Le contrat de travail est la convention par laquelle un travailleur s'engage à mettre son activité professionnelle sous l'autorité et la direction d'un employeur en contrepartie d'une rémunération* ». Trois éléments fondamentaux dans cette définition établissent l'effectivité d'un contrat de travail et donc de l'emploi : l'existence d'une activité professionnelle, la subordination du travailleur qui doit être sous l'autorité et la direction de l'employeur, ainsi que le versement d'une rémunération. Le lien de subordination juridique est caractérisé par l'exécution d'un travail sous l'autorité d'un employeur qui a le pouvoir de donner des ordres et des directives, d'en contrôler l'exécution et de sanctionner les manquements de son subordonné[81]. Le travail effectué devrait en outre soulever une contrepartie appelée salaire, qui doit pouvoir être distinguée de l'indemnité de fonction[82] ou des rémunérations exceptionnelles[83] perçues dans le cadre du mandat social. C'est l'agencement de ces trois éléments qui caractérise l'effectivité de l'emploi. Le juge OHADA[84] les a réitérés dans une affaire en posant sous le couvert de l'article 426 que « *…le cumul suppose que les fonctions salariées correspondent à un emploi effectif exercé dans un état de subordination à l'endroit de la société, en*

---

[79] Voir à cet effet les articles 438, 439 à 448 AUSCGIE desquels il ressort en substance que ces conventions doivent faire l'objet d'une autorisation préalable du conseil d'administration et d'une approbation *a posteriori* de l'assemblée générale ordinaire.

[80] M. COZIAN, A. VIANDIER, Fl. DEBOISSY, *Droit des sociétés, op.cit.*, n°557, p. 305.

[81] Cass.soc., 13 nov. 1996, *RJS*, 12/1996, n°1320 ; Cass. Soc., 29 janv. 2002, *Droit social*, 2002, p.494, chron. J. Savatier.

[82] Voir art. 431 AUSCGIE. L'assemblée générale ordinaire peut allouer aux administrateurs en rémunération de leurs activités, à titre d'indemnité de fonction une somme fixe annuelle qu'elle détermine souverainement.

[83] Art. 432 AUSCGIE. Le conseil d'administration peut également allouer à ses membres, des rémunérations exceptionnelles pour les missions et mandats qui leur sont confiés, ou autoriser le remboursement des frais de voyage, déplacements et dépenses engagés dans l'intérêt de la société.

[84] Cour d'appel de Dakar, chambre sociale 2, arrêt n°472 du 06 nov. 2007, ELTON SA. C/S. *Revue EDJA* n°76, janv-fév-mars 2008, p.80, note DOUDOU NDOYE, Avocat.

contrepartie d'une rémunération distincte de celle allouée comme mandataire social ».

L'existence de ces trois éléments soulève en retour la protection du droit social et conforte par conséquent le statut de dirigeant. Le juge OHADA a, de ce fait, dans une affaire, reconnu la compétence du tribunal du travail à déclarer abusive la rupture du contrat de travail d'un directeur général, puisque l'effectivité dudit contrat avait été établie[85]. Par contre, cette compétence a été rejetée dans une autre espèce où un emploi effectif distinct des tâches dévolues en qualité de directeur général n'a pu être établi[86]. Le cumul constitue en fait une arme efficace d'atténuation des effets de la révocation *ad nutum*. En effet, placé dans un état de subordination à l'entreprise, le mandataire salarié se retrouve dans une situation privilégiée, car le contrat de travail qui le lie à la société constitue un moyen de limitation des conséquences financières néfastes qui pourront l'atteindre au moment de sa révocation du poste de dirigeant social[87]. Ce faisant, le droit des sociétés ouvre la possibilité d'une sécurisation du statut de dirigeant social que la jurisprudence s'est toujours attelé à protéger.

2. Un contrôle judiciaire de plus en plus accentué de la révocation

L'on révèle de la part des juges, un contrôle sans cesse croissant aussi bien de la forme (a) que du fond de la révocation (b).

a. Le contrôle de la forme : la sanction de la révocation irrégulière

Il y a bien longtemps que les juges s'intéressent aux conditions dans lesquelles intervient la révocation des dirigeants pour éviter qu'ils ne fassent l'objet d'un acharnement de la part des actionnaires. Ce contrôle vise en fait la procédure de la révocation afin de sanctionner la révocation irrégulière en la forme. Le contrôle de la procédure repose sur trois points majeurs[88] : la

---

[85] Cour d'appel de Dakar, chambre social 2, Arrêt n°263 du 14 juin 2005, Bank of AFRICA c/BONNEAU, *Revue EDJA* n°76 janvier-février-mars 2008, p.75.

[86] Cour d'appel de Dakar, chambre sociale 2, arrêt n°472 du 06 nov. 2007, ELTON SA. C/S. op.cit.

[87] C. MONKAM, « Réflexions sur le cumul de fonctions en droit des sociétés anonymes de l'OHADA », *Uniform Law Review, 2015, doi : 10. 1093/ulr/unv001*, p. 11.

[88] Mais la question de la compétence de l'organe révoquant est préalable. Dans les SA avec administrateur général où il n'y a pas de conseil, c'est l'assemblée générale qui est compétente pour révoquer l'administrateur général et l'administrateur général adjoint.

fixation à l'ordre du jour de la révocation, les conditions de convocation et de délibération, et le respect du principe du contradictoire.

Tout d'abord, la question de la régularité de la révocation non inscrite à l'ordre du jour a été tranchée par le législateur. Il ressort en effet de l'article 522 AUSCGIE que l'assemblée peut, en toutes circonstances, révoquer un ou plusieurs membres du conseil, le cas échéant, l'administrateur général ou l'administrateur général adjoint et procéder à leur remplacement, même si cela ne figure pas à l'ordre du jour. En outre, l'AUSCGIE prévoit que le conseil peut à tout moment révoquer le président-directeur général, le président du conseil d'administration, le directeur général et le directeur général adjoint[89].

Ensuite, si la révocation n'a pas à être inscrite à l'ordre du jour pour être valide, les conditions de convocation et de délibération doivent néanmoins avoir été remplies, que la révocation émane du conseil d'administration ou de l'assemblée générale. Le législateur sanctionne ainsi désormais par la nullité toute convocation et toute délibération irrégulières de ces organes sociaux[90]. La jurisprudence OHADA s'y attelait déjà, puisqu'un arrêt rendu

---

Dans les SA avec conseil, c'est le conseil qui a la compétence directe de révoquer le président-directeur général, le président du conseil d'administration, le directeur général et le directeur général adjoint. Mais l'assemblée générale détient ce pouvoir indirectement, car en révoquant le mandat d'administrateur de ces derniers, sauf dans le cas d'un directeur général non actionnaire, elle leur fait automatiquement perdre la qualité de dirigeant. Mais encore faut-il déterminer laquelle des assemblées a la compétence. L'article 522 al 2 prévoit que l'assemblée, sans précision de laquelle, peut en toutes circonstances révoquer un ou plusieurs membres du conseil, le cas échéant, l'administrateur général ou l'administrateur général adjoint. Mais il s'agit de l'assemblée générale ordinaire, puisqu'il ressort clairement de l'article 433 alinéa 2 que les administrateurs sont révocables à tout moment par l'assemblée générale ordinaire. Mais l'on peut également fonder cette compétence sur les dispositions de l'article 546 al 1 AUSCGIE qui prévoit la compétence de l'assemblée générale ordinaire pour toutes les décisions qui ne relèvent pas de la compétence des assemblées extraordinaires et spéciales prévues aux articles 551 et 555 AUSCGIE. C'est ainsi que le juge OHADA a invalidé la révocation d'un président-directeur général et son équipe pour défaut de compétence de l'assemblée générale extraordinaire, partant des articles 546 et 555 AUSCGIE.

[89] Voir respectivement les articles 469, 484, 492 et 475 AUSCGIE.

[90] Les statuts déterminent les règles relatives à la convocation et aux délibérations du conseil d'administration (article 453 al 1). Mais l'AUSCGIE prévoit aussi des règles impératives. L'article 453 al 4 dispose que les délibérations du conseil sont nulles lorsque tous ses

par la cour d'appel d'Abidjan[91] avait annulé les délibérations d'un conseil d'administration visant la révocation de son président, pour avoir été signées par un seul administrateur, alors que la loi prévoit que le conseil ne peut valablement délibérer que si la moitié au moins de ses membres est présente.

Enfin, un principe emprunté au droit processuel est d'une importance capitale dans le processus de révocation : le principe du contradictoire. La question posée à propos est de savoir si le dirigeant peut être révoqué sans être préalablement informé et sans être invité à exposer des moyens de défense[92]. Appliqué au droit des sociétés, le principe de la contradiction impose de placer les dirigeants sociaux menacés de révocation en situation de faire entendre leurs explications[93]. Au départ, le principe de la révocation suppose seulement que l'administrateur ait été mis en demeure de présenter ses observations préalablement à la décision de révocation[94]. Mais la Cour de cassation française décidera plus tard dans un arrêt du 14 mai 2013[95] que ce dernier devrait être informé du motif de sa révocation avant qu'il soit procédé au vote. Cette exigence de la communication du motif permet à l'administrateur menacé de révocation de faire entendre utilement ses explications devant l'assemblée générale des actionnaires appelée à décider de son sort. Le juge français impose ainsi clairement une obligation de loyauté à la société dans le processus de révocation, obligation en général

membres n'ont pas été régulièrement convoqués. La violation des règles de quorum et de majorité entraîne aussi la nullité des délibérations aux termes de l'article 454 alinéa 3. En ce qui concerne la validité des délibérations de l'assemblée, après en avoir fixé les conditions aux articles 518 et 519, l'alinéa 4 de l'article 519 prévoit la nullité de toute assemblée irrégulièrement convoquée.

[91] Cour d'appel d'Abidjan, arrêt n°1176 du 24/08/2001, Koffi Victor Bergson c/ Loteny Télécom, *Ohadata J- 02-184.*

[92] R. NEMEDEU, *Le contrôle des dirigeants de la société anonyme*, thèse, *op. cit*, p. 114.

[93] Note A. Gaudemet sous Cass. com., 14 mai 2013, n°11-22845 PB, *BJS*, 2013, p. 634.

[94] Voir. notamment Cass. com., 24 janv. 1998, JCP E, 1998, I, 1306, obs. A. Viandier, et J.-J. Caussain : révocation jugée abusive parce que « décidée sans que l'intéressé ait été mis en mesure de présenter préalablement ses observations ; Cass. com., 29 mars 2011, n° 10-17667, *RJDA* juin 2011, n°538 ; Rev. Sociétés, 2011, p. 563, note J.-F., Barbieri, révocation d'un directeur général qui n'avait pas été mis en mesure de débattre contradictoirement des motifs de son éviction, ce qui lui a causé un préjudice moral devant être réparé.

[95] Cass. com., 14 mai 2013, *op. cit.*

plutôt requise du dirigeant social[96]. Il va plus tard la consacrer de façon expresse dans un arrêt du 24 septembre 2014 où la Cour de cassation exigera que l'exercice du droit de révocation *ad nutum* soit soumis à une obligation autonome, une obligation de loyauté de la part de la société[97]. Le principe de la libre révocation est alors combattu au nom des droits fondamentaux de l'homme[98], car la société ne peut plus abuser de son droit de révoquer.

b. Le contrôle du fond de la révocation : le recours à la théorie de l'abus de droit

Le principe la révocation *ad nutum* en lui-même dispense d'énoncer un quelconque motif à l'appui de la révocation[99]. C'est pourquoi l'examen de la jurisprudence OHADA ou même française, fait ressortir que les juges ne procèdent pas à un contrôle des motifs de la révocation. Mais plutôt, au nom de la théorie de l'abus de droit, les circonstances de la révocation peuvent conduire à la remettre en question. La jurisprudence aussi bien française[100] qu'OHADA[101] se sert de cette théorie pour contrôler les

---

[96] Au sujet de cette extension de l'obligation de loyauté, voir J.-M. GARINOT, « La loyauté en droit des sociétés : une obligation en clair-obscur », *RLDA*, mars 2014, p. 60 et s.

[97] Cass. com., 8 avr. 2014, n° 13-11.650 (F-D), Dr. sociétés, 2014, p. 725, note C. Tabourot-Hyest. Il est à noter qu'il s'agit dans cette espèce d'une SAS et que la cour a estimé que pour avoir mis Monsieur M. en demeure de présenter ses observations, la société *Akerys capital* n'avait pas manqué à son obligation de loyauté.

[98] C'est la conséquence de l'emprise croissante du droit européen sur les législations nationales qui a conduit à voir une transposition des garanties processuelles fondées sur l'art. 6.§1 de la convention européenne de sauvegarde des droits de l'Homme. Voir M. COZIAN, A. VIANDIER, F. DEBOISSY, *Droit des sociétés*, *op. cit.*, n°379, p. 217. Voir également, Cass. com., 14 mai 2013, préc.

[99] R. NEMEDEU, *Le contrôle des dirigeants de la société anonyme*, thèse, *op. cit.*, p. 119.

[100] Pour des exemples de révocations injurieuses ou vexatoires dont les faits sont exposés dans le manuel ci-dessus, voir CA Paris, 13oct. 2000, BJS, 2001, p. 176 ; CA Paris,28 janv. 2003 : *jurisData n° 2003-202612* ; CA Paris, 13 oct. 2006, *RJDA* juil. 2007, n° 742 ; CA Paris, 30 juin 2009, *RJDA*, 2010, n° 34 ; CA Paris, 9mars 2010, *RJDA*, 2010, n° 970 ; CA Paris, 29 janv. 2013, *BRDA*, avril 2013, n° 3.

[101] CA d'Abidjan, arrêt n°1247 du 28 novembre 2003,*Ohadata J-03-347* op. cit ; Cour suprême de Côte d'Ivoire, Chambre judiciaire, arrêt n°404/04 du 11 juil. 2004, Kone Kafongo c/ BHCI, Actualités juridiques, n°47/2005, p. 87, note KASSIA Bi Oula, *Ohadata J-05-344* (pour la révocation d'un directeur général sous l'empire de l'ancien AUSCGIE où elle était encore *ad nutum*) ; CCJA, Arrêt n° 032/2007 du 22 nov. 2007, affaire T. C. E.

circonstances d'intervention de la révocation. En effet, la révocation *ad nutum* n'autorise pas la malveillance, et le dirigeant est fondé à réclamer des dommages et intérêts sur le fondement de l'article 1382 du code civil (camerounais comme français), si son éviction intervient dans des circonstances brutales, injurieuses ou vexatoires : publicité tapageuse, accusations diffamatoires, injures, coups et blessures... C'est la théorie de l'abus de droit qui justifie la réparation du préjudice subi par le dirigeant ainsi « traîné dans la boue »[102]. Ce faisant, la jurisprudence a considérablement atténué le principe de la révocation *ad nutum* en assurant ainsi une certaine stabilité au statut de dirigeant social.

Conclusion

Les scandales financiers intervenus notamment dans les grandes firmes américaines vers la fin des années 80 ont conduit au phénomène de la "*corporate governance*" mettant un fort accent sur la direction et le contrôle de la gestion des entreprises. Il en a résulté une tendance générale à défendre une certaine éthique dans le droit des affaires, et qui a conduit à imposer une certaine rigueur au statut de dirigeant social. Mais, vu le caractère incontournable de cette fonction dans la performance de l'entreprise, il était opportun de chercher à savoir comment le droit OHADA l'aménage pour ne pas qu'elle perde son attractivité.

L'on a constaté que la fonction de dirigeant social est très contraignante au regard de la loyauté sans faille qui s'impose à celui-ci dans la gestion de la société. Même si le législateur de l'AUSCGIE n'a pas expressément consacré l'obligation de loyauté à son endroit, celle-ci transparaît dans la majorité des obligations et même au travers des sanctions attachées à la fonction de direction. Néanmoins, on a relevé que, le statut de dirigeant social n'est pas pour autant sans protection, car sous d'autres cieux, le droit, en prenant appui sur la théorie de la personne morale, a développé des mécanismes permettant de la stabiliser. Il s'agit de la notion de « faute détachable des

---

WIELEZYNSKI c/ COFIPA INVESTMENT BANK COTE D'IVOIRE S. A. *Ohadata J-08-242*. Dans tous ces cas, l'abus de droit dans la révocation n'ayant pas été démontré, les juges n'ont pas fait droit à la demande de dommages-intérêts.

[102] M. COZIAN, A. VIANDIER, F. DEBOISSY, *Droit des sociétés, op. cit.*, n°576, p. 317.

fonctions », et l'assurance-responsabilité civile dirigeant qui visent à exonérer le dirigeant de la responsabilité qui pèse par principe sur la société pour le compte de laquelle il a agi, à partir du moment où ses fautes n'ont pas été intentionnelles. Mais si ces mécanismes ne sont pas encore ancrés dans la pratique du droit OHADA, on reconnaît toutefois au législateur et au juge OHADA le mérite de recourir à des constructions juridiques tels que la révocation pour justes motifs, ou même encore la théorie de l'abus de droit pour ne pas laisser le dirigeant social à la merci des associés.

Ce faisant, le droit uniforme OHADA s'inscrit incontestablement dans la mouvance mondiale du droit des sociétés consistant à favoriser la théorie des *stakeholders*[103], qui prône une prise en considération des intérêts de toutes les personnes impliquées dans la vie d'une entreprise. Il y va de l'équilibre des intérêts en présence dans la société et de la stabilité même de celle-ci.

---

[103] Par opposition à la théorie des *shareholders* qui se préoccupe uniquement des intérêts des propriétaires de l'entreprise. Pour d'amples explications sur ces théories économiques, voir : F.G. TREBULLE, « *Stakeholders theory* et droit des sociétés » (première partie), Bulletin Joly Sociétés, déc.2006, N°12, p. 1337 et s. ; F.G. TREBULLE, « *Stakeholders theory* et droit des sociétés », (deuxième partie), Bulletin Joly Sociétés, janv. 2007, N°1, p. 7 et s.

LA JUSTICIABILITÉ DES AFRICAINS DEVANT LA COUR PÉNALE INTERNATIONALE : VERS UNE ÉCHAPPATOIRE

Cunégonde TCHAYA TCHATAT[1]

Résumé

Les ressortissants africains ont jusqu'ici été les seuls à être jugés par la Cour pénale internationale. Ils ont donc, à travers leurs dirigeants, souhaité qu'une solution soit trouvée à cette situation. Cet article présente, dans cette optique et au vu des règles de compétence posées par le statut de Rome, les échappatoires à la justiciabilité des Africains devant cette juridiction. Il en ressort que les États ont plusieurs options : les unes se ramènent à la contestation de la juridiction de la Cour pénale internationale et les autres visent à faire concurrence à cette cour. Ce dernier groupe de mesures semble pouvoir évincer plus efficacement la Cour pénale internationale. Mais, au-delà de la préoccupation sus-évoquées, cet article est un outil de sensibilisation sur le rôle déterminant des États dans la répression des crimes graves de droit international.

Mots clés : justiciabilité – Africains - Cour pénale internationale – échappatoire.

Introduction

1. La Cour pénale internationale (CPI) est fonctionnelle depuis 2002.[2] Elle tient sa compétence de la coordination par certains États de leur souveraineté[3] dans la poursuite des crimes qui portent atteinte à la paix et la

---

[1] **Chargée de Cours- FSJP, Université de Yaoundé II- Soa.**

[2] Le statut de Rome portant création de la CPI est entrée en vigueur le 7 juillet 2002 après la 60è ratification.

[3] La CPI est une juridiction internationale compétente quand les juridictions nationales sont défaillantes. Voir Préambule et art. 1 et 17 du statut de Rome.

sécurité de l'humanité.[4] Toutefois, son fonctionnement jusqu'ici a fait l'objet de beaucoup de critiques, particulièrement des États et des citoyens africains. Ces derniers estiment que la CPI serait en train de fonctionner à la carte et serait un instrument de néocolonialisme sur les États africains. Jusqu'ici, pensent-ils, et il convient de le constater, les poursuites engagées par la CPI sont dirigées contre des Africains que ce soit comme simple citoyens, commandants de guerre, hauts fonctionnaires ou chefs d'État [5], alors que la CPI aurait pu mener des poursuites contre des ressortissants d'autres continents[6]. M. Jean Ping par exemple, alors président de la Commission de l'Union africaine estimait que « *la justice internationale ne semble appliquer les règles de la lutte contre l'impunité qu'en Afrique, comme si*

---

[4] L'ensemble des infractions concernées se trouvent aux articles 5 et suivants du statut de Rome. Il s'agit des crimes de guerre, des crimes contre l'humanité, du génocide et du crime d'agression sous la condition de l'entrée en vigueur des amendements de Kampala.

[5] Depuis son entrée en vigueur, la CPI a été amenée à se prononcer sur huit (8) situations, toutes concernant des États africains : République démocratique du Congo (ICC-01/04), Ouganda (ICC-01/04), Darfour (Soudan) (ICC-02/05), République centrafricaine (ICC-01/05), République du Kenya (ICC-01/09), Libye (ICC-01/11), Côte d'Ivoire (ICC-02/11), Mali (ICC-01/12-01/15).

[6] Soit pour leur participation à la commission d'infractions relevant de la compétence de la CPI dans leur État ou dans d'autres États non africains (en Irak Afghanistan, etc.), ou encore du fait de leur participation à la commission d'infractions dans des États africains. Dans ce dernier contexte, des allégations de crimes de guerre commis par les forces de l'Organisation du traité atlantique nord (OTAN) en Libye ont été faites. Mais, le procureur de la CPI a déclaré dans l'un de ses rapports que « *rien ne permet au Bureau de conclure que les frappes aériennes de l'OTAN, qui ont pu faire des morts et des blessés civils ou détruire des biens civils, étaient dirigées contre la population civile en tant que telle ou des biens de caractère civil* ». *Troisième Rapport du Procureur de la Cour pénale internationale au Conseil de sécurité en application de la Résolution n°1970 (2011)*, rapport du 16 mai 2012, para. 55. Voir aussi la proposition de résolution du 26 juillet 2012 enregistrée à la présidence de l'Assemblée nationale française dans laquelle un groupe de dix parlementaires français demandait la création d'une commission d'enquête sur le rôle de la force Licorne en Côte d'Ivoire. Le groupe déclare dans sa proposition que la France s'est possiblement rendue coupable de complicité de meurtres de masse, voire d'épuration ethnique à Blolequin ou à Duékoué, en étant l'allié objectif et parfois agissant des forces présentées aujourd'hui comme républicaines. Ces rapport et proposition sont cités par J. B. Mbokani, « la Cour pénale internationale : une cour contre les Africains ou une cour attentive à la souffrance des victimes africaines », *Revue Québécoise de Droit international*, 26.2 (2013), p. 72.

rien ne se passait ailleurs en Irak, à Gaza, en Colombie ou dans le Caucase »[7]. Dans la même logique, Julian Fernandez observe avec une certaine ironie que « *[si] le Procureur répète souvent qu'il examine les cas de la Colombie, de l'Afghanistan ou de la Géorgie, la Cour demeure cantonnée au terrain africain* ».[8] Elle serait donc, selon les Africains, une Cour mise sur pied uniquement pour renforcer l'hégémonie de l'Occident sur l'Afrique.[9] Sous ce rapport, « *l'opposition symétrique entre Mars (les États-Unis) et Vénus (l'Europe), ou mieux, entre Achille (les États-Unis) et Ulysse (l'Europe) à propos de la justice internationale pénale se serait muée en mariage entre Achille et Ulysse contre les sortilèges qui caractérisent l'Afrique* ».[10] Un constat se dégage

---

[7]Propos rapportés par M. Meunier, « Cette Cour qui fait peur à tout le monde », *Jeune Afrique*, 9 mars 2009. Toutefois, l'abstention de la CPI dans certains cas peut s'expliquer juridiquement.

[8] J. Fernandez, *La politique juridique extérieure des États-Unis à l'égard de la Cour pénale internationale*, Paris, Pedone, 2010, pp. 48-48, cité par J. MOUANGUE KOBILA, « L'Afrique et les juridictions internationales pénales », *Cahier Thucydide*, n°10, Etude-Février 2012, p. 4. Voir aussi les déclarations du président rwandais, Paul Kagamé, réagissant à la décision du procureur de la CPI de mettre en accusation le président Omar el-Béchir : « *ICC is made for Africans and poor countries* » (D. Kezio-Musoke, « Kagame tells why he is against the ICC charging Bashir »). Il poursuit, Rwanda « *cannot party to ICC for one simple reason…with ICC all the injustices of the past including colonialism, imperialism, keep coming back in different forms. They control you. As long as you are poor, weak there is always some rope to hang you"* (Rwanda's kagame says ICC targeting poor African countries, Agence France Presse dépêche du 31 juillet 2008). Et de conclure, Rwanda cannot be part of that colonialism, slavery and imperialism" (Voir F. Soudan, "Tutu, Kagamé et le cas El-Béchir", mardi 17 mars 2009), tous cités par Pacifique Manirakiza, « L'Afrique et le système de justice pénale internationale », *African Journal of Legal Studies,* 3 (2009), pp. 21-52, p.32

[9] Ce n'est cependant pas l'avis de l'ancien procureur de la CPI Louis Moreno Ocampo. Pour ce dernier, « *les situations sélectionnées ont abouti à la perception douteuse de l'existence d'une stratégie de poursuites fondée intentionnellement sur un critère géographique* », pourtant, précise-t-il, « *l'équilibre régional ne figur[ait] pas parmi les critères de sélection d'une affaire dans le Statut* ». Voir Bureau du procureur, Rapport sur les activités mises en œuvre au cours des trois premières années (juin 2003-juin 2006), 12 septembre 2006, p. 7, http//www.icc-cpi.int/NR/rdonlyres/D76A5D89-FB64-47A9-9821-725747378AB2/143681/ OTP_3yearreport 20060914French.pdf

[10] Voir J. Mouangue Kobila, « L'Afrique et les juridictions internationales pénales », *op. cit.*, p. 36 ; S. SUR, « Ni Mars ni Vénus : Achille ou Ulysse », *Questions Internationales* n° 9, septembre –octobre 2004, http://www.sergesur.com/Ni-Mars-ni-Venus-Achille-ou-Ulysse.htlm (consulté le 14 janvier 2012), cité par J. Mouangue Kobila, « L'Afrique et les

de ce qui précède : nombre d'États africains soutenus par l'Union africaine ne désirent plus voir les Africains poursuivis devant la CPI.[11]

2. Les Africains sont les ressortissants du continent africain ou d'États africains. Mais pour l'intérêt de cette étude, l'accent sera mis sur leur qualité de ressortissants d'États africains dans la mesure où ce sont les États qui sont parties au statut de Rome et non les régions ou les continents, même si leurs actions peuvent être impulsées et influencées par des instances régionales. C'est en effet, la ratification du statut de Rome par les États qui confère la qualité de justiciable de la CPI à leurs ressortissants, c'est-à-dire qui leur donne la capacité d'être soumis à justice ou d'obtenir justice devant la CPI.[12]

3. La justiciabilité, renvoie donc, à la fois à l'adjectif « justiciable » et au substantif qui en est dérivé. Elle s'entend alors comme la faculté de prendre la qualité de justiciable. Elle peut aussi être considérée comme la possibilité d'être jugé par une juridiction.[13] Dans le second cas, sont concernées les

---

juridictions internationales pénales », *op. cit.*, p. 36 . Voir aussi, B. Muna, dans sa déclaration du 2 décembre 2011 sur les ondes de Radio France internationale (RFI) : « Je pense que Ocampo a malheureusement donné l'image de ce tribunal, comme un tribunal pour poursuivre les Africains. R il y a des violations des droits de l'homme dans tous les continents ». Entrevue de B. Muna par Nicolas Champeaux, déc. 2011 sur Invité Afrique, RFI Radio, France, RFI radio Archives, en ligne : RFI <htt://www.rfi.fr/emission/20111002-bernard-mouna-procureur-adjoint-tpir>.

[11] Pourtant les Etats africains ont joué un rôle de premier plan dans la mise en place d'une Cour pénale internationale permanente. En effet, sur les 53 États africains, 47 ont participé à la conférence internationale des plénipotentiaires tenue à Rome en 1998 sur la création de la CPI. De même, l'exigence de l'article 126 (60 ratifications pour l'entrée en vigueur de la Cour), a été remplie avec 20 ratifications, soit 1/3 venant des États africains ; le Sénégal était d'ailleurs le premier pays ayant ratifié le statut de la Cour (le 2 septembre 1999). Cela démontrait l'assentiment des pays africains pour cette juridiction. Et comme le rappelait le prof. Maluwa, conseiller juridique de l'ex-Organisation de l'unité africaine (OUA), « *Africa had a particular interest in the establishment of the Court, since its peoples had been the victims of large scale violations of human rights over the centuries: slavery, wars of colonial conquest and continued acts of war and violence, even in the post-colonial era*", Prof. Muluwa, cité par Pacifique Manirakiza, « L'Afrique et le système de justice pénale internationale », *op. cit.*, p.28.

[12] G. Cornu, *Vocabulaire Juridique*, Association Henri Capitant, 10e éd., PUF, janvier 2014, p. 592.

[13] C. Atias, « Justiciabilité », in L. Cadiet (dir.), *Dictionnaire de la justice*, PUF, 2004, pp. 798-800, p.798. Dans cette acception, elle a deux variantes : la justiciabilité objective qui a

personnes soupçonnées d'avoir commis des crimes relevant de la compétence de la CPI alors que dans le premier cas, il s'agit pour les victimes de ces crimes d'avoir le droit de recourir à la Cour pour obtenir réparation.[14] Ce dernier aspect ne pose pas particulièrement de problème en tant qu'il s'agirait d'un avantage pour les victimes africaines, par rapport aux victimes d'autres continents, si elles sont admises à raconter leur « misère » devant la CPI et à obtenir justice. C'est l'exercice par la CPI de sa compétence contre des Africains soupçonnés d'avoir commis des crimes graves de droit international qui pose problème, même si leur soumission à la juridiction de la CPI pourrait, dans certaines circonstances aller de pair avec celle de leurs éventuelles victimes que la juridiction en question est chargée de protéger de manière générale.

En effet, le statut de Rome ne reconnaît que trois (3) formes de compétence : la compétence territoriale (quand l'État sur le territoire duquel les crimes ont été commis est partie au statut) ; personnelle active (quand l'auteur du crime est ressortissant d'un État partie) et universelle conditionnée (quand la CPI est saisie d'une situation par le Conseil de sécurité des Nations unies alors même qu'il n'existe aucun lien de rattachement entre le crime et la CPI). Il n'est donc pas prévu de compétence personnelle de protection (passive) qui donne compétence à une juridiction lorsque les victimes d'une infraction ressortissent de l'État ayant un lien de rattachement avec la juridiction concernée (juridiction nationale de l'État ou juridiction internationale à laquelle l'État a cédé une partie de sa souveraineté pour la poursuite de certaines infractions). Si donc, la CPI accorde une place importante à l'indemnisation des victimes, la recherche d'une voie de contournement de sa compétence ne peut se faire de manière intéressante que sous le prisme de l'infracteur. Dans cette optique, il s'agira dans cette étude de déterminer les moyens, pour les présumés infracteurs, ressortissants d'États africains, d'échapper à la juridiction de la CPI.

4. La question qu'il convient dès lors de se poser est celle des moyens de contournement de la compétence de la CPI par les États africains.

---

trait à la matière relevant de la compétence d'une juridiction et la justiciabilité subjective qui se rattache aux personnes.

[14] C. Atias, « Justiciabilité », *op. cit.*, p. 799.

Autrement dit, que peuvent faire les États africains pour soustraire leurs ressortissants de la juridiction de la CPI ? Cette préoccupation présente un double intérêt.

Le premier intérêt réside dans le fait que plusieurs États africains sont parties à la convention de Rome instituant une Cour pénale internationale. En outre, la presque totalité des États africains est membre de l'Organisation des Nations unies (ONU) dont le Conseil de sécurité est en même d'actionner la CPI. Il s'ensuit donc un conflit entre les engagements internationaux des États africains et leur désir de soustraire leurs ressortissants de la compétence de la CPI.

Le second intérêt ressort du fait que cette étude permet de revenir sur cette institution judiciaire à vocation universelle qu'est la CPI, particulièrement ses règles de compétence et les défaillances inhérentes à sa création même. Aussi est-il possible de généraliser les résultats de cette recherche, à quelques exceptions près,[15] à tout État, même occidental, partie ou non à la convention de Rome. Toutefois, d'autres considérations extra-juridiques pourraient entraîner une variation sur la portée ou l'efficacité des moyens de contournement décelés. D'où l'intérêt à se limiter au cadre africain.

5. Pour répondre à la question précédemment posée, l'exégèse a été utilisée à travers la lecture combinée des dispositions du statut de Rome, appuyée par les éclairages de la doctrine et de la jurisprudence. Il en est ressorti qu'il existe plusieurs moyens de contournement de la compétence de la CPI à la disposition des États africains. Le premier moyen, relativement efficace, réside dans l'anéantissement de la compétence de la CPI par toute action visant à ne pas lui accorder la juridiction à l'égard des citoyens d'États africains ou à la lui retirer ou encore par toute action visant à gêner le bon exercice de sa compétence. Le second moyen se résume en la mise sur place d'un système de justice efficace et fiable pour connaître des infractions

[15] Si toutes les mesures ici énoncées sont exploitables par tout État, il pourrait y avoir des différences au niveau de leur efficacité selon que l'État concerné est membre ou non du Conseil de sécurité et à même de bloquer les décisions de ce dernier ; si l'État est un État développé dont les juridictions sont capables d'exercer avec efficacité et impartialité les poursuites pénales, etc.

relevant de la compétence de la CPI. Dans le premier cas, les mesures à prendre sont des mesures de contestation à l'égard de la CPI (I) alors que dans le second cas, il s'agit de mesures de concurrence avec la CPI (II).

I- Les mesures de contestation

Le statut de Rome est une convention et comme telle, elle est soumise à la ratification des États. Ce n'est en principe que la ratification ou l'acceptation de compétence qui soumet les citoyens de ces États à la juridiction de la CPI ou qui les met sous la protection de cette juridiction.[16] L'État qui s'abstient de ratifier ou d'accepter la compétence de la Cour ne saurait être lié en vertu du principe de l'effet relatif des conventions.[17] Aussi, celui qui est partie à une convention a-t-il la possibilité de la dénoncer selon les règles du droit international. Dès lors, le défaut de ratification ou la dénonciation de la ratification apparaissent comme des outils à la disposition des États africains afin d'éviter « l'acharnement » de la CPI à l'égard de leurs ressortissants. À côté de ces deux (2) mesures, existe une autre visant à bloquer l'action de la CPI dans les cas où elle est normalement compétente et décide de poursuivre. Il s'agit de la non coopération avec les organes de la CPI. Mais il convient de se poser la question de savoir si ces solutions sont en mesure de paralyser entièrement l'action de la CPI envers les ressortissants d'États africains. Pour la plupart des conventions, le défaut de ratification ou la dénonciation de la ratification sont des entraves totales à leur application à l'État tiers. Mais, dans le cas du statut de Rome, si les mesures sus-énumérées permettent de limiter la compétence de la CPI (A), elles ne constituent pas un obstacle total à l'exercice de la compétence de cette dernière. Ceci relativise ainsi l'efficacité de cette voie (B).

---

[16] Cas où les victimes sont ressortissantes d'un État ayant ratifié ou reconnu la compétence de la CPI.

[17] Sur le plan international, l'article 37 de la convention de Vienne sur le droit des traités de 1969 dispose qu'un traité ne crée ni obligations ni droits pour un État tiers sans son consentement. Avant la convention de Vienne, la CPJI et la CIJ avaient déjà consacré le principe de l'effet relatif des conventions internationales. Dans son arrêt n° 7 du 25 mai 1926 relatif à certains intérêts allemands en Haute Silésie polonaise, la CPJI déclarait : « un traité ne fait droit qu'entre Etats qui y sont parties ». La CIJ confirme aussi ce principe dans son arrêt rendu le 27/07/1945 dans l'affaire de l'incident aérien entre Israël et la Bulgarie, la Cour constate que l'art. 26 de son statut ne possède aucune force de droit pour les États non signataires.

A- Des mesures limitant la compétence de la CPI

7. Si les statuts des tribunaux pénaux internationaux *ad hoc* créés autoritairement par le Conseil de sécurité agissant en vertu du chapitre VII de la Charte des Nations unies (ci-après la Charte) s'imposent à l'ensemble des États membres des Nations unies grâce aux vertus conjuguées des articles 25 et 103 de la Charte, il n'en va pas de même du statut de la Cour pénale internationale ne liant, conformément au principe de l'effet relatif des traités, que les États parties.[18] Toutefois, ces derniers ont la possibilité de dénoncer leurs engagements (2). Les États non parties quant à eux peuvent rejeter la juridiction de la CPI en s'abstenant de ratifier ou en reportant la compétence de la CPI au moment de la ratification (1) s'ils décident de se joindre à la communauté des États parties. Mais, dans les deux situations, les États peuvent refuser leur coopération aux organes de la Cour (3).

1- Le rejet de la juridiction de la CPI pour les États non parties au statut de Rome

8. Le rejet de la juridiction de la CPI par les États non parties peut se faire par la non ratification du statut de Rome (a) ou par le report de la compétence de la CPI au moment de la ratification (b).

a- La non ratification du statut de Rome

9. Un État qui devient partie au statut reconnaît par là même la compétence de la Cour.[19] Cette compétence est automatique et intégrale.[20]

---

[18] Le traité est la loi commune des parties. La maxime bien connue *"Pacta sunt servenda"* précise que les accords ne peuvent ni imposer des obligations aux tiers ni leur conférer des droits, tels sont les deux aspects du principe qui sont confirmés par une jurisprudence abondante et constante. Les traités ne confèrent pas d'obligation à la charge des États tiers. Dans *l'affaire de l'île de Palmas* relative à un différend entre des États-Unis et les Pays-Bas qui se disputaient la souveraineté sur cette île, l'arbitre Max Huber a déclaré dans sa sentence : « Il semble en outre évident que les traités conclus par l'Espagne avec les tierces puissances et qui reconnaissent sa souveraineté sur les Philippines ne pourraient pas lier les Pays-Bas ». En l'espèce, l'île de Palmas faisant partie de Philippines, les États-Unis, successeurs de l'Espagne aux philippines après la guerre hispano-américaine en 1898 désiraient opposer lesdits traités aux Pays-Bas. Voir P. Daillier et A. Pellet, *Droit international Public*, 7e éd., Paris, LGDJ, EJA, 2002, p. 242.

[19] Art. 12 para. 1 du statut de Rome.

[20] Il n'est donc pas nécessaire que les États acceptent sa compétence spécifiquement pour chaque crime.

Cette reconnaissance peut aussi avoir lieu, au cas par cas, sans que l'État ait besoin de ratifier le Statut.[21] Dans un cas comme dans l'autre, les effets sont les mêmes. D'abord, la CPI est compétente à l'égard des faits commis sur le territoire de l'État ayant ratifié le statut de Rome ou ayant consenti à sa compétence (critère territorial). Sont assimilées aux infractions commises sur le territoire, les infractions commises à bord d'un navire ou d'un aéronef dont l'État de pavillon ou d'immatriculation est un État partie. Ensuite, la CPI est compétente à l'égard des ressortissants de l'État partie ou de celui ayant consenti à sa compétence qui se seraient rendus coupables de crimes réprimés dans le statut de Rome (critère de la nationalité-personnalité active).[22]

---

[21] Cf. art. 12 para. 3 du Statut de Rome : « *Si l'acceptation de la compétence de la Cour par un État qui n'est pas Partie au présent Statut est nécessaire aux fins du paragraphe 2, cet État peut, par déclaration déposée auprès du Greffier, consentir à ce que la Cour exerce sa compétence à l'égard du crime dont il s'agit…* » et Art. 4 (2) du Statut de Rome : « *La Cour peut exercer ses fonctions et ses pouvoirs, comme prévu dans le présent Statut, sur le territoire de tout État Partie et, par une convention à cet effet, sur le territoire de tout autre État* ». Voir la compétence de la CPI à l'égard des faits commis en Côte d'Ivoire alors que ce pays n'était pas encore partie à la convention de Rome. La Côte d'Ivoire n'étant pas partie au statut de Rome, la saisine de la Cour s'insère dans le cadre d'un élargissement et d'une acceptation de sa compétence. En conséquence, l'enquête menée par le procureur a été déclenchée sur la base du consentement des autorités ivoiriennes investies du pouvoir politique, conformément à l'art. 12 para.3 du statut de Rome. Aussi bien le président sortant en 2003 qu'Alassane Dramane Ouattara, par une lettre du 19 mai 2011, ont consenti à la compétence de la Cour par le truchement d'une déclaration *ad hoc*. Juridiquement, l'enquête aurait également pu être ouverte par le CS sur le fondement de l'art. 13 b) du statut de Rome ou par un État partie au titre de l'art. 13 a) du même statut. D'ailleurs, la saisine par un État partie sur laquelle misait le procureur par un souci d'efficacité présente, assurément, des avantages incontestables. En plus d'assurer une coopération consentie des États africains, cette modalité de saisine présentait au moins l'avantage virtuel de mettre la Cour à l'abri des suspicions d'instrumentalisation qu'une saisine par le CS aurait immanquablement entraînée tant l'Union africaine a toujours été rétive en la matière. La Côte d'Ivoire avait transmis au greffier de la CPI une déclaration de consentement pour les crimes commis sur son territoire depuis les évènements du 19 septembre 2002, c'est-à-dire, la tentative de coup d'État qui fut la base de la division du pays. Voir Communiqué de presse n° ICC-20050215-91-Fr, 15 fév. 2005.

[22] Le paragraphe 2 de l'article 12 dispose que « *…la Cour peut exercer sa compétence si l'un des États suivants ou les deux sont Parties au présent Statut ou ont accepté la compétence de la Cour conformément au paragraphe 3 :*

A contrario, un État qui ne ratifie pas le Statut, comme le Cameroun, l'Égypte, ou le Maroc, ne reconnaît pas la compétence de la CPI, bref ne lui délègue pas une partie de sa souveraineté en matière de poursuite pénale.[23] Ainsi, ses ressortissants ne peuvent, en principe, faire l'objet de poursuites devant la Cour. De même, la Cour ne peut connaître, en principe, des faits constitutifs de crimes qui se seraient produits sur son territoire. Dès lors, tout État africain non partie au statut de Rome, qui ne souhaiterait pas voir ses ressortissants poursuivis par la CPI, doit commencer par s'abstenir à ratifier le Statut.

10. L'option de non ratification a sa pleine portée lorsqu'il est question du crime d'agression. En effet, l'article 15 bis para 5 issu des amendements de Kampala[24], énonce qu'en ce qui concerne un État qui n'est pas partie au statut, la Cour n'exerce pas sa compétence à l'égard du crime d'agression[25] quand celui-ci est commis par des ressortissants de cet État ou sur son territoire. Il s'agit d'une première mesure qui pourrait par la suite être complétée par d'autres mesures.

À côté de cette solution globale existe une autre solution plus restreinte dans la mesure où elle ne vise qu'une catégorie de crimes :[26] le report de la compétence de la CPI par la souscription à la disposition d' « *opting out* ».

b- Le report de la compétence de la CPI par la souscription à la disposition d'« opting-out »

11. La clause d' « *opting out* » est, dans le statut de Rome la clause prévoyant la possibilité pou un État, au moment de la ratification de la

---

a) L'État sur le territoire duquel le comportement en cause a eu lieu ou, si le crime a été commis à bord d'un navire ou d'un aéronef, l'État du pavillon ou l'État d'immatriculation ;
b) L'État dont la personne accusée du crime est un ressortissant ».

[23] Sauf cas d'une reconnaissance expresse en dehors de toute ratification.

[24] En effet, du 31 mai au 11 juin 2010 s'est tenue la 1ère conférence de révision du statut de Rome à Kampala en Ouganda, conférence pendant laquelle le Statut a été modifié. Cependant, ces modifications n'entreront en vigueur que lorsque le nombre de ratifications nécessaires aura été atteint conformément à l'art. 121 du statut.

[25] Sous réserve de l'entrée en vigueur des amendements au statut de Rome issus de la conférence de révision de Kampala de 2010.

[26] C'est le résultat d'un compromis trouvé sous l'impulsion de la France et des États-Unis visant à protéger leurs militaires à l'étranger.

convention, de déclarer que les dispositions relatives aux crimes de guerre ne s'appliqueront pas à son égard. Elle est prévue à l'article 124 du statut de Rome. Après avoir survécu à la conférence de révision de Kampala de mai - juin 2010[27], cet article a été supprimé du statut de Rome par l'amendement issu de la Résolution ICC-ASP/14/Res.2, du 26 novembre 2015. Cette suppression n'entraîne cependant pas la disparition automatique de la clause. Il faudrait encore que l'amendement y relatif soit ratifié par les États conformément à l'article 121 (4)[28]. En attendant l'entrée en vigueur de cet amendement, cet article garde toute sa vigueur.

12. Il dispose que « *nonobstant les dispositions de l'article 12 paragraphe 1 un État qui devient partie au présent Statut peut déclarer que, pour une période de 7 ans à partir de l' entrée en vigueur du Statut à son égard, il n'accepte pas la compétence de la Cour en ce qui concerne la catégorie des crimes visés à l' article 8 lorsqu' il est allégué qu' un crime a été commis sur son territoire ou par ses ressortissants. Il peut à tout moment retirer cette déclaration...* » Il organise donc un régime transitoire permettant aux États d'écarter la compétence de la CPI pour une période de sept ans à compter de la ratification et uniquement pour les crimes de guerre commis par leurs ressortissants ou perpétrés sur leur territoire. Dès lors, une fois que l'État souscrit à cette disposition, il paralyse par la même occasion les actions qui viendraient d'autres États ou du procureur de la CPI, même si les faits sont commis par ses ressortissants sur le territoire d'un autre État partie. Beaucoup d'États en ont déjà fait usage.[29] Cela suppose en outre que l'État qui use de ce principe

---

[27] Les dispositions de cet article ont été examinées à la conférence de révision du statut de Rome à Kampala, convoquée conformément à l'article 123 paragraphe 1. Au terme de cette conférence, il a été décidé de ne pas amender l'article 124, mais d'examiner de nouveau ses dispositions lors de la quatorzième session de l'assemblée des États parties en 2015/de le réviser automatiquement dans cinq ans (résolution RC/Res.4).

[28] Art. 121, para 4 du statut de Rome: « *Sous réserve des dispositions du paragraphe 5, un amendement entre en vigueur à l'égard de tous les États Parties un an après que les sept huitièmes d'entre eux ont déposé leurs instruments de ratification ou d'acceptation auprès du Secrétaire général de l'Organisation des Nations Unies* ».

[29] Lors de la ratification du statut de la CPI, la France et la Colombie ont fait jouer la « déclaration de l'article 124 » du statut afin de protéger leurs ressortissants impliqués dans des opérations militaires à l'extérieur, et notamment les opérations de « maintien de la paix ». Cette déclaration a eu pour effet de suspendre la compétence de la CPI en France et

entend couvrir les crimes de guerre commis par ses forces. Les États africains impliqués dans les atrocités humanitaires peuvent dès lors utiliser cette disposition pour soustraire leurs ressortissants de la juridiction de la CPI. Mais cette déclaration doit être faite au moment de la ratification. Ainsi, cette solution ne sera valable que pour les États qui n'ont pas encore ratifié le Statut et qui désirent le faire. Les États parties quant à eux ont à leur disposition la possibilité de dénoncer le statut de Rome.

2- La dénonciation du statut de Rome pour les États parties

13. La dénonciation ou le retrait est un acte de procédure accompli unilatéralement par les autorités compétentes des États parties qui désirent se délier de leurs engagements.[30] La dénonciation met fin aux traités bilatéraux. Pour les traités multilatéraux, elle ne provoque, en principe que le « retrait » de son auteur de la communauté des parties contractantes, les autres parties conservant entre elles la relation conventionnelle. Le statut de Rome est l'une de ces conventions qui ont expressément prévu des modalités de retrait des États parties. En effet, l'article 127 intitulé « Retrait », énonce en son alinéa 1er que « *Tout État Partie peut,…, se retirer du présent Statut* ». Cet article peut être considéré comme une clause de dénonciation ou de retrait réglementée. Il implique en outre que la ratification du statut de Rome ne lie pas indéfiniment l'État qui a ratifié, lequel peut, quand il le désire, le dénoncer. C'est dans cette logique que les 11 et 12 octobre 2003, les dirigeants africains se sont réunis à Addis-Abeba, en sommet extraordinaire, pour discuter d'un éventuel retrait collectif du statut de Rome.[31] Ce désir a été réitéré au 26e sommet de l'UA, le 31 janvier 2016 à Addis-Abeba.[32] Le statut de Rome pose expressément les conditions du retrait.

---

en Colombie pour les crimes de guerre pendant une période de 7 ans à partir de l'entrée en vigueur, c'est-à-dire jusqu'au 1er juillet 2009. Mais la France a retiré sa déclaration en 2008.

[30] P. Daillier et A. Pellet, *Droit international Public*, *op. cit.*, p. 304, n° 194.

[31] Radio France internationale, « Addis-Abeba : Sommet de l'UA sur ses relations houleuses avec la CPI », Radio France Internationale, 11 octobre 2013, en ligne : RFI <http:/www.rfi.fr/afrique/20131010-sommet-ua-addis-abeba-cpi-kenya-ouganda-rwanda>.

[32] Le Président kenyan a plaidé en faveur du retrait des pays africains du Statut de Rome par « … *l'élaboration d'une feuille de route pour le retrait de la CPI, comme nécessaire* ». Voir discours du président kenyan Uhuru Kenyatta à la clôture du 26e sommet de l'UA, le 31 janv. 2016.

14. L'article 127 (1) précise que le retrait doit être fait « *par voie de notification écrite adressée au Secrétaire général de l'Organisation des Nations Unies* »[33]. À partir de cette disposition, on peut déterminer le mode de la dénonciation ainsi que l'autorité compétente pour recevoir la dénonciation. Dans le cas d'espèce, un État africain ayant ratifié la convention de Rome et désireux de ne plus voir appliquer la compétence de la CPI à l'égard de ses ressortissants, peut tout simplement l'exprimer par écrit et en notifier le Secrétaire général des Nations unies. Autrement dit, il n'est pas possible pour un État de se retirer par voie orale. Une fois la notification faite, en l'absence de dispositions exigeant d'autres formalités telle l'acceptation des autres États contractants, la dénonciation est valable. Toutefois, cette dénonciation ne prend pas immédiatement effet.

La partie désireuse de se retirer peut indiquer la date à laquelle elle aimerait que la dénonciation prenne effet. À défaut, le retrait produira effet un an après la date à laquelle la notification a été reçue. Aucun effet ne pourrait être produit avant ce délai même si l'État qui désire se retirer le prévoit expressément.[34] La date prise en compte ici suit la théorie de la réception en ce que c'est la date de réception de la notification par le Secrétaire général des Nations unies qui est considérée et non la date d'émission de la notification. Cela pourrait contribuer à repousser la date de prise d'effet de quelques jours si la réception est retardée.

15. Le retrait ne dégage pas l'État des obligations mises à sa charge par le Statut alors qu'il y était partie, y compris les obligations financières encourues, et n'affecte pas non plus la coopération établie avec la Cour à l'occasion des enquêtes et procédures pénales à l'égard desquelles l'État avait le devoir de coopérer et qui ont été commencées avant la date à laquelle le retrait a pris effet ; le retrait n'affecte en rien la poursuite de l'examen des affaires que la Cour avait déjà commencé à examiner avant la date à laquelle il a pris effet.

Ces dispositions de l'article 127 (2) s'inscrivent en droite ligne des règles du droit des conventions internationales qui prévoient que le retrait, en ce qui concerne les conventions multilatérales, n'affecte en principe que la

[33] Art. 127 (1) du statut de Rome instituant une Cour pénale internationale.
[34] Art. 127 (1).

partie qui l'a effectué.[35] Si donc un État africain se retire du statut de Rome, la CPI cessera d'être compétente à l'égard de ses ressortissants, mais conservera sa compétence à l'égard des ressortissants d'autres États parties.

La dénonciation du statut de Rome affecte ainsi la dévolution de compétence de la CPI, ce qui n'est pas le cas du refus de coopération.

3- Le refus de coopération avec la CPI

16. Le refus de coopération avec la CPI est une solution exploitable dans le but de soustraire les ressortissants africains de la compétence de cette dernière. Il affecte l'exercice par cette dernière de sa compétence. En effet, l'exercice de la compétence de la CPI ne peut être efficace qu'avec la coopération des États, que ce soit pour l'arrestation, les enquêtes, la recherche de preuves, le transfert des personnes poursuivies que pour l'exécution des peines.[36] Et même, le procureur ne peut prendre certaines mesures d'enquêtes dans un État sans s'assurer de la coopération de cet État, à moins que la chambre préliminaire ait déterminé qu'en l'espèce, celui-ci est manifestement incapable de donner suite à une demande de coopération parce qu'aucune autorité ou composante compétente de son appareil judiciaire national n'est disponible pour le faire.[37]

17. Le défaut de coopération des États est un frein à l'efficacité de la CPI. Dès lors, les États africains désireux de soustraire leurs ressortissants de la compétence de la CPI peuvent tout simplement, dans le cas où ces personnes se trouvent sur leur territoire, refuser de les livrer à la CPI, où refuser de coopérer dans la recherche des éléments de preuve pouvant servir à leur condamnation. Dans cette logique, certains États africains ont réussi, pour l'instant, à soustraire certains ressortissants de la juridiction de la CPI

---

[35] P. Daillier et A. Pellet, *Droit international Public*, *op. cit.*

[36] Voir les art. 86-111. Pour les autres formes de coopération, voir l'art. 93 du statut de Rome (identification des personnes, interrogatoire des personnes, signification de documents, examen de localités et de sites, exhumation et examen des cadavres enterrés dans des fosses communes, transmission de dossiers et de documents, protection des victimes et des témoins, préservation des éléments de preuve, identification, localisation, gel ou saisie du produit des crimes, des biens, des avoirs et des instruments liés aux crimes, aux fins de leur confiscation éventuelle...).

[37] Art. 57(3)(d). Toutefois, il pourrait se poser le problème d'interprétation. Le sens donné au concept de disponibilité pourrait en effet varier.

en lui refusant leur coopération. Cette solution est d'ailleurs exploitée au niveau régional entendu dans sa globalité. L'Union africaine, sous la seule réserve du Tchad, a par exemple décidé de ne pas coopérer avec la CPI en vue de l'arrestation du président soudanais Omar el-Béchir, objet d'un mandat d'arrêt de la CPI depuis le 4 mars 2009.[38] Depuis cette date, la volonté de la CPI de poursuivre Omar el-Béchir n'a pas pu se concrétiser faute de coopération des États africains.[39] Lors du 25e Sommet de l'Union africaine en Afrique du Sud du 07 au 15 juin 2015, la communauté africaine a craint que l'Afrique du Sud le transfère finalement à la CPI. Mais, cela n'a pas eu lieu et l'interdiction pour le président Omar el-Béchir de quitter le territoire sud-africain, précédemment décidée par les juridictions sud-africaines, a été purement et simplement levée.

18. Ainsi, la solution de refus de coopération semble efficace, à condition que l'État récalcitrant ait été le terrain des exactions reprochées aux personnes poursuivies, que ces personnes soient à sa disposition ou qu'il ait quelque élément que ce soit pouvant paralyser l'action de la CPI.[40]

---

[38] De manière générale, l'Union africaine n'apporte pas son concours à la CPI dans l'exercice de sa mission. Elle a d'ailleurs formellement rejeté l'examen de la demande de la CPI d'ouvrir un Bureau de liaison à Addis-Abeba, siège de l'UA. Voir la Décision sur la mise en œuvre de la Décision Assembly/AU/DEC.270(XIV) relative à la deuxième réunion ministérielle sur le statut de Rome de la Cour pénale internationale, *op. cit.*, point 8.

[39] Le Rapport de la Commission sur la réunion des États africains parties au statut de Rome précise en son point 10 que « *Les Etats membres de l'UA ne coopèrent pas [...] dans l'arrestation et le transfert du Président Omar El Bashir du Soudan à la CPI* ». Une position similaire a été adoptée par l'UA lors du sommet de Malabo en juillet 2011à la suite du mandat d'arrêt émis contre le colonel Kadhafi le 27 juin 2011. L'UA est allée plus loin en demandant au CS des Nations unies de mettre en œuvre les dispositions de l'art 16 du statut de Rome en vue d'annuler le processus de la CPI sur la iybye dans l'intérêt de la justice et de la paix dans ce pays. Voir.UA, Conférence de l'Union, 17ème Session ordinaire, 30 juin- 1er juillet 2011, Malabo (Guinée équatoriale), Décision sur la mise en œuvre des décisions de la conférence relative à la Cour pénale internationale, Assembly/AU/ Dec. 36 (XVII), Doc. EX CL/670(XIX), point 6.

[40] Voir le refus de coopérer des autorités libyennes et l'arrestation et la détention de quatre fonctionnaires du bureau public pour la défense de la CPI, affectés à la défense d'El-Islam Kadhafi, en territoire libyen durant pratiquement un mois. Pour plus de détails voir J. B. Bokani, « La Cour pénale internationale : une Cour contre les Africains ou une cour attentive à la souffrance des victimes africaines ? », *Revue québécoise de droit international*, 26.2, 2013, pp.47-100, p. 61.

19. Cette solution de non coopération n'est pas cependant sans porter de conséquence. En effet, les États africains, parties aux statut de Rome, comme tout État d'ailleurs, sont tenus par une obligation générale de coopérer avec la CPI.[41] Ils sont en outre tenus de prévoir dans leur législation nationale des procédures qui permettent la réalisation de toutes les formes de coopération visées dans le statut de Rome.[42] Les États sont par conséquent tenus de s'abstenir de toute attitude visant à faire obstacle au fonctionnement de la CPI.[43] Les États non parties sont tenus de coopérer lorsqu'ils ont signé des conventions de coopération avec la Cour ou en cas de saisine de cette dernière par le Conseil de sécurité des Nations unies (ci-après Conseil de sécurité ou CS).[44] Le refus de coopérer pourrait donc

---

[41] Voir art. 86 du statut de Rome qui énonce : « *Conformément aux dispositions du présent Statut, les Etats Parties coopèrent pleinement avec la Cour dans les enquêtes et poursuites qu'elle mène pour les crimes relevant de sa compétence* ». Cette obligation n'est que le reflet du principe de la force obligatoire des conventions internationales signées de bonne foi (*Pacta sunt servanda*) posée par l'article 26 de la convention de vienne sur le droit des traités du 23 mai 1969 et est valable pour tous les organes de la Cour.

[42] Art. 88 du statut de Rome.

[43] Voir aussi dans ce sens J.-L. Atangana Amougou, « Le refus de coopérer avec la Cour pénale internationale », *Revue Internationale de Droit Comparé*, n° 4, 2015, p. 973-994.

[44] En vertu de l'article 25 de la Charte des nations unies du 26 juin 1945, les membres de l'Organisation conviennent d'accepter et d'appliquer les décisions du Conseil de sécurité. Ainsi, dans ses Résolutions 1593 et 1970, il demande non seulement aux États concernés de coopérer avec la Cour, mais aussi, tout autre État partie ou non à la convention de Rome. Voir Résolution du CS 1970 (2011) du 26 février 2011, para. 5 : « *Décide que les autorités libyennes doivent coopérer pleinement avec la Cour et le Procureur et leur apporter toute l'assistance voulue, en application de la présente résolution et, tout en reconnaissant que le Statut de Rome n'impose aucune obligation aux États qui n'y sont pas parties, demande instamment à tous les États et à toutes les organisations régionales et internationales concernées de coopérer pleinement avec la Cour et le Procureur* »; et Résolution 1593 (2005) du 31 mars 2005 sur le Darfour, para. 2: « *Décide que le Gouvernement soudanais et toutes les autres parties au conflit du Darfour doivent coopérer pleinement avec la Cour et le Procureur et leur apporter toute l'assistance nécessaire conformément à la présente résolution et, tout en reconnaissant que le Statut de Rome n'impose aucune obligation aux États qui n'y sont pas parties, demande instamment à tous les États et à toutes les organisations régionales et internationales concernées de coopérer pleinement* ».

engendrer des sanctions diplomatiques[45] et économiques[46] venant soit de l'Assemblée des États parties au statut de Rome, soit du Conseil de sécurité.[47] Dans ce contexte, l'État récalcitrant, on l'imagine, sous-pèsera entre les conséquences en cas de non coopération et les conséquences d'une sanction.

20. Toutefois, les articles 97 et 98 du statut de Rome ouvrent une possibilité pour les États africains de refuser leur coopération sans encourir de sanction. En effet, l'article 97 dispose que lorsqu'un État partie est saisi d'une demande et constate qu'elle soulève des difficultés qui pourraient en gêner ou en empêcher l'exécution, il consulte la Cour sans tarder en vue de régler la question si « *l'État requis serait contraint, pour donner suite à la demande sous sa forme actuelle, de violer une obligation conventionnelle qu'il a déjà à l'égard d'un autre État* »[48]. L'article 98 quant à lui prévoit en son alinéa 1 que : « *La Cour ne peut poursuivre l'exécution d'une demande de remise ou d'assistance qui contraindrait l'État requis à agir de façon incompatible avec les obligations qui lui incombent en droit international en matière d'immunité des États ou d'immunité diplomatique d'une personne ou de biens d'un État tiers, à moins d'obtenir au préalable la coopération de cet État tiers en vue de la levée de l'immunité* ». L'alinéa 2 du même article énonce que « *La Cour ne peut poursuivre l'exécution d'une demande de remise qui contraindrait l'État requis à agir de façon incompatible avec les obligations qui lui incombent en vertu d'accords internationaux selon lesquels le consentement de l'État d'envoi est nécessaire pour que soit remise à la Cour une personne relevant de cet État, à moins que la Cour ne puisse au préalable obtenir la coopération de l'État d'envoi pour qu'il consente à la remise* ».

---

[45] Avertissement, rupture des relations diplomatiques, révocation de l'exequatur accordé aux consuls de l'État récalcitrant, suppression du droit de bénéficier des accords internationaux, interdiction d'être représenté à certaines institutions internationales, etc.

[46] Privation des avantages découlant de la solidarité économique internationale, isolement de la vie économique mondiale par blocus, boycottage, embargo, augmentation des droits de douane sur les produits provenant de l'État récalcitrant, refus d'accorder des emprunts, etc.

[47] Voir art. 87 para. 7 : « *Si un État Partie n'accède pas à une demande de coopération de la Cour contrairement à ce que prévoit le présent Statut, et l'empêche ainsi d'exercer les fonctions et les pouvoirs que lui confère le présent Statut, la Cour peut en prendre acte et en référer à l'Assemblée des États Parties ou au Conseil de sécurité lorsque c'est celui-ci qui l'a saisie* ».

[48] Art. 97 (c) du statut de Rome.

Ces deux articles donnent donc des alibis suffisants aux États pour ne pas coopérer avec la CPI. Ainsi, les États peuvent multiplier entre eux des conventions bilatérales et multilatérales de non coopération avec la CPI visant, de manière implicite ou explicite, à soustraire leurs ressortissants de la juridiction de la CPI.[49]

21. Cependant, pour certains auteurs, l'article 98 n'inclurait pas les États parties. En effet, ces derniers interprètent les termes « États tiers » comme renvoyant uniquement aux États non parties. Les États parties seraient donc considérés comme ayant renoncé à se prévaloir des immunités que le droit international reconnaît à leurs dirigeants.[50] Bien plus en vertu du principe de l'exécution de bonne foi des conventions légalement formées, un État qui prend de telles dispositions manifeste ouvertement sa mauvaise foi dans l'exécution de ses engagements conventionnels.

Mais les organes habilités à prononcer ou à mettre en œuvre des sanctions à l'égard des États récalcitrants ont manifesté jusqu'ici une inaction laissant penser que les États peuvent librement refuser leur coopération. Par exemple, le Conseil de sécurité qui a saisi la CPI de deux situations n'a pas pris de mesure visant à s'assurer de la coopération des États, notamment dans l'arrestation du président Omar el-Béchir du Soudan, malgré les multiples décisions d'information relatives au défaut de coopération des États. [51]

---

[49] Il convient cependant de noter que la signature de tels accords par des États parties à la convention de Rome après ratification, serait interprétée comme une violation de leurs engagements conventionnels.

[50] Voir dans ce sens P. Gaeta, « Official Capacity and Immunities », dans A. Cassese, P. Gaeta et J. RWD Jones (dir.), *The Rome Statute of the International Criminal Court : A commentary*, Oxford, Oxford University Press, 2002, pp. 992-995; B. Tranchant, « Les Immunités des Etats tiers devant la Cour pénale internationale », *RGDIP*, 3, 2013, pp. 643-644. *Contra*, D. Tladi, « The ICC Decisions on Chad and Malawi: on Cooperation, Immunities, and Article 98", *Journal of International Criminal Justice*, 11, 2013, 199.

[51] Voir *Procureur c. Ahmed Muhammad Harun et Ali Muhammed Ali Abd-Al-Rahman*, Décision informant le CS de la non coopération de la République du Soudan, Chambre préliminaire I, 26 mai 2010, ICC-02/05-01/07-57 ; *Procureur c. Omar Hassan Ahmad El Béchir*, décision informant le CS des Nations unies et l'assemblée des États parties de la visite récente de Omar el-Béchir en République du Tchad, Chambre préliminaire I, 27 août 2010, ICC-02/05-01/09-109 ; *Procureur c. Omar Hassan Ahmad El Béchir*, décision informant le CS des Nations unies et l'assemblée des États parties de la présence de Omar

Les solutions sus-évoquées ne permettent que de limiter la compétence de la CPI. Elles ne sont pas capables de la paralyser complètement.

B- Des mesures ayant un impact limité

Les solutions sus-évoquées ont un effet relatif dans la mesure où le statut de Rome renferme des dispositions qui permettent de les contourner. Dans la plupart des cas, force n'est pas donnée au principe de l'effet relatif des conventions. Il s'agit concrètement des situations où la CPI reste compétente malgré le refus de ratifier ou la dénonciation de la ratification par les États. On peut ainsi citer le cas de saisine de la CPI d'une situation par le Conseil de sécurité des Nations unies et le cas où les crimes sont commis sur le territoire d'un État partie par des ressortissants africains.

Dans ces deux (2) situations, la CPI conserve sa compétence (1). Dans le cas particulier du report de compétence, la limitation est plutôt matérielle et temporelle (2).

1- La conservation de la compétence de la CPI

23. Un État non partie au statut de Rome, c'est-à-dire celui qui n'a pas ratifié le statut ou celui qui a dénoncé sa ratification, peut toujours voir ses ressortissants tomber sous la juridiction de la CPI dans certaines circonstances. Ceci est possible lorsque le ressortissant d'un État non partie s'est rendu coupable de crimes graves sur le territoire d'un État partie (b) ou lorsque la CPI est saisie par le Conseil de sécurité des Nations unies (a). Même un retrait en masse des États africains n'est pas en même de produire l'effet escompté d'empêcher la compétence de la CPI dans ces deux situations (c).

---

el-Béchir sur le territoire de la République du Kenya, Chambre préliminaire I, 27 août 2010, ICC-02/05-01/09-107 ; *Procureur c. Omar Hassan Ahmad El Béchir*, décision informant le CS des Nations unies et l'assemblée des États parties de la visite récente de Omar el-Béchir à Djibouti, Chambre préliminaire I, 12 mai 2011, ICC-02/05-01/09-129.

a- Le cas de la saisine de la CPI par le Conseil de sécurité des Nations unies

24. La CPI ne peut exercer sa compétence que si elle est saisie par un État partie, le procureur ou le Conseil de sécurité.[52] Dans ce dernier cas, les conditions de l'article 12 sont inopérantes ; notamment la condition suivant laquelle l'un des États suivants doit être partie au statut de Rome : l'État sur le territoire duquel le comportement en cause s'est produit et l'État dont la personne accusée du crime est un national. Toutefois, la saisine par le Conseil de sécurité doit être effectuée sur la base du chapitre VII de la Charte des Nations unies, c'est-à-dire de sa mission de maintien de la paix et la sécurité internationales.[53] Il est ainsi établi que le Conseil de sécurité peut saisir la CPI d'un crime qui s'est produit sur le territoire d'un État ou censé être commis par le ressortissant d'un État qui n'est pas partie au statut de Rome ou qui a décliné la compétence de la CPI. Le droit commun conventionnel du statut peut être écarté dans ces deux volets : territorial (État sur le territoire duquel le crime a été commis) et personnel (État dont le ressortissant est accusé).[54] Dans les deux cas, la qualité d'État partie est neutralisée. Ainsi, un État africain qui refuse de ratifier le Statut, le dénonce ou qui choisit de souscrire à la clause d' « *opting out* » de l'article 124[55], ne pourra pas obtenir le résultat escompté, à savoir l'incompétence de la CPI à l'égard de ses ressortissants.

25. Les premiers pas du Conseil de sécurité dans l'accomplissement de son rôle « positif » à l'égard de la CPI a eu lieu par la Résolution 1593 du 31

---

[52] Voir art. 13 du Statut de Rome : « *La Cour peut exercer sa compétence à l'égard d'un crime visé à l'article 5, conformément aux dispositions du présent Statut:*

a) Si une situation dans laquelle un ou plusieurs de ces crimes paraissent avoir été commis est déférée au Procureur par un État Partie, comme prévu à l'article 14 ;

b) Si une situation dans laquelle un ou plusieurs de ces crimes paraissent avoir été commis est déférée au Procureur par le Conseil de sécurité agissant en vertu du chapitre VII de la Charte des Nations Unies ; ou

c) Si le Procureur a ouvert une enquête sur le crime en question en vertu de l'article 15 »

[53] Art. 13 b. du statut de Rome.

[54] Voir S. A. Ndiaye, Le Conseil de Sécurité et les Juridictions pénales internationales, thèse, Droit, Université d'Orléans, 2011, p. 277, disponible sur https://tel.archives-ouvertes.fr/telè00705886, consulté le 12 février 2015.

[55] Pour plus de détails, voir *infra*, p. 15.

mars 2005 qui déférait la situation du Darfour à la CPI alors que le Soudan n'avait pas ratifié le statut de Rome.[56] La décision de « *désignature* » prise par les autorités de Khartoum n'a eu aucun effet sur la compétence de la CPI qui continue de réclamer le président Omar el-Béchir à fin de jugement devant elle.

Dans la même logique, le CS a déféré la situation libyenne à la CPI. En effet, le 26 février 2011, le CS (Résolution 1970) a saisi la CPI de la situation en Libye depuis le 15 février 2011.[57] Conformément à la Résolution 1970, le procureur de la Cour a ouvert, dès le 03 mars 2011, une enquête sur les allégations de violences commises par le gouvernement libyen dans le cadre des répressions contre les civils lors des manifestations à l'encontre du régime de l'ancien guide libyen Mouammar Kadhafi alors que la Libye n'était pas partie au statut de Rome.[58]

26. La saisine par le Conseil de sécurité a d'ailleurs un impact plus important dans la mesure où elle oblige tous les membres de l'ONU à coopérer avec la CPI, même les États tiers au statut de Rome. En effet, l'article 25 de la Charte des Nations unies prévoit que les États membres de l'Organisation « *conviennent d'accepter et d'appliquer les décisions du Conseil de sécurité* » conformément à la Charte. Toutefois, le pouvoir de saisine de la CPI par le CS est indétachable de la diplomatie de ses membres permanents.[59]

27. Le pouvoir ainsi reconnu au Conseil de sécurité pose une multiplicité de questions : en premier lieu, celle de l'égalité entre les États. Les États membres du Conseil de sécurité qui n'auraient pas ratifié le Statut se

---

[56] Cette résolution a abouti au premier mandat d'arrêt international émis à l'encontre d'un chef d'État en exercice (mandat d'arrêt du 04 mars 2009, ICC-02/05-01/09.

[57] S/RES/1970 (2011) du 26 fév. 2011.

[58] La présidence de la CPI assigne cette situation à la chambre préliminaire I qui délivre, le 27 juin 2011, trois mandats d'arrêt à l'encontre de Mouammar Kadhafi, de son fils Saif Al-Islam Kadhafi et de l'ancien chef de l'intelligence militaire libyenne, Abdullah Al-Senussi. Ces derniers sont accusés d'avoir commis les crimes de meurtre et de persécution réprimés à l'art. 7.1(a) et (h) du statut de Rome et constitutifs de crimes contre l'humanité entre le 15 et le 18 février 2011.

[59] Ces derniers disposent d'un droit de veto qui leur permet individuellement de paralyser l'action du CS et donc de la CPI.

retrouveraient dans la situation confortable de mettre en cause les ressortissants d'autres États, sans courir le risque que leurs ressortissants soient également poursuivis par la CPI. En deuxième lieu, le pouvoir d'initiative du CS qui provoque une extension du domaine subjectif du statut aux États qui ne sont pas parties, donne un caractère universel à la Cour, et s'oppose au principe du fonctionnement consensuel de la Cour et, par ricochet, au principe *pacta sunt servenda* de façon générale. Il n'en est pas de même lorsqu' un ressortissant d'État non partie se déplace vers un État partie pour y commettre les infractions réprimées dans le statut de Rome.

b- Le cas de la commission de crimes sur le territoire d'un État ayant accepté la compétence de la CPI par des ressortissants africains

28. Le défaut de ratification du statut de Rome ne peut protéger les ressortissants d'États africains si ces derniers se rendaient coupables d'infractions relevant de la compétence de la CPI sur le territoire d'un autre État - non africain- ayant accepté la compétence de la CPI soit par la ratification du statut de Rome, soit par une convention spéciale.

La CPI est compétente pour toute infraction commise sur le territoire d'un État partie. Dans cette hypothèse, la nationalité de l'auteur de cette infraction est sans importance. Le bureau du procureur de la CPI le rappelle dans un rapport datant du 6 novembre 2014. Dans cette affaire où les ressortissants d'Israël étaient indexés, il précise que « *bien qu'Israël ne soit pas un État partie, au regard de l'article 12-2-a du Statut, la CPI peut exercer sa compétence à l'égard du comportement de ressortissants d'un État non partie qui auraient commis des crimes visés par le Statut de Rome sur le territoire d'un État partie à la CPI, à bord d'un navire battant pavillon d'un tel État ou à bord d'un aéronef immatriculé dans celui-ci* ».[60]

Le modèle de compétence retenu étend l'action de la CPI aux États tiers. Ce faisant, des ressortissants d'États non parties au statut de Rome peuvent être poursuivis devant la CPI dans l'hypothèse où ils commettraient ou seraient impliqués dans des crimes exécutés sur le territoire d'un État partie.

---

[60] Bureau du procureur, situation relative aux navires battant pavillons comorien, grec et cambodgien, Rapport établi au titre de l'article 53-1 du Statut, 6 novembre 2014, http://www.icc-cpi.int/iccdocs/otp/OTP-COM-Article_53(1)-Report-06Nov2014Fra.pdf, p. 4, consulté le 10 novembre 2015.

C'est d'ailleurs un des déterminants les plus solides qui explique l'opposition américaine.[61]

29. Les critères personnel et territorial sont retenus de manière alternative. Il suffit donc que l'État sur le territoire duquel les infractions ont été commises soit partie au statut de Rome. Dans ce cas, aucun autre critère de compétence n'est recherché.[62]La qualité et la nationalité de l'auteur de l'infraction deviennent sans importance.

En retenant les deux critères personnel et territorial de manière alternative et non pas cumulative, la CPI dispose de compétences à l' égard des ressortissants d'États tiers même si la saisine n'est pas le fait du CS. Cependant, une pareille hypothèse n'est possible que si le crime a été commis sur le territoire d'un État partie. La doctrine n'y voit pas une violation du principe de l'effet relatif des traités contenu dans l'article 34 de la convention de Vienne de 1969.[63]

30. Cette option peut donc rattraper les ressortissants d'États africains non parties qui auraient commis des crimes graves sur le territoire d'un État partie.

Les solutions de non ratification et de retrait ou de dénonciation du statut de Rome ne permettent donc pas de satisfaire pleinement le désir pour les États africains de soustraire leurs ressortissants de la compétence de la CPI. Toutefois, il est possible de se poser la question de l'effet d'un retrait en masse des États africains. Un tel retrait peut-il affecter l'existence même de la CPI ?

c- L'effet d'un retrait en masse tel qu'envisagé par les États de l'Union africaine

---

[61] D. Scheffer, « International Criminal Court: The Challenge of Jurisdiction", *Proceedings of the Annual Meeting of the ASIL*, vol. 93, 1999, pp. 68-72.

[62] Conformément aux dispositions de l'article 12 para 2, la Cour peut exercer sa compétence si **l'un** des États suivants ou les deux sont parties au statut de Rome : l'État territorial ou l'État dont la personne accusée du crime est un ressortissant.

[63] J. Verhoeven, « Vers un ordre répressif Universel ? Quelques observations », Annuaire de Droit International, 1999, vol. 45, n°1, pp. 55-71, p. 64. Disponible sur www.Persee.fr/doc/afdi_0066-3085_1999_num45_1_3553, consulté le 18 février 2016.

Certaines conventions internationales peuvent être considérées comme caduque dès le moment où les États membres restants atteignent un nombre minimum indiqué dans la convention[64] ou sont en dessous du nombre minimum initial requis pour l'entrée en vigueur de la convention.[65] Mais, il n'en est pas de même du statut de Rome de la Cour pénale internationale. Car aucune disposition ne prévoit l'extinction du traité pour de telles raisons ou pour toute autre raison. En effet, comme le pose l'article 55 de la Convention de Vienne du 23 mai 1969 sur le droit des traités, « *A moins que le traité n'en dispose autrement, un traité multilatéral ne prend pas fin pour le seul motif que le nombre des parties tombe en dessous du nombre nécessaire pour entrer en vigueur* ». Si donc tous les États africains parties au statut de Rome ou ayant accepté la compétence de la CPI décident de se retirer, ce retrait n'aura d'effet qu'à leur égard et n'affectera en rien l'existence même de la CPI. Bien plus, les modalités de saisine de la CPI, ainsi que son domaine de compétence, pourraient permettre qu'elle reste compétente pour connaître de certains faits ayant un lien de rattachement avec les pays africains. La CPI pourrait également conserver sa compétence si l'État africain choisit de souscrire à la disposition d' « *opting out* ».

2- La souscription à la disposition d' « *opting-out* » comme une solution limitée dans son étendue

31. La disposition d' « *opting out* » est limitée non seulement dans la matière, mais également dans le temps. En outre, elle n'empêcherait pas la CPI d'être compétente sur saisine du Conseil de sécurité.

32. L'article 124, tel qu'expliqué, donne la possibilité aux États de repousser la compétence de la CPI pour les crimes de guerre commis sur leur territoire ou par leurs ressortissants pendant une période de 7 ans. Mais, cette solution de report de compétence est une solution limitée dans la matière en ce qu'elle ne couvre qu'une catégorie de crimes relevant de la compétence de la CPI : les crimes de guerre. Dès lors, si les autres crimes

---

[64] Voir la Convention sur les droits politiques de la femme du 20 décembre 1952 (art. 8). Cet article dispose que la convention « *cessera d'être en vigueur à la date où aura pris effet la dénonciation qui ramènera à moins de six le nombre des parties* ». Voir aussi l'art. 15 de la Convention pour la prévention et la répression du crime de génocide du 9 décembre 1948, qui fixe à seize le nombre minimal des parties.

[65] P. Daillier et A. Pellet, *Droit international Public, op. cit.*

(crimes contre l'humanité et génocide) sont commis et constatés pendant cette période, la CPI exercera sa compétence.

Plus important est le fait que la situation de guerre peut renfermer pratiquement toutes les catégories de crimes réprimés dans le statut de Rome : le crime d'agression, les crimes de guerre, le génocide et les crimes contre l'humanité. Ainsi, la difficulté, bien que réelle, n'est pas insurmontable dans ces cas de qualification multiple où les juges retiendront sûrement la qualification la plus utile, celle justifiant la compétence de la Cour et faisant échec à la déclaration étatique excluant cette compétence pour crime de guerre.[66]

33. La disposition d'« *opting out* » est également limitée dans le temps. En effet, cette disposition n'est valable que pour sept (7) ans. À l'expiration de ce délai, l'État qui y avait souscrit reconnaît la compétence de la CPI à l'égard des crimes de guerre commis par ses forces. Ces derniers ne peuvent échapper à la juridiction de la CPI que si l'État en question renouvelle sa souscription à la disposition transitoire. En outre, le fait que cet article soit abrogé empêchera les renouvellements ou de nouvelles souscriptions, dès lors que l'amendement y relatif entrera en vigueur.

Une autre question vient à l'esprit : celle de l'effet de la saisine de la CPI par le Conseil de sécurité, d'une situation impliquant les ressortissants d'un État qui aurait souscrit à la clause d'« *opting out* ».

Le statut de Rome ne prévoit pas de disposition donnant une réponse claire à cette question. Toutefois, celle-ci peut être déterminée par une interprétation combinée des articles 124, 12 et 13 du statut. L'interprétation de l'article 124 fait penser que la Cour saisie par le CS devra connaître de l'affaire, malgré l'option de l'État en cause. En effet, cet article déroge aux dispositions de l'article 12 para. 1 et 2 sur les conditions préalables à l'exercice de la compétence de la CPI.

Le para. 1 a trait à la reconnaissance automatique de la compétence de la CPI à l'égard des crimes visés à l'article 5 par le fait de la ratification. L'article 124 semble exprimer, à travers ce paragraphe, la possibilité de ne

---

[66] S. A. Ndiaye, Le Conseil de Sécurité et les Juridictions pénales internationales, *op. cit.*, p. 278.

pas reconnaître la compétence de la CPI malgré la ratification, pour l'un des crimes de l'article 5, notamment les crimes de guerre.

Le para 2 de l'art. 12 relatif à l'exigence de l'adhésion de l'État au Statut de Rome[67] ne fait référence qu'aux cas visés à l'art. 13 para a) ou c), c'est-à-dire le cas où le Procureur est saisi par un État partie et le cas où le procureur se saisit *proprio motu*, excluant ainsi le cas de saisine par le CS. Ce n'est que par exception à ces deux cas qu'un État peut déclarer différer la compétence de la CPI pour une période de 7 ans. L'article 124 ne déroge pas au cas de l'article 13 (b) relatif à la saisine de la CPI par le CS, non mentionné par l'article 12 para. 2

Aussi, de manière logique, si le CS peut soumettre à la Cour des crimes présumés perpétrés sur le territoire ou par des ressortissants d'États tiers, on imagine mal qu'il ne puisse en faire autant dans le cas où les crimes auraient été perpétrés sur le territoire ou par des ressortissants d'États parties ayant souscrit au régime transitoire de l'article 124. On en arriverait à « *une situation ubuesque* »[68] où le CS se verrait reconnaître, par le statut, un pouvoir large d'intervention sur des ressortissants d'États tiers et non sur des ressortissants d'États parties.

35. Au terme de cette partie, il apparaît que les États africains ont la possibilité de limiter la compétence de la CPI à l'égard de leurs ressortissants, soit par leur non adhésion à la convention, soit par la dénonciation de cette dernière ou par l'exploitation des options qu'elle leur offre ou même le refus de coopérer avec les organes de cette juridiction. Toutefois, ces solutions dites de contestation ne résolvent pas entièrement le problème, la CPI demeurant compétente si elle est saisie par le CS ou si un ressortissant d'un État africain non partie commet des infractions sur le territoire d'un État partie. Il serait donc intéressant d'explorer une autre voie, celle de la concurrence.

II- La voie de la concurrence

[67] L'Etat sur le territoire duquel les crimes sont commis ou dont les ressortissants sont auteurs des crimes en cause doit être partie au statut.

[68] S. A. Ndiaye, Le Conseil de Sécurité et les Juridictions pénales internationales, *op. cit*, p. 281.

36. La création de la CPI et la ratification du statut de Rome par un Etat ne dessaisissent pas cet État de sa juridiction à l'égard des crimes graves de droit international qui s'y seraient commis. Les États ont transféré leur souveraineté à la CPI dans ce domaine, uniquement quand ils sont défaillants. Dès lors, ces États pris individuellement peuvent faire concurrence à la CPI dans la poursuite des crimes graves de droit international. La concurrence peut également se faire par des actions collectives et concertées des États africains.[69] Dans tous les cas, elle se manifestera par la mise sur pied d'un arsenal juridique permettant de réprimer les crimes relevant de la compétence de la CPI (A) et l'exercice par les juridictions nationales de leur priorité de compétence (B).

A- Le préalable : la mise sur pied d'un arsenal juridique permettant la répression des crimes relevant de la compétence de la CPI

37. La CPI ; selon l'article 1er du statut de Rome est une juridiction complémentaire des juridictions nationales. Elle ne peut en outre exercer sa compétence que dans le cas où l'État du territoire de l'infraction ou celui dont l'auteur est ressortissant est dans l'incapacité de poursuivre ou manque de volonté pour poursuivre les auteurs des crimes graves de droit international. Sur cette base, on peut imaginer que l'engagement d'un État africain à poursuivre les auteurs de ces infractions et leur poursuite effective peuvent servir de blocage à la compétence de la CPI. Pour le faire, il faut nécessairement que l'État ou les États en question en aient les moyens et que des mesures soient prises sur le plan interne à cet effet afin de ne pas violer certains principes sacro-saints du droit pénal à savoir le principe de légalité et le principe de non-rétroactivité de la loi pénale. Il s'agit donc de mettre sur pied un système de justice fiable et efficace. Ceci passe inévitablement par l'introduction en droit interne des infractions concernées (1) ainsi que leurs modalités de répression (2).

1- L'introduction en droit interne des infractions relevant de la compétence de la CPI

[69] Il faut préciser que ce sont les Etats qui sont parties à la Convention de Rome et non les institutions régionales, même s'il est possible que des accords soient signés entre ces dernières et la CPI.

38. Dans son avis du 21 février 1925 sur *l'Echange des populations turques et grecques*, la CPJI rappelait qu'*« un Etat qui a valablement contracté des obligations internationales est tenu d'apporter à sa législation les modifications nécessaires pour assurer l'exécution des engagements pris »*[70]. Pour ce faire, l'Etat doit abroger certaines normes internes qui sont en contradiction avec les obligations découlant du traité et surtout adopter de nouvelles lois incriminant des faits dénoncés dans la convention.[71]

En effet, la difficulté d'application est d'autant plus grande pour les conventions de nature pénale, en vertu du principe de la légalité des délits et des peines. [72] La conséquence de la non insertion des conventions en droit

[70] CPJI, avis du 21 février 1925, *Echange des populations turques et grecques*, série B, n°10, p. 20. La CPJI applique ainsi la théorie du dualisme entre l'ordre juridique interne et l'ordre juridique international. Cette dernière considère qu'il existe une certaine étanchéité entre ces deux ordres juridiques ; leur imbrication, qui ne va pas de soi, ne saurait donc résulter que d'un acte formel de l'Autorité nationale- souvent une loi- reprenant à son compte ce qui a été arrêté dans la sphère internationale. Mais à côté de cette théorie, se développe une autre appelée théorie du monisme pour laquelle le droit international s'intègre directement dans le droit interne des Etats, les rapports entre les deux ordres juridiques étant caractérisés par l'osmose. Voir A. Cisse critiquant la décision de la Cour de cassation sénégalaise relative à *l'affaire Hissène Habré.* Pour lui, les traités et conventions régulièrement ratifiés sont intégrés *de jure* au droit national et sont d'application immédiate selon les dispositions de l'article 79 de la Constitution sénégalaise. A. Cisse, « Droit sénégalais », in A. Cassese et M. Delmas Marty (dir.), *Juridictions nationales et crimes internationaux*, Paris, PUF, 2002, 673 p., pp. 437-450, p. 444.

[71] Parmi les Etats africains ayant ratifié le statut de Rome instituant la CPI, quelques-uns seulement ont pris de telles mesures : l'Afrique du Sud (*Implementation of the Rome Statute of the International Criminal Court Act 27 of 2002 amended by Judicial Matters Amendment Act 22 of 2005 et Implementation of the Rome Statute of the International Criminal Court Regulations GNR1089 in GG 23761 f 16 August 2002*) ; le Burundi (Loi n°1/004 du 8 mai 2003 portant répression du crime de génocide, des crimes contre l'humanité et des crimes de guerre) ; la République du Congo (Loi n° 8-98 du 31 octobre 1998) ; le Kenya (*The Internatinal Crimes Act, 2008* entrée en vigueur en janvier 2009) ; le Mali (Loi n° 01-079 du 20 août 2001 portant Code pénal, mis à jour au 31 mars 2005) ; le Niger (Loi n° 2003/025 du 13 juin 2003, modifiant la Loi n° 61-27 du 15 juillet 1961, portant institution du Code pénal ; le Sénégal (Loi n° 2007-02 du 12 février 2007 modifiant le Code pénal et Loi n° 2007-05 du 12 février 2007, modifiant le Code de procédure pénale, relative à la mise en œuvre du Traité de Rome instituant la Cour pénale internationale).

[72] V. les exemples égyptien (non adoption de lois internes relatives à l'application de la Convention contre le génocide et les Conventions de Genève de 1949) ; Marocain (non

interne est le refus par les juridictions d'exercer leur compétence.[73] À défaut, elles appliquent le droit pénal national– ordinaire ou militaire – déjà en vigueur, en prenant pour références les infractions à ce droit national (telles que meurtres, torture, lésions corporelles graves et autres crimes de droit commun) qui se rapprochent le plus des comportements jugés. Cette approche, relativement courante dans les procès qui ont suivi la Seconde Guerre mondiale, a été adoptée et continue d'être utilisée dans des affaires plus récentes de crimes internationaux. On pourrait citer l'exemple du procès en cour martiale, selon le Code pénal militaire américain, du lieutenant William L. Calley, accusé aux États-Unis de meurtre dans l'affaire du massacre de My Lai (1970).[74] Ou encore, plus récemment, les affaires des soldats américains jugés devant des cours martiales pour des crimes commis en Irak (présomption de recours généralisé à la torture contre des détenus irakiens en 2004). Dans un cas comme dans l'autre, les charges retenues contre les prévenus auraient pu être assimilées à des crimes de guerre ou des crimes contre l'humanité.[75]

39. Cette pratique comporte le risque de sanctionner des comportements totalement licites au regard du droit international pénal ou d'admettre des restrictions ou obstacles, telle la prescription ou l'amnistie, qui ne sont plus

publication des mêmes conventions dans le Bulletin officiel alors qu'au Maroc, les conventions internationales ne reçoivent application que lorsqu'elles sont publiées dans le Bulletin Officiel et absence d'insertion de la Convention sur la prévention et la répression du crime de Génocide) ; Camerounais (absence de lois d'insertion des Conventions de Genève).

[73] A défaut, elles appliquent le droit pénal national.

[74] *United States v. First Lieutenant William L. Calley, Jr. (1971),* 46 C.M.R. 1131(1973), cité dans W. Ferdinandusse, *Direct Application of International Criminal Law in National Courts,* T.M.C. Asser Press, The Hague, 2006, p. 19, cité par A. M. La Rosa, *Prévenir et réprimer les crimes internationaux : vers une approche « intégrée » fondée sur la pratique nationale,* Rapport de la troisième réunion universelle des Commissions nationales de mise en œuvre du Droit international humanitaire, vol. 1, CICR, juin 2013, p. 30. Pour un autre exemple ou, même après l'adoption d'une loi sur la CPI, il a été jugé nécessaire de se référer également au droit commun, voir le procès de Donald Paye et d'autres soldats devant la Cour martiale générale du Royaume-Uni, Centre Bulford (7 septembre 2006 au 30 avril 2007). Dans cette affaire, des sept membres des forces armées britanniques accusés, un seul (D. Payne) a été condamné.

[75] W. Ferdinandusse, *Direct Application of International Criminal Law in National Courts,* op. cit.

admises s'agissant de crimes internationaux. En outre, les peines prévues par le droit commun peuvent être sans adéquation avec les violations graves du droit international et leur contexte.

40. Il faut donc la prise de lois d'incrimination qui définissent l'infraction soit en reprenant la définition contenue dans la convention soit en renvoyant à la disposition de la convention incriminant les faits en question. Ne devraient pas être négligées les peines sanctionnant les infractions concernées.[76] Trois méthodes permettent de remplir cette obligation : l'adaptation par incorporation, l'adaptation par référence et une méthode mixte combinant les deux premières.

La première consiste à reprendre le texte international dans une loi interne et lui associer une sanction si cette dernière n'est pas prévue dans la convention internationale.[77]

La seconde méthode se fait par renvoi aux dispositions conventionnelles concernées assorti de règles de procédure et éventuellement de sanctions lorsqu'elles n'existent pas dans la convention. Cette option est privilégiée dans des constitutions nationales et des codes pénaux.[78] Tout comme l'option précédente, elle présente l'avantage d'offrir une base légale s'il n'existe rien d'autre. Elle peut dès lors aussi servir de solution transitoire avant que les réformes législatives nécessaires à la pleine mise en œuvre du statut de Rome au niveau national ne soient achevées. Elle est relativement simple et permet assez aisément de couvrir toutes les infractions graves, y compris celles qu'établit le droit coutumier. En outre, aucune nouvelle législation n'est nécessaire si les traités en question sont modifiés.[79]

---

[76] Il est à relever que dans la majorité des conventions, si l'incrimination est plus ou moins précise, il n'en est pas de même des sanctions qui y sont souvent absentes.

[77] Cette méthode a été adoptée par le Niger avec l'introduction du crime de génocide, des crimes contre l'humanité et crimes de guerre dans son Code pénal. Voir Loi N° 2003/025 précitée (art. 208 en ses différentes sections). Voir aussi l'art. 132 bis du Code pénal camerounais qui reproduit la définition de la torture telle que prévue à l'article 1 de la Convention des Nations Unies contre la torture ou les traitements cruels, inhumains et dégradants du 10 décembre 1984.

[78] Par exemple la *International Crimes Act* du Kenya précitée, *Section 6 (4)* sur la définition des crimes et *Section 7* sur les règles procédurales applicables.

[79] A.M. La Rosa, *Prévenir et réprimer les crimes internationaux : vers une approche « intégrée » fondée sur la pratique nationale*, *op. cit.*, p. 33.

En revanche, un procédé aussi simple peut se révéler inadapté au système de certains États, selon la façon dont est interprété le principe de légalité (en particulier dans ses formulations *nullum crimen sine lege scripta* et *nullum crimen sine lege certa*), qui veut que la sanction applicable à toute infraction soit connue et prévisible. Bien plus, le degré de spécificité requis au niveau national s'agissant des proscriptions pénales ne serait tout simplement pas atteint avec une telle approche. Celle-ci oblige aussi le juge national à déterminer le droit applicable dans le pays à la lumière des dispositions figurant dans certains traités, dans la coutume et dans la jurisprudence internationale, ce qui laisse aux tribunaux une grande marge de manœuvre (et, accessoirement, de confusion).[80]

La troisième méthode, fondée sur une approche mixte de la criminalisation, combine renvoi générique aux dispositions conventionnelles et intégration expresse dans le code pénal des Etats de certains crimes internationaux.[81] Cette méthode semble la meilleure parce qu'elle permet de respecter les principes de légalité et de spécificité tout en n'imposant pas d'amender les dispositions spécifiques à chaque modification ou développement du droit international pénal.[82] Cette méthode, fréquente dans la pratique nationale avant l'adoption du statut de Rome, permet à un État de satisfaire pleinement à ses obligations conventionnelles et, en même temps, de bien différencier les crimes. Elle exige cependant des juges qu'ils soient capables d'interpréter aussi bien des dispositions de droit interne et de droit international que l'interaction souvent déroutante qui existe entre les deux.

41. Lorsqu'un État manque alors d'incorporer dans son droit interne les crimes relevant de la compétence de la CPI, cela peut d'une certaine manière faire obstacle à l'exercice de sa juridiction surtout pour les traités qui ne sont pas « *self-executing* ». Et même, pour la catégorie des traités « *self-executing* », il faudra encore qu'il ait prévu des sanctions en cas de violation

[80] *Ibid.*, pp. 33-34.

[81] Voir la définition du génocide dans la Loi burundaise précitée, art. 2 et art. 431(5) du Code pénal sénégalais définissant le Crime de droit international et art. 431 (6) sur les sanctions applicables.

[82] A.M. La Rosa, *Prévenir et réprimer les crimes internationaux : vers une approche « intégrée » fondée sur la pratique nationale*, *op. cit.*, p. 36.

de ses dispositions. Cela suppose alors que les éléments de l'infraction soient précisés et les sanctions indiquées dans un texte écrit. [83] À cette mesure, devront s'ajouter les règles sur les modalités de répression.

2- La mise sur pied de modalités de répression

42. Le statut de Rome ainsi que le Règlement de procédure et de preuve de la CPI régissent le droit applicable devant cette juridiction. Il est donc nécessaire que les États s'approprient certaines de ces règles pour empêcher l'exercice par cette cour de sa compétence, en particulier l'adoption des règles procédurales (a) et l'adaptation des principes de droit pénal applicables au droit de la CPI (b).

a- La prévision des règles procédurales pour la mise en œuvre de la compétence des juridictions nationales

43. Le droit pénal processuel définit des règles permettant de mettre en application les règles de droit pénal, notamment la répression des infractions. L'absence de règles procédurales est une entrave majeure à la répression. Ainsi, même si certains faits sont incriminés, ceux-ci ne peuvent faire l'objet de répression que par la mise sur pied d'un ensemble de règles visant à indiquer la procédure à suivre pour la répression de ces faits. Dans les ordres judiciaires pénaux, il existe très souvent des règles de procédure générales ou de droit commun applicables à des infractions de droit commun. Mais à côté de ces règles, les organes législatifs mettent en place des règles particulières pour certaines infractions particulières. L'inexistence de ces règles est susceptible de paralyser la répression des crimes graves de droit international. C'est dans ce contexte qu'il est nécessaire, pour les États africains, d'introduire en droit interne des règles particulières pour la répression des crimes graves de droit international.[84]

Les crimes graves de droit international étant d'une particulière gravité, ils ne sauraient respecter toutes les règles de procédure posées pour les infractions de droit commun. En dehors de la procédure à suivre proprement dite, les règles de compétence doivent être posées. Il s'agit de

---

[83] **Mais reste toujours que pour plus de clarté, les dispositions conventionnelles devraient être insérées dans le droit interne.**

[84] Certains pays africains ayant ratifié le statut de Rome l'ont fait : Burundi, Kenya, Sénégal.

l'adoption de principes de compétence appropriés, y compris a portée extraterritoriale, notamment les compétences personnelles active et passive et surtout, la compétence universelle (territorialisée ou absolue).[85] Il serait même louable de créer de nouvelles juridictions chargées de la répression des crimes graves de droit international.

44. L'exemple le plus topique de paralysie de poursuite pour défaut de règles de procédure est celui du Sénégal appelé à juger l'ex-président tchadien Hissène Habré.

Dans cette affaire, la Cour de cassation sénégalaise, dans une décision du 20 mars 2001, a estimé que les juridictions sénégalaises n'étaient pas compétentes pour connaître des infractions de torture reprochées à Habré, celles-ci ayant été commises hors du territoire national. La Cour considérait que le Sénégal, après s'être conformé à l'article 4 de la convention de New York, en incriminant les actes de torture, à travers l'article 295-1 du code pénal, n'a pas pris parallèlement les dispositions nécessaires sur le plan de la procédure pénale. Le Sénégal ne s'étant donc pas encore acquitté de l'obligation également posée par l'article 5-2[86] de la convention de New York contre la torture, les juridictions sénégalaises ne peuvent pas exercer leur compétence sur des faits de torture commis en dehors du territoire sénégalais par des étrangers. La Cour souligne en effet « *Qu'aucun texte de procédure ne reconnaît une compétence universelle aux juridictions sénégalaises en vue de poursuivre et de juger, s'ils sont trouvés sur le territoire de la*

[85] La compétence universelle en matière pénale est l'affirmation par un État de sa compétence pour juger des infractions pénales qui auraient été commises sur le territoire d'un autre État par des ressortissants d'un autre État contre des ressortissants d'un autre État, lorsque l'infraction alléguée ne constitue pas une menace directe pour les intérêts vitaux de l'État qui affirme sa compétence. En d'autres termes, la compétence universelle équivaut à la revendication, par un État, du droit d'engager des poursuites dans des circonstances ou aucun des liens traditionnels que constituent la territorialité, la nationalité, la personnalité passive ou le principe de compétence réelle (ou de protection), n'est présent au moment où l'infraction alléguée est commise. Conseil de l'Union européenne, Rapport du groupe d'experts UA-EU sur le principe de la compétence universelle, doc. off. 8672/1/09 Rev. 1 (16 avril 2009), p. 7. Dans sa forme territorialisée, son exercice est conditionnée par la présence du suspect sur le territoire de l'Etat en question alors que dans sa forme absolue, elle s'exerce quel que soit le lieu où se trouve le suspect.

[86] Cet article énonce que les Etats parties à la Convention doivent prendre les mesures nécessaires en vue d'établir la compétence de leurs juridictions nationales.

République, les présumés auteurs ou complices de faits [de torture]...lorsque ces faits ont été commis hors du Sénégal par des étrangers; que la présence au Sénégal d'Hissène Habré ne saurait à elle seule justifier les poursuites intentées contre lui »[87]. Cet exemple démontre les problèmes que peut causer l'absence des règles procédurales dans la répression des infractions relevant de la compétence de la CPI. Ces règles devront surtout s'attarder sur les cas de compétence des juridictions internes et la répartition de compétence dans l'ordre judiciaire interne. Elles devront aussi, si nécessaire[88], prévoir des procédures à suivre, de la constatation de l'infraction jusqu'au prononcé de la sanction.

45. Pourtant, il est possible d'éviter tous ces problèmes d'interprétation en établissant les règles de compétence et en jugeant effectivement. Cela éviterait de se retrouver dans la situation du Sénégal avec l'affaire *Hissène Habré* où le problème s'est posé par rapport à l'admission qu'un juge d'une puissance européenne connaisse d'une affaire mettant en cause un ancien chef d'État africain. Au point où le Sénégal s'est finalement remis à l'Union africaine pour en décider. Or, si le Sénégal avait prévu des règles procédurales relatives à la répression de la torture, les juridictions sénégalaises auraient eu un fondement à l'exercice de leur compétence et ce problème ne se serait pas posé.

46. Toutefois, il ne suffit pas seulement d'incorporer. En fait, comme pour les lois internes, une diffusion est nécessaire pour une meilleure application de l'adage « *Nul n'est censé ignorer la loi* »[89]. Si en effet il est clair pour tout citoyen d'un village ou d'une ethnie X qu'en exterminant la population du village ou de l'ethnie Y, il commet un acte abominable, il reste que ce citoyen doit savoir que son fait est répréhensible par la loi et que la fourchette des sanctions se situe entre tel nombre d'années d'emprisonnement. Un habitant de Nguélémedouga (Cameroun), par exemple doit être mis au courant des conventions ratifiées par le Cameroun

---

[87] Cour de cassation, Crim., Arrêt n °14 du 20 mars 2001, *Souleymane Guengueng et autres contre Hissène Habré*, http://www.hrw.org/french/themes/habre cour_de_cass.html.

[8888] C'est-à-dire si l'on estime que les règles de procédure ordinaire ne devraient pas s'appliquer.

[89] A. akam Akam, « Libres propos sur l'adage « Nul n'est sensé ignorer la loi » », *Revue Africaine des Sciences Juridiques*, vol. 4, n° 1, 2007, pp. 31-54.

et des lois de mise en œuvre adoptées. De même, les principes généraux applicables doivent être adaptés au droit de la CPI.

b- L'adaptation des principes généraux de droit pénal aux exigences du droit de la CPI

47. Il serait judicieux que les États veillent à ce que les principes généraux de droit pénal énoncés dans leur législation soient adaptés aux exigences du droit de la CPI, du moins aux fins de la poursuite des crimes relevant de la compétence de cette juridiction. Quelques règles primordiales doivent être posées. Il s'agira de mettre à l'écart les arguments de défense qui ne sont pas retenus dans le statut de Rome et le Règlement de procédure et de preuve de la CPI, notamment la défense fondée sur l'obéissance à des ordres supérieurs manifestement illégaux.[90] Dans cette perspective, il conviendrait que les États africains adoptent des mesures qui garantissent notamment la non applicabilité des délais de prescription (lorsque le droit national prévoit la prescription)[91], la reconnaissance de certaines formes de responsabilité, dont celle des chefs militaires, la non-pertinence de la qualité officielle et des immunités[92], et la non-reconnaissance de l'amnistie[93] ou de la grâce pour les criminels de droit international.

---

[90] Voir Statut de Rome, art. 33.

[91] Art. 29 du Statut de Rome du 18 juillet 1998 : « Les crimes relevant du Statut de la Cour ne se prescrivent pas. »

[92] Art. 27 al. 1 du Statut de Rome qui dispose : « *Le présent Statut s'applique à tous de manière égale, sans aucune distinction fondée sur la qualité officielle. En particulier, la qualité officielle de chef d'Etat ou de gouvernement, de membre d'un gouvernement ou d'un parlement, de représentant élu ou d'agent d'un Etat, n'exonère en aucun cas de la responsabilité pénale …pas plus qu'elle ne constitue en tant que telle un motif de réduction de la peine* ». L'al. 2 du même article continue : « *Les immunités ou règles spéciales qui peuvent s'attacher à la qualité officielle d'une personne, en vertu du droit interne ou du droit international, n'empêchent pas la Cour d'exercer sa compétence à l'égard de cette personne* ».

[93] En ce qui concerne l'amnistie, La combinaison des articles 17 et 20 du Statut de la CPI laissent penser que l'amnistie accordée pour les crimes relevant de sa compétence ne saurait servir d'obstacle à la compétence de la Cour. Le premier mentionne le « *manque de volonté* » ou « *l'incapacité de l'Etat de mener véritablement à bien des poursuites* » alors que le second évoque le but recherché de « *soustraire la personne concernée à sa responsabilité pénale* ». L'amnistie pourrait donc être considérée si non, comme un manque de volonté ou une impossibilité de poursuivre, au moins comme ayant pour but de soustraire la personne concernée de sa responsabilité pénale. Relevons d'ailleurs que, lors des négociations relatives à l'autorité de la chose jugée de l'article 20 du Statut de la CPI, l'amnistie a été exclue

48. Les principes relatifs à la responsabilité pénale inscrits dans le droit national doivent être au moins aussi stricts que ceux énoncés dans la troisième partie du statut de Rome. Ainsi, tous les crimes relevant de la responsabilité pénale conjointe tels que la complicité et l'incitation directe et publique visées à l'article 25 doivent être punissables au titre du droit national.

49. Or, si sur le plan interne, les États africains continuent de donner droit aux immunités, à adopter des lois d'amnistie sur des actes commis constitutifs de crimes relevant de la compétence de la CPI ou à leur appliquer les règles ordinaires de prescription, il va sans dire que la CPI constatera leur impossibilité ou leur manque de volonté à poursuivre et à punir les auteurs de ces crimes. C'est ainsi que dans le cadre de la polémique suscitée par les poursuites exercées par la CPI contre le président soudanais el-Béchir, l'UA avait institué un groupe de haut niveau sur le Darfour présidé par l'ancien président sud-africain Thabo Mbeki. Le rapport établi par ce groupe (Rapport du groupe de haut niveau de l'Union africaine sur le Darfour)[94] avait constaté les faiblesses du système judiciaire soudanais pour réprimer les crimes du Darfour. Il a alors proposé une série de mesures: premièrement, des réformes législatives et judiciaires pour renforcer la capacité du système judiciaire soudanais afin de réprimer efficacement les crimes du Darfour et d'accorder des réparations aux victimes desdits crimes; deuxièmement, la création d'un tribunal hybride pour le Darfour, lequel tribunal serait composé de juges et procureurs dont certains seraient nommés par le gouvernement soudanais et d'autres par l'UA[95]. Cette recommandation, qui était pourtant une des voies de satisfaire le critère de complémentarité de la CPI, est toutefois restée lettre morte, justifiant l'intervention de la CPI au Darfour.

50. Il faudrait donc que les États africains, peut-être individuellement, mais mieux encore de manière synergique, répriment les crimes relevant de

---

comme disposition ayant valeur d'un jugement, en mesure d'empêcher un nouveau procès devant la Cour.

[94] Rapport du groupe de haut niveau de l'Union africaine sur le Darfour (GUAD), Doc off CPS UA, 207e réunion, Doc UAPSC/AHG/2(CCVII) (2009) [Rapport Mbeki].

[95] Rapport du groupe de haut niveau de l'Union africaine sur le Darfour (GUAD), précité, para 324, 330-333.

la compétence de la CPI et reconnaissent les caractères qui leur sont attachés.

Cette démarche est nécessaire, car le risque d'aménagements épars et diversifiés est d'aggraver les inégalités entre États et de favoriser une sorte de « *forum shopping* ». Il consistera pour les victimes à privilégier les pays ayant adopté compétence universelle, normes internationales et intégré les principes reconnus dans le statut de Rome pour y déposer leur plainte ;[96] et pour les criminels de se réfugier dans les États n'ayant pas pris de telles mesures ou les ayant fortement limitées. Il s'ensuit qu'il devrait y avoir un consensus général sur les modalités de répression des crimes graves de droit international. [97]

51. C'est dans cette logique que les États africains, à travers l'Union africaine, ont décidé de faire concurrence avec la CPI en s'opposant à la poursuite de certains ressortissants africains par la CPI.[98] Dans ce contexte, des textes ont été adoptés visant la répression des crimes graves de droit international et mettant sur pied des institutions ayant pour but de participer à la répression desdits crimes.

---

[96] On en veut pour preuve l'afflux des plaintes avec constitution de partie civile en Belgique après l'adoption de la loi de 1993. Des plaintes ont été déposées en Belgique contre le président mauritanien Maouya ould Sid'Ahmed Taya, le président irakien Saddam Hussein, le premier ministre israélien Ariel Sharon, le président de Côte d'Ivoire Laurent Gbagbo, le président rwandais Paul Kagamé, le président cubain Fidel Castro, le président de la République centrafricaine Ange Félix Patassé, le président de la République du Congo Denis Sassou Nguesso, le président de l'Autorité palestinienne Yasser Arafat, l'ancien président tchadien Hissène Habré, l'ancien président chilien le général Augusto Pinochet, l'ancien président iranien Hashemi Rafsanjani, l'ancien ministre de l'Intérieur du Maroc Driss Basri, l'ancien ministre des Affaires étrangères de la République démocratique du Congo Abdoulaye Yerodia Ndombasi, entre autres. Les plaintes déposées contre Laurent Gbagbo ont finalement été retirées.

[97] C. Tchaya Tchatat, Essai sur Le Statut pénal du Chef d'Etat, thèse, Droit, Faculté des Sciences Juridiques et Politiques, Université de Yaoundé II-Soa, 2009, 590p, p. 505.

[98] Dans la même logique d'opposition aux forces occidentales, l'Union africaine, par un accord avec le gouvernement de la République du Sénégal daté du 22 août 2012, a créé des chambres extraordinaires au sein des juridictions sénégalaises, pour résoudre le problème de la poursuite d'Hissène Habré et des responsables de crimes commis au Tchad durant la période du 7 juin 1982 au 1er décembre 1990 par la Belgique.

Dans le protocole portant amendements au protocole portant statut de la Cour africaine de justice et des droits de l'homme du 27 juin 2014, les États africains rappellent leur engagement à intervenir dans un État membre dans des circonstances graves telles que les crimes de guerre, le génocide, les crimes contre l'humanité ainsi qu'en cas de menace sérieuse à l'ordre légitime pour restaurer la paix et la stabilité dans l'État membre de l'union sur recommandation du Conseil de paix et de sécurité.[99] Ils ont réitéré leur respect du caractère sacré de la vie humaine, de la condamnation et du rejet de l'impunité et des assassinats politiques, des actes de terrorisme et des activités subversives, des changements anticonstitutionnels de gouvernements et des actes d'agression,[100] ils décident de compléter les institutions nationales, régionales et continentales dans la prévention des violations sérieuses et massives des droits de l'Homme et des peuples par la garantie de rendre compte pour ces violations partout où elles sont commises.[101] C'est partant de cela qu'ils ont ajouté une section de droit international pénal à la Cour africaine de justice et des droits de l'homme et des peuples.[102] Selon le statut de cette juridiction tel que modifié en annexe du protocole sus-évoqué, la section de droit international pénal est chargée des affaires relatives aux crimes définis dans le statut.[103] Les crimes visés sont : le génocide, les crimes contre l'humanité, les crimes de guerre, le crime relatif au changement anticonstitutionnel de gouvernement, la piraterie, le terrorisme, le mercenariat, la corruption, le blanchiment d'argent, la traite des personnes, le trafic illicite de stupéfiants, le trafic illicite de déchets dangereux, l'exploitation illicite des ressources naturelles et le crime d'agression.[104] Cette liste paraît nettement plus longue que la liste des infractions réprimées dans le statut de Rome et les inclut toutes. Elle a en outre tenu compte du contexte socio- économique et politique de

---

[99] Préambule, para. 8.

[100] Préambule, para. 10.

[101] Préambule, para. 16.

[102] Article 16 (1) modifié du Statut : « la Cour est composée de trois (3) sections : une Section des affaires générales, une Section des droits de l'homme et des peuples et une Section du droit international pénal. »

[103] Art. 17 para. 3

[104] L'article 28 A (2) laisse la porte ouverte à de possibles extensions de compétence de cette section par la Conférence des chefs d'Etat et de gouvernement de l'Union africaine sur consensus des Etats parties.

l'Afrique en réprimant les crimes relatifs au changement anticonstitutionnel de gouvernement, à l'exploitation illégale des ressources naturelles. Ce texte offre en outre l'avantage de la clarté et de la simplicité dans la mesure où les crimes graves sont prévus dans un texte juridique unique de référence ; ce qui faciliterait la tâche aux organes chargés de la répression des crimes qui, autrement, recouraient à plusieurs textes juridiques distincts régissant les crimes en question.

52. Malheureusement, l'article 46 A bis institue une immunité des chefs d'État ou de gouvernement de l'UA en fonction ou toute autre personne agissant ou habilitée à agir en cette qualité ou tout haut responsable public en raison de ses fonctions. Or, en instituant ces immunités personnelles et fonctionnelles, elle donne la possibilité à la CPI d'attraire devant elle les ressortissants africains ayant cette qualité s'ils ne sont pas jugés par les juridictions nationales.

Ainsi, malgré les acquis constatés, les États africains ont encore du chemin à faire. Il reste qu'ils acceptent de soumettre les chefs d'État et de gouvernement en exercice au droit pénal international même si cela se faisait sous une procédure spéciale[105], qu'ils ratifient le protocole portant amendements au protocole portant statut de la Cour africaine de justice et des droits de l'homme du 27 juin 2014. Ceci permettra que la machine judiciaire régionale se mette en marche. Il faut en outre que l'Union africaine ouvre des négociations avec l'assemblée des États parties au traité de Rome pour que la section de droit international pénal de la Cour africaine soit reconnue comme un deuxième échelon de la justice pénale internationale après les juridictions nationales de sorte que des conflits positifs de compétence soient évités entre cette juridiction et la CPI.

Les mesures sus-évoquées ne sont qu'un préalable à l'exercice effectif, par les juridictions nationales africaines, de leur priorité de compétence.

B- Le subséquent : l'exercice par les juridictions nationales africaines de leur priorité de compétence

[105] Privilège de procédure, en demandant par exemple l'assentiment de l'autorité sous-régionale ou régionale.

53. Le préambule du statut de Rome dispose en son para. 6 qu' « il est du devoir de chaque État de soumettre à sa juridiction criminelle les responsables des crimes internationaux »[106]. La résolution RC/Res.1 issue du sommet de Kampala le rappelle ainsi : « il revient en premier lieu à chaque Etat d'enquêter et de poursuivre les crimes les plus graves ayant des retombées internationales »[107]. Dès lors, la CPI ne sera compétente que si les États faillissent à leur mission. L'exercice de cette priorité de compétence issue du principe de complémentarité est donc une voie de contournement de la compétence de la CPI. Cette dernière est tributaire de la défaillance des juridictions nationales (1). Toutefois, des difficultés de mise en œuvre peuvent être constatées compte tenu du contexte socio- économique des pays africains (2).

1- La compétence de la Cour pénale internationale : une compétence tributaire de la défaillance des juridictions nationales

54. La compétence de la CPI est tributaire de la défaillance des juridictions nationales, qu'elle soit saisie par les États, sur initiative personnelle du procureur de la Cour ou sur renvoi d'une situation par le CS.

À la différence des deux tribunaux pénaux internationaux *ad hoc* organisés sous le régime de la primauté et de la hiérarchie des normes de compétence[108], les relations entre la CPI et les juridictions nationales sont gouvernées par le principe de complémentarité. Cette complémentarité de la CPI à l'égard des juridictions nationales est déclarée dès le préambule du statut de Rome.[109] Elle est confirmée à l'article 1er du même statut : « *Il est créé une Cour pénale internationale.... Elle est complémentaire des juridictions pénales nationales...* » En conséquence, la CPI ne connaîtra d'une affaire que si les Etats n'ont pas la volonté ou la capacité de juger eux-mêmes les auteurs des crimes allégués. En cas de défaillance des États, les seuls éléments qui pourraient empêcher que la Cour connaisse des faits allégués sont la

---

[106] Statut de Rome, UN Doc A/Conf.183/9 du 17 juillet 1998.

[107] Résolution RC/Res.1, para. 1er , adoptée à la neuvième séance plénière, le 8 juin 2010, par consensus.

[108] Voir art. 9 para. 2 et 8 para. 2 respectivement des Statuts du TPIY et du TPIR.

[109] Voir Préambule, al. 10ème : « Soulignant que la Cour pénale internationale dont le présent Statut porte création est complémentaire des juridictions pénales nationales ».

suspension de la procédure par le CS[110] et si la Cour estime que la situation « *n'est pas suffisamment grave pour que [elle] y donne suite* »[111].

55. Le principe de complémentarité tire sa substance du régime de la recevabilité des affaires qui sont soumises à compétence juridictionnelle de la CPI. L'art. 17 para. 1 du statut de Rome pose en filigrane les conditions d'applicabilité du principe. Ainsi, la Cour sera incompétente si :

« a) l'affaire fait l'objet d'une enquête ou de poursuites de la part d'un État ayant compétence en l'espèce, à moins que cet État n'ait pas la volonté ou soit dans l'incapacité de mener véritablement à bien l'enquête ou les poursuites ; b) l'affaire a fait l'objet d'une enquête de la part d'un État ayant compétence en l'espèce et que cet État a décidé de ne pas poursuivre la personne concernée, à moins que cette décision ne soit l'effet du manque de volonté ou de l'incapacité de l'État de mener véritablement à bien les poursuites ; c) la personne concernée a déjà été jugée pour le comportement faisant l'objet de la plainte, et qu'elle ne peut être jugée par la Cour en vertu de l'art. 20 paragraphe 3 ... ».[112]

La compétence de la CPI n'est donc qu'une compétence résiduelle et subsidiaire. Elle ne connaîtra de l'affaire que si le cas est suffisamment grave, si la personne n'a pas encore été jugée pour le crime en question ou si les juges nationaux n'ont pas déclenché la procédure de poursuite. Le procureur a d'ailleurs l'obligation de notifier toute situation qui lui est soumise à tous les États parties et aux États qui, selon les renseignements disponibles, auraient normalement compétence à l'égard des crimes dont il s'agit.[113] Dès

---

[110] Voir art. 16 du Statut de Rome : « « *Aucune enquête ni aucune poursuite ne peuvent être engagées ni menées en vertu du présent Statut pendant les douze mois qui suivent la date à laquelle le Conseil de Sécurité en a fait la demande à la Cour dans une résolution adoptée en vertu du Chapitre VII de la Charte des Nations Unies* ». Cet article poursuit à la fin que « *cette demande peut être renouvelée par le Conseil dans les mêmes conditions* ».

[111]Art. 17, para. 1 d) du Statut de Rome.

[112] Rappelons que l'art. 20 para. 3 est relatif au principe *Ne bis in idem* applicable devant la CPI.

[113] L'art. 18 prévoit que le Procureur notifie toute situation qui lui est soumise à tous les Etats parties et aux Etats qui, selon les renseignements disponibles, auraient normalement compétence à l'égard des crimes dont il s'agit. Et dans le mois qui suit la réception de cette notification, un Etat peut informer la Cour qu'il ouvre ou a ouvert une enquête sur ses ressortissants ou d'autres personnes sous sa juridiction pour des actes incriminés dans le statut de Rome. Si l'Etat le lui demande, le Procureur lui défère le soin de l'enquête.

lors, les États africains désireux de soustraire leurs ressortissants de la juridiction de la CPI ont intérêt à exercer les poursuites et s'assurer que ces poursuites sont effectives et ne visent pas à soustraire les suspects de leur responsabilité pénale, que les décisions et la procédure suivent les délais raisonnables, évitant ainsi à la procédure de subir des retards injustifiés incompatibles avec l'intention de traduire en justice la personne concernée ; que la procédure est menée de manière indépendante et impartiale et non d'une manière qui est incompatible avec l'intention de traduire en justice la personne concernée.[114] Ce n'est que dans ces conditions que le principe *non bis in idem* posé par l'article 20 du statut de Rome pourrait s'appliquer. Ce principe pourrait également s'appliquer si le jugement émane d'une juridiction régionale ou sous régionale.

56. Toutefois, dans le cas où un État se trouverait dans l'incapacité de procéder aux enquêtes ou aux poursuites, il pourrait faire appel à un autre État pour le faire ou à la Cour africaine de justice et des droits de l'homme et des peuples si elle est déjà entrée en vigueur. En effet, la poursuite des ressortissants africains par une cour africaine telle que projetée pourrait aussi paralyser l'action de la CPI à l'égard des ressortissants africains en vertu du principe *ne bis in idem*. À défaut, c'est la CPI qui se saisira de l'affaire.

L'incapacité à poursuivre se vérifie par la décrépitude, l'affaissement ou l'indisponibilité de l'appareil judiciaire d'un État l'empêchant de se saisir de l'accusé ou de réunir des éléments suffisamment probants pour engager la machine pénale.

57. Dès lors que l'Etat mène ou a mené l'enquête ou qu'il a effectivement exercé les poursuites, il peut contester la recevabilité de l'affaire devant la CPI.[115] Ceci permettra qu'on n'en arrive pas à une sorte de « subsidiarité inversée » au profit de la CPI.

---

[114] Voir art. 17 para. 2 du Statut de Rome. Voir aussi l'art. 20 para. 3 posant des exceptions au principe *Ne bis in idem* dans les cas où la procédure avait pour but de soustraire la personne concernée de sa responsabilité pénale ou n'a pas été menée de manière indépendante ou impartiale dans le respect des garanties d'un procès équitable prévues par le droit international.

[115] Voir art. 19 para. 2 b) du Statut de Rome.

C'est dans cette logique qu'à la suite de l'ouverture des poursuites contre de hauts responsables kenyans suspectés de crimes contre l'humanité[116], le gouvernement de la République du Kenya a déposé une demande visant à contester l'admissibilité des dossiers devant la CPI sur le fondement du principe de complémentarité. Concrètement, le gouvernement kenyan invoque l'imminence de certaines réformes constitutionnelles et législatives d'envergure et notamment la nouvelle Constitution adoptée en août 2010 qui incorpore le droit à un procès équitable et des garanties procédurales dans le système judiciaire national. En outre, il fait état de l'existence d'une enquête ouverte par les instances judiciaires nationales sur les violences postélectorales. Le Kenya appuie sa requête visant à prouver sa capacité et sa volonté de juger les responsables des violations du droit humanitaire commises en manifestant son intention de rapporter les résultats de cette enquête devant la chambre préliminaire.[117]

Cependant, cette contestation est demeurée infructueuse, non pas parce que le procureur et la chambre préliminaire ont remis en question la volonté du Kenya de poursuivre, mais parce que les personnes poursuivies au niveau national étaient différentes de celles visées dans la procédure ouverte par la chambre préliminaire de la CPI. Cette dernière précise d'ailleurs à l'encontre de l'argumentaire du Kenya que la chambre détermine si l'enquête couvre les mêmes faits, mais aussi les mêmes personnes que celles identifiées dans la procédure ouverte devant la Cour.[118] Une telle condition vaut également à

---

[116] Il s'agit d'Uhuru Kenyatta, vice-premier ministre et ministre des Finances devenu par la suite président de la République du Kenya, William Ruto, Francis Muthaura, Hussein Ali, Henry Kosgey et Joshua Arap Sang.

[117] Voir la requête du gouvernement kenyan contestant la compétence de la CPI dans les affaires à l'encontre de Ruto, Kosgey, Sang, Muthaura, Kenyatta et Ali pour leur rôle présumé dans les violences postélectorales kényanes de 2007-2008, en date du 31 mars 2011

[118] Voir ICC-01/09-01/11, case *The prosecutor v. William Samoei Ruto, Henri Kiprono Kosgey* and *Joshua Arap Sang* et ICC-01/09-02/11, case *The prosecutor v. Francis Kirini Muthaura, Uhuru Muigai Kenyatta and Mohammed Hussein Ali* du 30 mai 2011 ; l'Arrêt relatif à l'appel interjeté par la République du Kenya contre la Décision relative à l'exception d'irrecevabilité de l'affaire soulevée par le Gouvernement kényan en vertu de l'article 19-2-b du Statut rendue par la Chambre préliminaire II le 30 mai 2011, ICC-01/09-01/11 OA, *Affaire Le Procureur C. William Samoei Ruto, Henry Kiprono Kosgey et Joshua Arap Sang*, 30 août 2011.Voir aussi Chambre préliminaire I de la CPI, *le Procureur*

l'égard des États non parties au statut, qui n'ont pas effectué de déclaration de compétence, mais poursuivent l'auteur d'un crime relevant de l'article 5 qui se trouverait sur leur territoire. Ils peuvent, dans le mois suivant la notification d'une enquête par la Cour l'informer qu'ils ouvrent ou ont ouvert une enquête.[119]

58. La volonté de poursuivre et les poursuites effectives s'apprécient au moment de la procédure devant la chambre préliminaire. Ainsi, tout changement de circonstance en instance d'appel est inopérant sur la décision de recevabilité devant la Cour.[120] Dès lors, les juridictions nationales africaines devraient éviter d'attendre que les organes de la CPI s'intéressent à la situation dans leur pays pour faire usage de leur priorité de compétence.

Sur le plan pratique en revanche, certains États africains, pour certaines raisons, ont favorisé le renversement du principe de complémentarité au profit de la CPI. On pourrait ainsi citer les exemples ougandais, congolais et centrafricain. L'Ouganda avait soumis la situation qui régnait sur son territoire au procureur de la CPI sans justifier cette saisine par son incapacité à mener l'enquête ou les poursuites.[121] Les cas de la RDC[122] et de la RCA[123]

---

c/ Saif Al-Islam Gaddafi et Abdullah Al-Senussi, ICC-01/11-01/11, du 31 mai 2013, para. 77 et s. Dans ce cas, la Chambre décide que les poursuites en Lybie ne couvraient pas les mêmes faits que ceux reprochés aux personnes poursuivies devant la CPI.

[119] Art. 18, para. 2 du Statut de Rome.

[120] Voir CPI, Chambre d'appel, ICC-02/11-01/12, *le Procureur c. Simone Gbagbo*, arrêt du 27 mai 2015, confirmant la décision de la Chambre préliminaire I relative à l'exception d'irrecevabilité soulevée par la Côte d'ivoire du 11 déc. 2014 alors que Simone Gbagbo avait été condamné, le 10 mars 2015 à 20 ans de prison ferme et 10 ans de privation des droits civiques. La Chambre d'appel estime, dans cette affaire, que « *A titre de mesure de correction, la portée de la procédure d'appel est fixée par celle de la procédure s'étant déroulée devant la Chambre préliminaire. Cette procédure devant la Chambre préliminaire s'est conclue avec la Décision attaquée. Les faits postérieurs à la Décision attaquée ne relèvent pas de la portée de la procédure devant la Chambre préliminaire et par conséquent de celle de la procédure d'appel* ».

[121] En décembre 2003, le président ougandais a déféré la situation concernant l'Armée de résistance du seigneur (ARS) à la CPI. Voir Communiqué de presse, 29 janvier 2004, ICC-20040129-44. Cette situation concerne le conflit armé interne qui a sévi au nord de l'Ouganda. Le président Museveni avait clairement identifié les responsables de crimes et n'avait aucunement relevé l'incapacité de l'Etat ougandais à poursuivre pour fonder la saisine de la CPI. Voir K. P. Apuili, « The ICC's Possible deferal of the LRA case to Uganda", JICJ, vol. 6 2008, pp. 25-40.

sont en revanche différents en ce sens qu'ils ont expressément précisé qu'ils étaient dans l'incapacité de mener les enquêtes conformément à l'article 17 para. 3 du statut de Rome.

59. Ces cas énumérés contredisent la volonté des États africains de soustraire de la juridiction de la CPI les ressortissants africains. On pourrait ainsi penser que le problème se trouverait ailleurs; par exemple reposerait sur la qualité des personnes poursuivies. On peut en effet constater que les cas dans lesquels la CPI a suscité le plus d'opposition et de résistance sont des cas de chefs d'État en fonction.[124]

60. Si le principe de complémentarité est un principe incontesté dans le fonctionnement de la CPI permettant aux Africains d'échapper à sa compétence à travers l'exercice par les juridictions nationales africaines de leur priorité de compétence, on pourrait se poser la question de savoir si cette complémentarité reste de vigueur lorsque c'est le CS qui saisit la CPI d'une situation. Le principe de complémentarité se transforme-t-il en une primauté de la CPI.

Une réponse négative s'impose à cette question même si le statut de Rome ne renferme pas de disposition expresse en ce sens. En effet, ni l'article 17 ni les articles 19 et 53 ne font de distinction entre les modalités d'activation de la compétence de la CPI.

---

[122] CPI, Communiqué de presse du 19 avril 2004, Renvoi devant le Procureur de la situation en République démocratique du Congo, ICC-OTP-20040419-50-Fr. Dans ce cas, le renvoi de la RDC confirme les communications des ONG qui ont été portées à la connaissance du procureur relativement à la situation en Ituri. Sur la base de la fiabilité de ces informations, le Procureur entendait ouvrir une enquête de sa propre initiative, même s'il préconisait la voie d'une saisine par les autorités congolaises pour des raisons d'efficacité. Voir CPI, Communiqué de presse du 23 juin 2004, le Bureau du Procureur de la Cour pénale internationale ouvre sa première enquête, ICC-OTP-20040623-59-Fr.

[123] CPI, communiqué de presse du 7 janvier 2005, Renvoi devant le Procureur de la situation en République centrafricaine, ICC-OTP620050107-86-Fr. Sur la déclaration d'incapacité de jugement faite par les juges nationaux, voir C. A. E. Bakker, « Le principe de complémentarité et les auto-saisines : un regard critique sur la pratique de la Cour pénale internationale », Paris, *RGDIP*, tome 112, n°2, 2008, pp. 361-378, p. 372.

[124] Voir le cas du président soudanais Omar el-Béchir. Toutefois, d'autres cas ont suscité également la résistance des autorités nationales comme le cas de l'ex-première dame ivoirienne Simone Gbagbo.

L'article 53 para. 3 a) particulièrement prévoit que le Conseil de sécurité, lorsqu'il est à l'origine du déclenchement des activités de la Cour, peut demander à la chambre préliminaire « d'examiner la décision de ne pas poursuivre prise par le Procureur en vertu des para. 1 ou 2 ». Les paragraphes visés prévoient que le procureur, afin de décider d'ouvrir une enquête ou de poursuivre, examine si l'affaire est recevable au titre de l'article 17. Or, l'article 17 précise les modalités d'application du principe de complémentarité.

Il n'y a que l'article 18 qui sème un petit doute. Cet article prévoit la notification de toute enquête à tous les États parties et aux États qui, selon les renseignements disponibles, auraient normalement compétence à l'égard des crimes dont il s'agit. Mais cette obligation ne lui incombe que dans les cas de saisine étatique (article 13 (a) et de saisine par le Procureur agissant *proprio motu* (article 13 c). Aucune référence n'est faite à l'article 13 (b) relatif à la saisine par le Conseil de sécurité.

Cependant, cette omission n'implique pas nécessairement que la compétence de la CPI devient prioritaire. Tout simplement, la complémentarité n'agira plus dans sa pleine mesure du fait de la soustraction de certaines obligations, notamment l'obligation d'information des États pour susciter leur intérêt à poursuivre.[125] Dès lors, si les tribunaux nationaux veulent poursuivre en pareille circonstance, la CPI n'est pas légitimée à agir. En conséquence, l'exercice par les juridictions africaines de leur priorité de compétence pourrait concourir efficacement à soustraire les ressortissants africains de la juridiction de la CPI. Il ne s'agit pas seulement de ceux des États territoriaux, mais de tout tribunal national qui peut asseoir sa compétence sur la base de tout critère de rattachement reconnu en droit pénal international.

61. L'institution d'une section de droit pénal international à la Cour africaine de justice et des droits de l'homme et des peuples ne libère pas les

[125] Le Procureur reste le *dominus* de l'action pénale. Le CS ne saisit la CPI que d'une situation et il revient au procureur de décider d'ouvrir ou non des enquêtes ou des poursuites sur des affaires particulières.

États africains de cette obligation, car cette Cour est elle-même complémentaire des juridictions nationales.[126]

Bien plus, les juridictions nationales paraissent pouvoir entreprendre virtuellement de manière plus efficace des poursuites à l'encontre des criminels qui, pour la plupart, ont commis leur forfait sur leur territoire. Il semble aussi plus évident de réunir, au niveau étatique, les renseignements et les témoignages, rendant possible l'ouverture d'un procès pénal international. Or, l'efficacité de la CPI dépend presque entièrement des États (contribution financière, coopération en vue de l'arrestation, enquêtes, transfert, détention et emprisonnement, etc.).

En outre, la CPI, pour l'instant, s'est surtout occupée du cas des grands criminels, les donneurs d'ordre ; laissant de côté les exécutants. Pourtant, si les donneurs d'ordre sont souvent à l'origine de conflits, ils ne sont pas ceux qui commettent directement les crimes. Il est même possible qu'ils constatent au même moment que les observateurs et la communauté internationale, la commission de ces crimes.[127] La classe des exécutants est une classe qui mérite donc tout autant l'attention de la justice pénale. Or, si toutes les enquêtes et poursuites sont dirigées vers la CPI, elle sera très rapidement débordée.[128]

La réduction du nombre d'affaires portées devant la CPI résultant de l'exercice par les juridictions nationales de leur compétence serait une preuve de succès de la communauté internationale dans la lutte contre l'impunité. L'ancien procureur en chef de la CPI Luis Moreno-Ocampo, le faisait déjà savoir lors de sa prestation de serment quand il déclarait : « *the effectiveness of the International Criminal Court should not be measured by the number of cases that reach it. On the contrary, complementarity implies that the absence of trials before this Court, as a consequence of the regular functioning of national*

[126] Voir art. 46 H du protocole portant amendements au Protocole portant Statut de la Cour africaine de Justice et des Droits de l'homme du 27 juin 2014.

[127] Par exemple, dans le cas des crimes de guerre.

[128] Elle diffère en effet des juridictions pénales internationales qui sont créées pour des situations particulières.

institutions, would be a major success"[129]. Toutefois, l'administration d'une telle justice ne manque pas de poser des difficultés.

2- Les difficultés envisagées

62. Les difficultés de mise en œuvre de la compétence des juridictions nationales africaines sont nombreuses.

63. La première difficulté, longtemps décriée et valant même pour certaines juridictions internationales est le risque de règlement de comptes, de politisation de la justice et de partialité des juges. De façon générale, on peut imaginer que la poursuite des personnes dans un pays dans lequel il s'est perpétré des crimes graves de droit international ne soit pas exempte de l'intrusion de considérations extra juridiques.

Pour être plus explicite, les juridictions et les juges qui les composent trouveront certainement des obstacles qui les empêcheraient de mener des poursuites à l'encontre de personnes ayant des connexions personnelles ou politiques avec le pouvoir en place. Il s'agit de ce qui est souvent appelé la justice des vainqueurs caractérisée par la sélectivité des poursuites. Ces derniers visent alors uniquement les criminels affiliés au pouvoir précédent. Ainsi, les tribunaux risqueraient de servir de forum répressif des opposants politiques. Ce risque est d'autant plus grand que la plupart des gouvernements sont caractérisés par l'absence de foi dans les valeurs incarnées par la notion d'État de droit.[130] Le cas du Rwanda, de l'Éthiopie et de la Côte d'Ivoire sont révélateurs de cette logique.

À côté de l'hypothèse de politisation de la justice pénale, se trouve le risque de partialité des juges. Ces derniers peuvent, étant originaires du pays en conflit ou du pays dans lequel les faits ont eu lieu, se laisser influencer par leurs sentiments personnels. Il est donc important et souhaitable que ces juridictions soient indépendantes, compétentes, efficaces et équitables.

64. La deuxième difficulté réside dans la situation socio-économique des États africains et se pose en termes de défaut de moyens humains et

---

[129] L. Moreno-Ocampo, lors de la cérémonie d'engagement solennel du Procureur de la CPI, La Haye, Pays-Bas, 16 juin 2003, p. 3, http//www2.icc-2673648B4896/143586/030616 moreno-ocampo-Français.pdf.

[130] P. Manirakiza, « L'Afrique et le système de justice pénale internationale », *op. cit.*, p. 44.

financiers. Ils sont pour la plupart des pays en développement qui ont encore des difficultés à satisfaire les besoins basiques de leurs citoyens. Les juridictions sont peu nombreuses et les infractions de droit commun à elles seules réussissent déjà à engorger les tribunaux. La plupart des magistrats sont formés pour juger les infractions de droit commun. Il y a donc lieu de constater une absence criante d'expertise locale en droit pénal international, droit applicable à la répression des crimes internationaux et qui est une combinaison des règles et principes en vigueur dans plusieurs branches du droit international et parfois même découlant des systèmes juridiques étrangers à certains juges nationaux. Il pourrait dès lors se poser un problème de moyen humain en termes de qualité et de quantité. Il en va de même des enquêteurs (police judiciaire).

Le problème de la qualité pourrait se résorber par les séminaires de renforcement des capacités, des stages de formation et l'introduction de modules de formation sur le droit pénal international dans les écoles de magistrature, ou mieux la formation de magistrats spécialisés en droit pénal international. Toutefois, la formation du personnel judiciaire et de police ne doit pas se limiter aux questions de droit, mais aussi couvrir les aspects militaires ou tout autre aspect nécessaire à la compréhension des crimes de droit international et du contexte de leur commission. Cette formation peut d'ailleurs s'étendre aux avocats, aux fonctionnaires de l'armée, de la justice et des affaires étrangères[131], au public, afin que les autorités se sentent soutenues dans leurs enquêtes et les poursuites de personnes devant les tribunaux nationaux.[132]

Pour ce qui est de la quantité, elle va de pair avec le problème des moyens financiers. L'accroissement en nombre du personnel judiciaire implique un coût de formation et une augmentation de la masse salariale.

---

[131] Citons l'exemple du tribunal de district de l'Etat du Texas, aux États-Unis dont l'ignorance des obligations de son pays en matière de coopération avec le Tribunal pénal international pour le Rwanda a pu l'amener à refuser de répondre à la requête du tribunal, qui lui demandait de lui remettre un ressortissant rwandais. Cas cité par Amnesty International, *Liste actualisée des principes à respecter en vue d'une mise en œuvre efficace de la Cour pénale internationale. Campagne pour la justice internationale*, Doc. Public, IOR 53/009/2010, EFAI, Mai 2010, p. 26.

[132] Amnesty International, *Liste actualisée des principes à respecter en vue d'une mise en œuvre efficace de la Cour pénale internationale. Campagne pour la justice internationale, op. cit.*

Les pays africains risquent aussi de manquer de moyens financiers pour mener les enquêtes et les poursuites. En fait, les crimes graves de droit international sont souvent commis dans un contexte généralisé et impliquent l'interrogation d'un grand nombre de personnes, les descentes sur les lieux de crimes qui parfois couvrent toute l'étendue du territoire et les territoires voisins, la protection des témoins dont le coût est non négligeable. Il pourrait donc être difficile pour un État en reconstruction (la plupart du temps) de supporter de tels coûts.[133]

65. La troisième difficulté est liée aux problèmes d'accès, de langue et de compatibilité des systèmes et traditions juridiques. Ces derniers ne font que renforcer l'ampleur des difficultés. Anne Marie La Rosa, dans un rapport, explique qu'un juge, qui avait eu à présider une affaire concernant la commission d'actes de génocide 0 des dizaines de milliers de kilomètres de son tribunal, a souligné l'impact psychologique d'une telle entreprise et indiqué qu'il en resterait probablement marqué pour le reste de ses jours.[134]

66. La solution à tous ces problèmes, pour les États africains, est de conjuguer leurs efforts et d'instituer entre eux une coopération et entraide judiciaire et un fonds d'aide régional à la répression des crimes graves de droit international.

En ce qui concerne la coopération, si les règles pénales de fond et de forme sont posées, il reste que leur efficacité doit être assurée par l'élaboration d'un système de coopération entre États d'une part et entre les États avec la section de droit pénal international de la Cour africaine d'autre part. Cette coopération donnera alors la possibilité à l'État du *forum déprehensionis* ou à la Cour africaine, d'avoir tous les éléments de l'infraction, et de procéder à l'exécution de sa décision ou des mesures conservatoires tel le gel des avoirs si ceux-ci se trouvent dans un État différent.[135]

---

133 Le coût sera d'autant plus élevé si ce sont les juridictions d'un Etat étranger africain qui décident de mener les poursuites. Par exemple, le Sénégal a demandé la somme de 27,4 millions d'euros pour financer le procès contre Hussein Habré.

134 A.M. LA ROSA, *Prévenir et réprimer les crimes internationaux : Vers une approche « intégrée » fondée sur la pratique nationale*, *op. cit.*, p. 55.

135 C. Tchaya Tchatat, *Essai sur le Statut pénal du Chef d'Etat*, *op. cit.*, p. 506.

Le statut de la Cour africaine de justice et des droits de l'homme pose déjà l'obligation pour les États parties de coopérer avec elle et de l'assister dans la poursuite des crimes qui relèvent de sa compétence.[136] Ce principe de coopération avec la Cour africaine étant posé, il revient maintenant aux États de signer des accords bilatéraux, mieux multilatéraux de coopération et de s'assurer qu'une telle coopération ait effectivement lieu lorsque sont poursuivis, au niveau national, les auteurs de crimes graves réprimés dans le statut de Rome de la Cour pénale internationale.[137]

En effet, Il ne s'agit pas de s'opposer uniquement à la compétence de la CPI, mais de se mettre ensemble pour faire en sorte que les crimes graves de droit international soient effectivement jugés, soit par les juridictions nationales africaines, soit par la Cour africaine.

En ce qui concerne le fonds d'aide à la répression des crimes graves de droit international, les États africains devraient mettre de côté, à l'aide des contributions nationales et des aides qui pourraient provenir des Organisations non gouvernementales et d'autres institutions nationales et internationales ou de particuliers, un fonds qui pourrait être débloqué pour un État qui désire poursuivre des crimes graves commis sans avoir les moyens financiers suffisants.

---

[136] Il s'agit de la coopération pour : l'identification et la localisation des personnes ; la réunion des témoignages et la production des preuves ; le service des documents ; l'arrestation, la détention ou l'extradition des personnes, la cession ou le transfert de l'accusé devant la Cour ; l'identification, le suivi, le blocage et la saisie des produits, biens, avoirs et instruments des crimes dans le but d'une éventuelle confiscation, sans préjudicier les droits d'autrui ; toute autre forme d'assistance qui n'est pas interdite par la loi de l'Etat sollicité en vue de faciliter l'enquête et le jugement des crimes tombant sous la compétence de la Cour. Art. 46 L du statut de la Cour africaine de justice et des droits de l'Homme.

[137] Quelques accords de coopération bilatéraux ou multilatéraux en matière judiciaire et d'extradition existent déjà, même s'ils n'ont pas pour principal objet la facilitation de la répression des crimes graves de droit international. Pour ne citer que quelques unes, voir Accord de coopération en matière de police entre le Cameroun et le Nigeria du 27 mars 1972 ; Accord de coopération judiciaire entre le Cameroun et le Nigeria du 27 mars 1972 ; Traité bilatéral d'entraide judiciaire entre le Burkina Faso et la Côte d'Ivoire de juillet 2014 ; Accord d'extradition entre les Etats membres de la CEMAC du 28 janvier 2004 ; Accord de coopération judiciaire entre les Etats membres de la CEMAC du 28 janvier 2004 ;

67. La coopération et l'entraide judiciaires, couplées avec le fonds d'aide à la répression des crimes graves, permettront aux juridictions nationales de réprimer efficacement les crimes graves de droit international et de bloquer par la même occasion l'action de la CPI qui est tributaire de leur défaillance.

La répression effective des crimes graves relevant de la compétence de la CPI par les juridictions africaines (nationales ou régionales) est donc un moyen de contrecarrer l'action de la CPI à l'encontre des ressortissants africains. Toutefois, si la voie répressive semble être une voie permettant de réduire les interventions de cette juridiction en Afrique, il reste que cette voie ne devrait être utilisée qu'en dernier recours, en aval lorsque les atrocités ont déjà été commises.

68. Il serait en effet également possible de paralyser l'action de la CPI par des actions en amont ayant pour objectif de prévenir la commission des crimes graves relevant de la compétence de la CPI. Ceci passe par une priorité donnée par les politiques africains aux voies pacifiques de résolution de conflits (il s'agit par exemple d'éviter des situations de guerre) ; de la formation des soldats et citoyens au droit humanitaire. De manière générale, les États doivent prendre toutes les mesures nécessaires pour que les règles et les sanctions applicables soient intégrées dans leur système de référence, et pour qu'elles soient connues et dûment appliquées. Il convient aussi, par le biais de mesures éducatives, d'inculquer aux individus ce qui est autorisé et ce qui ne l'est pas. En fait, l'efficacité du message de la sanction dépend du degré d'intériorisation de la norme sanctionnée par les personnes susceptibles de la violer, en particulier les porteurs d'armes.[138] Le droit international pénal doit avoir été intégré au point que le respect de ses règles soit devenu un véritable réflexe[139].

Conclusion

69. Il était question dans cette étude de déterminer les moyens que peuvent utiliser les États africains pour soustraire leurs ressortissants de la compétence de la CPI. Le statut de Rome, étant une convention soumise à

---

[138] A. M. La ROSA, *op. cit*, p. 64.
[139] *Idem.*

ratification des Etats, ce n'est en principe que cette ratification qui rend les ressortissants d'un État justiciables de la CPI. L'acceptation de la compétence de la CPI sans que l'Etat soit partie à la Convention produit le même effet. Dans ce contexte, pour permettre à leurs ressortissants d'échapper à la compétence de la CPI, les États africains doivent s'abstenir de ratifier le statut de Rome ou d'accepter la compétence de la CPI, dénoncer la ratification si elle avait déjà eu lieu. Ils peuvent également choisir de se limiter à un certain type d'infraction, notamment le report de la compétence de la Cour pour les crimes de guerre. À côté de ces mesures affectant la dévolution de compétence à la CPI, existe une autre qui empêche, au contraire l'exercice libre par la CPI de sa compétence. Il s'agit du défaut de coopération avec les organes de la CPI. Ces mesures ne permettent cependant pas de bloquer entièrement l'action de la CPI envers les ressortissants d'États africains.

70. En effet, si pour la plupart des conventions, le défaut de ratification ou la dénonciation de la ratification sont des entraves totales à leur application à l'État tiers, dans le cas du statut de Rome, les mesures sus-énumérées permettent de limiter la compétence de la CPI sans pour autant la paralyser entièrement. La CPI reste compétente dans plusieurs cas de figure : lorsqu'une situation lui est soumise par le Conseil de sécurité des Nations unies dans l'exercice de sa mission de maintien de la paix ou lorsque l'infraction est commise sur le territoire d'un État partie à la convention de Rome par des ressortissants africains. Dans ces hypothèses, aucun lien de rattachement n'est recherché entre l'Africain infracteur et la CPI.

71. Il a cependant été relevé que la création de la CPI et la ratification du statut de Rome par un État ne dessaisissent pas cet État de sa juridiction à l'égard des crimes réprimés dans le statut qui s'y seraient commis ou qui tomberaient sous le coup de sa compétence telle que définie par ses lois internes. La CPI ne peut intervenir, selon les termes de la convention de Rome que si l'Etat normalement compétent est défaillant. Dès lors, les États africains peuvent choisir la voie de concurrence. Cette dernière peut se faire individuellement ou de manière concertée. Elle consiste pour les États africains à s'assurer que leurs juridictions nationales poursuivent effectivement et efficacement les crimes graves de droit international. Pour ce faire, un certain nombre de mesures doivent être prises, notamment la mise sur pied d'un arsenal juridique permettant de réprimer les infractions visées et la poursuite effective des auteurs de tels crimes.

72. Ces mesures ne sont pas cependant sans poser des difficultés. Ces difficultés ont trait au risque de règlement de comptes, de partialité des juges et de politisation de la justice ; au défaut des moyens humains et financiers.

Ces difficultés peuvent se résoudre par : la formation des autorités intervenant dans la chaîne judiciaire au droit pénal international, à défaut de formation de magistrats spécialisés et de la création de juridictions spécialisées ; la coopération interétatique ; la création d'un fonds d'aide à la répression des crimes graves de droit international.

73. À côté de ces voies intervenant en aval, des actions de sensibilisation et d'éducation doivent avoir lieu en amont pour éviter que les ressortissants africains commettent les crimes relevant de la compétence de la CPI. Mais une fois que le crime a été commis, l'éviction de la compétence de la CPI ne peut se faire de manière efficace qu'autant que les moyens choisis tendent à la répression des crimes et partant, à la lutte contre l'impunité des auteurs d'infractions portant atteinte à l'intérêt de l'humanité ; ce pour quoi la CPI a été créée en complément aux juridictions nationales.

74. Dans cette optique, son intérêt pour les crimes commis en Afrique lui confère un rôle de protection des peuples africains. Mais, il faut bien que le peuple africain soit protégé non seulement des dangers du dedans, mais également des dangers du dehors, que la CPI s'intéresse à d'autres populations qui subissent des crimes similaires à ceux perpétrés en Afrique ; qu'elle n'intervienne vraiment qu'en cas de défaillance constatée des juridictions nationales compétentes. Ce n'est qu'ainsi qu'elle remplirait sa mission de départ, c'est-à-dire poursuivre les crimes qui menacent la paix et la sécurité de l'humanité quels qu'en soient la provenance et les auteurs en complément des juridictions nationales. On imagine donc que des poursuites dirigées contre des ressortissants d'autres continents pourraient redonner confiance aux Africains envers cette institution.

Cependant, la révolte manifestée par les États africains, qui en apparence n'est que la résultante de l'intervention de la CPI en Afrique, ne cacherait-elle pas autre chose ?

75. En effet, dans cinq (5) cas sur les huit (8) situations connues par la CPI, ce sont les pays eux- mêmes qui ont demandé à la Cour de prendre en charge des procédures qu'ils ne pouvaient assumer, et pour certains au moment même où la polémique sur la partialité de la CPI battait son plein.[140]

Il paraît alors que les États africains sont prompts à réagir contre l'exercice de la compétence de la CPI lorsque sont en cause des dirigeants en exercice. Dans le cas contraire, la CPI reçoit leur coopération et souvent ce sont les États eux-mêmes qui la saisissent des affaires mettant en cause des dirigeants déchus et leurs partenaires dans le crime. On pourrait ainsi imaginer que c'est plutôt l'article 27, sur la non pertinence de la qualité officielle et des immunités, en particulier la non pertinence de la qualité de chef d'État en exercice, qui fait problème.[141]

---

[140] C'est le cas de l'Ouganda (voir lettre de renvoi émanant du gouvernement ougandais reçue à la CPI le 22 décembre 2003), de la RDC (voir lettre du gouvernement de la RDC datant du 19 avril 2004 déférant la situation dans ce pays à la CPI. Quoique intervenu après la menace d'ouverture de poursuites *proprio motu* par le Procureur de la CPI), de la République centrafricaine (voir Lettres de saisine de la CPI, Gouvernement de la République centrafricaine, du 22 décembre 2004 et de la présidente de la République centrafricaine du 30 mai 2014), de la Côte d'ivoire (Voir les lettres du gouvernement ivoirien du 14 décembre 2010 et du 03 mai 2011) et du Mali (voir la lettre de renvoi du ministre de la Justice garde des Sceaux malien datant du 13 juillet 2012). Le CS a déféré deux des trois affaires restantes à la CPI (situation au Soudan et situation en Libye) ; ce n'est que dans le cas du Kenya que la Chambre préliminaire a autorisé le Procureur à ouvrir des enquêtes « *proprio motu* ».

[141] Le Protocole portant amendements au Protocole portant Statut de la Cour africaine de Justice et des Droits de l'Homme du 27 juin 2014 créant une Section de Droit pénal international à la Cour africaine de Justice et des droits de l'Homme et des peuples, tout en reconnaissant dans son article 46 B, le principe de la non pertinence de la qualité officielle, exonère les chefs d'Etat ou de gouvernement en fonction ou tout autre haut responsable public en raison de ses fonctions. Voir l'article 46 A Bis de ce texte intitulé « immunités », qui dispose : « *Aucune procédure pénale n'est engagée ni poursuivie contre un chef d'État ou de gouvernement de l'UA en fonction, ou toute personne agissant ou habilitée à agir en cette qualité ou tout autre haut Responsable public en raison de ses fonctions* ».

LA RÉPONSE DE L'UNION AFRICAINE À « L'OFFENSIVE » DE LA COUR PÉNALE INTERNATIONALE : UNE APPROCHE JURIDICO-INSTITUTIONNELLE.

RASJPR N° 20

TCHEJIP TCHATCHOUANG

Résumé

Les critiques répétées de l'Union africaine à l'égard de la Cour pénale internationale (CPI), peuvent laisser croire que celle-ci est en faveur de la tolérance face aux crimes internationaux : c'est pourquoi il a semblé nécessaire d'effectuer une analyse des actes, qui tendent à démontrer sa ferme volonté de lutter contre les crimes graves affectant la société internationale. Elle le fait à travers une réforme institutionnelle qui attribue les compétences jadis reconnues à la Cour pénale internationale à une section de droit international pénal, nouvellement créée au sein de la Cour africaine de justice et des droits de l'homme. Concrètement, il pourrait s'agir d'une riposte de l'organisation sous régionale, à la « surdi-mutité » de la Cour pénale internationale, en ce qui concerne ses appels au respect de l'immunité des chefs d'État et de gouvernement en fonction. L'Union africaine, en affichant un certain degré d'engagement pour la lutte contre l'impunité, reste tout aussi partisane du respect du droit international coutumier quant aux immunités. C'est donc cette lecture différente du droit qui explique la réponse de l'Union face à l'offensive de la Cour pénale internationale.

Introduction

1- Nul ne peut dire aujourd'hui, encore moins penser quel avenir l'Union africaine réserve à la Cour pénale internationale. Pourtant, il y a quelques années dans la ferveur et l'euphorie des délégations présentes à

Rome[1], plusieurs délégués africains engageaient leurs pays respectifs au soutien de la mise en place d'une justice pénale internationale permanente. Ils y voyaient certainement une promotion des valeurs éthiques universelles, la lutte contre l'impunité et une plus grande contribution à la mise en œuvre effective du droit international humanitaire.

2- Sortis de l'individualisme[2] qui caractérisait les discussions avant Rome, les organismes régionaux, telle l'Union africaine semblaient avoir pris le relais pour convaincre ceux de leurs membres encore réticents à signer sans réserve les accords de Rome. Outre le plan régional, il en a été aussi le cas dans les organisations sous régionales comme la SADC[3] qui a adopté en juillet 1999 une loi-modèle permettant d'adapter les législations nationales aux exigences du statut de Rome : cela devrait faciliter l'harmonisation des législations et rendre plus aisée la ratification par les États membres. Les pays de l'Afrique de l'Ouest se sont également concertés en décembre 2000 à travers une conférence ouest-africaine sur la signature et la ratification du statut de la Cour pénale internationale tenue à Bamako sous les auspices de la CEDEAO.

---

[1]Le 10 juin 1998, les délégations de plus de 140 pays et des représentants de centaines d'organisations non gouvernementales et d'organismes intergouvernementaux divers se sont réunis à Rome pour traiter de la création d'une cour pénale internationale. Le 17 juillet 1998, 120 pays, par l'entremise de leurs hauts fonctionnaires et spécialistes, ont adopté sous forme de traité le *Statut de la Cour pénale internationale* (CPI).

[2] La négociation a été menée essentiellement par les gouvernements, mais tous les observateurs ont souligné le rôle essentiel joué par les ONG très bien organisées en une très puissante « coalition » utilisant largement les moyens de diffusion modernes (internet) et fournissant même une aide technique à certaines délégations gouvernementales de petits pays sans ressources humaines et diplomatiques suffisantes. Voir ; Serge Sur, « Vers une Cour pénale internationale : la Convention de Rome entre les ONG et le Conseil de sécurité », RGDIP, 1999, no 1, p. 29 (présentation critique). Pour une appréciation positive : William R. Pace, « The relationship between the International Criminal Court and Non-Governmental Organizations », p. 189, in Herman A.M. von Hebel, Johan G. Lammers et Jolien Schukking, Reflections on the International Criminal Court. Essays in Honour of Adriaan Bos, La Haye : T.M.C. Asser Press, 1999, xvii (l'auteur a été le président de la coalition des ONG).

[3]Southern African Development Community, Communauté de développement de l'Afrique australe.

3- L'Union africaine, préoccupée par de nombreuses violations des droits de l'Homme dans des parties du continent ; notamment que les hommes, femmes et enfants en Afrique ont été victimes de génocide, de crimes de guerre, de crimes contre l'humanité et d'autres crimes reconnus par les termes du droit international des droits de l'Homme et du droit international humanitaire; notant que les auteurs de ces crimes sont rarement traduits en justice et qu'un recours efficace est fréquemment nié aux victimes, voulait marquer d'une pierre blanche son rejet de l'impunité. Pour ce faire, elle a noté par elle-même que vingt-sept (27) États africains ont ratifié le statut de Rome et que des efforts sont déployés par certains d'entre eux pour donner un effet légal à l'application du statut de Rome au niveau national. Elle n'a pas caché sa profonde préoccupation quant au fait que certains gouvernements africains ayant ratifié le statut de Rome n'ont pas pris les mesures nécessaires pour en intégrer les dispositions dans le régime de droit au niveau national. L'Union africaine exhortait ainsi ses membres qui n'ont pas encore ratifié le statut de Rome à le faire et à adopter un plan d'action national pour une mise en œuvre efficace de statut de Rome au niveau national. Elle est même allée plus loin dans ses recommandations en demandant le retrait l'article 98[4] des accords bilatéraux sur l'immunité et s'abstenir de s'engager dans des actes qui réduiraient l'efficacité de la Cour, conformément à leurs obligations internationales[5].

4- Cette position de l'Union correspondait bien au souhait de l'institution quant à la coopération avec les autres institutions internationales. En effet, la Charte africaine des droits de l'homme et des peuples recommandait déjà dans son préambule de favoriser la coopération

---

[4] Selon cet article, « *1. La Cour ne peut poursuivre l'exécution d'une demande de remise ou d'assistance qui contraindrait l'État requis à agir de façon incompatible avec les obligations qui lui incombent en droit international en matière d'immunité des États ou d'immunité diplomatique d'une personne ou de biens d'un État tiers, à moins d'obtenir au préalable la coopération de cet État tiers en vue de la levée de l'immunité.*
2. La Cour ne peut poursuivre l'exécution d'une demande de remise qui contraindrait l'État requis à agir de façon incompatible avec les obligations qui lui incombent en vertu d'accords internationaux selon lesquels le consentement de l'État d'envoi est nécessaire pour que soit remise à la Cour une personne relevant de cet État, à moins que la Cour ne puisse au préalable obtenir la coopération de l'État d'envoi pour qu'il consente à la remise.

[5] Voir la résolution pour mettre un terme à l'impunité en Afrique et sur l'incorporation et la mise en œuvre du statut de Rome de la Cour pénale internationale (2005).

internationale en tenant dûment compte de la Charte des Nations unies et de la Déclaration universelle des droits de l'homme. Les États y reconnaissaient par ailleurs que les droits fondamentaux sont fondés sur les attributs de la personne humaine. Ce qui justifiait leur protection internationale. C'est donc cette protection que la juridiction criminelle internationale aspire à mettre en œuvre en réprimant les crimes les plus graves du droit humanitaire.

5- Depuis quelques années déjà, les premières poursuites devant cette juridiction ont été ouvertes. Plus qu'un secret de polichinelle, on constate que les seuls présumés criminels sont des Africains[6]. Comme si des crimes de guerre, des crimes contre l'humanité, des génocides et encore plus des crimes d'agression ne se commettaient pas ailleurs[7], l'Union africaine a semble-t-il considéré le continent comme une zone d'expérimentation des mécanismes de la CPI, mais encore plus comme *un instrument de punition des chefs d'État africains*[8]. Ce qui à ses yeux devient une offensive, une agression, voire une croisade contre des valeurs protégées comme l'institution qu'est le chef de l'État ou de gouvernement.

6- L'opinion publique africaine voyait en la seule existence de la Cour une mesure devant contribuer à la paix, à la sécurité et au bien-être du monde, qui étaient menacés par des crimes graves. La Cour, créée par un traité auquel les adhésions seraient volontaires pour ne pas être marquée du stigmate d'une justice imposée par un groupe d'États à l'égard d'un autre,

---

[6] Cinq situations ont été déférées à la Cour depuis 2003 : la République démocratique du Congo (RDC), l'Ouganda, la République centrafricaine (RCA), le Darfour-Soudan et la Jamahiriya arabe libyenne. Le Conseil de sécurité a déféré celles du Darfour et de la Libye à la Cour ; les autres situations n'ont pas été déférées par des Etats tiers, mais par les Etats concernés eux-mêmes, pratique généralement qualifiée d'« auto-saisines » (self-referrals). Enfin, après une autorisation de la chambre préliminaire II qui faisait suite à une demande du Procureur, une enquête a désormais été ouverte dans le cadre d'une sixième situation concernant les violences postélectorales au Kenya. En vertu d'une autorisation de la chambre préliminaire III, le Procureur a ouvert une septième enquête concernant la situation en Côte d'Ivoire.

[7] En effet, on pourrait se demander le pourquoi des renvois des situations du Soudan et de la Libye, à la différence de la Tchétchénie, de Gaza, de la Syrie, de l'Irak, etc.

[8] MOUANDJO (S.M), « Les institutions internationales, les pays du sud et la démocratie », Le journal de Tanger.

paraît aujourd'hui plus un élément d'expression de la puissance que du droit. En effet, l'une des particularités de la Cour pénale internationale dans le régime international semblait l'attachement à un certain égalitarisme, à *l'« indifférence des positions statutaires des criminels poursuivis »*[9]. Il s'agissait en quelque sorte de traiter « *les cas semblables de la même façon et les cas différents de façon différente* »[10], sans que la différence en cause ne soit fonction de la qualité de ressortissant d'une grande puissance. Pour beaucoup se jouait alors le passage d'une culture de l'impunité à une culture de la responsabilité, de la dissuasion sauvage à la dissuasion judiciaire, voire d'une société interétatique à une « *humanité souveraine* »[11]. Mais les espoirs suscités par le régime de Rome et son « esprit » d'origine demeurent pour l'instant inaccomplis. La Cour pénale internationale connaît nombre de difficultés depuis son entrée en vigueur. Son fonctionnement délicat trouve son explication majeure dans les résistances qu'elle a dû et qu'elle doit encore affronter. Notamment celle récente de l'Union africaine.

7- Le début du désamour entre les deux institutions commence effectivement avec les résolutions qui s'enchaînent[12] jusqu'à la résolution 1593 du 31 mars 2005 par laquelle le Conseil de sécurité décide de déférer la situation au Darfour au procureur de la CPI afin que la juridiction pénale internationale permanente reconnaisse les crimes commis depuis le 1er juillet 2002[13]. L'affaire Al Bashir, ainsi qualifiée, va sans doute marquer un tournant dans les relations entre l'Afrique et la juridiction criminelle de La Haye. Cette affaire a compromis sérieusement les relations entre cette cour et l'Union africaine qui, il y a peu d'années encore, exhortait ses États

---

[9]COTTEREAU (G), « Statut en vigueur, la Cour pénale internationale s'installe », A.F.D.I., 2002, pp. 129-161, p. 130.

[10] Selon l'adage qualifié par Herbert HART de premier fondement de l'idée de justice, in *Le concept de droit*, (trad. Michel Van de KERCHOVE), Bruxelles, Facultés universitaires Saint-Louis, 2005, p. 177.

[11]De FROUVILLE (O), « La Cour pénale internationale : une humanité souveraine ? », Les Temps Modernes, n° 610, 2000, pp. 257-288.

[12] La résolution 1547, S/RES/1547/2004, la résolution 1556, S/RES/1556/2004, et la résolution 1564S/RES/1564/2004.

[13] La résolution 1593 du 1er juillet 2005 du Conseil de sécurité, UN.Doc.S/RES.

membres non encore parties au statut de Rome à y adhérer[14]. La divergence est devenue tellement grande que lors de son 15e sommet et après des débats animés, l'Union africaine a reporté l'ouverture d'un bureau de liaison de la Cour pénale internationale à Addis-Abeba, et réitéré l'injonction faite à ses membres de ne pas coopérer dans l'affaire Bashir[15]. Les évènements au Kenya[16] et en Côte d'Ivoire[17] sont venus renforcer les craintes que l'Union africaine avait déjà de la Cour pénale internationale. Encore plus, au-delà de l'Union elle-même, les États membres, pris individuellement, ne dissimulent plus leur grande phobie à l'égard de la Cour pénale internationale[18]. Le 25e

---

[14] KAMTO (M), « L'affaire Al Bashir et les relations de l'Afrique avec la Cour pénale internationale », in Maurice KAMGA et Makane Moise MBENGUE (dir), *L'Afrique et le droit international. Variations sur l'organisation internationale (Liber Amicorum en l'honneur de Raymond Ranjeva)*, Paris, Ed., A. Pedone, 2013, P. 156.

[15] Voir « Décision, déclarations et résolution adoptées par la quinzième session ordinaire de la Conférence à Kampala (Ouganda) », le 27 juillet 2010, disponible sur le site http://www.africaunion.org/root/ua/Conferences/2010/juillet/Summit_2010_b/doc/DECISIONS/Assembly p. 23 (juin 2011).

[16]Sur autorisation de la Chambre préliminaire II donnée le 31 mars 2010, le Procureur de la CPI avait ouvert une enquête sur les violences à caractère politico-ethnique dont le bilan est de 1200 morts et plus de 300 000 déplaces, notamment dans la vallée du Rift. Le 15 décembre 2010, il a déposé devant les juges deux requêtes dans lesquelles il a demandé l'émission de citations à comparaître contre six responsables kenyans accusés d'avoir commis des crimes contre l'humanité. Parmi les responsables poursuivis, l'on compte trois ministres de l'actuel gouvernement d'union: le vice-premier ministre et ministre des Finances, Uhuru Kenyatta, aujourd'hui président de la République, le ministre de l'Enseignement supérieur, William Ruto et le ministre de l'Industrialisation, Henry KipronoKosgey.

[17] Le président Alassane Ouattara, rival de Laurent Gbagbo, avait demandé à la CPI, le 3 mai 2011, d'enquêter sur les « crimes graves » commis lors des violences postélectorales qui se sont produites entre décembre 2010 et avril 2011. La Chambre préliminaire III a par la suite autorisé, le 3 octobre 2011, le Procureur à enquêter dans ce pays pour les crimes commis depuis le 28 novembre 2010 ainsi que sur les crimes susceptibles d'avoir été commis ultérieurement dans le cadre de cette situation.

[18]Auparavant, le sommet extraordinaire de l'UA tenu les 11 et 12 octobre 2013 à Addis-Abeba en Éthiopie avait déjà mis en exergue les rapports houleux qui prévalent entre l'Afrique et cette juridiction. À l'occasion, certains pays dénonçant un acharnement, ont même menacé de quitter la CPI. Dans un propos dur, HAILE MARIAM DESALEGN, premier ministre éthiopien, a qualifié la CPI de « chasse raciale ». « *Le traitement inique que nous avons subi de la part de la CPI est totalement inacceptable* », avait-il alors déploré. Lors d'un discours officiel, le président UHURU KENYATTA, qui a déféré le 12 novembre

sommet de l'Union africaine, tenu en juin 2015 à Johannesburg en Afrique du Sud, a donné une fois de plus l'occasion de comprendre à quel point la fracture entre les deux camps est profonde. La demande formulée par la CPI au pays hôte d'arrêter le président soudanais en séjour sur son territoire n'a pas reçu d'écho favorable. M. Béchir est retourné dans son pays sans en être inquiété. Comme pour davantage enfoncer le clou, Pretoria a fait savoir, lors d'un débat parlementaire, son intention de réclamer des réformes de la CPI[19]. Le 26e sommet tenu tout récemment à Addis-Abeba (janvier-février 2016), ne s'est non plus détourné de la question[20].

8- Comment comprendre donc que des États ou groupe d'États, qui clamaient tambour battant la fin de l'impunité des auteurs des crimes graves au début des années 2000, en viennent moins de deux décennies plus tard à rejeter celle-là qui apparaissait comme véritable rempart contre les atteintes massives aux droits de l'Homme ? Aux hypothèses de réponses, on ne saurait passer outre l'acharnement réel ou supposé de la Cour contre les Africains qui sans doute aura entraîné cette réaction virulente de l'Union africaine à savoir le contenu de l'article 46 *A bis : « Aucune procédure pénale n'est engagée ni poursuivie contre un chef d'État ou de gouvernement de l'UA en fonction, ou toute personne agissant ou habilitée à agir en cette qualité ou tout autre haut Responsable public en raison de ses fonctions »*.Issu de la réforme de la Cour africaine de justice et des droits de l'homme, cet article vient en réponse à l'article 27 du statut de Rome qui dispose : « 1-*Le présent Statut s'applique à tous de manière égale, sans aucune distinction fondée sur la qualité officielle. En*

2014 à La Haye à une convocation du Procureur FATOU BENSOUDA, s'est montré plus violent contre ce qu'il qualifie de « simple jouet » au service des Occidentaux. « *Les chefs d'Etat et de gouvernement en exercice ne devraient pas être poursuivis quand ils sont en fonction. Nous avons décidé de parler d'une seule voix afin d'être sûrs que nos préoccupations soient clairement entendues* ». « *Elle n'est plus le lieu de la justice, mais le jouet des pouvoirs impérialistes en déclin. Cette Cour agit sur demande des gouvernements européens et américain contre la souveraineté des Etats et peuples africains* », s'est-il insurgé.

[19] BAPELA (O), ministre adjoint des Affaires traditionnelles, qui s'exprimait au nom du gouvernement sud-africain, a affirmé devant les députés que si ces réformes n'étaient pas acceptées, son pays n'aurait pas d'autre choix que de reconsidérer son adhésion à la CPI.

[20] Le président Ouattara de Côte d'Ivoire affirmait en ce sens que la Côte d'Ivoire n'enverrait plus d'Ivoirien devant la Cour pénale internationale. Il précisait par la même occasion que l'Union africaine devrait développer les mécanismes pour que les Africains soient jugés en Afrique devant une cour africaine (interview France 24 du 4 février 2016).

particulier, la qualité officielle de chef d'État ou de gouvernement, de membre d'un gouvernement ou d'un parlement, de représentant élu ou d'agent d'un État, n'exonère en aucun cas de la responsabilité pénale au regard du présent Statut, pas plus qu'elle ne constitue en tant que telle un motif de réduction de la peine. 2- Les immunités ou règles de procédure spéciales qui peuvent s'attacher à la qualité officielle d'une personne, en vertu du droit interne ou du droit international, n'empêchent pas la Cour d'exercer sa compétence à l'égard de cette personne ».

9- La position issue du protocole portant amendements au protocole portant statut de la Cour africaine de justice et des droits de l'homme, qui par la même occasion créait une section criminelle au sein de cette institution, vient consacrer le « divorce » avec la Cour pénale internationale[21]. L'Union africaine, pour ainsi se démarquer des aspirations de la Cour pénale internationale, va choisir de procéder à une réforme de la structure juridictionnelle qui existait en son sein. On va ainsi fusionner la Commission africaine des droits de l'homme et des peuples et la Cour de justice de l'Union africaine pour aboutir à la Cour africaine de justice et des droits de l'homme de l'Union africaine. Ce qui sera le plus visible dans cette réforme est l'introduction au sein de la Cour d'une section de droit international pénal (I), qui laisse hautement place à une pluralité d'interprétations sur le plan juridique (II).

I- L'introduction d'une section de droit international pénal au sein de la Cour africaine de justice des droits de l'homme

10- La protection des droits de l'Homme est une préoccupation permanente de l'Union africaine. Toute une charte, certes inspirée d'autres textes internationaux, mais aussi bien adaptée à son aire géographique que novatrice, s'en charge. Au-delà des simples prescriptions de la Charte, un organe juridictionnel est prévu pour la sanction des violations desdits droits. L'organe, de nos jours réformé, est la Cour africaine de justice des droits de

[21]Le professeur Marcelin NGUELE ABADA en évoquant ce fameux article 27 affirmait qu'il s'agit là d'une disposition qui à elle seule justifierait les réticences et les résistances à la ratification du statut de la Cour pénale internationale, in « Les enjeux pour le Cameroun de la ratification du statut de la cour pénale internationale »,
Séminaire national sur la mise en œuvre du droit international humanitaire au Cameroun, Yaoundé, 22-23 mars 2000, p. 4.

l'homme, fusion de la Commission africaine des droits de l'homme et des peuples[22] et de la Cour africaine des droits de l'homme[23]. Cette institution nouvelle se subdivise en trois sections: une section des affaires générales, une section des droits de l'Homme et des peuples et une section du droit international pénal. La section du droit international pénal, comme son nom l'indique, est celle qui est en charge de la mise en œuvre du droit international humanitaire et donc une concurrente ou une semblable à la Cour pénale internationale. Il est donc nécessaire de se pencher sur sa compétence matérielle (A) et personnelle (B).

A- La compétence *rationae materiae* de la section de droit international pénal

11- La compétence d'attribution de la section de droit international pénal n'est pas exhaustive comme l'indique l'article 28 A du statut de la Cour africaine. Cependant, nous pouvons observer une double grille d'analyse de la compétence d'attribution de la section de droit international. La compétence concurrente avec la Cour pénale internationale (1) et la compétence propre ou exclusive de la section (2).

1- La compétence concurrente avec la Cour pénale internationale

12- La Cour établit sa compétence s'agissant des quatre crimes retenus par la Cour pénale internationale. En effet, les deux organes ont une conception identique desdits crimes. On peut néanmoins noter quelques modifications. Par exemple, dans la définition du crime d'agression, la Cour africaine préfère le terme "caractéristique" à celui de "nature" utilisé dans le statut de Rome, elle choisit ne pas faire allusion à la résolution 3314 (XXIX) du 14 décembre 1974, mais plutôt à l'acte constitutif de l'Union africaine et à la Charte des Nations unies. Le crime d'agression n'est pas selon la Cour africaine le seul acte de l'Etat, les organismes politiques qu'ils soient liés ou non à l'Etat sont de potentiels auteurs.

---

[22] La commission fut formellement installée le 2 novembre 1987 à Addis-Abeba. Elle était entre autres chargée de la promotion des droits de l'Homme et des peuples, de leur protection, de l'interprétation de toutes dispositions de la Charte et de l'exécution de toutes tâches que la Conférence des chefs d'Etat et de gouvernement pourrait lui confier. Voir article 30 et 45 de la Charte.

[23] Le protocole donnant naissance à la Cour africaine fut adopté le 10 juin 1998 à Ouagadougou. La Cour est entrée en vigueur le 25 janvier 2004.

13- En évoquant ainsi l'acte constitutif de l'Union, on doit y voir le respect des textes de l'institution notamment le pacte de non-agression et de défense commune du 31 janvier 2005[24]. Ce texte contient une définition de l'agression qui va au-delà de la définition retenue par l'Assemblée générale de l'ONU et par la conférence de révision de Kampala sur le statut de Rome. Le pacte y ajoute des éléments comme les actes d'espionnage qui pourraient être utilisés à des fins d'agression militaire contre un État membre, l'assistance technologique de toute nature, les renseignements et la formation au profit d'un autre État, pour utilisation aux fins de commettre des actes d'agression contre un État membre, l'encouragement, le soutien, l'acceptation ou la fourniture de toute assistance aux fins de commettre des actes terroristes et autres crimes transfrontaliers violents organisés contre un État membre. Le professeur KAMTO qualifie cette extension de douteuse[25]. Il remarque par la même occasion qu'elle dilue cette notion juridique dont les contours n'étaient déjà pas très précis[26].

14- Dans cette même veine, le professeur KAMTO trouve d'autres notions plutôt controversées. Il s'agit par exemple des notions de menace d'agression et d'action préventive[27]. Il faut certes remarquer que toutes ces notions, à la fois controversées et douteuses, ne figurent pas dans la définition donnée par l'article 28M de la Cour africaine. Cependant, les alinéas 2 et 3 de l'article 28 A en disent long sur les possibilités de compétence matérielle de la section de droit international pénal de la Cour africaine. Ils précisent entre autres que « *La Conférence peut étendre, sur consensus des États Parties, la compétence de la Cour à d'autres crimes afin de refléter le développement du droit international* »[28]. « *Les crimes relevant de la compétence ou dévolution à la Cour ne doivent souffrir d'aucune limitation* »[29].

---

[24] Voir le texte sur le site de l'union africaine, WWW. africa-union.org/official _documents.

[25] Voir KAMTO (M), *L'agression en droit international*, Pedone, Paris, 2010, p.63.

[26] *Ibid.*

[27] *Ibid.*

[28] Article 28 A al. 2.

[29] Article 28 A al. 3.

15- Cette texture ouverte des normes[30] de l'Union peut s'étendre aux autres crimes et notamment le crime contre l'humanité[31]. S'agissant de ce crime, la phrase introductive se lit ainsi ; « *Aux fins du présent Statut, on entend par « crime contre l'humanité » l'un quelconque des actes ci-après lorsqu'il est commis dans le cadre d'une attaque* ***ou d'une activité généralisée*** *ou systématique lancée contre toute population civile et en connaissance de cette attaque ou activité* ». Le terme « ***d'une activité généralisée*** » qui ne figure pas dans le statut de Rome laisse présumer un élargissement de facteurs pouvant conduire à la qualification du crime contre l'humanité[32]. Il scelle définitivement la controverse sur le contexte de commission de ce crime. Comme pour le crime d'agression, les alinéas ci-haut énumérés sont aisément applicables au regard de l'énoncé de sa définition. "*Les autres actes inhumains de caractère analogue causant intentionnellement de grandes souffrances ou des atteintes graves à l'intégrité physique ou à la santé physique ou mentale*" contenus aussi bien dans les statuts de Rome que de la Cour africaine attestent de l'ouverture du crime à d'autres éléments. En l'envisageant dans sa composante axiologique, l'incrimination porte sur le caractère fondamental des valeurs protégées par les conventions des droits de l'Homme y compris la Charte africaine des droits de l'homme et des peuples. Le crime rassemblera de ce fait les valeurs protégées par les droits étatiques, mais aussi les valeurs non désignées *expressiver bis* par les textes internationaux et même nationaux. Il en va ainsi de tout crime susceptible de porter atteinte à la dignité humaine. Et pour rejoindre LE GUHENEC, « *le crime qui n'a pas seulement pour objet de blesser ou de donner la mort, mais*

---

[30] Sur la notion de texture ouverte des normes, voir H. J. A. HART, The concept of Law, Bruxelles, 1976, pp. 55 et s.

[31] Voir TSIMI NTONO (G), *Le paradigme du crime contre l'humanité et la renaissance du pluralisme juridique dans les droits pénaux africains ; contribution à une théorie de l'inter normativité des systèmes pénaux nationaux en transition,* Université de Yaoundé II, 2012, 699p.

[32] C'est avec la jurisprudence Tadic II que l'exigence d'un contexte martial a cessé d'être un élément constitutif du crime contre l'humanité. Il suffit que les actes soient commis dans le cadre d'une attaque généralisée ou systématique contre des populations civiles quelle qu'elles soient. L'Union africaine vient ainsi en élargir le contexte par le terme activité généralisée, car il ne semble pas évident d'établir une synonymie entre attaque et activité généralisée. Même si l'une peut englober l'autre, on peut y déceler la réduction du seuil d'intention.

celui qui accompagne ces blessures et cette mort d'une violation volontaire, délibérée et gratuite de la dignité de celles ou de ceux qui en sont les victimes »[33].

16- Pour les crimes de guerre et de génocide, l'Union africaine consacre la définition retenue par la Cour pénale internationale[34]. En consacrant les crimes du statut de Rome, l'Union africaine manifeste son attachement à la promotion de l'éthique universelle et à l'impunité des crimes graves du droit international humanitaire. Cependant, la Cour africaine, comme pour se démarquer de la Cour pénale internationale, consacre d'autres crimes dont la section de droit international pénal dispose d'une compétence exclusive.

2- La compétence propre ou exclusive de la section de droit international pénal

17- Outre les crimes pour lesquels la Cour pénale internationale et la section de droit international de la Cour africaine peuvent établir de façon concurrente leur compétence, la section de droit international pénal de la Cour africaine a choisi de se démarquer de la Cour pénale internationale en prévoyant d'autres crimes dont elle serait compétente. Il s'agit des crimes relatifs au changement anticonstitutionnel de gouvernement[35], de la Piraterie[36], du Terrorisme[37], du Mercenariat[38], de la Corruption[39], du

---

[33]DESPORTES (F) et LE GUHENEC (F), *Droit pénal général*, Paris, Economica, coll., « corpus droit privé », 15e éd., 2008, p. 21-27.

[34] Ces deux entités consacrent la définition retenue à l'article 2 de la Convention pour la prévention et la répression du crime de génocide de 1948.

[35] Charte africaine de la démocratie, des élections, et de la gouvernance (2007/2012) ; Déclaration sur les changements anticonstitutionnels de gouvernement (2000).

[36] Convention de 1958 sur la haute mer, Convention relative aux infractions et à certains autres actes survenant à bord des aéronefs du 14 septembre 1963. Convention sur le droit de la mer du 10 décembre 1982.

[37] Voir les conventions et protocoles ci-après ; Convention de l'OUA sur la prévention et la lutte contre le terrorisme (1999/2002) et le protocole à la convention de l'OUA sur la prévention et la lutte contre le terrorisme

[38] Convention internationale contre le recrutement, l'utilisation, le financement et l'instruction de mercenaires du 4 décembre 1989. Convention de l'OUA sur l'élimination du mercenariat en Afrique du 3 juillet 1977.

[39] Convention de l'Union africaine sur la prévention et la lutte contre la corruption (2003/2006) ; Convention internationale pour la répression des attentats terroristes à l'explosif, 1997 ; Convention internationale pour la répression du financement du terrorisme, 1999 ; Convention internationale pour la répression des actes de terrorisme

Blanchiment d'argent[40], de la Traite des personnes[41], du Trafic illicite de stupéfiants[42], du Trafic illicite de déchets dangereux[43], de l'exploitation illicite des ressources naturelles[44]. Le choix de l'abondance opéré par la Cour africaine de justice et des droits de l'homme peut faire peser le doute sur la capacité de cette dernière à pouvoir poursuivre ces crimes. La Cour pénale internationale, en se limitant en son temps à quatre crimes, estimait qu'aller au-delà, en embrassant tous les crimes faisant l'objet de conventions internationales, pourrait entraîner des risques de justiciabilité devant la Cour. Nous nous attarderons uniquement sur les crimes relatifs au changement anticonstitutionnel de gouvernement dans la mesure où tous les autres ont fait l'objet de définition conventionnelle au niveau universel.

18- Ce crime est défini à l'article 28 E comme suit; « *1. Aux fins du présent Statut, « changement anticonstitutionnel de gouvernement » signifie le fait de commettre ou d'ordonner de commettre les actes suivants, avec l'intention d'accéder ou de se maintenir illégalement au pouvoir : a) un putsch ou un coup d'État militaire perpétré contre un gouvernement démocratiquement élu ; b) toute intervention de mercenaires visant à renverser un gouvernement démocratiquement élu ; c) toute intervention de dissidents armés ou de mouvements rebelles ou à travers l'assassinat politique destinée à renverser un gouvernement démocratiquement élu ; d) tout refus d'un gouvernement en place de remettre le pouvoir au parti ou au candidat sorti vainqueur d'élections libres, justes et régulières ;e) tout amendement ou révision de la Constitution ou des instruments juridiques, considéré comme une violation des principes du changement démocratique de gouvernement ou non conforme à la Constitution.*

---

nucléaire 2005, *Convention de Maputo* du 11 juillet 2003 sur la prévention et la lutte contre la corruption ; *Convention des Nation Unies contre la corruption,* 9 décembre 2003.

[40] Résolution sur la fuite illicite des capitaux en provenance d'Afrique (2013).

[41] Protocole additionnel à la Convention des Nations Unies contre la criminalité internationale visant à prévenir, réprimer et punir la traite des personnes, en particulier des femmes et des enfants du 15 novembre 2000 ; Protocole additionnel à la Convention des Nations Unies contre la criminalité internationale visant à prévenir, réprimer et punir le trafic de migrants par terre, air et mer du 15 novembre 2000.

[42] Convention des Nations Unies contre le trafic illicite de stupéfiants et de substances psychotropes du 19 décembre 1988.

[43] Convention pour la prévention de la pollution par les navires du 2 novembre 1973.

[44]Convention africaine sur la conservation de la nature et des ressources naturelles (Révisée) (2003).

f) toute modification substantielle des lois électorales durant les six (6) mois précédant les élections sans le consentement de la majorité des acteurs politiques. 2. Aux fins du présent Statut « un gouvernement démocratiquement élu » est défini conformément aux instruments juridiques de l'Union africaine.

19- En faisant une brève analyse de ce crime, il en ressort deux catégories d'auteurs. D'abord les gouvernants. Ils sont les seuls susceptibles de commettre les éléments constitutifs du crime tels que définis par l'alinéa 1 d, e et f. L'autre catégorie est constituée de toute personne capable de diriger un groupe ayant des velléités de conquérir le pouvoir par des mécanismes non démocratiques. Il s'agit ici des putschistes et des chefs rebelles. Ce crime est-il réellement susceptible de poursuites ? Loin de constituer une question anodine, il est un fait constant que les régimes africains sont très régulièrement confrontés au changement de Constitution dans le but de se maintenir au pouvoir[45]. Sans vite aller en besogne, l'opérationnalité de la Cour permettra de comprendre la politique de l'Union africaine face à ce fléau qui mine l'idéal démocratique sur le continent. À l'aune de cette analyse, on peut aussi s'interroger sur la réalité de la compétence personnelle de la Cour africaine de Justice qui semblait être le véritable point de démarcation avec la Cour pénale internationale.

B- La compétence *rationae personae* de la section de droit international pénal

20- À l'observation et à l'analyse des crimes retenus, il serait impossible de penser qu'il y a une véritable démarcation en termes de compétence matérielle entre la Cour pénale internationale et la Cour africaine dans sa section de droit international pénal. En effet les crimes, qui semblent pour la Cour africaine constituer un élargissement de compétence, ne sont pas essentiellement ceux tournés vers la sauvegarde de la morale de l'humanité et donc les plus graves du droit international. Cependant, la rupture avec la Cour pénale internationale apparaît dans la compétence personnelle des

[45] Depuis le changement constitutionnel de 2008 au Cameroun, plusieurs autres Etats sont rentrés dans la danse parfois avec des fortunes diverses. C'est le cas au Burkina Faso, en République du Congo, au Burundi, au Rwanda, en République démocratique du Congo etc.

deux entités juridiques. Il y apparaît une réelle opposition (1) qui n'est pas sans effet sur la relation entre les deux entités (2).

1- L'opposition réelle de la compétence *rationae personae* de la section de droit international pénal à celle de la Cour pénale internationale

21- L'Union africaine ne s'éloigne pas de la Cour pénale internationale uniquement par l'attribution à la section de droit international pénal d'une compétence élargie sur le plan *rationae materiae. Rationae personae,* la section de droit international pénal de la Cour africaine élargit encore, contrairement à la CPI, sa compétence aux personnes morales autres que les États. Ce n'est pourtant pas là le point de rupture entre les deux institutions. La pomme de discorde est la question de l'immunité des chefs d'État et de gouvernement en fonction.

22- Le statut de Rome est on ne peut plus clair sur les questions liées à l'immunité. Il déclare : « *1. Le présent Statut s'applique à tous, de manière égale, sans aucune distinction fondée sur la qualité officielle. En particulier, la qualité officielle de chef d'État ou de gouvernement, de membre d'un gouvernement ou d'un parlement, de représentant élu ou d'agent d'un État, n'exonère en aucun cas de la responsabilité pénale au regard du présent Statut, pas plus qu'elle ne constitue en tant que telle un motif de réduction de la peine. 2- Les immunités ou règles de procédure spéciales qui peuvent s'attacher à la qualité officielle d'une personne, en vertu du droit interne ou du droit international, n'empêchent pas la Cour d'exercer sa compétence à l'égard de cette personne* »[46]. À l'opposé de cet article, le statut de la Cour africaine de justice accorde une immunité absolue au dirigeant en fonction. Il dispose : « *Aucune procédure pénale n'est engagée ni poursuivie contre un chef d'État ou de gouvernement de l'Union africaine en fonction, ou toute personne agissant ou habilitée à agir en cette qualité ou tout autre haut Responsable public en raison de ses fonctions* »[47]. Cet article apparaît selon les observateurs comme un bouclier contre les poursuites engagées contre les chefs d'État africains en fonction. Toutefois, il n'est pas précisé que la Cour africaine n'est compétente que pour les crimes commis par les Africains. Par contre, l'immunité ne concerne elle que les chefs d'État et de gouvernement

[46] Article 27 Statut de Rome de la Cour pénale internationale.

[47] *Article 46A bis.*

africains. Cela suppose donc que tout autre chef d'État ou de gouvernement pourrait faire l'objet de poursuites de la Cour si jamais le procureur venait à démontrer qu'il a :

i- incité, encouragé, organisé, ordonné, aidé, financé, conseillé ou participé en tant qu'auteur principal, coauteur principal ou est complice de n'importe laquelle des infractions énoncées dans le présent Statut ;

ii- aidé, ou soutenu la perpétration de n'importe laquelle des infractions énoncées dans le présent Statut.

Ou est :

iii- un complice avant ou après tout fait ou de quelque manière que ce soit participe à une collaboration ou conspiration à la commission de n'importe laquelle des infractions énoncées dans le présent Statut ;

iv- iv. tenté de commettre n'importe laquelle des infractions énoncées dans le présent Statut[48].

23- Cette rédaction, que nous pouvons qualifier de maladroite, montre à profusion l'intention de rupture qui anime les dirigeants africains à l'égard de la Cour pénale internationale. Il s'agit d'une volonté hâtive de soustraire les dirigeants africains la justice pénale universelle et d'une démonstration de son incapacité à faire entendre sa voix sur la scène internationale qui se manifeste par un repli sur soi et une non-participation à la mise en place des mécanismes de la justice universelle.

2- Les effets de l'opposition des compétences personnelles

24- L'antinomie des articles 27 et 46 des statuts de la Cour pénale internationale et de Cour africaine de justice et des droits de l'homme peut produire des effets néfastes en ce qui concerne les relations entre les deux institutions. Surtout, le statut de la juridiction universelle ne prévoit pas un mode de coopération avec les organismes internationaux régionaux. On peut donc voir à travers la création de la section de droit international pénal au sein de la Cour africaine un rejet de l'universalité de la Cour pénale internationale (a), mais, surtout une mise à mal de la coopération avec la juridiction criminelle universelle (b).

---

[48] Article 28N.

a- Le rejet de l'universalité de la Cour pénale internationale par l'Union africaine

25- La mise en place par l'Union africaine d'une Section de droit international pénal recèle un sentiment de rejet de la Cour pénale internationale et par conséquent de ses aspirations comme véritable juridiction à compétence universelle. En effet, la Cour pénale internationale est compétente pour les crimes commis sur le territoire des États parties, ou de ceux qui, sans être partie, défèrent la situation devant elle. De plus, le procureur peut engager d'office des poursuites.

26- L'un des éléments caractéristiques de l'universalité de la Cour pénale internationale est la possibilité de saisine par le Conseil de sécurité de l'ONU[49]. La reconnaissance d'un pouvoir d'intervention du Conseil de sécurité dans l'action des juridictions pénales internationales est rendue possible par la consubstantialité réciproque entre les considérations liées au maintien de la paix et celles relatives à la justice pénale internationale[50]. C'est donc dans ce sens qu'elle fonde ses pouvoirs sur le chapitre VII de la Charte des Nations unies.

27- En croisant les regards, il ne fait aucun doute que l'Union africaine désire mettre à mal le principe d'universalité reconnu à la Cour pénale internationale. Il ressort clairement du protocole portant amendement du statut de la Cour africaine que les crimes commis sont soumis au procureur soit par un État partie, par la conférence des chefs d'État et de gouvernement de l'Union africaine ou le Conseil de paix et de sécurité de

---

[49] Selon l'article 13 b) La Cour peut exercer sa compétence à l'égard d'un crime visé à l'article 5, conformément aux dispositions du présent Statut : Si une situation dans laquelle un ou plusieurs de ces crimes paraissent avoir été commis est déférée au Procureur par le Conseil de sécurité agissant en vertu du Chapitre VII de la Charte des Nations Unies.

[50] À l'analyse, l'intervention du Conseil de sécurité dans la création ou dans le fonctionnement des juridictions pénales internationales ou internationalisées répond à des préoccupations qui ne sont pas exclusivement juridiques. En effet, en l'absence d'intervention du Conseil de sécurité, la juridiction pénale internationale constitue potentiellement une menace pour les membres permanents très réticents à l'idée de voir leur personnel militaire investi dans les théâtres d'opérations militaires soumis à la compétence d'un organe judiciaire extérieur. C'est dans ce cadre que se comprend l'adoption de mécanismes d'articulation ou de neutralisation permettant au Conseil de sécurité d'intervenir dans la procédure devant la Cour pénale internationale.

l'Union africaine. Le bureau du procureur peut ordonner d'office des enquêtes sur la base d'informations sur des crimes relevant de la compétence de la Cour[51]. Cette attitude traduit sans ambages un rejet systématique des mécanismes de poursuites extra-africaines[52]. Aussi, la non-exécution d'un mandat d'arrêt de la Cour pénale internationale pris sur saisine du Conseil de sécurité par des États membres des Nations unies parties au statut de Rome ne serait-elle pas constitutive d'une violation du droit international et spécifiquement, une violation des droits et obligations des autres parties au statut de Rome, si les conditions requises pour l'exécution du mandat d'arrêt en cause sont remplies[53]. D'autant plus que le mandat d'arrêt de la Cour pénale internationale participe des règles secondaires de mise en œuvre d'obligations *erga omnes*. Le refus itératif de coopérer à l'arrestation et à la remise d'Omar el-Béchir témoigne avec éclat du refus des États africains de coopérer pour les procédures devant les juridictions internationales pénales résultant d'initiatives extra-africaines. Pierre BERTHELOT observe à ce compte qu' « *aucun* (des "États" africains) *n'a apporté son soutien à la* [...] *décision de la Cour Pénale Internationale, du moins au niveau officiel* »[54].

28- Ce rejet est justifié par la posture politique du Conseil de sécurité qui, selon les Africains, manque d'objectivité dans le traitement des situations susceptibles d'entraîner des poursuites devant la Cour pénale internationale[55]. Un tel rejet ne pourra se traduire en pratique que par une

---

[51] Art. 46 H et 46 G.

[52] Voir sur la question : MOUANGUE KOBILA (J), « L'Afrique et les juridictions internationales pénales », Cahier Thucydide n°10, 2012 ; pp 17 et s.

[53]KELSEN (H) écrit ainsi que « *si l'Etat est oblige par le traité de se conformer à la décision du tribunal, l'inexécution de la décision peut être considérée comme une violation du traité par lequel le tribunal a été établi* » et il envisage en conséquence « *l'application de sanctions par les autres Etats contractants contre l'Etat responsable de l'acte illicite*. Voir de cet auteur, *Théorie du droit international public, RCADI*, 1953, III, vol. 84, pp.97.

[54]BERTHELOT (P) « La CPI face à la tragédie du Darfour », Géopolitique africaine, n° 35, juillet, septembre 2009, pp. 245.

[55] L'exclusivité du pouvoir au Conseil de sécurité des Nations Unies de renvoyer des cas à la CPI, lorsqu'on sait que c'est en vertu de ce pouvoir que le Conseil a saisi la CPI de la situation au Darfour le 31 mars 2005, et de la situation en Libye le 26 février 2011 sur la base du chapitre VII de la Charte des Nations Unies, a conduit l'UA à envisager dans un premier temps l'amendement de l'article 13 du Statut de Rome ; un peu plus tard, l'article 16 du Statut de Rome « *pour permettre à l'Assemblée générale des Nations Unies de surseoir à*

réticence, voire un refus systématique de coopérer avec la juridiction pénale universelle.

b- La mise à mal de la coopération avec la Cour pénale internationale

29- La question du rapport de l'Union africaine avec la Cour pénale internationale est de tout intérêt depuis que cette dernière a décidé de ne pas coopérer en vue de l'arrestation du président soudanais Omar el-Béchir, objet de plusieurs mandats d'arrêt de la Cour pénale internationale depuis le 4 mars 2009. D'autant plus qu'une position similaire a été adoptée par l'Union africaine à la suite du mandat d'arrêt émis contre le colonel Kadhafi 27 juin 2011. Lors du sommet de Malabo en juillet 2011, l'Union africaine a engagé ses États membres à ne pas collaborer à l'exécution de ces mandats d'arrêt. Elle jugeait en effet que « *le mandat d'arrêt publié par la Chambre préliminaire contre le Colonel Kadhafi complique sérieusement les efforts visant à trouver une solution politique négociée à la crise en Libye, et à traiter les questions d'impunité et de réconciliation de manière à prendre en compte l'intérêt mutuel des parties concernées.* » Elle a dès lors recommandé « *aux États membres de ne pas coopérer à l'exécution du mandat d'arrêt et* a *demandé au Conseil de Sécurité des Nations Unies de mettre en œuvre les dispositions de l'article 16 du Statut de Rome en vue d'annuler le processus de la CPI sur la Libye dans l'intérêt de la justice ainsi que de la paix dans ce pays* »[56].

30- En effet, n'étant pas partie au statut de Rome[57], l'organisation panafricaine n'a pas non plus conclu d'accord de coopération avec la Cour

enquêter ou à poursuivre, pour une (1) année, au cas où le Conseil de sécurité n'aurait pas pris de décision dans un délai spécifique ».

[56]Voir UA, Conférence de l'Union, 17e Session ordinaire, 30 juin–1er juillet 2011, Malabo (Guinée Equatoriale), Décision sur la mise en œuvre des décisions de la Conférence relatives à la Cour Pénale Internationale, Assembly/AU/Dec.366(XVII), Doc.EX.CL/670(XIX), point 6 ; cf. également http://fr.rian.ru/world/20110702/190023677. html (consulte le 21 Novembre 2011).

[57]VANDEPOORTER (A) dans le contexte de l'application des décisions du Conseil de sécurité au sein de l'Union européenne considère que les auteurs s'accordent généralement sur ce qu'une organisation internationale n'est pas directement liée par les décisions d'une autre organisation internationale à laquelle tous ses Etats membres appartiennent. In « L'application communautaire des décisions du Conseil de sécurité », AFDI, 2006, pp. 102,136.

pénale internationale[58]. Au contraire, elle a formellement rejeté l'examen de la demande de la Cour pénale internationale d'ouvrir un bureau de liaison à Addis-Abeba, son siège, consacrant ainsi son opposition à la Cour pénale internationale. Aussi, les articles 9, 10, 86 et 111 du statut de Rome, conçu dans une perspective wesphalienne, imposent aux seuls États de coopérer avec la Cour pénale internationale. Cette lecture est spécifiquement corroborée par l'article 90 du statut de Rome, dédié aux demandes concurrentes. Ces dispositions laissent libre champ aux organisations régionales, tiers imprévu dans ce diptyque classique, de contester la compétence de la Cour pénale internationale et d'entraver la mise en œuvre de ses actes judiciaires. On pouvait bien se douter de l'extension de cette résistance aux États membres de l'Union africaine.

31- Sommé de s'expliquer par la Cour pénale internationale sur son refus d'arrêter le président soudanais, le Tchad a répondu qu'étant membre de l'Union africaine, il devait se plier à la décision prise par cette organisation interdisant à ses États membres de coopérer avec la Cour pénale internationale aux fins de la remise du président Omar el-Béchir. Dans le même ordre d'idées, le Malawi a également sur ce cas fondé son refus de coopérer sur l'incompatibilité entre l'arrestation d'un chef d'État et l'immunité que celui-ci tient du droit international coutumier ainsi que sur l'incompatibilité de la position de l'Union africaine avec la coopération attendue par la Cour pénale internationale. Lors du sommet de l'Union africaine en juillet 2010, le président en exercice, le malawite Bingu WA MUTHARIKA déclarait déjà que mettre un chef d'État en exercice sous le coup d'un mandat d'arrêt porte atteinte à la solidarité africaine, ainsi qu'à la paix et à la sécurité en Afrique pour lesquelles nous nous sommes battus pendant des années[59]. Cette option, si elle venait à être suivie, aiderait à

[58]En comparaison, la CPI a conclu un accord de coopération et d'assistance avec l'Union européenne le 10 avril 2006. Il est entre en vigueur le 1er mai de la même année.

[59] BAYAMASISSAO, « La CPI : l'Occident juge l'Afrique », Africa 24 Magazine, n° 3, juillet 2011, p. 144. Il est à noter cependant que des Etats voulant améliorer leur image coopèrent ou choisissent simplement de ne pas s'attirer des ennuis. C'est le cas du Malawi qui, dans le but de s'attirer les faveurs des investisseurs étrangers, décida de ne pas organiser le sommet de l'Union africaine. La raison de ce refus est simple : il ne veut pas recevoir un second blâme de la Cour pour réception d'Al Bashir sur son sol. Le changement d'attitude est le fruit d'une alternance politique. Le nouveau gouvernement cherche à se démarquer

imposer la posture de l'Union africaine. Une posture qui mérite juridiquement d'être interprétée.

II- L'interprétation de la posture de l'Union africaine vis-à-vis de la Cour pénale internationale

32- La relation Union africaine – Cour pénale internationale est de plus en plus tumultueuse. Cela s'est matérialisé, comme on l'a vu plus haut, par la réforme de la Cour africaine de justice et des droits de l'homme. Cette réforme, à l'issue de laquelle est née une section de droit international pénal, dit long sur les intentions de l'Union africaine à l'égard de la Cour pénale internationale. Pourquoi ne pas consacrer une section criminelle tout court ? Le droit criminel est un des domaines de souveraineté de l'État. Parler de section criminelle serait comme instaurer une juridiction supérieure devant connaître des affaires nationales qui seraient contestées devant elle. C'est donc dire que le choix de section de droit international pénal, accompagné de la notion de compétence internationale pénale, n'est pas anodin.

33- En effet, les compléments« droit international pénal »et « compétence internationale pénale »rattachés à la section renvoient aux infractions pénales définies au niveau international, aux crimes qui transcendent l'espace national et à ceux qui peuvent aussi être réprimés par les droits nationaux[60]. On retrouve dans cette dénomination, une volonté certaine de l'organisation d'attribuer à la section de sa cour, les compétences autrefois dévolues à la seule Cour pénale internationale. Si c'est le cas en ce qui concerne la compétence *rationae materiae*, l'Union africaine voulait par cette réforme manifester son mécontentement quant à la violation du sacro-

---

du précédent. L'aide extérieure constitue 40% du budget du Malawi. La précédente administration en perdant le soutien des bailleurs de fonds a ainsi compromis le fonctionnement de l'Etat. Des membres du Sénat américains avaient demandé au président OBAMA la suspension de l'aide américaine en faveur du Malawi.

[60]Une esquisse de la définition du droit international pénal peut être donnée en se focalisant sur son objet, à savoir la poursuite « *des crimes les plus graves qui touchent l'ensemble de la communauté internationale* ». Monsieur Olivier DE FROUVILLE, quant à lui, estime que « *le droit international pénal recouvre l'ensemble des normes de droit international public qui ont pour but la protection de l'ordre public international par la prohibition de certains comportements qui y portent atteinte, sous peine de sanction exécutoire, ainsi que la répression de ces comportements* » in *Droit international pénal, Sources, Incriminations, Responsabilité,* éd. Pédone, 2012, p.3.

saint principe de l'immunité des chefs d'État et de gouvernement consacré par le droit international coutumier (A). Ce qui ne constitue pas une entrave de l'Union africaine à la lutte contre l'impunité des crimes graves du droit humanitaire, encore moins aux espoirs des victimes d'obtenir réparation (B).

A- L'idéal africain du respect du principe coutumier des immunités des chefs d'État et de gouvernement

34- Le droit international coutumier, crée une exception à l'immunité des chefs d'État si des juridictions internationales demandent leur arrestation, pour la commission de crimes internationaux. À ce titre, appliquer certaines dispositions du statut de Rome soulève de nombreux problèmes pour les États. Le droit international en général n'y échappe pas non plus. La Commission du droit international, relativement à certaines de ces questions, conclut que la norme postérieure n'annule pas automatiquement la norme antérieure en droit coutumier, tout au moins et particulièrement dans les cas où les traités visés ont des États parties différents[61]. La doctrine est divisée sur la question des immunités, la position choisie dans le statut de Rome n'est pas exempte de critiques. Il semble donc important d'analyser la position de Cour internationale de justice (1) avant la consécration sibylline du respect des immunités dans le statut de Rome (2).

1- La position de la Cour internationale de justice

35- La priorité doit-elle être accordée au droit international ou à la poursuite pénale ? Le moment véridique de le savoir a été fixé par la Cour internationale de justice le 14 février 2002. En effet, la justice internationale avait été saisie par la République démocratique du Congo, contestant le mandat d'arrêt émis contre son ministre des Affaires étrangères, en raison du respect des règles du droit international coutumier consacrant l'immunité aux dirigeants et représentants d'États. La CIJ, dans un *obiter dictum* a énoncé qu'il n'existe pas, « *en droit international coutumier [...] une exception quelconque à la règle consacrant l'immunité de juridiction pénale et*

---

[61]KOSKENNIEMI (M), « Fragmentation du droit international: difficultés découlant de la diversification et de l'expansion du droit international », Rapport du Groupe d'étude de la Commission du droit international, établi sous sa forme définitive par Genève, 1er mai-9 juin et 3 juillet-11 août 2006, A/CN.4/L.682.

l'inviolabilité des ministres des Affaires étrangères en exercice, lorsqu'ils sont soupçonnés d'avoir commis des crimes de guerre ou des crimes contre l'humanité »[62]. Ce principe s'applique *a fortiori* à l'immunité des chefs d'État, des chefs de gouvernement et des agents diplomatiques en fonction. Selon le *dictum* de la CIJ dans l'affaire du mandat d'arrêt précité : « *Un ministre des affaires étrangères ou un ancien ministre des affaires étrangères peut faire l'objet de poursuites pénales devant certaines juridictions pénales internationales dès lors que celles-ci sont compétentes »*[63]. Mais il est entendu, que cette compétence ne peut s'exercer que « *conformément au droit international »*[64], comme rappelé dans la déclaration de Kampala[65].

36- L'émission et la diffusion, par les autorités belges, du mandat d'arrêt du 11 avril 2000, constituent, pour la CIJ, une méconnaissance de l'immunité du ministre des Affaires étrangères en exercice du Congo et, plus particulièrement, viole l'immunité de juridiction pénale et l'inviolabilité dont jouissait alors M. Yerodia en vertu du droit international. Ces actes ont engagé la responsabilité internationale de la Belgique[66]. Dès lors, la Cour estime que la Belgique doit, par les moyens de son choix, mettre à néant le

---

[62]Voir CIJ, affaire du *Mandat d'arrêt du 11 avril 2000 République démocratique du Congo c. Belgique*, Arrêt du 14 février 2002, par. 60.

[63]*Ibid.*

[64]*Ibid*, paragraphe 58. Une décision allant dans le sens du respect des immunités internationales de l'Etat, même accusé des crimes internationaux les plus graves a été rendue dans l'affaire des *Immunités juridictionnelles de l'Etat (Allemagne c. Italie); Grèce intervenant*, tranchée le 3 février 2012. Au point 1 du dispositif de cet arrêt, la CIJ a dit pour droit *que la République italienne a manqué à son obligation de respecter l'immunité reconnue à la République d'Allemagne par le droit international coutumier en permettant que soient intentées à son encontre des actions civiles fondées sur des violations du droit international humanitaire commises par le Reich allemand entre 1943 et1945*. Au point 2 de cet important arrêt, la CIJ énonce que *la République italienne a manqué à son obligation de respecter l'immunité reconnue à la République fédérale d'Allemagne par le droit international en prenant des mesures d'exécution forcée visant la Villa Vigoni.*

[65]Voir Conférence de Révision du Statut de Rome de la Cour Pénale Internationale, Kampala, 31 mai –11 juin 2010, Documents officiels, le deuxième considérant du préambule de la Déclaration de Kampala, RC/Décl. 1, doc. RC/11, http://www.icc,cpi.int/Menus/ASP/Sessions/Official+Records/Review+Conference.htm" (consultee"le"19"fevrier"2012),"p."25."

[66] Mandat d'arrêt du 11 avril 2000 (République démocratique du Congo c. Belgique), arrêt, C. I. J. Recueil 2002. Par75

mandat en question, en informer les autorités auprès desquelles ce mandat a été diffusé[67]. Il [le ministre des Affaires étrangères] bénéficie d'une immunité de juridiction pénale et d'une inviolabilité totale à l'étranger[68]. La Cour, à cet égard, ne reconnaît pas l'existence d'une exception en droit coutumier à l'inviolabilité du ministre des Affaires étrangères en exercice. Ils peuvent être accusés de crimes de guerre ou crimes contre l'humanité, leur protection demeure inchangée.

37- Dans le même ordre d'idées, la CIJ a affirmé que les immunités de fonction ne protégeaient pas les hauts fonctionnaires qui en bénéficient face aux crimes internationaux contre l'humanité qu'ils auraient commis, et ce même pendant leur mandat, puisque ceux-ci ne peuvent être considérés comme faisant partie de leur fonction officielle, mais plutôt comme des actes privés. En ce qui concerne les immunités personnelles en revanche, la CIJ est arrivée à la conclusion que, la personne qui en bénéficie est intouchable tant qu'elle exerce sa fonction. Mais que celles-ci ne devraient pas faire obstacle à ce que sa responsabilité pénale pour des crimes internationaux soit engagée après son mandat[69].

38- La Cour pénale internationale, semble confondre la question de la *responsabilité pénale individuelle des chefs d'État*, qui est un acquis en droit international pénal, avec celle des mesures judiciaires contre un chef d'État en fonction, alors même qu'il est protégé par une immunité personnelle[70].

---

[67] Par76 ; La CIJ refusera de se prononcer sur les conséquences pour les Etats tiers d'un différend entre la Belgique et le Congo, tout en s'estimant consciente des répercussions que sa décision pourrait avoir.

[68] *Ibidem*, Par 53

[69] *Ibidem* note 124, pp. 322-325. Certaines juridictions nationales ont eu à agir dans le même sens : voir notamment Regina v. Bartle and the Commissioner of Police for the Metropolis and others EX Parte Pinochet, Chambre des *Lords*, 25 novembre 1998.

[70] La question de l'étendue de la protection octroyée par ces immunités face à des crimes de droit international humanitaire s'est relativement vite posée. Comme l'expose P. GAETA, le problème est de mettre en balance deux intérêts opposés : « *the need to stem or at leastrestrain impunity, which requires that immunities accruing to state agents and officials forforms of 'state criminality' do not apply, and the necessity to guarantee the smooth functioning of international relations and the discharge of official functions on behalf of states"* in 'Immunities and Genocide', in: GAETA Paola (édit.), *Oxford Commentaries on International Law: The UN Genocide Convention,* Oxford, Oxford University Press, 2009, p. 312. Voir aussi, DONNEDIEU de VABRES Henry, 'The Nuremberg Trial and the

Salvatore ZAPPALA note ainsi qu' « *on peut déduire de la Jurisprudence dominante que les organes situés au sommet de la hiérarchie d'un État, avec fonction de représentation de l'État en tant que tel à l'étranger* [...] *jouissent d'immunités personnelles pour toute la durée de leur mandat* »[71]. Le droit international coutumier confère à chaque chef d'État ou membre de gouvernement une immunité absolue. Il faut tout de même dire que immunité ne signifie pas impunité, mais il faut aussi remarquer que la fronde des États africains a commencé avec ce mandat d'arrêt.

39- L'Union africaine épouse l'idéologie de l'immunité absolue et l'admet comme fondement de la non-coopération avec la Cour pénale internationale. Il est cependant difficile de présager de l'attitude des Etats, leur réaction face à l'immunité des chefs d'État dépendra de leur appartenance au traité. Ainsi, "*while the Statute of the ICC denies immunity to Heads of State, in principle it cannot affect the immunity of Heads of States of non-parties. States that are parties to the Statute would violate international law if they hand over a Head of State of a non-party to the ICC. The situation for the SCLS seems to be the same*"[72]. De même, un État tiers au Statut n'a pas à respecter un tel mandat d'arrêt et livrer un suspect à la Cour pénale internationale. Ainsi, le Tchad n'aurait par exemple pas à arrêter Al Bashir. Bien plus, en s'abstenant, il respecte le droit, estimant qu'il crée une exception au principe de l'immunité du chef de l'État, lorsqu'une juridiction internationale demande l'arrestation de celui-ci pour la commission de crimes internationaux.

Modern Principles of International Criminal Law', in: METTRAUX Guénaël (édit.), *Perspectives on the Nuremberg Trial*, Oxford, Oxford University Press, 2008, pp. 265-266. Les affaires *Le Procureur c. Anto Furundzija*, Chambre de première instance, 10 décembre 1998, Affaire n° IT-95-17/1-T, par. 140 et *Le Procureur c. Slobodan Milosevi"*, Chambre de première instance III, 8 novembre 2001, Affaire n° IT-99-37-PT, par. 26-34.

[71] ZAPPALA (S), *La justice pénale internationale*, Paris, Montchrestien, coll. Clefs politique, 2007, p.98.

[72]ROMANO (P-R.C) et André NOLLKAEMPER, The Arrest Warrant Against The Liberian President, Charles Taylor, The American Society of International Law, juin 2003, http://www.asil.org/insigh110.cfm

2- La consécration sibylline dans le statut de Rome

40- L'article 98 du statut de Rome pose en effet le principe du respect de l'immunité, ainsi que l'exigence procédurale de la levée de l'immunité avant l'exécution d'une demande de remise ou d'assistance faite à un État. Il s'agit là d'un bémol à l'application systématique et sans réserve de l'article 27 al. 2 dudit statut. L'article 98 est lu comme impliquant que, « *l'État requis doit faire prévaloir l'immunité d'une personne recherchée ou de ses biens sur une demande d'assistance de la Cour* »[73]. Seule une lecture biaisée[74] du Statut de Rome pourrait déboucher sur le sens de la reconnaissance d'un tel droit de poursuite sur la base de l'article 27 al. 2 de cet instrument.

41- La question de la compatibilité des deux règles s'est largement posée en doctrine. Quant à la portée et à l'étendue de l'article 98 paragraphe 1, deux interprétations sont possibles. La première consiste à penser que les "*États tiers*", qui sont visés par cet article ne concernent pas seulement les États non parties, mais incluent aussi les États parties. Cette première interprétation neutraliserait l'effet voulu par l'article 27 paragraphe 2, puisque la renonciation de cet « *État tiers* » serait alors la condition *sine qua non* à l'accomplissement d'une demande d'assistance judiciaire faite par la Cour, et prendrait de ce fait la forme d'une restriction aux obligations tant générales que spécifiques de coopération contenues dans le statut de Rome.

42- La deuxième interprétation consiste au contraire à considérer que les "*États tiers*" visés par l'article 98 paragraphe 1 concernent uniquement les États non parties au statut de Rome. Cette dernière interprétation a pour effet de rendre le principe contenu dans l'article 27 paragraphe 2 effectif, puisqu'elle obligerait alors l'État requis à exécuter une demande de coopération faite par la Cour, sans avoir à obtenir préalablement l'accord de l'« *État tiers* » dans tous les cas où cet État est également partie au statut[75]. À l'égard des États non parties cependant, la situation ne diffère en rien de celle exposée plus haut, puisque l'accord préalable de celui-ci serait alors

---

[73] Voir DAVID (E), *La Cour pénale internationale*, RCADI, vol. 313, 2005, pp. 441,442.

[74] MOUANGUE KOBILA (J), *op cit.*, p. 24.

[75]KRESS Claus / PROBST Kimberly, « Commentaire de l'article 98 du Statut de Rome », in:TRIFFTERER Otto (édit.), *Commentary of the Rome Statute of the International Criminal Court, Observers'notes, articleby article*, Baden-Baden, Nomos, 2e éd., 2008, pp. 1607-1608.

indispensable, étant donné que les obligations légales qui découlent du statut ne s'imposent pas à lui, et ne pourraient permettre à la Cour de déroger au droit international en matière d'immunité.

43- Dans le communiqué consécutif aux décisions de la Cour pénale internationale, sur la non coopération alléguée du Tchad et du Malawi, la Commission de l'Union africaine avait indiqué que : *"[a]rticle 27 appearsunder the part of the Statute setting out general principles of criminal law and appliesonly in the relationship between the Court and the suspect. In the relationship between the Court and states, article 98(1) applies"*[76].Quoi qu'il en soit, l'article 98 fait expressément échec à toute mesure d'exécution contre les personnes protégées par le droit international, la Cour internationale de justice ayant conclu que « *la compétence n'implique pas l'absence d'immunité et l'absence d'immunité n'implique pas la compétence* »[77]. L'Union africaine ne s'est donc pas trompée, en repoussant les décisions de la Cour pénale internationale relatives à la non coopération alléguée du Malawi et du Tchad dans un communiqué solidement argumenté[78]. En dépit de toutes ces vicissitudes normatives, l'Union africaine ne se détourne pas de la question de l'impunité des crimes du droit humanitaire.

B- L'attachement de l'Union africaine à la lutte contre l'impunité des crimes graves du droit humanitaire

[76]Voir Press release on the decisions of pre-trial Chamber 1 of the International Criminal Court (ICC) pursuant to article 87(7) of the Rome Statute on the alleged failure by the Republic of Chad and the Republic of Malawi to comply with the cooperation requests Issued by the Court with respect to the arrest and surrender of President Omar Hassan al Bashir of the Republic of the Sudan, Addis-Ababa, 9 January 2012, http://www.au.int/fr/content/press,release,decisions,pre,trial,chamber,i,international,criminal,court,icc, pursuant, article (consultee"le"13"fevrier"2012).

[77] Affaire du *Mandat d'arrêt*, *op. cit.*Paragraphe, 59.

[78]Voir le Communiqué du 9 janvier 2012, Press Release on the Decisions of Pre-Trial Chamber I of the International Criminal Court (ICC) Pursuant to Article 87(7) of the Rome Statute on the Alleged Failure by the Republic of Chad and the Republic of Malawi to Comply with the Cooperation Requests Issued by the Court With Respect to the Arrest and Surrender of President Omar Hassan Al Bashir of the Republic of the Sudan, http://www.au.int/fr/content/press,release,decisions,pre,trial,chamber,i,international,criminal,court,icc,pursuant,article (consulte le 15 janvier 2012).

44- La position des États africains et de l'Union africaine vis-à-vis de la Cour pénale internationale, qui se situe, dans la tension entre la paix et la justice, à mi-chemin entre une impunité de facto et la responsabilité pénale des plus hauts responsables de l'État, s'apparente à une survivance de l'ambivalence originelle du *jus in bello* dans l'Afrique noire précoloniale, entre le respect d'une « esquisse » de droit humanitaire et sa méconnaissance répétée[79]. Pourtant, à l'observation de l'attitude des membres de l'Union africaine, la priorité semble être accordée au maintien de la paix (1), la justice apparaissant comme l'ultime solution (2).

1- La priorité au maintien de la paix

45- La pacification complète du continent africain constitue la finalité première de l'Union africaine. Elle veut ainsi sur le plan régional, continuer la vieille pratique de l'ONU. Mais il faut dire que l'organisme sous régional reste bien dans ce cadre sous tutelle de cette dernière. Certes les deux se fixent des objectifs de maintien de la paix, aucun d'eux n'a pourtant donné une définition du concept. Il s'agirait donc d'une notion entourée de flou terminologique. Elle conduit à une multitude de sens : rétablissement de la paix, imposition de la paix, stabilisation de la paix, etc. On doit tout de même situer ce concept entre les mécanismes traditionnels de résolution pacifique des conflits, que sont la médiation, l'établissement des faits, et même des mesures d'intervention militaire[80].

46- BERLIA Georges pense que le maintien de la paix est « *la limitation de la compétence de la guerre* »[81]. Mieux vaudrait dans ce contexte, considérer la définition de INDAR JIT RIKE qui entend par maintien de la paix, l'idée de « *prévention, confinement, apaisement et arrêt des hostilités entre États par l'intermédiaire de l'intervention d'une tierce partie organisée et dirigée internationalement et faisant usage de personnel militaire, policier et civil…* »[82]. L'histoire démontre certes l'échec de l'Organisation de l'unité africaine quant à la mise en œuvre des mécanismes de maintien de la paix

---

[79]MOUANGUE KOBILA (J), « L'Afrique et les juridictions internationales pénales », Cahier Thucydide n°10,Etude – Février, 2012.

[80] La notion est donc située entre le Chapitre VI et VII de la Charte des Nations Unies.

[81] BERLIA (G), *Le maintien de la paix : Doctrine et problèmes*, Montchrestien, Paris, 1976, p. 20.

[82] INDAR (J R), *The theory and practice of peacekeeping*, London, C. HURST & CO, 1984.

sur le continent[83]. On n'en dira pas autant pour son successeur, sauf à penser que la résolution des conflits en Afrique est un travail de Sisyphe. Que non, l'Union africaine, en rupture avec le passé, a choisi d'instaurer un Conseil de paix et de sécurité en son sein, comme pour faire du maintien de la paix sa priorité.

47- La sonnette d'alarme lancée par Kofi Annan, alors Secrétaire général des Nations unies : « *tant que l'Afrique ne sera pas venue à bout de ses conflits, les progrès resteront précaires même dans les pays éloignés du théâtre des hostilités* »[84], aurait permis de comprendre que paix et développement sont indissociables. C'est dans ce sens que les articles 3 et 4 de l'Acte constitutif de l'Union africaine, bien que reprenant les objectifs de l'Organisation de l'unité africaine, en ajoutent des considérations nouvelles comme la démocratie, l'État de droit, la bonne gouvernance, qui sont des éléments pouvant entraîner la rupture de la paix. L'innovation fondamentale en matière de maintien de la paix consiste dans le droit pour l'Union africaine, d'« *intervenir dans un pays membre sur décision de la Conférence dans certaines circonstances graves comme les crimes de guerre, le génocide et les crimes contre l'humanité et le droit des États membres de solliciter l'intervention de l'union pour restaurer la paix et la sécurité* »[85]. Il y a ici une révélation de la volonté de l'Union africaine de recourir d'abord au maintien de la paix, avant la justice. Cette volonté est plus ressentie dans le pacte de non-agression et de défense commune de 2005 où sont consacrées les notions de « menace d'agression » et « d'action préventive ».

2- Le recours secondaire à la justice

48- L'Afrique s'oppose-t-elle comme le pensent certaines organisations[86] à la lutte contre l'impunité, engagée depuis la Première Guerre mondiale

---

[83] Voir ATCHE BESSOU (R), *Les conflits armés internes en Afrique et le droit international*, Thèse, Université Cergy Pantoise, 2008, 482P.

[84] KOFFI (A), « Afrique, plaidoyer pour un nouveau départ », in *Jeune Afrique Economie*, n°297, p.110.

[85] Art. 4 alinéa h de l'Acte constitutif de l'UA.

[86] BAUDOUIN (P), Président d'honneur et responsable du Groupe d'action judiciaire de la FIDH, a déclaré que « ***Cette décision ternit tous les efforts de l'UA en faveur de la justice sur le continent et constitue un retour en arrière inquiétant, qui risque de servir de précédent et d'alibi pour de chefs d'Etat d'autres régions. Elle enfreint les dispositions de l'Acte constitutif de l'UA, va à l'encontre de l'intérêt et des obligations des États qui ont***

contre les responsables des crimes graves ? Nous ne le pensons pas. En effet, la rupture de la collaboration avec la Cour pénale internationale ne devrait pas être perçue comme favorable à l'impunité. L'Union africaine n'a pas cessé sa collaboration, elle a juste mis en place un organe concurrent capable de sanctionner les présumés coupables de crimes graves. Dans l'impossibilité de « *séparer l'individu criminel de l'Etat responsable* », l'on ne saurait engager des poursuites contre les intéressés qu'après la cessation de leurs fonctions, l'Etat ne pouvant jamais être criminel[87]. Cette option ne marque pas moins l'attachement de l'Afrique à la répression des crimes graves. Son comportement, lors de la mise en œuvre de certaines poursuites, confirme bien ce choix.

49- Dans l'affaire Gbagbo par exemple, la position de l'Union africaine n'était pas anti-collaborationniste. L'Union africaine n'est pas montée au créneau pour s'insurger contre les poursuites entamées contre ce dernier et d'autres de ses collaborateurs. Il en va de même des situations déférées à maintes reprises par les États africains devant la Cour pénale internationale. Cette attitude de l'Union montre qu'elle n'est pas contre des poursuites, qui portent naturellement sur la mise en œuvre des responsabilités pénales individuelles, que l'on reconnaît acquises en droit international coutumier.

***ratifié le Statut de Rome, elle porte atteinte à l'indépendance de la CPI, elle viole le droit international pénal qui exclut toute exemption de responsabilité pour les crimes de guerre, les crimes de contre l'humanité et les crimes de génocide* ». Aussi**, MABASSA FALL, représentant permanent de la FIDH auprès de l'UA déclarait que « ***L'UA aurait dû rappeler à ses États membres qu'aucune poursuite de la CPI n'aurait été possible si les autorités nationales concernées avaient montré leur volonté et capacité de juger les auteurs des crimes les plus graves commis dans leur pays.* », voir aussi**, Moussa Bienvenu Haba, « L'offensive de l'Union africaine contre la Cour pénale internationale : La remise en cause de la lutte contre l'impunité », 9 décembre 2013.

[87]Voir LEJBOWICS (A), *Philosophie du droit international. L'impossible capture de l'humanité*, Paris, PUF, 1999, p. 353. Pour une analyse critique de cette immunité de l'Etat pour crime, Cf. MAHMOUD MOHAMED SALAH,« Interrogations sur l'évolution du droit international pénal », *JDI*, juil-août-sept. 2009, pp. 754 et s; l'affaire des *Activités militaires et paramilitaires au Nicaragua et contre celui-ci, Nicaragua c. Etats-Unis d'Amérique*, arrêt du 27 juin 1986 (par. 110 et 111); l'affaire relative à l'*Application de la Convention pour la prévention et la répression du crime de génocide (Bosnie-Herzégovine c. Serbie et Monténégro)*, arrêt du 26 février 2007 (§ 2 du dispositif).

50- Dans d'autres cas, l'Union africaine a elle-même décidé de mettre en œuvre la répression des crimes graves du droit international humanitaire. C'est la jurisprudence Hissène Habbré. En l'espèce, l'organisation sous régionale décide de mettre sur pied les Chambres africaines extraordinaires, pour juger les crimes commis par cet ancien chef d'État dans son pays entre 1982 et 1990. Les Chambres sont logées au sein de la juridiction sénégalaise, pays d'accueil du présumé coupable[88]. Elles sont chargées comme l'indiquent leurs statuts, de mettre en œuvre la décision de l'Union africaine, relative à la poursuite par la République du Sénégal des crimes internationaux commis au Tchad entre le 7 juin 1982 et le 1er décembre 1990, et conformément aux engagements internationaux du Sénégal[89]. Les Chambres sont à cet effet, compétentes pour connaître des crimes de génocide[90], des crimes contre l'humanité[91], des crimes de guerre[92] et du crime de torture[93]. La remarque qui peut être faite ici est la définition réductrice, voire lapidaire des crimes retenus. Malgré cela, il est plus important de s'attarder sur la volonté de l'Union africaine de poursuivre les crimes graves, que sur l'étendue de la définition desdits crimes. Aussi, serait-il intéressant que les Chambres africaines ne s'arrêtent pas seulement à la poursuite de Habré[94], elles devraient, pour une justice tous azimuts, étendre leurs enquêtes au complice, planificateur, instigateur et autres coauteurs des crimes présumés.

Conclusion

51- En somme, l'Union africaine, dans une volonté de se réapproprier les poursuites des crimes graves commis sur son sol, laissés, il y a quelques années à la Cour pénale internationale, établit une nouvelle grille de lecture dans la lutte contre l'impunité des crimes graves du droit humanitaire. Non

---

[88] Article premier.

[89] Article 2.

[90] Article 6.

[91] Article 7.

[92] Article 8.

[93] Article 9.

[94] Notons qu'il a récemment fait l'objet d'une condamnation à perpétuité. Nous y reviendrons pour des analyses critiques.

sans s'interroger sur les capacités présumées ou réelles du continent à assumer cette responsabilité, on doit aussi se demander avec qui les États doivent coopérer. Qui se saisira de la poursuite des crimes lorsqu'il sera impossible pour un État de mettre en œuvre les poursuites ? Quelle pourra être la réelle influence de la Cour pénale internationale sur le continent ? Toutes ces questions, qui ne pourront trouver une véritable solution qu'avec le fonctionnement effectif de la section de droit international pénal, nous obligent à tourner notre réflexion vers la téléologie, que porteraient la réaction et le choix de l'Union africaine de créer une juridiction concurrente de la Cour pénale internationale.

52- Outre une volonté de s'approprier les poursuites des crimes graves commis sur le continent africain, la position africaine est surtout celle du respect des règles d'immunité qui se distinguent de la responsabilité pénale individuelle. L'Afrique estime que la Cour pénale internationale viole constamment la règle de l'immunité accordée aux dirigeants en fonction, avec un acharnement contre les dirigeants africains. Si les autres États ont pu se soustraire de la Cour pénale internationale, soit par la non ratification de ses statuts[95], soit par une convention particulière[96], ou enfin par la clause dite *d'op out*[97], l'Afrique elle, a choisi la voie de la rupture de collaboration,

---

[95] Chine, Cameroun, Etats-Unis, Inde, Israël, Bahreïn, Qatar, Soudan, Vietnam, etc.

[96]Du point vue unilatéral, les Etats-Unis ont voté l'*American Service-Members' Protection Act of 2002,* dit loi *ASPA*. Ce texte pose d'abord l'interdiction de principe de toute coopération avec la Cour, que ce soit au niveau des juridictions américaines ou du gouvernement fédéral. Ce qui, d'un point de vue interne, a pour effet de soustraire de la compétence de la Cour tout citoyen américain présent sur le territoire des Etats-Unis. Ensuite, sur le plan international, la loi subordonne la participation américaine aux opérations de maintien de la paix au vote par le Conseil de sécurité d'une résolution garantissant l'immunité des forces armées américaines si la CPI peut exercer sa compétence sur le territoire de l'Etat où se déroule l'opération ou s'il n'existe pas d'accord bilatéral garantissant l'immunité des troupes américaines entre les Etats-Unis et l'Etat partie au statut de Rome sur le territoire duquel est menée l'opération.

[97] L'article 124 du statut de Rome qui consacre cette clause dispose que « *Nonobstant les dispositions de l'article 12, paragraphes 1 et 2, un État qui devient partie au présent Statut peut déclarer que, pour une période de sept ans à partir de l'entrée en vigueur du Statut à son égard, il n'accepte pas la compétence de la Cour en ce qui concerne la catégorie de crimes visée à l'article 8 lorsqu'il est allégué qu'un crime a été commis sur son territoire ou par ses ressortissants. Il peut à tout moment retirer cette déclaration. Les dispositions du présent article seront réexaminées à la conférence de révision convoquée conformément à l'article 123, paragraphe 1* ».

pour faire entendre sa voix. Il n'est un secret pour personne, que la position africaine est une contestation de la politique, et par ricochet du pouvoir du Conseil de sécurité tel que prévu par l'article 16 du statut de Rome. Il est donc venu le moment de la réforme des institutions internationales, pour permettre une présence équitable de toutes les zones géographiques dans le noyau de prise des décisions au plan universel.

Note bibliographique

ASSOGBAVI D., L'Afrique au cœur de la Cour pénale internationale, CPI-Afrique, Bulletin d'information de la Coalition pour la Cour pénale internationale n°1, juillet 2006.

ASSOGBAVI D., Les États africains doivent respecter leur engagement, Le Moniteur de la Cour pénale internationale n°29, avril 2005.

BAYAMASISSAO, « La CPI : l'Occident juge l'Afrique », *Africa 24 Magazine*, n° 3, juillet 2011.

BERTHELOT (P) ; « La CPI face à la tragédie du Darfour », Géopolitique africaine, n° 35, juillet, septembre 2009.

BOKA (M), La Cour Pénale Internationale entre droit et relations internationales, les faiblesses de la Cour à l'épreuve de la politique des États, Thèse Université Paris-Est, 2013.

CESONI (M L) et SCALIA (D), « Juridictions pénales internationales et conseil de sécurité : Une justice politisée », *Revue québécoise de droit international*, 2012.

CHILE EBOE-OSUJI, « Le rôle du Conseil de sécurité dans les poursuites pour crime d'agression : perspective africaine », Le Moniteur, Journal de la Coalition pour la Cour pénale internationale n°34/mai-octobre 2007.

COTTEREAU (G), « Statut en vigueur, la Cour Pénale Internationale s'installe », A.F.D.I., 2002.

DAEMERS (J) ; « Justice pénale internationale : (im) pressions africaines », Institut d'Études de Sécurité de l'Union européenne, 2014.

De FROUVILLE (O), « La Cour pénale internationale : une humanité souveraine ? », *Les Temps Modernes*, n° 610, 2000.

FOKOU (F.M), « Union africaine - Cour Pénale Internationale : De la collusion à la collision *comprendre la radicalisation du discours africain* », Institut de Recherche et d'Enseignement sur la Paix n° 23 – janvier 2015.

KAMBALE KALUME (P.), « Un nouvel élan et de nouveaux défis pour la campagne de ratification en Afrique », Le Moniteur de la Cour pénale internationale, avril 2002.

KAMTO (M), « L'affaire Al Bashir et les relations de l'Afrique avec la Cour pénale internationale », in Maurice KAMGA et Makane Moise MBENGUE (dir*), L'Afrique et le droit international. Variations sur l'organisation internationale (Liber Amicorum en l'honneur de Raymond Ranjeva*), Paris, Ed., A. Pedone, 2013.

KIRSCH (Ph.), « La Cour pénale internationale face à la souveraineté des États », CASSESE (A.) et DELMAS-MARTY (M.) (dir.), *Crimes internationaux et juridictions internationales,* Paris, PUF, 2002.

MOUANDJO (S M), « Les institutions internationales, les pays du sud et la démocratie », *Le journal de Tanger.*

MOUANGUE KOBILA (J), « L'Afrique et les juridictions internationales pénales », Cahier Thucydide n°10, 2012.

MUXART (A), « Immunité de l'ex-chef d'état et compétence universelle : quelques réflexions à propos de l'affaire Pinochet », Revue ADI, 1998.

ONDO (T.), « Réflexions sur la responsabilité pénale internationale du chef de l'État », *Rev.*

trim. dr. h., vol. 67, 2007.

ONDO (T.), La responsabilité introuvable du chef d'État africain. Analyse comparée de la contestation du pouvoir en Afrique noire francophone (Les exemples du Camerounais, Gabonais, Tchadien et Togolais), Thèse, Université de Reims, 2005.

SASSOLI (M.), « L'arrêt Yerodia: quelques remarques sur une affaire au point de collision entre les deux couches du droit international », *RGDIP*, 2002.

SUR S., Le droit international pénal entre l'Etat et la société internationale, Actualité et droit international, Revue d'analyse juridique de l'actualité internationale, octobre 2001.

VERHOEVEN (J.), « M. Pinochet, la coutume internationale et la compétence universelle », *Journal des Tribunaux*, 1999.

VERHOEVEN (J.), « Mandat d'arrêt international et statut de ministre », *Journal des procès*, 19 avril 2002.

ZORGBIBE (C.), « L'Afrique et la justice internationale », *Géopolitique africaine* n°11, juillet 2003.

II.

DROIT PUBLIC

LA QUALIFICATION INSTITUTIONNELLE DE LA SOCIÉTÉ D'ÉCONOMIE MIXTE AU CAMEROUN : CONTRIBUTION À L'ÉTUDE DES CATÉGORIES JURIDIQUES EN DROIT ADMINISTRATIF

Daniel MBARGA NYATTE[1]

RÉSUMÉ

Il y a un intérêt à étudier la société d'économie mixte dans le cadre camerounais, et l'existence d'un fait, d'un élément inséré dans des catégories juridiques différentes ne saurait alors surprendre. Qualifiée d'abord par le législateur d'entreprise du secteur public et parapublic, et ensuite considérée comme un mode de gestion déléguée des services publics locaux, la société d'économie mixte est :

- d'une part un mode imparfait de délégation de service public dans la mesure où il y a non seulement une inclusion insuffisante des critères des délégations du service public, en l'occurrence l'admission inachevée du critère formel, la satisfaction incomplète du critère organique, la présence insatisfaisante du critère matériel, mais aussi une pénible correspondance aux catégories de délégation de service public, avec une distanciation à l'égard de la concession, une impossible assimilation à l'affermage et à la régie intéressée.

- d'autre part, elle apparaît plutôt comme une catégorie parfaite d'entreprise publique, dès lors qu'il y a intégration des éléments communs aux entreprises parapubliques comme la personnalité morale, l'accomplissement des activités industrielles et commerciales, l'administration du personnel et le contrôle de l'État même si, par ailleurs, il y a renfermement des traits spécifiques, la démarquant clairement de l'établissement public administratif, avec une impossible confusion avec la

[1] **Chargé de cours, Habilité à diriger les recherches – Université de Yaoundé II.**

société à capital public, et une distinction entre la société d'économie mixte et les sociétés purement privées.

D'une manière générale, une réforme législative ou une précision jurisprudentielle s'imposent afin de positionner avec souplesse la société d'économie mixte dans sa catégorie correspondante.

INTRODUCTION

La qualification juridique est nécessaire pour le travail du juriste. Comme le souligne Gérard TIMSIT, « *la tâche du juriste est plus modeste que celle du philosophe ou du sociologue du droit; il s'agit pour lui d'ordonner, de classifier de façon immédiate les éléments juridiques* ... »[2]. Elle permet au juriste d'insérer les faits dans les catégories juridiques, mais n'est pas définitive, et René Savatier relève justement que « *le caractère à la fois passionnant et décevant de la tâche des juristes vient de ce que le droit est sans cesse à reconstruire (...). Ainsi, les compartiments qu'il établit ne sont jamais étanches, ni définitifs* »[32].

L'existence d'un fait, d'un élément inséré dans des catégories juridiques différentes ne saurait alors surprendre. La société d'économie mixte traduit cette situation, car qualifiée par le législateur camerounais d'abord d'entreprise du secteur public et parapublic[4] et ensuite considéré comme un mode de gestion déléguée des services publics locaux[5]. Entreprise parapublique et délégation de service publie relèvent pourtant de logiques historiques et conceptuelles différentes.

D'un point de vue historique, la délégation de service public est plus récente que l'entreprise parapublique. La délégation de service public, instituée en France par la loi n°91-3 du 3 janvier 1991 relative à la transparence et à la régularité des procédures de marchés, et soumettant la

---

[2]Gérard Timsit, *Le rôle de la notion de fonction administrative en droit administratif français*, Thèse de Doctorat en droit, Université de Paris, LGDJ, 1962, p. 19.

[3]René Savatier, cité in LECLERQ(C) et CHALVIDAN PTERRE(H), *Travaux dirigés de droit constitutionnel*, 5ème éd.,Litec, 19S9,p.S.

[4]Article 2 de Sa loi N° 99/016 du 22 décembre Ï999 portant statut général des établissements publics et des entreprises du secteur public et parapublic.

[5]Article 82(2) de la loi N" 2009/011 du 10 juillet 2009 portant régime financier des collectivités territoriales décentralisées.

passation de certains contrats à des règles de publicité et de mise en concurrence, modifiée par la loi Sapin[6] n°93-122 du 29 janvier 1993, n'a été définie que par la loi Murcef du 11 décembre 2001. Au Cameroun, le premier texte en la matière est le décret n° 2004/275 du 24 septembre 2004 portant code des marchés publics, suivi par la loi n° 2009/011 du 10 juillet 2009 portant régime financier des collectivités territoriales décentralisées.

La société d'économie mixte quant à elle est plus ancienne. Elle apparaît dans les catégories juridiques au début du XXe siècle. Au Cameroun, elle fut utilisée pour la première fois avant l'indépendance à travers le décret du 30 juin 1955 dans le cadre des plans de modernisation des colonies initiés par la France. Elle sera régie par la suite par de nombreux textes[7] avant de voir son régime harmonisé par la loi N° 99/016 du 22 décembre 1999 portant statut général des établissements publics et des entreprises du secteur public et parapublic, et plus récemment par la loi n° 2009/011 du 10 juillet 2009 portant régime financier des collectivités territoriales décentralisées.

D'un point de vue conceptuel, délégation de service public et entreprise parapublique revêtent des significations différentes. La loi française du 29 janvier 1993[8] définit les contrats de délégation de service public comme des contrats par lesquels une personne morale de droit public confie la gestion d'un service public dont elle a la responsabilité, à un délégataire public ou privé dont la rémunération est substantiellement liée au résultat d'exploitation du service. La définition du code des marchés publics camerounais est quasiment la même à savoir « *la délégation de la gestion d'un service public à un tiers dont la rémunération est substantiellement liée au résultat de l'exploitation du service* »[9] .

---

[6] Il s'agit de La loi Sapin n°93-122 du 29 janvier 1993 relative à la prévention de la corruption et à fa transparence de la vie économique et des procédures publiques.

[7]Sans être exhaustif, on peut citer la loi N° 6S/LF du 11 juin 1968 et le décret n° 68/DF du 15 juillet 1968JT.O.C juillet 1968 P.1347 ;arrêté du 29 septembre 1971,J.O.C,15 janvier 192JM28 ;décret no 78/462 du 24 octobre 1978₃IO.C 1er juin 1980,p.8871 ;décret N° 77 du 04 août 1977;mod. par le décret No 79/200 du 25 mai 1979J.0.0,1er juin 1979,P_623 ;décret No 78/103 du 26 mars 1979J.O.C,*1*™avril 1979₃P.386.

[8]Selon les termes de la loi Murcef du 11 décembre 2001, insérant un alinéa supplémentaire dans la loi Sapin n° 93-122 du 29 janvier 1993.

[9]Article 5 ail (a) du décret n° 2004/275 du 24 septembre 2004 portant Code des Marchés Publics.

À travers ces définitions transparaissent les traits communs aux conventions de délégation de service public : les critères de qualification, le pouvoir de contrôle de l'autorité délégante et le régime de la compétence contentieuse. Les conventions de délégation de service public satisfont en effet les critères du contrat administratif à savoir : le critère organique permanent[10] (présence d'une personne publique) et les critères alternatifs[11] (le critère finaliste ou la participation à l'exécution du service public et le critère matériel ou la présence des clauses exorbitantes du droit commun). Le contrôle permet à l'autorité délégante de s'assurer de l'exécution régulière du service public par le délégataire. Le contentieux des conventions de délégation de service public relève en principe de la compétence du juge administratif[12].

La définition de l'entreprise parapublique quant à elle ne va pas de soi. Le terme secteur parapublic fait pourtant traditionnellement « référence à un ensemble hétérogène d'entreprises et établissements : les établissements publics à caractère industriel et commercial (EPIC) d'une part, et d'autre part, les entreprises dans lesquelles l'État détient directement ou non, plus de la moitié du capital, avec ou sans droits de vote. Parallèlement, il est systématiquement fait référence à toutes les autres formes que peut revêtir l'intervention paraétatique, perçue dans une acception plus générale. Il s'agit notamment des établissements publics à caractère administratif (EPA) et des participations publiques minoritaires, dans lesquelles la puissance publique détient plus de 10% du capital… »[13].

---

[10] T.C, 8 juillet 1963, Entreprises Peyrot.

[11] Le juge administratif camerounais semble toutefois avoir consacré le cumul des critères matériel et finaliste. Cf jugement n°147/04-05/ADD, UM NTJIAM François de la chambre administrative de la Cour suprême du 31 août 2005.

[12] Le juge judiciaire peut exceptionnellement apprécier la légalité d'un acte administratif dans les cas limitativement admis : d'une part en matière fiscale ou en cas d'atteinte grave au droit de propriété et d'autre part en matière pénale (TC, 5 juillet 1991, Avranches et Desmarets, Rc., p.638).

[13] Voir dans ce sens A. M. Sagna, *Les relations publiques dans une entreprise de service public audiovisuel : cas de la RTSI*, Mémoire de fin d'étude pour l'obtention du diplôme d'étude en information et communication, option Relations publiques, Institut Supérieur des Sciences de l'Information et de la Communication, 2007, p.17.

Bien plus encore, traditionnellement, on distingue l'entreprise privée de l'entreprise publique par le critère de la détention de capital. L'entreprise publique a pour seul actionnaire l'État alors que le capital de l'entreprise privée provient de différents actionnaires privés. L'entreprise parapublique dite aussi entreprise d'économie mixte est une société anonyme de capitaux privés et publics. Les entreprises publiques ou « parapubliques » sont des « entreprises à statut privé(...), mais dont le capital est détenu majoritairement par une personne publique ou une entreprise du secteur public. Le contrôle sur la gestion de l'entreprise est aussi un critère de qualification de l'entreprise parapublique, si le capital *n'est pas majoritairement public* »[14]. Plus précisément, la société d'économie mixte a deux « *caractères distinctifs que l'on retrouve dans toutes les législations (...). D'une part, il existe une double participation à leur capital de l'État ou des collectivités publiques et des personnes privées ou assimilées; d'autre part, ces mêmes catégories de personnes se retrouvent dans les organes de la société* »[15]. Ces précisions terminologiques semblent toutefois n'avoir pas été prises en compte par certains Etats comme la France et le Cameroun.

En France déjà, « *il n'existe pas une, mais plusieurs définitions ou précisément plusieurs approches de la notion d'entreprise publique* »[16]. Au Cameroun, le concept d'entreprise parapublique ne pouvait être convenablement défini avant 1995 à cause de l'incertitude sur l'existence même du droit de l'entreprise publique. L'ordonnance du 17 août 1995 portant statut des entreprises du secteur public et parapublic, qui ouvre la période de codification du droit des entreprises publiques, bien qu'innovatrice à plusieurs titres, ne sera pas adoptée par l'Assemblée nationale. Elle ne fait pas de différence entre entreprise publique et entreprise du secteur parapublic. L'établissement public administratif y est même considéré comme une forme d'entreprise publique[17] contrairement à

---

[14]Voir dans ce sens (A. M) Sagna, *op cit.* p. 17.

[15]Voir Sawadogo (M.F), *Le régime juridique des sociétés d'économie mixte en Haute-Volta*, Thèse pour le Doctorat d'Etat, mention droit, Université de Paris 1-Paotheon-Sokbokise, Sciences économiques Sciences humaines- Sciences juridiques, 1981. p. 7.

[16]PAYET(M), *Le contrôle de l'entreprise publique, Essai sur Le cas français*, Thèse de Doctorat, Droit public, Université de Saint-Etienne, 2001, p. 12.

[17]Article 2 de l'ordonnance de 1994.

l'opinion de la doctrine unanime française et africaine[18]. Elle se contente d'énumérer les formes d'entreprises du secteur public et parapublic (établissement public administratif, société à capital public et société d'économie mixte) et de fixer les critères d'identification (l'autonomie administrative et financière, la tutelle et le patrimoine d'affectation).

La loi N° 99/016 du 22 décembre 1999 portant statut général des établissements publics et des entreprises du secteur public et parapublic va reprendre les grandes lignes de l'ordonnance du 17 août 1995 portant statut général des entreprises du secteur public et parapublic. Si, d'un point de vue sémantique, elle distingue les établissements publics des entreprises du secteur public et parapublic, il reste qu'elle ne définit pas clairement la notion d'entreprise parapublique et soumet les composantes du secteur public[19] à un ensemble de dispositions communes. C'est dire que la loi de 1999 semble faire correspondre à une même réalité l'entreprise du secteur public et parapublic et l'entreprise parapublique.

Une chose est toutefois sûre. Si la loi parle des établissements publics et parapublics, il est possible d'identifier l'entreprise parapublique. Négativement, l'entreprise parapublique n'est pas un établissement public administratif. Positivement, si l'autonomie administrative et financière[20], la tutelle[21] et le patrimoine d'affectation[22] permettent d'identifier les

---

[18]La précision est apportée par (L.N) MAKANDA, « *La liquidation des entreprises publiques en droit camerounais* », biblio.ohada.org, le 4 juin 2013.

[19] L'article 3(1) dispose que « Le secteur public et parapublic est essentiellement constitué d'établissements publics administratifs, de sociétés à capital public et de sociétés d'économie mixte, sans préjudice des dispositions de l'article *1*er alinéa (2) ci-dessus ». C'est-à-dire que des lois particulières peuvent, en tant que de besoin, créer d'autres formes d'établissement public ou parapublic.

[20] L'autonomie financière est définie à l'article *2(1}* comme la capacité pour une personne morale d'administrer et de gérer librement les biens meubles ou immeubles, corporels ou incorporels ou en numéraire constituant son patrimoine propre, en vue de réaliser son objet social.

[21]La tutelle est définie à l'article 2(8} comme le pouvoir dont dispose l'Etat pour définir et orienter la politique du gouvernement dans le secteur où évolue l'établissement publie administratif ou l'entreprise du secteur public ou parapublic en vue de la sauvegarde de l'intérêt général. Elle s'exerce sur le plan technique et sur le plan financier par un département ministériel ou par tout autre administration ou organe désigné dans les statuts.

établissements publics et les entreprises du secteur public et para public, seule l'autonomie administrative et financière permet de définir l'entreprise du secteur public et parapublic, le patrimoine d'affectation étant employé uniquement pour les établissements publics administratifs. Plus précisément encore, l'entreprise du secteur public et parapublic est identifiée à travers ses formes que sont la société à capital public et la société d'économie mixte.

La société à capital public est définie comme une « *personne morale de droit privé, dotée de l'autonomie financière et d'un capital-actions intégralement détenu par l'État, une ou plusieurs collectivités territoriales décentralisées ou une ou plusieurs autres sociétés à capital public, en vue de l'exécution dans l'intérêt général, d'activités présentant un caractère industriel, commercial et financier* »[23]. La société d'économie mixte est plus clairement définie[24] comme une « *personne morale de droit privé, dotée de l'autonomie financière et d'un capital-actions détenu partiellement d'une part, par l'État, les collectivités territoriales décentralisées, ou les sociétés à capital public et d'autre part, par les personnes morales ou physiques de droit privé* »[25].

La tutelle technique a pour objet de fixer les objectifs assignés à l'ensemble des entreprises du secteur considéré et, en tant que de besoin, d'en assurer la régulation, en vue d'un fonctionnement normal. La tutelle financière a pour objet d'apprécier les opérations de gestion à incidence financière des établissements publics administratifs, et d'examiner *a posteriori les* comptes des autres catégories d'entreprises du secteur public et parapublic. Elle est exercée par le ministère *chargé* des finances pour les établissements publics administratifs, les sociétés à capital public ayant l'Etat comme unique actionnaire, ainsi que les sociétés à capital public et les sociétés d'économie mixte où l'Etat détient au minium vingt-cinq pour cent (25 *%) du* capital.

[22]Le patrimoine d'affectation est défini à l'article 2(4) comme l'ensemble des biens meubles ou immeubles, corporels ou *incorporels* ou en numéraire, mis par l'Etat et les collectivités territoriales décentralisées à la disposition d'un établissement public administratif.

[23]Art 2.al.5 de la loi da 1999, *op cit.*

[24]Avant l'ordonnance du 17 août 1995 portant statut généra! des entreprises du secteur public et parapublic, les sociétés d'économie mixtes sont approximativement définies entre autres par l'art. 2 al.4 de la loi n° 74/18 du 5 décembre 1974 relative au contrôle des ordonnateurs, des gestionnaires et gérants des crédits publics et des entreprises d'Etat définissant les sociétés d'économie mixte comme « les sociétés présentant un intérêt stratégique pour la défense nationale quelle que soit la participation de la puissance publique ».

[25]Article 2al.6de la loi de 1999, *op cit.*

Une précision doit être faite. L'intitulé de la loi de 1999 est clair : elle porte statut général des établissements publics et des entreprises du secteur public et parapublic. La société à capital public et la société d'économie mixte sont des entreprises du secteur public et parapublic. La société à capital public se caractérise par l'entière souscription publique du capital[26]. Les capitaux de la société d'économie mixte ne sont que partiellement publics[27]. Le législateur parle des « entreprises du secteur public et parapublic ». Il semble logique de considérer pour le moment que l'entreprise publique renvoie à la société à capital public, et l'entreprise parapublique à la société d'économie mixte.

Cette déduction semble toutefois trop catégorique et précipitée. Dans certains pays comme le Cameroun, le législateur considère depuis 2009 la société d'économie mixte comme un mode de gestion déléguée des services publics locaux[28]. La question que l'on peut alors se poser peut être formulée comme suit: la société d'économie mixte est-elle une délégation de service public ou une entreprise parapublique ?

Déterminer la catégorie juridique d'appartenance de la société d'économie mixte permet à coup sûr de faciliter sa compréhension. .De la sorte, il sera plus aisé de déterminer son régime juridique et, en conséquence, de mieux cerner les relations entre personnes publiques et personnes privées dans la société d'économie mixte. À ce sujet, le constat fait au regard des considérations sus-évoquées est que la société d'économie mixte n'est pas un mode parfait de délégation de service public(I), mais est une catégorie parfaite d'entreprise parapublique(II).

I) LA SOCIÉTÉ D'ÉCONOMIE MIXTE, MODE IMPARFAIT DE DÉLÉGATION DE SERVICE PUBLIC.

La société d'économie mixte n'est pas généralement considérée comme un mode de délégation de service public. Elle est cependant considérée par le législateur camerounais comme un mode de gestion déléguée des services

---

[26]La précision qui découle de l'interprétation de l'art.2 al 2 de l'ordonnance du 17 août 1995 précité est apportée par (L.N) MAKANDA, *op cit.*, p.94.

[27](L.N) MAKANDA, *op cit.*, p.94.

[28]Article 82 al-2 de la loi de 2009 portant régime financier des collectivités territoriales décentralisées.

publics locaux. En tant qu'interprète authentique du droit[29], sa décision devrait mettre fin à tout débat. Elle suscite tout de même des interrogations, car la société d'économie mixte ne regorge pas irréprochablement des critères des délégations de **service** public(A) et **ne correspond** aisément à aucun type de délégation de service public (B).

A) L'inclusion insuffisante des critères des délégations de service public

Les délégations de service public, il faut le rappeler, sont des contrats par lesquels une personne morale de droit public confie la gestion d'un service public dont elle a la responsabilité, à un délégataire public ou privé dont la rémunération est substantiellement liée au résultat d'exploitation du service. Une analyse de cette définition permet de ressortir trois critères des conventions de délégations de service public à savoir le critère formel(l), le critère organique (2) et le critère matériel(3) qui ne permettent pas d'identifier clairement la société d'économie mixte.

1) L'admission inachevée du critère formel

La société d'économie mixte ne satisfait pas complètement le critère formel des délégations de service public. Mais déjà à quoi renvoie ce critère formel ? Il signifie simplement que les conventions de délégation se présentent sous la' forme d'une convention ou d'un contrat qui est un contrat administratif.

La base contractuelle fait déjà défaut à la société d'économie mixte. La société d'économie mixte est créée par décision unilatérale de l'autorité administrative. La volonté de création émane en principe exclusivement de la personne publique. La société d'économie mixte peut toutefois être créée par voie contractuelle[30]. Le contrat de création sera-t-il un contrat administratif ?

---

[29] «Dans le vocabulaire de Kelsen, l'interprétation authentique n'est pas seulement celle qui émane de l'auteur de l'acte, mais plus généralement celle qui est donnée par une autorité habilitée à interpréter ou encore celle à qui Porche juridique fait produire des effets, même si elle n'est pas formellement habilitée » cité par M.Troper, *La philosophie du droit.* 1ère éd., Paris, Que sais-je, 2003, p.100.

[30] Le professeur Jean Rivero, *in Droit administratif, I2tmtt*éd., Paris, Précis Dalloz, 1983, p.605, relève que l'entreprise d'économie mixte peut résulter de la transformation d'une société privée. La transformation peut se réaliser soit par voie contractuelle (achat d'action

Le contrat administratif est défini sur la base de la combinaison du critère organique permanent et des critères alternatifs. Au plan organique, le contrat administratif est conclu par au moins une personne publique. Les critères alternatifs[31] (critère finaliste et critère matériel) exigent que la convention conclue ait pour finalité la participation du cocontractant de l'administration à l'exécution du service public ou contienne des clauses exorbitantes du droit commun. La convention qui remplit ces critères est un contrat administratif soumis en principe à la compétence contentieuse du juge administratif.

Les sociétés d'économie mixte peuvent bien être créées par un contrat administratif. Cependant, elles demeurent des organismes privés[32] gérant certes un service public, mais conjointement avec la personne publique. Plus précisément, elles sont en droit camerounais soumises au droit OHADA sur les sociétés anonymes[33]. La société d'économie mixte ne remplit donc qu'imparfaitement le critère formel des délégations de service public. Ce qui déteint sur la satisfaction du critère organique des délégations de service public.

2) La satisfaction incomplète du critère organique

Le critère organique met en exergue la relation entre l'autorité délégante et le délégataire. L'autorité délégante est une personne publique. Il peut s'agir de l'État, d'une collectivité territoriale décentralisée, d'un établissement public[34] ou d'un groupement d'intérêt public[35]. Le délégataire

---

en bourse ou convention entre la société d'Etat réglant les modalités d'association), soit par acte unilatéral, l'Etat imposant son intervention et en fixant les modalités, soit par combinaison des deux procédés.

[31]Le juge administratif camerounais semble toutefois avoir consacré le cumul des critères matériel et finaliste.

[32]DE LAUBADERE (A), VENEZIA (J C), GAUDEMET(Y) : *Traité de droit administratif*, Tome ï, 13ème éd., Paris, LGDJ, 1992, p. 540.

[33]Voir POUGOUE (P.G), « Les sociétés d'Etat à l'épreuve du droit OHADA », *Juridis périodique*, N° 65, Janvier mars 2006, p. 100.

[34]Au Cameroun, l'établissement public délégante ne peut être pour le moment qu'un établissement public administratif. La catégorie d'établissement public industriel et commercial disparaît au profit de la société d'économie mixte et de la société à capital public avec la loi N° 99/016 du *22* décembre Î999 portant statut général des établissements publics et des entreprises du secteur public et parapublic.

peut être une personne publique ou une personne privée. La relation entre ces parties laisse entrevoir qu'au départ elles sont séparées, mais décident par la suite d'établir des relations contractuelles dans le cadre de la gestion du service public. Le délégant confie alors la gestion du service public au délégataire.

La société d'économie mixte semble ne pas obéir à cette logique. Elle est certes constituée de personnes publiques et de personnes privées. De plus, la société d'économie mixte peut être délégataire de la gestion d'un service public, mais elle est souvent constituée de manière unilatérale comme une entité à part entière, la personnalité morale cachant les personnes qui la composent. De la sorte, c'est la société d'économie mixte qui agit lorsqu'elle conclut un contrat par exemple et non la personne publique ou la personne privée. En réalité, les deux parties deviennent une seule entité. Les parties peuvent donc être les mêmes dans la cadre d'une société d'économie mixte et d'une délégation de service public, mais elles s'inscrivent dans deux logiques différentes.

Il faut aussi relever que les délégations de service public peuvent mettre en présence uniquement des personnes publiques contrairement à la société d'économie mixte qui est une société anonyme de droit privé dans laquelle le capital est détenu en partie d'une part par l'État, les collectivités territoriales décentralisées, ou les sociétés à capital public et d'autre part, par les personnes morales ou physiques de droit privé. La composition de la société d'économie mixte l'éloigne ainsi des délégations de service public. Son contenu y contribue aussi.

3) La présence insatisfaisante du critère matériel

Le critère matériel des délégations de service public met en exergue leur contenu. Le professeur Jacques BIAKAN relève que « *d'un point de vue matériel, la gestion déléguée des services publics se présente sous la forme d'un contrat synallagmatique construit sur deux obligations qui se font face :la remise du délégant au délégataire du droit d'exploiter ou de gérer une activité de service public et la possibilité d'une rémunération du délégataire en contrepartie de ce*

[35]Voir la loi n° 2010/023 du 21 décembre 2010 fixant le statut du groupement d'intérêt public.

droit d'exploiter et de gérer »[36]. Le désengagement de la personne publique n'est toutefois pas total. Le contrôle permet à l'autorité délégante de s'assurer de l'exécution régulière du service public par le délégataire.

La société d'économie mixte ne correspond pas exactement à cette logique. Les droits et obligations des parties n'existent pas dans le cadre d'une délégation de service public. Les parties ont certes des obligations les unes envers les autres, mais elles ont en général pour obligation majeure de réaliser l'objet social de la société d'économie mixte, cette dernière étant avant tout une société anonyme. En tant que société de droit privé, elle se doit de réaliser des bénéfices. Les personnes publiques l'utilisent généralement comme moyen d'intervention dans l'action économique- En participant à la société d'économie mixte, la personne publique et les personnes privées se confondent dans une même entité pour gérer, exploiter conjointement une activité d'intérêt général donnée.

Nous sommes ainsi loin de la logique des délégations de service public lorsqu'on est en présence de la société d'économie mixte. Elle ne satisfait pas suffisamment ses critères. Il est par voie de conséquence logique qu'elle ne corresponde pas irréprochablement aux types de délégations de service public.

B) La pénible correspondance aux catégories de délégations de service public

La société d'économie s'insère difficilement dans trois types[37] de délégations de service public que sont la concession(l), l'affermage(2), la régie intéressée(3).

1) La distanciation à l'égard de la concession

La concession est un mode de gestion déléguée du service public par lequel la personne publique confie à une personne physique ou morale, la charge d'exécuter un service public à ses frais, avec ou sans subvention ou sans garantie d'intérêt, et que l'on rémunère en lui confiant l'exploitation

[36]**Biakan (J)**, « La délégation des services publics en droit camerounais », ***RASJ***, **Vol.7**, N°.1, 2010, p.221.

[37]Le choix de ces trois modes de gestion du service public se justifie par leur appartenance originaire et incontestable aux conventions de délégation de service public.

d'un ouvrage ou l'exécution d'un service avec le droit de percevoir des redevances sur les usagers de l'ouvrage, ou ceux qui bénéficient du service. Ce qui veut dire que le concessionnaire crée les conditions d'exploitation du service public, gère l'activité de service public à ses risques et périls et est rémunéré par les usagers. De plus, la durée du contrat doit permettre au concessionnaire de recouvrer les sommes investies.

La logique de la société d'économie mixte n'est pas la même. La personne publique ici ne confie pas la gestion du service public à un délégataire. Elle gère conjointement le service public avec d'autres personnes physiques ou morales. S'il est vrai que la société d'économie mixte peut être concessionnaire., il reste que le personnel de la société d'économie mixte est soumis au Cameroun au droit privé, y compris pour leur rémunération sous réserve des dispositions du statut général de la fonction publique relatives à la retraite, à l'avancement et à la fin du détachement[38]. La société d'économie mixte ne peut ainsi pas être considérée comme une concession de service public. Il en est de même de l'affermage.

2) L'impossible assimilation à l'affermage

L'affermage est un mode de gestion déléguée du service public par lequel la personne publique choisit librement le fermier en vue d'assurer le service public qui lui est délégué par contrat, moyennant le versement à la personne publique d'une redevance déterminée. La différence entre le montant de cette redevance et les recettes qu'il réalisera représente sa rémunération. En outre, lorsque l'utilisation d'ouvrages est nécessaire pour l'exécution du service, leur construction n'est pas à la charge du fermier qui les reçoit de la personne publique.

C'est dire que dans l'affermage, c'est la personne publique et non le fermier qui crée les conditions d'exploitation du service public. La rémunération du fermier repose sur les redevances payées par les usagers. En revanche, il doit verser une contribution destinée à couvrir l'amortissement des frais initiaux engagés par la personne publique. Dans le cadre de la société mixte, les parties n'ont pas à verser une contribution pour amortir les investissements de la personne publique. Généralement, elles recherchent les

[38]Art.16 de la loi N° 99/016 du 22 décembre 1999 portant statut général des établissements publics et des entreprises du secteur public et parapublic.

bénéfices qui constituent en fin de compte une bonne part de leur rémunération. La société d'économie mixte ne peut donc valablement pas être qualifiée d'affermage. On peut en dire autant pour la régie intéressée.

3) L'impossible assimilation à la régie intéressée

La régie intéressée est un mode de gestion déléguée du service public par lequel « *le soin d'assurer le service public est confié par contrat à un organisme, public ou privé, qui va se trouver, non dans la situation (comme le concessionnaire) d'un entrepreneur, mais celle d'un gérant et, plus exactement d'un gérant intéressé* »[39]. Le régisseur n'assume pas les risques et périls de la gestion, il effectue les travaux de petit entretien. Sa rémunération, versée par l'administration, comprend un forfait minimum garanti et un pourcentage variable sur les résultats de l'exploitation.

La société d'économie mixte n'épouse pas cette logique. Les parties sont rémunérées principalement par les bénéfices réalisés. De plus, les parties peuvent investir pour démarrer l'activité d'une société d'économie mixte, ce qui n'est pas le cas dans la régie intéressée.

La société d'économie mixte ne peut pas être considérée comme une véritable délégation de service public. En réalité, l'institution-organe n'est pas en elle-même une modalité. C'est une action initiée par elle-même ou par une entité qui lui est extérieure qui en est une. Si la société d'économie mixte peut être délégataire ou gérer un service public délégué, elle ne se retrouve pas en elle-même dans les traits et les types de délégations de service public. Si son rattachement à la catégorie juridique de délégations de service public fait problème, une autre qu'est l'entreprise parapublique la reçoit à merveille.

II) LA SOCIÉTÉ D'ÉCONOMIE MIXTE, CATÉGORIE PARFAITE D'ENTREPRISE PARAPUBLIQUE

La société d'économie mixte s'insère **parfaitement** dans la catégorie juridique d'entreprise parapublique parce qu'elle intègre les éléments communs à celles-ci (A) même si elles regorgent des traits qui la particularisent(B).

A) L'intégration des éléments communs aux entreprises parapubliques

[39]R. Chapus, *Droit administratif général*, 15ème éd, Montchrestien, Paris, 2001, p. 644.

Une catégorie juridique est un « *ensemble de droits, de choses, de personnes, de faits, ou d'actes ayant entre eux, des traits communs caractéristiques et obéissant à un régime commun* »[40]. Parler d'entreprise parapublique suppose qu'il existe des éléments communs aux entreprises parapubliques. S'il peut paraître difficile de dégager l'essence de la catégorie juridique d'entreprises publiques en général, il est toutefois possible de recenser quatre[41] éléments communs[42] aux entreprises publiques et parapubliques: la personnalité morale(l), l'accomplissement des activités industrielles et commerciales (2), l'administration du personnel et le contrôle de l'État(3) qu'intègre la société d'économie mixte.

1) La personnalité morale

La personnalité morale représente le critère juridique[43] de l'entreprise publique. Les entreprises du secteur public et parapublic en général et la société d'économie mixte en particulier sont des institutions investies de la personnalité morale. Plus précisément, ces entités disposent d'une personnalité juridique distincte de celle de la collectivité publique dont elles relèvent. Ils disposent de tous les attributs attachés à la personnalité morale : l'individualité administrative, l'individualité patrimoniale, l'individualité financière et l'individualité juridique[44]. Les entreprises du secteur public et parapublic disposent ainsi d'une autonomie administrative et financière, d'un patrimoine et du droit d'ester en justice.

Lorsque l'entreprise du secteur public et parapublic est constituée sous la forme d'une personne morale de droit public (cas de l'établissement public administratif au Cameroun), elle a en plus de ces attributs, la possibilité d'exercer certains droits comme être propriétaire des biens du domaine

[40]BERGEL (J L): *Théorie générale du droit*, 4ème éd., Paris, Dalloz, 2003, p.210.

[41]Le quatrième élément qui est l'administration du personnel est précisé par (M) POYET, *Le contrôle de l'entreprise publique, Essai sur le cas français*, Thèse de Doctorat, Droit public, Université de Saint-Etienne, 2001, p.17.

[42]Au Cameroun, ces éléments sont contenus dans le chapitre 11 la loi du 22 décembre 1999 consacré aux dispositions communes aux établissements publics administratifs, sociétés à capital public, sociétés d'économie mixte et aux autres formes d'établissement public ou parapublic qui peuvent être créés par la loi.

[43]L'expression est de DE LAUBADERE (A), VENEZÏA (J.C),GAUDEMET(Y) : *Traité de droit administratif*, Tome 1, 13èmeéd.. Parts, LGDJ. I992,p,252.

[44]C .E,19 déc. 1950,BDF S.1950,111,6l NoteBoulouïs.

public, exercer le droit d'expropriation, être investi du pouvoir de police administrative et bénéficier du privilège du préalable. Exception faite de l'établissement public administratif, les attributs attachés à la personnalité morale sont reconnus aux entreprises du secteur public et parapublic en général pour exercer des missions à caractère industriel et commercial.

2) L'accomplissement des activités industrielles et commerciales

L'exercice des activités industrielles et commerciales représente le critère économique des entreprises publiques. L'entreprise publique, en intervenant dans le commerce et l'industrie, « *...se distingue d'autres pans du secteur public comme la fonction publique ou les établissements publics de type administratif* »[45]. Il n'existerait alors que deux types d'entreprises du secteur public et parapublic : la société à capital public et la société d'économie mixte.

La réalité est tout autre chose. L'établissement public administratif est considéré au Cameroun comme une composante du secteur public et parapublic[46]. La particularité n'est toutefois pas uniquement camerounaise. Ce problème de la forme commerciale ou non de l'entreprise publique est rencontré par d'autres pays. En France et en Allemagne, « *l'étude comparative prouve que partout l'entreprise publique apparaît (...) simultanément sous deux formes différentes. La première est celle d'un organisme administratif institutionnalisé, ayant de par la loi une certaine indépendance sur le plan de la gestion et un patrimoine soustrait à l'application des règles domaniales* »[47]. Par conséquent, comme l'a dit Franklin D. Roosevelt, une telle entité est « *reliée au pouvoir gouvernemental, tout en possédant la flexibilité et l'initiative de l'entreprise privée* »[48]. Elle est ainsi « *foncièrement hybride : mi -autorité (parce que toujours encore en régie et représentant, dans une certaine mesure, le pouvoir) et mi- commerçant...* »[49] .

---

[45] (M) POYET, *op cit.*, p.25.

[46]Art.3 de la loi de la loi de 1999, *op cit.*, p.3.

[47](M.G)Langrod, « L'entreprise publique en droit administratif comparé », *In Revue internationale de droit comparé.* Vol. 8 N°2, Avril-juin 1956, p. 219.

[48]Message au Congrès de 1944 au sujet de la TennesseValleyAuthority (T.V.A.). Cité par (M.G) Langrod, *op cit*,, p-2I9.

[49] (M.G) Langrod, *op cit.*, p.219.

La deuxième forme est celle d'une société commerciale dont le capital est rattaché exclusivement à l'État. Ce phénomène d'interpénétration du privé et du public se transforme le plus souvent en fiction : certaines règles du droit commercial sont écartées par la force des choses, par suite du caractère légal *sui generis* d'une telle société à propriétaire unique, qui exerce en surplus librement le contrôle de l'exploitation. Comme cela est révélé par l'histoire des sociétés d'économie mixte, « *la pénétration du contrôle gouvernemental reste essentielle et va en croissant, en dépit de toute façade* ».[50]

Dans les pays de Common Law, au Pakistan, l'Inde, Israël ou l'Australie, on se méfie de la société commerciale créée par l'Etat ou avec sa participation effective. Il est toutefois, à vrai dire, difficile de distinguer ces deux formes d'entreprise publique en tenant compte du caractère commercial de leur action. Cette réalité pousse à admettre que la distinction service public administratif et service public industriel et commercial[51] n'est pas toujours opératoire ici, car l'entreprise du secteur public et parapublic peut ne pas exercer une action industrielle et commerciale. Cette difficulté est toutefois atténuée par la certitude sur l'administration du personnel et le contrôle de l'État dans les entreprises du secteur public et parapublic.

3) L'administration du personnel et le contrôle de l'État

Le personnel des entreprises du secteur public et parapublic et le contrôle de l'État sont aussi des éléments communs aux entreprises parapubliques en général et aux sociétés d'économie mixte en particulier.

Le personnel des sociétés d'économie mixte est soumis en général au droit privé. Un régime marginal de droit public leur est toutefois appliqué dans certains pays[52] . De plus, les fonctions des autorités dirigeantes (président du conseil d'administration) de ces personnes morales de droit privé sont incompatibles avec celles de membre du gouvernement, de parlementaire, de directeur général ou de directeur général adjoint des

---

[50] (M.G) Langrod, *op cit.*, p,29.

[51]CE, 16 novembre 1956, Union syndicale des industries aéronautiques.

[52]Au Cameroun par exemple, l'article 16 de la loi de 1999 sur le statut des entreprises publiques précité les soumet pendant toute la durée de leur emploi à la législation du travail sauf sous réserve des dispositions du statut général de la fonction publique relatives à la retraite, à l'avancement et à la fin du détachement.

établissements publics administratifs et des entreprises du secteur public et parapublic. Ceci certainement pour un exercice efficace des missions de l'entreprise concernée et un contrôle adéquat de la puissance publique.

Le contrôle de l'État a pour but d'assurer « *la mainmise de la puissance publique* »[53]sur la société d'économie mixte. Le contrôle peut être financier, parlementaire ou économique. Seulement le régime du contrôle est très diversifié en raison des spécificités, des préoccupations nationales et de chaque type d'entreprise du secteur public et parapublic. Ceci n'entame en rien l'existence des traits communs aux entreprises. C'est que chaque type d'entreprise du secteur public et parapublic en général, la société d'économie mixte en particulier, regorge en plus de ces éléments communs, des éléments qui la particularisent.

B) Le renfermement des traits spécifiques

Il est important dans la détermination d'une catégorie juridique de « *dégager les liens qui unissent entre eux les éléments qui la composent et les traits qui la distinguent des autres phénomènes* »[54]. Considérer la société d'économie mixte comme catégorie juridique revient à constater qu'elle regorge en plus des éléments communs aux entreprises du secteur public et parapublic sus évoqués, des caractéristiques propres qui permettent de la distinguer d'autres entités comme l'établissement public administratif(1)., la société à capital public(2) et les entreprises privées(3).

1) La démarcation claire de l'établissement public administratif

La société d'économie mixte se distingue en principe de l'établissement public administratif par sa nature, son but et son régime. Claude DEVES définit la Société d'économie mixte (SEM) comme une société dans laquelle des capitaux privés sont associés à des capitaux publics en vue de gérer une activité d'intérêt général[55]. Charles ALBOUY précise alors que *"la société*

---

[53]Poyet (M), *op.cit.*, p.26.

[54]Bergel (J L), *op cit.*, p.210.

[55]7 Deves(C), « A quoi sert l'économie mixte? »*Revue française d'administration publique*, avril -juin 1987. p. 229. cité par Darold (J), *Les sociétés d'économie mixte locales: acteurs et témoins des politiques urbaines et territoriales " Quelle légitimité entre Partenariat Public/Privé et Entreprise Publique Locale* ? "Thèse de Doctorat en aménagement de l'espace et

d'économie mixte est (...) une institution de droit privé". Sociétés anonymes, les SEM disposent ainsi d'une gestion et d'une logique d'entreprise avec « *prise en compte de l'intérêt général dans ses objectifs* »[56]. C'est dire que la SEM est une personne morale de droit privé gérant un service public et soumise au droit privé.

L'établissement public administratif est une personne publique spécialisée dans l'exercice d'une mission de service public à caractère administratif, rattachée à une administration, soumise au contrôle de l'État et ayant reçu un patrimoine d'affectation. Elle est, contrairement à la société d'économie mixte, une personne publique contrôlée par la personne publique et soumise au droit public. Tel n'est pas toujours le cas, car au Cameroun, elle est considérée comme une forme d'entreprise du secteur public et parapublic, et est par conséquent soumise partiellement sur certains aspects au droit privé[57].

L'établissement public administratif est créé et dissout par l'exécutif ou par décision de l'organe délibérant de la collectivité publique décentralisée concernée. La création de la société d'économie mixte en France peut être contractuelle ou unilatérale[58]. Au Cameroun, les textes sont silencieux sur la création de la société d'économie mixte. Il est toutefois possible de penser qu'elles peuvent être créées par voie réglementaire ou selon les modalités de droit commun[59].

L'établissement public administratif en droit camerounais reçoit un patrimoine d'affectation. Ce qui n'est pas le cas des sociétés d'économie

---

urbanisme, Université de Bordeaux 3 - Michel de Montaigne. Institut d'aménagement, de tourisme et d'urbanisme, 2008, p.18.

[56]ALBOUY (C), *Sociétés d'économie mixte locales.* MASSON, 1991. p. 7. cité par Darold(J), *op cit.*

[57]C'est Je cas du personnel soumis pendant toute la durée de son emploi à la législation du travail sauf sous réserve des dispositions du statut général de la fonction publique relatives à la retraite, à l'avancement et à la fin du détachement.

[58]La précision est apportée par le professeur Jean Rivero, *op cit.*, p. 605.

[59]La déduction est faite par le professeur Biakan (J), in « Les innovations fondamentales de l'ordonnance du 17 août 1995 portant statut général des entreprises du secteur public et parapublic au Cameroun », *RJPIC,* N°2 – Mai – Août 1996. p.191-199.

mixte. La société d'économie mixte se distingue ainsi de l'établissement public administratif. Elle est aussi différente de la société à capital public.

2) L'impossible confusion entre la société d'économie mixte et la société à capital public

La société à capital public est une personne morale de droit privé constituée de capitaux publics en vue de l'exécution, dans l'intérêt général, d'activités présentant un caractère industriel, commercial et financier. La société d'économie mixte par contre connaît une double participation à leur capital de l'État ou des collectivités publiques et des personnes privées. De plus, les sociétés à capitaux publics sont créées par voie unilatérale et les collectivités publiques sont prépondérantes dans leurs organes[60]. La société d'économie mixte par contre peut être créée par transformation d'une société existante, de manière unilatérale par une collectivité publique ou alors sur une base contractuelle associant les personnes publiques et les personnes privées. Ces mêmes catégories de personnes se retrouvent dans les organes de la société. La société d'économie mixte ne saurait par ailleurs être confondue aux sociétés purement privées.

3) La distinction entre la société d'économie mixte et les sociétés purement privées

La société d'économie mixte ne saurait être confondue aux sociétés purement privées, qu'elles soient commerciales ou civiles. Ces dernières ont un régime de création, d'organisation et de fonctionnement largement dominé par le droit privé. La société d'économie mixte a par contre un régime en principe dérogatoire au commun. Les organes des sociétés d'économie mixte sont composés des collectivités publiques et des personnes

[60]Au Cameroun par exemple, l'article 30 de la loi de 1999 précitée précise que lorsque l'Etat est actionnaire unique d'une société à capital public, le rôle de l'assemblée générale est dévolu à un collège de cinq (5) membres dont la composition est fixée par les statuts. Ce collège comprend obligatoirement un représentant du ministre chargé des finances et un représentant du ministre chargé de la tutelle technique. Le représentant du ministre chargé des finances assure la présidence de l'assemblée générale. L'article 31 précise que lorsqu'une collectivité territoriale décentralisée est unique actionnaire, le rôle de l'assemblée générale est dévolu à un collège de cinq(5) membres désignés par son organe délibérant. L'article 32 dispose que lorsque la société à capital public a plusieurs actionnaires, l'assemblée générale est composée des représentants des actionnaires.

privées. Celles des sociétés purement de droit privé sont en principe composées de personnes privées.

CONCLUSION

La société d'économie mixte n'est au demeurant pas une forme achevée de délégation de service public. Elle peut pourtant être délégataire d'un service public .Elle ne correspond toutefois pas suffisamment à la concession, l'affermage et la régie intéressée. La raison est que, en elle-même, la société d'économie mixte est une entreprise parapublique. Toutefois, il est toujours possible de la rattacher aux délégations de service public. Seulement, ce n'est pas la société d'économie mixte en elle-même qui sera prise en considération, mais l'activité de service public qu'elle gère ou exploite. De la sorte, c'est la gestion déléguée du service public par une société d'économie mixte sur habilitation contractuelle de la personne publique qui peut être considérée comme un mode de délégation de service public.

Une réforme législative ou une précision jurisprudentielle de la qualification de la société d'économie mixte serait alors salutaire pour le droit camerounais des entreprises du secteur public et parapublic. Ceci afin de positionner avec souplesse la société d'économie mixte dans sa catégorie correspondante, surtout qu'elle peut toujours être habilitée par la personne publique à gérer ou exploiter un service public. Il s'agit là d'une interpénétration du secteur public et du secteur privé qui n'est toutefois pas totale, car « *le droit fonctionne comme du caoutchouc. Il plie sous la pression des réalités socio-économiques nouvelles, mais il ne cède pas. La dichotomie du public et du privé (...) ne va pourtant pas jusqu'à la rupture* »[61].

Il ne faudrait toutefois pas minorer l'importance du mode de création et des modalités d'action de la société d'économie mixte dans son rattachement aux conventions de délégation de service public. Sa création peut résulter d'un contrat administratif, mais si elle n'est pas habilitée contractuellement par une personne publique à exploiter un service public, elle ne correspond

---

[61]Simar (C)« *Les entreprises publiques : éléments d'analyse et de réflexion* », Cahiers de recherche sociologique, n° 15,1990, p. 112.

pas aux délégations de service public, mais davantage à une gestion mutualisée du service public. Si par contre elle est créée unilatéralement par la personne publique pour gérer une activité de service public, on parlera certainement de « *délégation unilatérale du service public* ».

LE RESPECT DES DROITS DE LA DÉFENSE DANS LE CONTENTIEUX DISCIPLINAIRE DE LA FONCTION PUBLIQUE AU CAMEROUN

AIME DOUNIAN[1]

RÉSUMÉ *:* Notion en général dégagée par la jurisprudence, dont la doctrine a conceptualisé les décisions, les droits de la défense sont un ensemble très vaste de prérogatives accordées à un justiciable en procès pour lui permettre d'assurer la sauvegarde de ses intérêts face à l'autre partie. Au Cameroun, la Constitution a consacré ce principe à travers son préambule en ces termes « *tout prévenu est présumé innocent jusqu'à ce que sa culpabilité soit établie au cours d'un procès conduit dans le strict respect des droits de la défense* ». Au regard de la Constitution, c'est théoriquement le juge constitutionnel qui est habilité à garantir ce droit. En l'absence de son œuvre jurisprudentielle dans ce domaine, il faut se tourner vers le juge administratif pour découvrir l'immense travail abattu par ce dernier dans la protection des droits de la défense. Il est parvenu ainsi à donner un sens et un contenu au respect des droits de la défense. C'est précisément ce regard du juge que nous nous sommes proposé d'examiner dans le champ du contentieux disciplinaire de la fonction publique. Il en ressort que le juge administratif camerounais assure le respect du principe des droits de la défense à travers la garantie des droits du mis en cause d'une part et la régularité de la procédure d'autre part.

Dans une de ses communications, le doyen Louis FAVOREU déclarait : « *la protection des droits fondamentaux nécessite, pour être assurée contre les pouvoirs exécutif et législatif, en application de textes constitutionnels(ou*

---

[1] Docteur/Ph.D en Droit public, Chargé de Cours à l'Université de Ngaoundéré (Cameroun) où il dispense les enseignements tels que le Droit administratif, le droit de l'environnement et le droit de l'urbanisme. Il est actuellement le Coordonnateur de l'Annexe de la Faculté des Sciences juridiques et politiques de l'Université de Ngaoundéré à Garoua.

internationaux), qu'en soient chargés, non plus seulement les juges ordinaires, mais aussi les juges constitutionnels et même les juges internationaux »[2]. C'est précisément dans ce sillage que s'inscrit cette contribution sur le respect du principe des droits de la défense dans le contentieux disciplinaire de la fonction publique. En effet, évoquer le principe des droits de la défense, c'est mettre en relief l'une des zones grises du constitutionnalisme à savoir la garantie des droits fondamentaux.

Issue du droit allemand[3], la notion de droit fondamental renvoie à deux acceptions principales. D'une part elle désigne les droits et libertés attachés à l'individu qui fonde le primat ontologique de l'être humain sur la société et le groupe ; c'est la définition substantielle. D'autre part, les droits fondamentaux sont les droits et libertés qui s'imposent aux pouvoirs législatif, exécutif et juridictionnel parce qu'ils sont protégés par la constitution de l'État et les traités auxquels celui-ci est partie[4] : c'est la définition formelle. En d'autres termes, les droits fondamentaux désignent une catégorie de droits qui se distinguent soit par leur fondamentalité substantielle -propriété constitutive des normes supérieures- soit par le caractère formel de leur fondamentalité en tant que droits inscrits dans la norme fondamentale[5]. Diverses classifications ont été opérées au sein des droits fondamentaux. L'on peut citer les droits inhérents à l'être, les droits du citoyen, les droits de l'acteur économique et les droits du justiciable. S'agissant de cette dernière catégorie, l'on peut énumérer-la liste n'étant point exhaustive, mais purement indicative- le droit d'accès à la justice, le droit à un tribunal impartial, la présomption d'innocence et les droits de la défense. C'est ce dernier droit fondamental qui constitue la matrice de notre analyse dans le contentieux disciplinaire de la fonction publique au

---

[2] FAVOREU (L.), « Universalité des droits fondamentaux et diversité culturelle » in *L'effectivité des droits fondamentaux dans les pays de la communauté francophone*, QUEBEC, AUPELF-UREF, 1994, p.48.

[3]FAVOREU (L.), *op. cit.*, p.37.

[4] DORD (O.), « Droits fondamentaux, notion de droits fondamentaux et théorie des droits fondamentaux » in ANDRIANTSIMBAZOVINA (J.) (Sous la dir.), *Dictionnaire des droits de l'homme,* Paris, QUADRIGE/PUF, 2012, p.332.

[5]PREUB (U.), « La garantie des droits : « les droits horizontaux » » in *Traité international De Droit constitutionnel,* Paris, Dalloz, 2012, p.234.

Cameroun. Il a été consacré sur le plan international, régional, voire national.

Au niveau international, l'article 10 de la Déclaration universelle des droits de l'homme stipule : « *toute personne a droit, en pleine égalité, à ce que sa cause soit entendue équitablement, et publiquement par un tribunal indépendant et impartial qui décidera, soit de ses droits et obligations, soit du bien-fondé de toute accusation en matière pénale dirigée contre elle* »[6]. L'article 11 dispose : « *toute personne accusée d'un acte délictueux est présumée innocente jusqu'à ce que sa culpabilité ait été légalement établie au cours d'un procès public où toutes les garanties nécessaires à sa défense lui auront été assurées* »[7].

Dans le cadre régional, l'article 6 de la Convention européenne des droits de l'homme abonde dans le même sens[8]. La Charte africaine des droits de l'homme et des peuples dispose à son tour « *Toute personne a droit à ce que sa cause soit entendue. Ce droit comprend(...) Le droit à la présomption d'innocence, jusqu'à ce que sa culpabilité soit établie par une juridiction compétente ; le droit à la défense, y compris celui de se faire assister par un défenseur de son choix ; le droit d'être jugé dans un délai raisonnable par une juridiction impartiale* »[9].

---

[6] Article 10 de la Déclaration universelle des droits de l'homme du 10 décembre 1948.

[7] Article 11 de la Déclaration universelle des droits de l'homme du 10 décembre 1948.

[8] Selon l'article 6 en effet « *Toute personne a droit à ce que sa cause soit entendue équitablement, publiquement et dans un délai raisonnable par un tribunal indépendant et impartial établi par la loi, qui décidera, soit des contestations sur ses droits et obligations de caractère civil, soit du bien-fondé de toute accusation en matière pénale dirigée contre elle(...).Tout accusé a droit notamment à être informé, dans le plus court délai, dans une langue qu'il comprend et d'une manière détaillée, de la nature et de la cause de l'accusation portée contre lui ; de disposer du temps et des facilités nécessaires à la préparation de sa défense ; de se défendre lui-même ou avoir l'assistance d'un défenseur de son choix et, s'il n'a pas les moyens de rémunérer un défenseur, pouvoir être assisté gratuitement par un avocat d'office, lorsque, les intérêts l'exigent, d'interroger ou de faire interroger les témoins à charge gratuitement par un avocat d'office, lorsque les intérêts de la justice l'exigent, d'interroger ou de faire interroger les témoins à charge et obtenir la convocation et l'interrogation des témoins à décharge dans les mêmes conditions que les témoins à charge ; de se faire assister gratuitement d'un interprète, s'il ne comprend pas ou ne parle pas la langue employée à l'audience* ».

[9] Article 7 de la Charte africaine des droits de l'homme et des peuples adoptée le 27 juin 1981 à Nairobi et ratifiée le 21 octobre 1986.

Sur un plan purement national, à travers un instrument juridique français en l'occurrence la Déclaration des droits de l'homme et du citoyen du 26 août 1789, l'on peut déjà percevoir les prémices du respect des droits de la défense[10]. la Constitution de la République tchadienne dispose « *tout prévenu est présumé innocent jusqu'à l'établissement de sa culpabilité à la suite d'un procès régulier offrant des garanties indispensables à sa défense* »[11].L'article 1er(4) de la Constitution gabonaise dispose que « *la République gabonaise reconnaît et garantit les droits inviolables et imprescriptibles de l'homme, qui lient obligatoirement les pouvoirs publics(...)les droits de la défense, dans le cadre d'un procès, sont garantis à tous* »[12].

La Constitution camerounaise consacre le principe des droits de la défense dans son préambule en ces termes « *tout prévenu est présumé innocent jusqu'à ce que sa culpabilité soit établie au cours d'un procès conduit dans le strict respect des droits de la défense* »[13]. Ce droit fondamental, comme tous les autres droits fondamentaux, est garanti par le juge constitutionnel. Au Cameroun, en principe, c'est le juge constitutionnel qui est habilité à garantir ce droit[14]. En l'absence de son œuvre jurisprudentielle en la matière, il faut interroger le juge administratif pour s'apercevoir que celui-ci a élaboré un travail fort intéressant à propos de la garantie des droits de la défense. En effet, celui-ci est parvenu à donner un sens et un contenu au principe des droits de la défense. C'est précisément la manière dont le juge a traité de ce principe que nous nous proposons d'examiner dans le champ du contentieux disciplinaire de la fonction publique.

---

[10] Il s'agit des articles 7 à 9 de la Déclaration des droits de l'homme et du citoyen du 26 août 1789.

[11] Article 24 de la Constitution tchadienne adoptée par référendum le 31 mars 1996 et révisée par la Loi constitutionnelle n°08/PR/2005 du 15 juillet 2005.

[12] Article 1er(4) de la Constitution de la République gabonaise modifiée par la loi n°13/2003 du 19 août 2003.

[13]Préambule de la de la Loi n°96/06 du 18 janvier 1996 portant révision de la Constitution du 02 juin 1972 modifiée par la Loi n°2008/001 du 14 avril 2008.

[14] Son homologue béninois est plutôt très avancé dans ce domaine. Cf. DCC 00-024 du 10 mars 2000 (aff.SOVI, obs. DJOGBENOU(J.), pp.605-609,in Association Béninoise de Justice Constitutionnelle, *Annuaire Béninois de Justice Constitutionnelle*, Cotonou, PUB, I-2013.

Principe dominant en procédure, les droits de la défense ne sont pas définis par la loi[15]; notion en général dégagée par la jurisprudence, dont la doctrine a conceptualisé les décisions, les droits de la défense sont un ensemble très vaste de prérogatives accordées à une personne en procès pour lui permettre d'assurer la sauvegarde de ses intérêts face à son adversaire[16]. Certains auteurs parlent, non de droits de la défense, mais de principe de contradictoire alors qu'en réalité celui-ci, qui implique la participation d'une personne à la procédure, n'est qu'un aspect de celui-là. En France, les droits de la défense existent dans les procédures pénale, civile et administrative et sur la base des sources distinctes[17]. En clair, ils s'appliquent désormais à toutes les règles qui ont la nature d'une punition[18].

Ainsi, en procédure pénale, la construction des droits de la défense émane de la jurisprudence et de la loi ; d'abord la jurisprudence qui a vu dans cette notion un principe général avec un arrêt de la chambre criminelle en date du 12 juin 1952[19]. Ensuite, de la loi qui, depuis celle du 8 décembre 1897, n'a cessé d'apporter de nouvelles pierres à l'édifice, les deux lois des 4 janvier et 24 août 1993, et celle du 15 juin 2000 étant pour l'heure les plus importantes. Aujourd'hui, les principaux aspects des droits de la défense sont au cours de l'enquête, la visite d'un avocat, l'instruction préparatoire, l'assistance d'un avocat, la consultation du dossier et le plaidoyer qui intervient au cours du jugement. Par ailleurs, les décisions sont motivées et susceptibles de recours. La violation des droits de la défense entraîne la nullité de l'acte.

En droit judiciaire privé, le climat est différent puisqu'il n'y a point de mis en examen, mais seulement des parties demanderesse et défenderesse. Ces parties bénéficient cependant d'un ensemble de garanties fondamentales pour défendre leurs intérêts qui ne sont pas toujours différentes des précédentes. Bien plus, très tôt, et en dehors de tout texte, le principe des

---

[15] PRADEL(J), « Droits de la défense », in ALLAND (D.) ET RIALS(S.), (Sous la dir.), *Dictionnaire de la Culture Juridique*, *op. cit.*, p.538.

[16]*Ibidem.*

[17] *Ibidem.*

[18] GINESTET(C), « Les droits de la défense en procédure pénale » in CABRILLAC(R) ET alii, *Libertés et droits fondamentaux*, Paris, Dalloz, 16e ed. 2010, p.546.

[19]*Ch.crim. 12 juin 1952, arrêt Imbert, JCP 1952, II, 7241, note Bronchot.*

droits de la défense s'est imposé dans le procès civil. Dès 1828, la Cour suprême d'alors en France, a solennellement proclamé que « *la défense étant de droit naturel, personne ne doit être condamné sans avoir été interpellé et mis en demeure de se défendre* »[20] .Ces garanties ou droits de la défense constituent un principe général de droit et selon certains arrêts du Conseil constitutionnel un principe à valeur constitutionnelle[21].Elles mobilisent le principe du contradictoire et les voies de recours. De plus, les décisions doivent être nécessairement motivées.

Le contentieux administratif pour sa part connaît la notion de droits de la défense, dégagée par la jurisprudence : d'abord par celle du Conseil d'État français avec un arrêt du 23 janvier 1924[22] ; ensuite, par celle du Conseil constitutionnel français avec un arrêt du 2 décembre 1976 affirmant que le respect des droits de la défense résulte des principes fondamentaux reconnus par les lois de la République, ce qui leur confère une valeur constitutionnelle[23].

Il faut au préalable noter que les prémices du principe des droits de la défense ont été érigées par l'article 65 de la loi du 22 avril 1905, qui dispose que tous les fonctionnaires, employés ou ouvriers de toutes les administrations publiques ont droit à la communication personnelle et confidentielle de tous documents composant leur dossier avant d'être l'objet d'une mesure disciplinaire ou d'un déplacement d'office.

C'est justement à ce propos qu'une analyse du principe du respect des droits de la défense à l'aune de la jurisprudence administrative camerounaise trouve tout son sens. Il ne s'agit pas ici, d'égrener le chapelet de toutes les décisions de justice administrative en matière des droits de la défense. Mais par un choix se basant sur l'historique de la justice administrative camerounaise et la pertinence de certaines décisions de justice, l'on a trouvé judicieux de s'intéresser au principe du respect des droits de la défense dans

---

[20] *Cass.civ.7 mai 1828, S.1828, I, 329.*

[21] GINESTET(C), « Les droits de la défense en procédure pénale », *op.cit.*, p.539.

[22] *C.E. 23 janvier 1924, Petit Colas.*

[23] FAVOREU (L.) et PHILIP (L.), *Les grandes décisions du Conseil Constitutionnel*, Paris, Dalloz, 2003, p.577.

le contentieux disciplinaire de la fonction publique[24]. Dans cette optique, l'examen d'une cinquantaine de décisions de justice administrative à travers les décisions du Conseil du contentieux administratif, du tribunal d'Etat, de la Cour fédérale de justice et de la Cour suprême entre 1952 et 1993 a permis d'analyser comment le juge administratif camerounais appréhende le principe des droits de la défense dans le champ du contentieux disciplinaire de la fonction publique.

Relativement à la jurisprudence, les auteurs ne sont pas d'accord sur l'autorité de la jurisprudence comme source de droit. Pour certains, les tribunaux ayant reçu mission d'interpréter la loi, ont en même temps le pouvoir, à côté du législateur, de créer la règle de droit, chaque fois au moins que cette règle n'est pas contraire à la loi[25]. D'autres refusent à la jurisprudence tout pouvoir créateur : les tribunaux doivent se borner à appliquer la loi et à constater la coutume ; leurs décisions n'ont qu'une autorité indirecte, tirée des sources directes sur lesquelles elles reposent[26]. Aujourd'hui, la jurisprudence est devenue une source de droit considérable[27].En effet, le pouvoir créateur du juge est une des questions qui divisent le plus les systèmes et la pensée juridiques[28]. La jurisprudence est la

---

[24]En effet, le contentieux de la fonction publique constitue à lui seul plus de la moitié du contentieux administratif à côté du contentieux électoral, du domaine de l'Etat, du contrat administratif, des accidents de circulation etc. Voir à ce sujet GUESSELE ISSEME (L.P.), *L'apport de la Cour Suprême au droit administratif,* thèse de doctorat en droit public, Université de Yaoundé II(Soa), septembre 2010, 664 pages. Plus précisément dans la deuxième partie de la thèse.

[25]Pour les partisans de cette thèse, l'on peut citer Hans KELSEN, Michel TROPER.

[26]Comme chef de file, l'on peut mentionner le Doyen CARBONNIER.

[27] Pour s'en convaincre, les multiples contributions scientifiques à ce sujet. L'on peut citer *la jurisprudence aujourd'hui* par les Professeurs Jean Luc AUBERT, BRANDAC, Jean Marie BRETON, Le Doyen CARBONNIER, Gérard CORNU, GOBERT, François TERRE, TUNC, ZENATI, *Rev.trim.dr.civ.*1992.337 et les réponses :d'autres propos sur la jurisprudence par Les professeurs TRICOT RONDEAU-RIVIER, SERVERIN ET JEAMMEAUD,BEROUJON in EISMEIN (P), « La jurisprudence et la loi », *Rev.trim.dr.civ.*1952,p.17 ; DUPEYROUX(O), « La jurisprudence, source abusive de droit », Mélanges Maury,p.349 ; « La doctrine française et le problème de la jurisprudence source du droit », Mélanges Gabriel MARTY ; la liste n'étant que purement indicative.

[28]« Nature et rôle de la jurisprudence dans les systèmes juridiques », Actes du 3e Congrès de l'Association internationale de Méthodologie juridique, Rabat 1993, PUAM, *RRJ,1993*-4,

source, d'abord exclusive puis principale des droits anglo-saxons. Elle fut en France, au temps où les parlements rendaient des arrêts de règlement, un germe important du droit de l'ancien régime[29]. Certains droits modernes, bien qu'étrangers à la Common law, reconnaissent au juge un pouvoir para-législatif[30]. En droit français, bien que selon l'article 4 du code civil, le juge ne puisse pas refuser de juger sous prétexte du silence, de l'obscurité ou de l'insuffisance de loi, certains hésitent à voir dans la jurisprudence une véritable source du droit[31]. On ne saurait nier toutefois que, quel que soit le système considéré, les solutions jurisprudentielles finissent par s'imposer, au-delà des parties, à la communauté juridique et à tous les citoyens.

En droit public, le juge administratif a été conduit à élaborer un droit prétorien suite à son affranchissement de l'application des règles de droit privé. Il a dû consacrer les principes généraux et créer le droit. Ainsi les règles les plus importantes du droit administratif ont été posées par le juge[32]. Il en est de même du statut de la fonction publique qui a été élaboré par le Conseil d'État et le législateur n'est intervenu qu'après coup pour consolider les règles ainsi établies. De ce fait, le rôle du juge est essentiel pour appliquer la loi, l'interpréter, en combler les lacunes, mais aussi pour la rajeunir, la vivifier, l'estomper, voire l'ignorer. Fort de tout cela, l'on considérera dans le cadre de cette contribution scientifique, la jurisprudence comme source de droit[33].

Ainsi, dans le langage du droit, le terme contentieux est largement polysémique et ne prend sens qu'en fonction du terme auquel on le confronte. En procédure civile, le contentieux s'oppose au gracieux, alors que pour les spécialistes de droit administratif, il s'oppose au traitement non juridictionnel d'un différend(non contentieux ou pré-contentieux).Si l'on s'intéresse aux sources du droit, le terme « *contentieux* » peut être opposé à

Cahiers de méthodologie juridique, n°8. ZENATI(F), *La jurisprudence*, Dalloz, coll. « Méthodes du droit », 1991.

[29]BERGEL (J-L), *Théorie générale du droit*, Paris, Dalloz, 5e ed, 2012, p.83.

[30]*Ibidem.*

[31] Il s'agit du Doyen Carbonnier qui reconnaît quand même la jurisprudence comme une autorité considérable du droit.

[32]VEDEL(G) ET DELVOLVE(P),*Droit administratif*, Paris, PUF,7e éd,1989, p.105 et suiv.

[33]CHABAS(F), *Introduction à l'étude du droit*, Paris, Montchrestien, 12e ed, 2000,p .177.

celui de jurisprudence, le terme désignant alors, toutes procédures confondues, l'activité des appareils juridictionnels et le produit de cette activité. Lié à la notion de contestation, le contentieux a nécessairement à voir avec le litige, le conflit, les procédures et les organes par lesquels un système juridique entend fournir des modes de résolution d'un différend[34]. Vu sous ce prisme, le contentieux disciplinaire renvoie au régime qui a pour objet d'assurer la répression des fautes commises par les fonctionnaires et autres agents publics, quand ces fautes ont un caractère professionnel, c'est-à-dire quand elles résultent d'un manquement aux obligations qui s'imposent aux membres de la fonction publique[35].Pour le célèbre auteur, il s'agit d'un régime susceptible d'emporter un effet de prévention, la crainte de sanctions incitant les agents à se comporter comme ils le doivent[36].Bien plus, un tel régime se distingue de celui de la responsabilité pécuniaire des agents publics. Sa mise en œuvre débouche sur le prononcé de sanctions, dont la sévérité est fonction de la gravité de la faute commise ; alors que celle de l'autre régime se concrétise par une obligation de verser à la victime d'un préjudice une indemnité dont le montant dépend de l'importance du préjudice causé[37].

C'est le Conseil du contentieux administratif qui pose les jalons du contentieux disciplinaire à partir des années 50[38].La connaissance de ce type de contentieux va se perpétuer avec le tribunal d'État, la Cour fédérale de justice et va se consolider avec la Cour suprême. C'est à travers cet ensemble de décisions de justice que transparaît l'œuvre constructive du principe des droits de la défense. Si la construction s'entend comme l'action de construire, l'édification[39], il s'agit surtout de l'élaboration intellectuelle, d'une création prétorienne ou d'un système explicatif[40]. En d'autres termes,

[34] ANCEL(P.) « Contentieux », in CADIET (sous la dir.), *Dictionnaire de la justice*, Paris, PUF, 2004, p.227.
[35] CHAPUS(R.),*Droit administratif général*, T.2,Paris, Montchrestien, 15e ed,2001,p.330.
[36] *Ibidem.*
[37] *Ibidem.*
[38] C'est véritablement à partir des années 50 que le juge administratif camerounais, sous l'égide du Conseil d'Etat français, commence à construire ses propres décisions en la matière.
[39] CORNU (G.), (Sous la dir.), *Vocabulaire juridique*, Paris, PUF, 10e ed., 2014, p.253.
[40] *Ibidem.*

l'action d'assembler selon un plan les éléments d'un édifice, d'un appareil, d'un ouvrage de l'esprit[41].

Ainsi, l'apport de cette étude en droit administratif et même en droit processuel est significatif d'autant que pour la doctrine, les principes des droits de la défense représentent un vocable ambigu. D'ailleurs, Mme Geneviève GIUDICELLI-DELAGE s'exclamait à la suite du professeur Georges BOLARD en ces termes : « *Est-il plus beau principe que celui (du respect) des droits de la défense ?* » Certes pas[42] . Et pourtant est-il vocable aussi ambigu que celui de « *droits de la défense* » ? Si ambigu que les rédacteurs du nouveau code de procédure civile l'ont, par « *une abstention résolue* » écarté, que la doctrine lui fait un sort tellement divers qu'il en devient, tout autant que son contenu, introuvable ; que, face à l'apparition de nouveaux concepts, alors qu'il exprime l'essence même du procès, il semble ne plus servir qu'à désigner quelques droits subjectifs processuels[43]. Sur un plan strictement jurisprudentiel, ce principe qui innerve toutes les procédures[44] est reconnu tantôt comme un principe général de droit aussi bien en France qu'au Cameroun, tantôt comme un principe à valeur constitutionnelle[45] ou encore comme un principe communautaire[46].

C'est fort de ces considérations qu'il paraît judicieux d'analyser le traitement que le juge administratif camerounais fait du respect du principe

---

[41] DUBOIS (J.), *Dictionnaire Lexis*, Paris, EAN, 2014, p.412.

[42] GIUDICELLI-DELAGE (G.), « Droits de la défense », in CADIET (L.), (Sous la dir.), *Dictionnaire de la justice*, op.cit., p.364.

[43] *Idem., p.364.*

[44] Voir en ce sens PRADEL(J), « Droits de la défense », in ALLAND (D.) ET RIALS(S.), (Sous la dir.), *Dictionnaire de la Culture Juridique, op.cit.*, p.538.

[45] FAVOREU (L.) et PHILIP (L.), *les grandes décisions du Conseil Constitutionnel*, op.cit., p.577.

[46] *Arrêt n°012/2011 du 31 mars 2011, Aff. Banque Atlantique du Cameroun-COBAC-Autorité monétaire du Cameroun-Amity Bank Cameroon PLC C/Arrêt n°010/CJ/CEMAC/CJ/09 du 13 novembre 2009 ;voir également Arrêt n°0031 CJ/CEMAC/CJ/03 du 03 juillet 2003, affaire TASHA LOWEH Lawrence ; Décision COBAC D-2000/22 et Amity bank Cameroon PLC ; Amity bank Cameroon PLC C/ arrêt n°010 /CJ/09 du 13 novembre 2009 ;arrêt n°003/CJ/CEMAC/CJ/09 du 25 juin 2009 affaire GUEREZEBANGA. En Europe, CJUE, 1ere ch.,2 novembre 2012, M.M C/Minister for justice, Equality and lawreform, aff.C-277/11 ; CJCE du 5 avril 1979, RATTI, C-148/78 ;CJCE du 16 juillet 1992, Banca Privada, C-67/91.*

des droits de la défense dans le contentieux disciplinaire de la fonction publique. Aussi la question principale qui retient notre attention est celle de savoir comment le juge administratif camerounais assure le respect des droits de la défense. Cette question se justifie sur le plan historique par le procédé par lequel ce principe a été consacré et implémenté, car il s'agit d'une œuvre du juge que le législateur a par la suite codifiée. Sur le plan théorique, ce principe demeure pour la doctrine un véritable vocable ambigu d'après une partie de la doctrine[47]. Il se justifie également sur le plan pratique, au regard de sa forte présence et même sa prégnance dans tous les procès de nos jours.

C'est ainsi que dans une démarche qui se veut réaliste d'approche hypothético-déductive, l'on démontrera que le juge administratif camerounais assure le respect du principe des droits de la défense à travers deux techniques principales à savoir d'une part la garantie des droits du mis en cause (I) et d'autre part la régularité de la procédure (II).

I- LA GARANTIE DES DROITS DU MIS EN CAUSE

Le contentieux disciplinaire oppose généralement deux parties à savoir l'administration d'un côté et le mis en cause de l'autre côté. Celui-ci est la personne contre qui une mesure disciplinaire est requise. Ce dernier a des droits qu'il faut garantir. Il s'agit du droit de se faire communiquer le dossier (A) et du droit de présenter sa défense(B).

A- LE DROIT DE SE FAIRE COMMUNIQUER LE DOSSIER

L'obligation de communication du dossier est un des grands principes généraux du droit de la fonction publique qui concerne tous les agents publics y compris les militaires et les préfets[48].En vertu de ce droit, lorsque l'action disciplinaire est engagée, le fonctionnaire a la possibilité de solliciter et d'obtenir la communication intégrale de son dossier individuel et des documents annexes. L'administration ne doit pas le lui refuser. Elle est en outre tenue de lui laisser tout le temps nécessaire pour prendre connaissance de chacune des pièces du dossier afin de préparer sa défense.

---

[47]Voir les déclarations de Mme Giudicelli Delage et du Professeur Georges Bolard sus évoquées.

[48] AUBY (J.M.) et alii, *Droit de la fonction publique*, Paris, Dalloz, 5e ed., 2005, p.378.

En d'autres termes, afin de présenter sa défense, le mis en cause doit se faire communiquer son dossier. Cette communication se déroule selon un procédé(1) bien déterminé et vise un but bien précis (2).

La communication a également pour procédé de faire connaître à l'agent la mesure disciplinaire et ses motifs.

1) Le procédé : faire connaître à l'agent la mesure disciplinaire et ses motifs

Le procédé est une méthode qui permet d'obtenir un certain résultat[49]. La méthode adoptée par le juge administratif pour la communication du dossier se traduit par l'usage d'une procédure et l'adoption des formes de communication. Le procédé se résume ainsi en la convocation de l'intéressé et la communication du dossier.

S'agissant du premier point, le juge administratif ne paraît pas explicite sur la question de la convocation du mis en cause. Il évoque juste celle-ci comme un élément de la procédure. Il affirme à cet effet « *Attendu que tout fonctionnaire traduit devant le conseil de discipline a droit à la défense (convocation…) ; Que la violation de ce droit est sanctionnée par le juge administratif par l'annulation de l'acte incriminé* »[50]. À y regarder de près, la convocation dont fait montre le juge administratif est l'information. Il l'affirme d'ailleurs en ces termes : « *attendu(…) qu'il appartient au fonctionnaire informé de l'action disciplinaire entreprise à son égard, de solliciter de l'Administration la communication de son dossier* »[51]. Le juge administratif français l'affirme également en ces termes « *Considérant(…) que la requérante, n'ayant pas été préalablement invitée à présenter sa défense, est fondée à soutenir que la décision attaquée a été prise dans des conditions irrégulières par le préfet de la Seine et est, dès lors, entachée d'excès de pouvoir ;* »[52].

---

[49] DUBOIS (J.), *Dictionnaire Lexis*, *op.cit.*, p.1501.

[50] *Jugement n°64/90-91 du 26 août 1990, AMOUGOU Linus C/ Etat du Cameroun(MFPCE).*

[51] *Jugement n°56/CS/CA/84-85 du 28 février 1985, MBANG Nicolas C/ Etat du Cameroun. En France cette position a été définie par le Conseil d'Etat (C.E. 26 juillet 1952, Rec. Lebon, p.415 ou encore C.E sect.5 mai 1944, Dame Veuve TROMPIER-GRAVIER, Rec.133.).*

[52] *C.E Sect.5 mai 1944, Dame Veuve TROMPIER-GRAVIER, Rec.133.*

La doctrine[53] va également dans le même sens que le juge administratif. En effet, pour le professeur René CHAPUS l'autorité administrative est d'abord tenue de mettre l'intéressé*« en mesure » ou « en même »* de présenter sa défense[54].Poursuivant sa réflexion, il affirme que s'agissant des fonctionnaires relevant du statut général de la fonction publique, la loi prescrit que l'Administration doit les informer de leur droit à demander la communication de leur dossier. En ce qui concerne les autres agents publics et hors de la fonction publique, on peut croire au vu de certaines décisions de justice, qu'il suffit que l'intéressé ait été avisé du projet de sanction, ou même que les circonstances n'aient pas pu lui permettre d'ignorer l'imminence d'une sanction. Selon d'autres arrêts qu'on voudrait croire mieux représentatifs de l'état actuel du droit, l'Administration est, de plus, tenue d'inviter explicitement l'intéressé à présenter ses moyens de défense, ou à demander la communication du dossier[55]. C'est le sens du décret portant organisation et fonctionnement du conseil permanent de discipline[56].

Aussi pour la doctrine, le déroulement de la procédure disciplinaire est-il structuré par un certain nombre d'étapes. La première est l'information de l'agent. Le principe même de l'information du fonctionnaire avant le prononcé de toute sanction puise ses racines dans le célèbre arrêt d'assemblée du Conseil d'État du 26 octobre 1945, *Aramu* dans lequel la haute juridiction a souligné qu' *« il résulte des principes généraux du droit applicable même en l'absence de texte qu'une sanction ne peut(...) être prononcée légalement sans que l'intéressé ait été mis en mesure de présenter utilement sa défense ;qu'il doit par suite, au préalable, recevoir connaissance(...)*

---

[53] Il s'agit du professeur René CHAPUS et MARCEAU Long et alii. Cf. CHAPUS(R.), *Droit administratif général*, T.1, *op.cit.*, p.1119 ; MARCEAU Long et alii, *Les grands arrêts de la jurisprudence administrative*, *op cit.*, commentaire de l'arrêt Dame Veuve Trompier-Gravier.

[54] CHAPUS(R.), *ibidem.*

[55] *Ibidem.* Pour les jurisprudences citées pour renchérir sa position, il s'agit des espèces *C.E. 7 avril 1975, BOUCHE et 28 octobre 1983, FOGELGESANG.Voir également C.E., Sect.4 mai 1962,Dme Ruard.*

[56]Article 16 du Décret n°2000/685/PM du 13 septembre 2000 portant organisation et fonctionnement du Conseil permanent de discipline de la fonction publique et fixant les règles de la procédure disciplinaire.

de l'essentiel des griefs qui y sont contenus, de manière à être en état de formuler toutes observations qu'il juge nécessaires »[57]. L'information de l'agent est la déclinaison naturelle du principe de la garantie des droits de la défense[58].

Pour certains auteurs, l'intéressé doit être informé qu'une procédure est engagée contre lui. Cette information, qui doit le mettre en mesure de présenter utilement sa défense, doit intervenir dans un délai raisonnable avant l'édiction de la sanction ou de la mesure le concernant[59], c'est-à-dire ni trop tôt[60] ni trop tard[61].

La position du juge administratif camerounais paraît floue quant à la forme de l'information. Il insiste tout comme la doctrine sur le délai et la procédure de l'information. À ce sujet, il déclare« *Considérant(…) qu'ainsi le requérant est fondé à se plaindre de n'avoir pas été mis à même de se disculper, et de n'avoir pas pu présenter, en temps utile, sa défense à l'autorité chargée du pouvoir disciplinaire »*[62]. Sur la question de la procédure, le juge camerounais a adopté la position classique que ne partage plus, selon les propos du professeur René CHAPUS, la jurisprudence française[63]. En effet, si en France l'administration a l'obligation d'informer, pour le juge administratif camerounais, l'Administration peut porter à l'intention de l'intéressé l'information. Bien plus, celui-ci est également obligé de requérir de l'administration l'information lorsqu'il a connaissance d'une action disciplinaire retenue contre lui. Il l'affirme d'autant en ces termes : « *Attendu qu'il appartient au fonctionnaire informé de l'action disciplinaire entreprise à son égard, de solliciter de l'Administration la communication de son dossier ;Attendu que MBANG Nicolas ne rapporte nulle part la preuve et n'offre pas de rapporter, qu'il ait sollicité la communication de son dossier et que l'administration le lui ait refusé, Qu'au demeurant, ce fonctionnaire ayant*

---

[57] *C.E. 26 octobre 1945, Aramu, Lebon 213, S.196.3.1 ; concl.Odent*

[58]MARC(E.), « les agents publics », in GONOD(P.) et alii, *Traité de droit administratif*, T.2, Paris, Dalloz, 2011, p.390.

[59] MARCEAU Long et alii, *Les Grands arrêts de la Jurisprudence administrative*, Paris, Dalloz, 19e éd, 2013, p.348.

[60] *C.E. Sect. 8 novembre 1963, Ministre de l'agriculture C/coopérative d'insémination artificielle de la Vienne.*

[61] *C.E. Sect.20 janvier 1956, Nègre.*

[62] *CCA n°250 du 25 septembre 1953, MFOULOU Jacques C/ Administration du territoire.*

[63] Cf. CHAPUS(R.), *Droit administratif général, op.cit.*, p.1119.

comparu devant le Conseil de discipline sans faire la moindre réserve, est non recevable à se prévaloir devant la chambre du vice de forme résultant du défaut de communication de son dossier personnel ; »[64]. Le juge étend l'application de cette double mesure aussi bien aux fonctionnaires qu'aux agents non fonctionnaires[65].

C'est dire que pour le juge administratif camerounais, la convocation tient à l'obligation d'informer. Celle-ci peut se faire par l'administration qui s'engage à déclencher une procédure disciplinaire contre un mis en cause, ou se faire sur l'initiative de l'intéressé lorsque celui-ci a connaissance d'une mesure disciplinaire retenue contre lui. Cette étape est le préalable à la communication du dossier à l'intéressé.

Quant au second point, en France, le droit à la communication du dossier a été consacré suite à l'affaire dite « *des fiches* », par l'article 65 de la loi de finances du 22 avril 1905 qui dispose que : « *tous les fonctionnaires civils et militaires, tous les employés et ouvriers de toutes les administrations publiques ont droit à la communication personnelle et confidentielle de toutes les notes, feuilles signalétiques et tous autres documents composant leur dossier, soit avant d'être l'objet d'une mesure disciplinaire ou d'un déplacement d'office, soit avant d'être retardés dans leur avancement à l'ancienneté* »[66].

Le droit à la communication est, certes, une simple règle de procédure, mais le juge administratif, par une véritable politique jurisprudentielle, lui a conféré une portée essentielle et une jurisprudence très abondante. Ainsi, l'administration est tenue d'informer le fonctionnaire de son droit à la communication de son dossier. Toutefois, c'est l'intéressé lui-même qui doit demander ensuite cette communication[67].

---

[64]Jugement n°56/CS/CA/84-85 du 28 février 1985, MBANG Nicolas C/ Etat du Cameroun.

[65] Dans une autre affaire, il déclare : « *Considérant(...) qu'ainsi le Sieur OBAM ETEME n'ayant pas été préalablement invité à présenter ses moyens de défense ; l'arrêté attaqué a été pris en violation du principe du respect des droits de la défense ; qu'il est de ce point de vue aussi, entaché d'excès de pouvoir* ; » *Arrêt n°98/CFJ/CAY du 27 janvier 1970, OBAM ETEME Joseph C/ République fédérale du Cameroun.*

[66] Article 65 de la loi de finances du 22 avril 1905.

[67] MARC(E.), « Les agents publics », in GONOD(P.), *Traité de droit administratif*, T.2., *op. cit.*, p.391.

Pour le professeur René CHAPUS, l'intéressé ayant demandé à présenter sa défense, l'autorité administrative doit lui communiquer son dossier ou les griefs existant contre lui[68].La communication doit être faite de façon utile, c'est-à-dire d'une part, l'intéressé doit pouvoir prendre connaissance de l'intégralité des pièces de son dossier (y compris, bien entendu, les documents intéressant la poursuite disciplinaire) ou être informé de l'ensemble des griefs ;d'autre part, il doit disposer pour préparer sa défense d'un délai convenable, en rapport avec la complexité et les particularités de l'affaire[69]. Il doit enfin être informé de son droit à se faire assister d'un ou plusieurs conseils de son choix[70].

C'est d'ailleurs dans ce sens que le juge administratif camerounais abonde quand il déclare« *Mais considérant, en droit qu'aux termes d'une jurisprudence constante et abondante du Conseil d'État, aucune sanction disciplinaire ne peut être prise sans observer les formalités prévues par l'article 65 de la Loi du 22 avril 1905, qui dispose que tous les fonctionnaires, employés ou ouvriers de toutes les administrations publiques ont droit à la communication personnelle et confidentielle de tous documents composant leur dossier avant d'être l'objet d'une mesure disciplinaire ou d'un déplacement d'office ;(...) Considérant, que dans le cas d'espèce, il n'existe au dossier aucune trace prouvant que le dossier administratif a été communiqué au sieur MEKOK, ni que notification de la sanction envisagée et de ses motifs a été notifiée à l'intéressé par l'autorité compétente ; Qu'ainsi le requérant n'a pas été mis à même de se disculper et n'a pu présenter en temps utile sa défense à l'autorité chargée du pouvoir disciplinaire ; Qu'il échet dès lors, d'annuler la décision attaquée* »[71].

C'est dire que la communication du dossier requiert un certain nombre de modalités à savoir le mode et la forme de communication du dossier, le contenu du dossier et le délai de communication. L'absence d'une des modalités entraîne l'annulation de la décision.

---

[68] CHAPUS(R.), *Droit administratif général, op.cit.*, p.1120.

[69] *C.E 7 mai 1975, Le jeune ; C.E 4octobre 1996, Elections municipales de Saint-André ou encore C.E. 28 juillet 1999, Commission nationale des comptes de campagne.*

[70] *C.E.17 juin 1988, Labrosse ; 21 juin 1996, Collery ou encore 26 juillet 1996, CPAM de Montpellier, DA 196, n°498 ; 27 octobre 1999, Ministre de la défense C/Recart, D.2000, SC, p.148, RFDA 1999, p.1296.*

[71] *CCA n°259 du 27 novembre 1953, MEKOK Luc C/ Administration du territoire.*

Pour ce qui est de la procédure et de la forme du dossier, le juge affirme que la communication du dossier doit être personnelle et confidentielle. En outre, le dossier doit être constitué du dossier de l'affaire et du dossier personnel du mis en cause. Il l'affirme d'ailleurs en ces termes « *Attendu que tout fonctionnaire traduit devant le conseil de discipline a droit à la défense (...communication des dossiers personnels et de l'affaire...)* »[72].En plus des dossiers personnels et de l'affaire, le juge, pour certaines affaires, a exigé que soit transmis également le rapport du chef de service[73].

S'agissant du délai et des modalités de communication, la communication du dossier doit se faire avant la comparution. Le juge administratif déclare à cet effet, « *Considérant qu'il est également fait grief aux premiers juges d'avoir rejeté son recours comme non fondé alors que les autorités de la gendarmerie nationale dans la procédure disciplinaire engagée contre lui, avaient violé grossièrement les droits de la défense en omettant de lui communiquer préalablement à sa comparution devant la commission de discipline, son dossier disciplinaire comme l'exigent les articles 140 et 146 du Décret n°75/700 du 06 novembre 1975 suscité ;* »[74]. Il poursuit en affirmant que « *Considérant(...) que d'autre part, l'article 146 dispose* : « *outre le droit précise dans le présent chapitre de s'expliquer verbalement ou par écrit, le militaire présumé fautif doit recevoir communication préalable de son dossier avant sa passation devant tout organisme disciplinaire ;* ». Cette communication du dossier avant la date de la comparution du mis en cause doit se faire dans les conditions telles qu'il puisse valablement assurer sa défense[75].

---

[72] *Jugement n°64/90-91 du 26 août 1990, AMOUGOU Linus C/Etat du Cameroun(MFPCE).*

[73] Il affirme d'ailleurs en ces termes « *Attendu(...) que préparer sa défense c'est pour le stagiaire fonctionnaire, prendre connaissance de son dossier et du rapport de son chef de service(...) ;* », *Arrêt n°9 du 16 octobre 1968, Etat du Cameroun C/BABA Youssoufa.*

[74] *Arrêt n°1/A du 18 février 1993, TCHOUPNJOU Jean Jacques C/ Etat du Cameroun(MINFA).*

[75] À ce propos, le juge affirme que « *Considérant au surplus(...) que les conseils du contentieux saisis de la question de la régularité de la procédure suivie devant les conseils de discipline doivent rechercher si, en fait, d'une part les fonctionnaires qui ont été déférés devant eux ont effectivement eu communication de leur dossier et dans les conditions telles qu'ils aient pu valablement assurer leur défense* », CCA n°318/A du 3 septembre 1954, EBANGOM Benoît C/ Administration du territoire.

La doctrine pense à cet effet que la communication doit se faire dans les conditions qui puissent permettre à l'intéressé de disposer d'un délai convenable pour préparer sa défense[76]. Pour MARCEAU Long et les autres, l'information doit intervenir dans un délai raisonnable avant l'édiction de la sanction ou de la mesure concernant le mis en cause[77], c'est-à-dire ni trop tôt[78] ni trop tard[79]. C'est précisément dans ce sens que converge le juge administratif lorsqu'il affirme « *Considérant(...) qu'ainsi le requérant est fondé à se plaindre de n'avoir pas été mis à même de se disculper, et de n'avoir pas pu présenter, en temps utile, sa défense à l'autorité chargée du pouvoir disciplinaire* »[80]. L'inobservation de cette condition est sanctionnée par l'annulation de la décision attaquée[81]. Il en est de même du contenu du dossier.

En effet, l'intéressé doit pouvoir prendre connaissance de l'intégralité des pièces du dossier ou être informé de l'ensemble des griefs formulés contre lui[82].Le juge administratif utilise plusieurs formules pour exprimer cette exigence. En effet, il déclare « *Mais considérant, en droit qu'aux termes d'une jurisprudence constante et abondante du Conseil d'État, aucune sanction disciplinaire ne peut être prise sans observer les formalités prévues par l'article 65 de la Loi du 22 avril 1905, qui dispose que tous les fonctionnaires, employés ou ouvriers de toutes les administrations publiques ont droit à la communication personnelle et confidentielle de tous documents composant leur dossier avant d'être l'objet d'une mesure disciplinaire ou d'un déplacement d'office* »[83]. Dans

---

76 CHAPUS (R.), *Droit administratif général*, op.cit., p.1120.

77 LONG (M.) et alii, *Les grands arrêts de la jurisprudence administrative*, op.cit.,p.348.

78 *C.E. Sect.8 novembre 1963, Ministre de l'agriculture C/Coopérative d'insémination artificielle de la Vienne.*

79 *C.E. Sect.20 janvier 1956, Nègre.*

80 *CCA n°20 du 25 septembre 1953, MFOULOU Jacques C/ Administration du territoire.*

81 Le juge déclare à ce sujet « *Considérant(...) qu'ainsi le requérant n'a pas été mis à même de se disculper et n'a pas pu présenter en temps utile sa défense à l'autorité chargée du pouvoir disciplinaire ; qu'il échet dès lors, d'annuler la décision attaquée* », *CCA n° 259 du 27 novembre 1953, MEKOK Luc C/ Administration du territoire*

82 CHAPUS (R.), *Droit administratif général, op.cit.*, p.1120

83 CCA n°259 du 27 novembre 1953, MEKOK Luc C/ Administration du territoire.

le même sens, il affirme que l'intégralité du dossier consiste en la production de chaque pièce contenant un grief distinct[84].

Comme la doctrine, la jurisprudence retient deux modes de communication de l'intégralité du dossier à savoir la voie écrite et la voie orale. En effet, le juge déclare pour ce qui est de la voie orale « *Considérant qu'à l'appui de son moyen le requérant a fait valoir que la circulaire du ministre des colonies en date du 25 février 1909 prescrit qu'il doit être donné lecture de toutes pièces du dossier dont l'examen leur est soumis aux membres du conseil de discipline* »[85]. C'est la raison pour laquelle le dossier doit être intégral et complet[86] .

La communication de l'intégralité du dossier a pour objectif non seulement de porter à la connaissance de l'intéressé les griefs retenus contre lui et lui permettre de mieux préparer sa défense en discutant de la régularité des documents et le bien-fondé des faits qui y sont rapportés, mais également de permettre aux membres du conseil de discipline de formuler leur avis en toute connaissance de cause[87].

Pour le juge administratif français, cherchant à développer progressivement une protection efficace de l'agent, il a conféré à la communication un certain nombre de caractéristiques tout en exigeant qu'elle soit complète[88]. L'agent public a droit à la communication de toutes

---

[84] C'est dans une de ses décisions qu'il déclare cela en ces termes « *Mais considérant que la communication du dossier a pour but, en faisant connaître au fonctionnaire la mesure disciplinaire envisagée contre lui, ainsi que ses motifs, de le mettre en mesure de se disculper ;qu'en exigeant qu'elle soit intégrale, on entend que chaque pièce contenant un grief distinct, doit être communiquée ;* » ;Jugement n°65/CFJ/CAY du 30 septembre 1969, EVINA ADA Christophe C/Etat du Cameroun oriental.

[85] *CCA n°318/A du 3 septembre 1954, EBANGOM Benoît C/Administration du territoire.*

[86] *Jugement n°2/CS/CA/78-79 du 2 novembre 1978, SO'O Georges C/ Etat du Cameroun.*

[87] Le juge affirme cela en ces termes « *Considérant(…) qu'il doit être donné lecture de toutes pièces du dossier(…) ;Considérant que ces prescriptions tendent à assumer la défense des droits du fonctionnaire incriminé en portant à sa connaissance qu'à celle du défenseur qui l'assiste et des membres du conseil qui n'ont pas encore pris lecture du dossier, les documents figurant dans celui-ci, et de permettre aux uns de formuler leur avis en toute connaissance de cause et aux autres de discuter la régularité de ces documents et le bien-fondé des faits qui y sont rapportés* ; », CCA n°318/A du 3 septembre 1954, EBANGOM Benoît C/Administration du territoire.

[88] *C.E. 23 mai 1952, Trèbes, Lebon 277.*

les pièces de son dossier utilisées par l'autorité investie du pouvoir disciplinaire à l'appui de son projet de sanction. La communication doit également être utile, c'est-à-dire intervenir suffisamment tôt pour que l'agent puisse vraiment prendre connaissance du contenu de son dossier et préparer au mieux sa défense[89].Cette condition est appréciée en fonction des circonstances de l'espèce[90].Enfin la communication doit être personnelle et confidentielle[91]. Le défenseur choisi par l'agent peut, toutefois, exercer le droit à communication s'il y a été autorisé.

Toutefois le juge administratif camerounais déclare que si certains documents devant se trouver dans le dossier sont absents et si les documents défaillants n'ont aucune incidence sur la solution de l'affaire, la communication peut toujours être considérée comme intégrale[92]. Cette communication vise un but précis.

2) Le but : mettre le mis en cause en mesure de se disculper

Originairement, la règle de la communication du dossier a été instaurée par l'article 65 de la Loi du 22 avril 1905[93]. Ce texte indique que « *tous les fonctionnaires civils et militaires, tous les employés et ouvriers de toutes les administrations publiques ont droit à la communication personnelle et confidentielle de toutes les notes, feuilles signalétiques et tous autres documents composant leur dossier avant d'être l'objet d'une mesure disciplinaire* ». En France, ce principe est repris dans l'article 19 du titre 1 du statut général de la fonction publique au terme duquel « *le fonctionnaire à l'encontre duquel une procédure disciplinaire est engagée a droit à la communication de*

---

[89] *C.E.16 octobre 1936, Bonny, Lebon 881.*

[90] *MARC (E.), « les agents publics », in GONOD (P.), Traité de droit administratif, op.cit., p.391.*

[91] *C.E.13 mars 1962, Mast, AJDA, 1962.311.*

[92] Il le déclare en ces termes « *Attendu que le grief tiré du défaut de communication intégrale du dossier personnel n'est irrecevable devant la section du contentieux administratif que si d'une part, il résulte des pièces du dossier que le demandeur qui l'invoque n'a au moment de sa comparution devant le Conseil de Discipline, émis aucune réserve quant aux documents ne figurant pas dans ledit dossier et si d'autre part les documents défaillants n'ont aucune incidence sur la solution de l'affaire ;* » Arrêt n°22/CFJ/SCAY du 15 novembre 1966, DIWOUTA LOTH Pierre C/ Etat du Cameroun oriental.

[93]BIGLIONE (F.) et GUILLAUMONT (O.), *Droit de la fonction publique en QCM*, Paris, Ellipses, 2006, pp.132-133

l'intégralité de son dossier individuel et de tous les documents annexes(...). L'administration doit informer le fonctionnaire de son droit à communication du dossier ». Ainsi, si le fonctionnaire n'est pas tenu d'accéder à son dossier avant la sanction, l'administration est cependant tenue de l'informer de son droit à communication et de faire droit à toute demande en ce sens[94].Le juge administratif français est particulièrement attaché à ce principe et a imposé son respect même pour les emplois à la décision du gouvernement[95].

Pour le juge administratif camerounais, la communication du dossier a pour but de mettre l'agent en mesure de se disculper. En effet, le juge administratif déclare « *Considérant que la garantie de la communication du dossier a pour but de mettre l'agent en mesure de se disculper, elle ne peut être éludée sous aucun prétexte (C.E.30 juillet 1941, COMIS), lorsqu'il n'existe pas de dossier, l'intéressé doit être prévenu de la mesure disciplinaire envisagée et de ses motifs. Il ne peut être suppléé à l'absence de cette formalité essentielle par la connaissance de l'imminence de la sanction (C.E.27 juillet 1945-REVERDY) »*[96]. La communication du dossier ne peut être écartée sous aucun prétexte[97]. Il confirme ce but en ces termes « *mais considérant que la communication du dossier a pour but, en faisant connaître au fonctionnaire la mesure disciplinaire envisagée contre lui, ainsi que ses motifs, de le mettre en mesure de se disculper »*[98].

Toutefois, ce but est tempéré par les mesures de police. Ainsi, lorsqu'il s'agit d'une décision de police, par exemple un arrêté d'expulsion, l'autorité chargée de cette mesure peut passer outre le respect du principe des droits de

---

[94] *C.E. 21 juin 1996, Commune de Buchères, RFDA, 1996, p.851.*

[95] *C.E. 5 juillet 2000, Mermet, RFDA, 2000, p.1159.*

[96] *CCA n°250 du 25 septembre 1953, MFOULOU JACQUES C/Administration du territoire*

[97] Le juge déclare « *Considérant qu'enfin et surtout l'administration doit respecter les droits de la défense en cas de licenciement pour insuffisance professionnelle résultant d'incapacité notoire, d'éthylisme ou sénilité en mettant le fonctionnaire intéressé en mesure de connaitre les griefs qui lui sont reprochés et de formuler le cas échéant des observations ; »,Arrêt n°3/75/CS/CAG du 19 décembre 1975, MENDOUGA Gérard C/ Etat du Cameroun ; voir également Affaire MFOULOU JACQUES précité.*

[98] *Jugement n°65/CFJ/CAY du 30 septembre 1969, EVINA ADA CHRISTOPHE C/Etat du Cameroun.*

la défense[99] . Il en est également des circonstances exceptionnelles qui peuvent exclure ou restreindre le respect de ce droit[100]. Bien plus, l'autorité compétente pour la sanction n'est pas tenue au respect du principe des droits de la défense en cas d'absence irrégulière constatée. Le juge administratif l'affirme d'ailleurs en ces termes « *Attendu que le requérant n'a pas seulement refusé de se plier à l'ordre d'affectation, il a été absent de son poste pendant près de huit mois à compter du 22 juin 1979, date à laquelle il avait reçu l'ordre de se rendre à Kousseri où il était affecté. D'où il suit que c'est à juste titre que la sanction prévue à l'article 164(2) du décret suscité a été appliquée à son encontre et l'article stipule que « le fonctionnaire qui abandonne son poste pour une durée de plus de six mois est d'office révoqué sans consultation du Conseil de discipline* »[101]. Ces préalables remplis, le mis en cause peut présenter sa défense.

B- LE DROIT DE PRÉSENTER SA DÉFENSE

À l'issue de la communication du dossier, le mis en cause, après avoir préparé sa défense doit la présenter. Le juge administratif a déterminé les modalités de présentation(1), ses objectifs, ainsi que la sanction de l'inobservation de ces modalités articulée autour du débat contradictoire(2).

1) Les modalités de présentation des droits de la défense

Le mis en cause doit, pour se disculper, présenter sa défense. Il peut le faire, soit par écrit, soit verbalement. Il peut également recourir à l'assistance d'un défendeur ou d'un conseil qu'il peut consulter à tout moment. La question des modalités soulève également l'épineux problème du délai. Le juge résume toutes ces modalités en affirmant que, « *Considérant que toute personne qui est appelée à comparaitre devant une instance disciplinaire doit, en vertu des droits de la défense, pouvoir à tout moment, communiquer avec son défenseur ou son conseil, procédure qui est la garantie naturelle de tout*

---

[99]Il l'affirme d'ailleurs en ces termes « *Considérant que la règle qui découle des principes généraux du droit administratif et qui exige de l'autorité compétente de mettre l'intéressé à même de s'expliquer, de présenter sa défense avant toute mesure de sanction, est inapplicable, lorsque, comme dans le cas d'espèce, il s'agit d'une décision de police ;* », *CCA n°208/A du 30 janvier 1953, Jean BOONE C/Administration du territoire.*

[100] *C.E 28 juin 1918 Heyries, GAJA, Paris, Dalloz, 16e ed., 2007, n°32, p.198.*

[101] *CS/CA, jugement n°76-82/83 du 30 juin 1983, MEYONGO Christophe C/ Etat du Cameroun.*

particulier traduit devant le conseil de discipline ; »[102]. Il est donc nécessaire de procéder au décryptage de ces modalités.

Ainsi, la communication par voie écrite a été consacrée par les textes et entérinée par le juge. Celui-ci déclare dans une de ses décisions que « *Considérant que d'autre part, l'article 146 dispose que outre le droit précisé dans le présent chapitre, de s'expliquer verbalement...* »[103].

La communication par voie orale est également autorisée suivant le même procédé que la communication par voie écrite. Poursuivant sur la même lancée, le juge réaffirme que « *Considérant que d'autre part, l'article 146 dispose que outre le droit précisé dans le présent chapitre, de s'expliquer verbalement ou par écrit(...)* »[104].

Le juge administratif déclare par ailleurs que le mis en cause peut se faire assister d'un défenseur de son choix. Il l'affirme en ces termes « *Considérant que(...), il peut avoir recours à un défenseur en se faisant assister par un militaire de son choix afin, non seulement de se justifier de certains actes, mais de faire admettre qu'ils ne sont répréhensibles ou à tout le moins que la sanction proposée par le commandant est trop forte* »[105].

Pour ce qui est du délai, le juge déclare que la présentation de la défense doit se faire en temps utile. Il affirme à ce sujet que « *Considérant(...) qu'ainsi le requérant n'a pas été mis à même de se disculper et n'a pu présenter en temps utile sa défense à l'autorité chargée du pouvoir disciplinaire* »[106].

Finalement, le juge traduit toutes ces modalités par l'expression « *mettre l'intéressé à mesure de discuter les moyens et tous les éléments retenus contre lui pour étayer l'accusation* »[107].

---

[102] *Jugement n°71/CS/CA du 13 mai 1976, BENE BELLA Lambert C/Etat du Cameroun.*

[103] *Arrêt n°°1/A du 18 février 1993, TCHOUPNJOU Jean Jacques C/ Etat du Cameroun (MINFA).*

[104] *Arrêt TCHOUPNJOU Jean Jacques C/ Etat du Cameroun (MINFA) précité.*

[105] *Arrêt n°1/A du 18 février 1993, TCHOUPNJOU Jean Jacques C/ Etat du Cameroun (MINFA).*

[106] *CCA n°250 du 25 septembre 1953, MFOULOU Jacques C/ Administration du territoire ; voir également CCA n°259 du 27 novembre 1953, MEKOK Luc C/ Administration du territoire.*

[107] Il l'affirme en ces termes « *Considérant que l'administration n'ignore pas qu'il faut mettre le fonctionnaire traduit devant le conseil de discipline dans les conditions lui permettant de discuter*

L'inobservation de cette mesure est sanctionnée pour ce qui est du mis en cause par une irrecevabilité[108] et pour l'administration par l'annulation de la décision attaquée[109]. Les modalités remplies, le débat peut avoir lieu.

2) Le débat contradictoire[110]

Il s'agit de l'application de la règle « *audi alteram partem* » traduite littéralement par l'expression « *écoute l'autre partie* ».C'est une règle essentielle de la procédure contentieuse qui a été reprise en procédure administrative non contentieuse[111]. Il s'agit de la nécessité de la procédure contradictoire qui veut que l'Administration ne puisse jamais prendre une décision défavorable à l'endroit d'un administré sans l'avoir au préalable mis en demeure de présenter ses observations[112]. La procédure devant le conseil est garante des droits de la défense. C'est ce qui explique son caractère contradictoire[113].

Ainsi, présenter sa défense revient à la préparer dans un délai convenable, être assisté le cas échéant par un défenseur ou un conseil. C'est du moins ce

---

les griefs retenus contre lui ; que cela signifie que le fonctionnaire doit être mis en mesure de discuter les moyens et tous les éléments retenus pour étayer l'accusation ; », jugement n°2/CS/CA/78-79 du 2 novembre 1978, SO'O Georges C/ Etat du Cameroun.

108 « *Considérant(...) qu'au demeurant, ce fonctionnaire ayant comparu devant le conseil de discipline sans faire la moindre réserve, est non recevable à se prévaloir devant la chambre administrative du vice de forme résultant du défaut de communication de son dossier personnel »,jugement n°56/CS/CA/84-85 du 28 février 1985, MBANG Nicolas C/ Etat du Cameroun.*

109 « *Considérant(...) qu'ainsi le requérant n'a pas été mis à même de se disculper et n'a pu présenter en temps utile sa défense à l'autorité chargée du pouvoir disciplinaire ;*
Qu'il échet, dès lors, d'annuler la décision attaquée », CCA n°259 du 27 novembre 1953, MEKOK Luc C/ Administration du territoire.

110 Encore appelé principe du contradictoire, celui-ci a fait l'objet d'une rencontre scientifique organisée par le tribunal administratif et la Faculté de droit de Pau et regroupé dans un ouvrage intitulé *Le principe du contradictoire dans le procès administratif* sous la direction de Jean GOURDOU, Olivier LECUCQ et Jean-Yves MADEC paru aux Éditions L'Harmattan, Paris, en 2010 et compte 193 pages.

111 DE VILLIERS (M.), (sous la dir.), *Droit public général, op.cit.*, p.562

112 RIVERO (J.) et WALINE (J.), *Droit administratif*, Paris, Dalloz, 21e ed.,2006,p.355

113 Article 14(1) du Décret n°2000/685/PM du 13 septembre 2000 portant organisation et fonctionnement du Conseil permanent de discipline de la fonction publique et fixant les règles de la procédure disciplinaire.

qui ressort de la position du juge quand il déclare que « *Considérant(...) qu'il peut avoir recours à un défenseur en se faisant assister par un militaire de son choix afin, non seulement de se justifier de certains actes, mais de faire admettre qu'ils ne sont répréhensibles à tout le moins que la sanction proposée par le commandant est trop forte* »[114]. Il réitère cela dans un autre jugement en ces termes « *Ainsi le requérant n'a pas été mis à même de se disculper et n'a pu présenter en temps utile sa défense à l'autorité chargée du pouvoir disciplinaire* »[115].Il poursuit en affirmant que « *Considérant au surplus(...) que les conseils du contentieux saisis de la question de la régularité de la procédure suivie devant les conseils de discipline doivent rechercher si, en fait, d'une part les fonctionnaires qui ont été déférés devant eux ont effectivement eu communication de leur dossier et dans des conditions telles qu'ils aient pu valablement assurer leur défense* »[116]. Il renchérit cette position dans une autre affaire lorsqu'il déclare « *Considérant enfin qu'une sanction telle que celle qui a frappé le requérant ne pouvait légalement intervenir sans que ce dernier ait été mis à même de discuter les griefs articulés contre lui ; qu'ainsi le sieur OBAM ETEME n'ayant pas préalablement été invité à présenter ses moyens de défense, l'arrêt attaqué a été pris en violation du principe du respect des droits de la défense ; qu'il est de ce point de vue aussi, entaché d'excès de pouvoir* »[117]. C'est dire que l'intéressé doit être mis dans des conditions lui permettant de présenter sa défense. Si le mis en cause peut assurer lui-même sa défense, la possibilité lui est offerte d'avoir un défenseur ou un conseil. Il le déclare dans une de ses décisions en ces termes « *Considérant que toute personne qui est appelée à comparaître devant une instance disciplinaire, doit, en vertu des droits de la défense, pouvoir à tout moment, communiquer avec son défenseur ou son conseil, procédure qui est la garantie naturelle de tout particulier traduit devant le conseil de discipline* »[118]. Il peut se faire assister, à ses frais, par un avocat ou tout autre mandataire de son choix. Il peut également désigner les

---

[114] *Arrêt n°1/A du 18 février 1993, TCHOUPNJOU Jean Jacques C/ Etat du Cameroun(MINFA).*

[115] *CCA n°259 du 27 novembre 1953, MEKOK Luc C/ Administration du territoire.*

[116] *CCA n°318/A du 3 septembre 1954, EBANGOM Benoît C/Administration du territoire.*

[117] *Arrêt n°98/CFJ/CAY du 27 janvier 1970, OBAM ETEME Joseph C/ République fédérale du Cameroun.*

[118] *Jugement n°71/CS/CA du 13 mai 1976, BENE B'ELLA Lambert C/Etat du Cameroun.*

témoins pour sa cause. C'est du moins la position du pouvoir réglementaire agissant dans le contentieux disciplinaire[119].

Par ailleurs afin de mieux présenter sa défense qui peut se faire sous forme écrite ou verbale, il doit être donné lecture de toutes les pièces du dossier dont l'examen est soumis aux membres du conseil. Cette mesure permet à l'intéressé ainsi qu'à son défenseur qui l'assiste de discuter la régularité des documents présentés et le bien-fondé des faits qui y sont rapportés[120].

Il ressort de cette position du juge administratif que l'idée de construire le principe du respect des droits de la défense devrait indéniablement reposer sur le droit à un procès équitable qui se décline par l'obligation de communication du dossier et le droit pour le mis en cause de présenter sa défense. Cette idée conçue par le juge administratif camerounais se matérialise à travers un aménagement articulé autour de la garantie de la régularité de la procédure.

II- LA RÉGULARITÉ DE LA PROCÉDURE

L'ensemble des règles procédurales s'articule autour de trois points à savoir la convocation qui se réduit à l'obligation de communication du dossier, la séance (débat contradictoire) et l'avis du conseil. La régularité de la procédure renvoie ainsi à la régularité dans la communication du dossier(A) et la régularité dans la comparution(B).

---

[119] *Article 25(1) du Décret n°2000/685/PM du 13 septembre 2000 portant organisation et fonctionnement du Conseil permanent de discipline de la fonction publique et fixant les règles de la procédure disciplinaire.*

[120] Il déclare en effet *« Considérant qu'à l'appui de son moyen le requérant a fait valoir que la circulaire du ministre des colonies en date du 25 février 1909 prescrit qu'il doit être donné lecture de toutes pièces du dossier dont l'examen leur est soumis aux membres du conseil de discipline ;Considérant que ces prescriptions tendent à assumer la défense des droits du fonctionnaire incriminé en portant à sa connaissance qu'à celle du défenseur qui l'assiste(...) de discuter la régularité de ces documents et le bien-fondé des faits qui y sont rapportés ; », CCA n°318/A du 3 septembre 1954, EBANGOM Benoît C/Administration du territoire.*

A- La régularité dans la procédure de communication du dossier

Pour qu'il y ait régularité dans la communication du dossier, il faut que la décision revête le caractère d'une sanction disciplinaire[121] . Cette régularité se traduit par un objectif(1) assorti de garanties(2).

1) L'objectif de la régularité dans la procédure de communication du dossier

Il s'agit de permettre au mis en cause de discuter de tous les éléments retenus contre lui. Le juge administratif affirme d'ailleurs à cet effet « *Considérant que l'Administration n'ignore pas qu'il faut mettre le fonctionnaire traduit devant le conseil de discipline dans des conditions lui permettant de discuter les griefs retenus contre lui ;que cela signifie que le fonctionnaire doit être mis en mesure de discuter les moyens et tous les éléments retenus pour étayer l'accusation ;que c'est une des conditions de la régularité de la procédure, aussi le dossier doit-il être complet ;qu'il est clair que l'omission de l'Administration qui constitue une irrégularité a eu une influence déterminante aux dépens du recourant sur la décision attaquée* »[122].

Il est un aspect de la procédure d'élaboration des décisions administratives en ce qu'elle intéresse également la procédure administrative non contentieuse. En effet l'Administration bénéficie du privilège de la décision exécutoire, c'est-à-dire du droit de prendre sous sa seule signature des décisions obligatoires pour les administrés. Il est absolument nécessaire que ceux-ci, tout au long de la procédure, bénéficient de très solides garanties et notamment celle de faire valoir leur point de vue auprès de l'Administration avant qu'une décision ne soit retenue contre eux[123]. Historiquement, il y a eu peu de textes venant donner des garanties aux administrés dans la procédure administrative. Le plus célèbre est l'article 65 de la loi du 22 avril 1905 imposant la communication du dossier dans toute sanction disciplinaire. Dans le silence des textes, c'est donc le juge qui a

[121] Le juge l'affirme d'ailleurs en ces termes « *Attendu que cette décision, qui ne revêtait pas le caractère d'une sanction disciplinaire, n'avait pas à être précédée de la communication du dossier* », *Arrêt n°14/CFJ/AP du 16 mars 1967, KOLLE MOUANGUE Louis C/ Etat du Cameroun.*

[122] *Jugement n°2/CS/CA/78-79 du 2 novembre 1978, SO'O Georges C/Etat du Cameroun.*

[123] RIVERO (J.) ET WALINE (J.) *op.cit.*, p.355.

dégagé les principales règles de la procédure administrative non contentieuse en général et de la procédure disciplinaire en particulier[124].

Ainsi, la finalité de la procédure disciplinaire est double :elle doit permettre la détermination objective des faits ou des omissions qui ont motivé le déclenchement des poursuites, tout en permettant à l'agent d'assurer convenablement sa défense et de compenser en quelque sorte le caractère nécessairement inégalitaire des rapports de l'agent accusé à l'institution accusatrice[125].

Il y a longtemps déjà, le célèbre juriste Bonnard écrivait que la procédure disciplinaire dans la fonction publique était en voie de juridictionnalisation[126]. À ce jour, ce chemin n'est pas entièrement parcouru et seuls certains traits essentiels de la procédure juridictionnelle sont applicables (par exemple l'audition de l'intéressé, la possibilité de présenter des observations écrites ou orales, l'audition de témoins, l'assistance d'un défenseur, la possibilité de prescrire des enquêtes, etc.).Il reste que sur certains points capitaux, la procédure disciplinaire diffère de la procédure juridictionnelle et notamment les débats du conseil de discipline ne sont pas autres que celles donnant lieu aux poursuites[127]. C'est dans ce sens que converge le juge administratif camerounais lorsqu'il affirme « *Considérant qu'aux termes d'une jurisprudence constante, les membres du conseil de discipline ne peuvent être récusés, qu'en effet, si les conseils se rapprochent à certains points de vue de véritables juridictions, l'assimilation est loin d'être complétée, c'est ainsi que les conseils peuvent statuer ultra petita, ils n'émettent qu'un simple avis, les débats ne sont pas publics et leurs membres ne peuvent être récusés* »[128]. La régularité de la communication est assortie d'un certain nombre de garanties.

---

[124] Le juge l'affirme d'ailleurs en ces termes « *Considérant en ce qui concerne le non-respect du principe « non bis in idem », qu'en matière de discipline des agents publics, une certaine procédure doit être suivie avant d'aboutir à la sanction, que tel n'a pas été le cas d'espèce ;puisque la décision d'affectation litigieuse a été prise par les supérieurs hiérarchiques du Sieur BILAE sans une quelconque procédure préalable* ; »,*Arrêt n°120/CFJ/CAY du 8 décembre 1970, BILAE Jean C/ Etat du Cameroun oriental.*

[125] DE VILLIERS (M.), (sous la dir.), *Droit public général, op.cit.*, p.408.

[126] AUBY (J.M.) et alii, *Droit de la fonction publique, op.cit.*, p.389.

[127] *Op.cit.*, p.390.

[128] *CCA n°294/A du 27 mars 1954, MOUCHILI Isaac C/Administration du territoire.*

2) Les garanties de la régularité de la communication

La première garantie de la régularité est la communication préalable de son dossier. En France, cette règle, formulée par l'article 65 de la loi de finances du 22 avril 1905 a été suffisamment amplifiée par les arrêts de principe *Aramu* et *Dame Veuve Trompier-Gravier*[129].

Aujourd'hui, le Conseil d'État français fait de cette garantie un principe général de droit. La garantie de ce principe est assurée par la procédure disciplinaire elle-même. En effet, lors de la séance de réunion du conseil de discipline, son président doit en premier lieu exposer les conditions dans lesquelles la communication du dossier a pu être réalisée[130]. Il s'agit d'ailleurs, d'après la jurisprudence, d'une formalité substantielle, autrement dit, sa méconnaissance entraîne l'annulation automatique de la décision, même si cette méconnaissance n'a eu en l'espèce aucune incidence sur la décision. C'est dans le même sens que converge le juge administratif camerounais[131].Pour ce dernier, la communication du dossier doit être le préalable à toute forme de poursuite disciplinaire. Il déclare à ce sujet « *Mais considérant qu'aux termes d'une jurisprudence constante et abondante du Conseil d'État, aucune sanction disciplinaire ne peut être prise sans observer les formalités prévues par l'article 65 de la Loi du 22 avril qui dispose que tous les fonctionnaires, employés ou ouvriers de toutes les administrations publiques ont droit à la communication personnelle et confidentielle de tous documents composant leur dossier avant d'être l'objet d'une mesure disciplinaire ou d'un déplacement d'office ;* »[132]. En outre, lorsqu'il n'existe pas de dossier,

---

[129]*C.E. 26 octobre 1945, Aramu, Lebon 213, S.196.3.1 ; concl.Odent ; C.E Sect.5 mai 1944, Dame Veuve TROMPIER-GRAVIER, Rec.133.*

[130] DE VILLIERS (M.), (sous la dir.), *Droit public général, op.cit.*, p.409.

[131] Il déclare en effet « *Considérant enfin, que le dossier personnel administratif n'a pas été communiqué par le rapporteur à l'intéressé avant la réunion de la commission ; qu'ainsi et contrairement aux prescriptions impératives de l'article 65 de la loi du 22 avril 1905, les droits de la défense ont été violés par l'autorité chargée de la procédure disciplinaire ; Qu'il suit de là que les faits reprochés au requérant n'ont pas été prouvés et que la formalité substantielle de la communication du dossier a été omise ;Qu'il échet en conséquence, d'annuler la décision susvisée* ; », *CCA, Arrêt n°266 du 27 novembre 1953, BAMA Jacques C/ Administration du territoire.*

[132]*CCA n°259 du 27 novembre 1953, MEKOK Luc C/ Administration du territoire.*

l'intéressé doit être prévenu de la mesure disciplinaire envisagée et de ses motifs[133].

Par ailleurs, l'agent informé des poursuites disciplinaires doit demander lui-même la communication du dossier[134]. S'il ne le fait pas, il ne peut pas se prévaloir de l'irrégularité de la procédure[135].En France, l'article 19 du Titre I du statut général de la fonction publique contraint l'Administration à prévenir l'agent que des poursuites vont être engagées et qu'il peut demander la communication de son dossier[136].

Au Cameroun, cette communication doit être intégrale, en ce sens que toute pièce contenant un grief disciplinaire distinct doit être connue du fonctionnaire mis en cause afin qu'il puisse valablement se défendre[137]. Le mis en cause doit reconnaître par une attestation, qu'il a eu communication du dossier[138]. La communication du dossier doit être confidentielle et personnelle[139].

Pour le juge, la communication du dossier qui passe par l'obligation d'informer le mis en cause doit être régulière. Dans une des décisions, il déclare en effet que « *Considérant que ces prescriptions tendent à assurer la défense des droits du fonctionnaire incriminé en portant à sa connaissance qu'à celle du défenseur qui l'assiste et des membres du conseil(...)que les éléments du dossier de la présente affaire permettent d'affirmer que le Sieur EBANGOM a régulièrement eu communication de son dossier et pu assurer sa défense et que le conseil a prononcé en toute connaissance de cause ; qu'ainsi donc le moyen soulevé manque tant en droit qu'en fait* ». Il précise cette position dans une autre décision en ces termes « *Considérant qu'il est également fait grief aux premiers juges d'avoir rejeté son recours comme non fondé alors que les autorités de la gendarmerie nationale dans la procédure disciplinaire engagée contre lui,*

---

[133] *CCA n°250 du 25 septembre 1953, MFOULOU Jacques C/ Administration du territoire.*

[134] *C.E., 27 avril 1966, Choux, Dalloz, 1966, II, p.261.*

[135] *C.E., 5 janvier 1966, Cazaux.*

[136] AUBY et alii, *Droit de la fonction publique, op.cit.*, p.380.

[137] Article 16(4) du Décret n°2000/685/PM du 13 septembre 2000 portant organisation et fonctionnement du Conseil Permanent de Discipline de la Fonction Publique et fixant les règles de la procédure disciplinaire

[138] Article 16(5) du décret suscité.

[139] *CCA n°259 du 27 novembre 1953, MEKOK Luc C/ Administration du territoire.*

avaient violé grossièrement les droits de la défense en omettant de lui communiquer préalablement à sa comparution devant la commission de discipline, son dossier disciplinaire(...) »[140]. La sanction de cette obligation de communication est l'annulation de la décision attaquée[141]. Dans le même sens, la communication du dossier doit se faire en temps utile, c'est-à-dire l'Administration doit donner suffisamment du temps au mis en cause pour préparer sa défense. Le non-respect de cette formalité entraîne l'annulation de la décision de sanction[142]. Cependant, la communication d'un dossier incomplet peut être régulière si la pièce manquante n'est pas de nature à exercer une influence déterminante sur la décision prise[143].Ainsi la régularité de la communication du dossier précède la régularité de la comparution.

B- La régularité de la comparution

Une autre phase caractérisée par la régularité de la procédure est la comparution. En effet, la comparution regorge trois phases cruciales à savoir : la présentation de la défense, l'avis du conseil et la prise de la sanction. Seule la régularité de l'avis du conseil fera l'objet d'analyse ; les autres aspects ayant été déjà abordés plus haut. Peut-être faut-il rappeler que le juge administratif camerounais en évoquant la sanction a fait de la faute professionnelle la condition du déclenchement de la procédure de prise de la sanction[144] . Il ressort de cette décision la définition *in globo* de la faute

---

[140]*Arrêt n°1/A du 18 février 1993, TCHOUPNJOU Jean Jacques C/ Etat du Cameroun (MINFA).*

[141] Cf. *supra.*

[142]*Jugement n°35/CS/CA du 03 mai 1990, EDZOA Georges Maurice C/ Etat du Cameroun.*

[143] Il l'affirme d'ailleurs en ces termes « *Considérant que la communication incomplète du dossier résulte de la disparition d'une pièce dont l'analyse est donnée(...) ;qu'il résulte du fait même que cette pièce non essentielle n'a pas été communiquée au Conseil d'enquête, qu'elle n'aurait pu en aucune façon influencer son avis ;que l'incorrection relevée dans l'accomplissement d'une formalité par ailleurs substantielle n'est pas de nature à avoir exercé une influence déterminante sur la décision prise ;qu'il n'y a donc aucun détournement de pouvoir(Cf. Conseil d'Etat arrêt LEROUX.9.4.1948) » ;CCA n°90 du 22 mars 1952, MAZE REMY C/Administration du territoire.*

[144] Il déclare d'ailleurs « *Attendu certes qu'il a été jugé que la sanction disciplinaire ne peut être motivée que par la faute commise par un fonctionnaire dans l'exercice ou à l'occasion de l'exercice de ses fonctions ; Que cependant, il a été aussi jugé qu'en raison de la nature des fonctions exercées, des fonctionnaires peuvent faire l'objet de sanction disciplinaire en raison de leur comportement privé, dès lors que celui-ci est de nature à jeter le discrédit sur la fonction qui*

pouvant donner lieu à sanction. En d'autres termes, il définit la faute professionnelle en ces termes « *Attendu que(...) constitue une faute administrative, tout manquement à ses obligations de nature à porter atteinte à l'honorabilité et la considération de l'agent et susceptible par répercussion, de nuire au prestige de la fonction publique ;* »[145] . Il précise le sens de cette définition en l'étendant aux activités se déroulant en dehors du cadre professionnel, mais qui en raison de leur particularité ou de leur sensibilité peuvent jeter un discrédit sur la fonction de l'agent public[146].

Ainsi, la procédure normale avant de prononcer une sanction à l'encontre d'un fonctionnaire fait intervenir un conseil de discipline[147]. Il s'agit d'analyser sa saisine et son avis(1) et la problématique de la récusation du conseil(2).

1) La saisine et l'avis du conseil de discipline

En France comme au Cameroun, la saisine du conseil de discipline est obligatoire[148].Le conseil délibère à huis clos hors de la présence du fonctionnaire et de ses défenseurs. C'est ce qui ressort également du décret

---

leur est confiée ou sur la fonction publique, », *jugement n°99/82-83 du 29 septembre 1983, ATEBA Victor C/ Etat du Cameroun.*

[145]*CFJ/AP, arrêt n°14/A du 19 mars 1969, MOUKOKO James Emmanuel C/ Etat du Cameroun oriental . Voir dans le même sens, jugement n°76/85-86 du 26 juin 1986, FOUDA Gothard C/Etat du Cameroun.*

[146] Il déclare à ce sujet « *Mais attendu que si l'on peut considérer que la faute professionnelle est celle qui est commise dans l'exercice ou à l'occasion de l'exercice des fonctions, les statuts particuliers édictent pour chaque corps de fonctionnaire de l'Etat des obligations spéciales inhérentes à la nature des fonctions assumées. C'est ainsi que, par exemple, des agissements étrangers au service des fonctionnaires de la police peuvent constituer des fautes professionnelles lorsque ces agissements sont de nature à jeter le discrédit sur la fonction* ; », *Arrêt n°56/84-85 du 28 février 1985, MBANG Nicolas C/ Etat du Cameroun*

[147] AUBY(J.M) et alii, *Droit de la fonction publique, op. cit.*, p.382.

[148] S'agissant de leur constitution en France, pour les fonctionnaires civils, l'organe en question est la commission administrative paritaire siégeant en formation restreinte, composée pour moitié des représentants de l'Administration et des représentants du personnel, de grade supérieur ou égal à celui du fonctionnaire poursuivi. Les membres du CAP sont tenus au secret professionnel, ils doivent être indépendants et impartiaux ; pour l'armée, il s'agit de commissions d'enquête non paritaires. Voir à ce sujet, DE VILLIERS(M),(sous la dir.,), *Droit public général, op.cit.* ., p.409.

portant organisation et fonctionnement du conseil permanent de discipline de la fonction publique[149].

Ainsi, l'avis du conseil de discipline est indispensable pour la régularité de la procédure dans le principe du respect des droits de la défense. Cette mesure est prévue à peine de nullité. C'est du moins ce qui ressort des moyens invoqués par le juge dans plusieurs affaires. Il déclare en effet « *Considérant par ailleurs que si l'autorité qui prononce la sanction doit obligatoirement consulter une commission(...)* ; »[150] . En outre, la consultation du conseil par l'autorité habilitée à prononcer la sanction est prescrite à peine de nullité. C'est ce qu'il déclare dans un de ses jugements en ces termes « *Considérant que l'article 31 du Décret n°66/22/COR du 20 janvier 1966 susvisé exige la réunion du conseil de discipline qui doit émettre un avis sur le point duquel une sanction doit être prise par l'autorité compétente ;*

Considérant qu'en prenant sa décision d'exclusion définitive du sieur SITAMZE sans avoir recueilli au préalable l'avis du conseil de discipline, le Secrétaire d'État à l'Enseignement a violé le texte susvisé ; Considérant qu'en matière de discipline des agents publics, cette formalité est prescrite à peine de nullité ; qu'il échet dès lors de prononcer l'annulation de l'arrêté n°185/SECRE/ENS du 21 juin 1968 attaqué pour vice de forme »[151].

En France, la garantie résultant de l'intervention d'un conseil de discipline ne s'applique que si un texte le prévoit. C'est donc le cas pour la fonction publique de l'État selon l'article 19 du Titre I du statut. L'autorité

[149] Voir les articles 4 à 28 du Décret n°2000/685/PM du 13 septembre 2000 portant organisation et fonctionnement du Conseil permanent de discipline de la fonction publique et fixant les règles de la procédure disciplinaire.

[150] *CCA n°270/A du 27 novembre 1953, EKONG Yves Adolphe C/ Administration du territoire.*

[151] *Arrêt n° 121/CFJ/CAY du 8 décembre 1970, SITAMZE Urbain C/ Etat du Cameroun oriental.* Il réitère cette position dans une autre affaire en ces termes « *Considérant qu'en prenant une décision d'exclusion du sieur BISSIONGOL de l'Ecole normale d'instituteurs sans prendre au préalable l'avis du conseil de discipline, le Secrétaire d'Etat a violé le texte susvisé ; Considérant qu'en matière des discipline des agents publics, cette formalité est prescrite à peine de nullité ; qu'il échet dès lors de prononcer l'annulation de l'arrêté attaqué pour vice de forme* », *Arrêt n°122/CFJ/CAY du 8 décembre 1970, BISSIONGOL Boniface C/ Etat du Cameroun oriental.*

disciplinaire ne peut pas, sauf exception, y déroger par l'usage d'autres formalités[152].

Cependant, si l'autorité habilitée à prendre la sanction est liée par la sollicitation de l'avis du conseil, il n'est par contre pas lié par l'avis du conseil. Il s'agit alors d'un avis obligatoire. Le juge l'affirme d'ailleurs en ces termes « *Considérant par ailleurs, que si l'autorité qui prononce la sanction doit obligatoirement consulter une commission d'enquête, elle n'est pas liée par l'avis émis par celle-ci, qu'en effet, elle jouit en cette matière d'un large pouvoir discrétionnaire qui lui permet d'infliger une sanction autre, même plus grave que celle à laquelle s'est arrêtée la commission* »[153]. Sur ce dernier point, la jurisprudence administrative camerounaise s'écarte de son homologue qui affirme que l'autorité administrative dans l'exercice de son pouvoir disciplinaire ne peut infliger de sanctions plus sévères que celles qui lui sont proposées par le conseil de discipline[154].Ce constat pose la problématique de la récusation du conseil.

2) La problématique de la récusation du conseil de discipline

Pour ce qui est de la compétence des membres du conseil, ceux-ci ne peuvent être récusés et le conseil se rapproche à certains points d'une véritable juridiction. Toutefois, il s'en écarte sur certains points[155].C'est d'ailleurs la position adoptée par le juge administratif quand il déclare « *Considérant qu'aux termes d'une jurisprudence constante les membres du conseil de discipline ne peuvent être récusés, qu'en effet, si les conseils se rapprochent à certains points de vue de véritables juridictions, l'assimilation est loin d'être complétée, c'est ainsi que les conseils peuvent statuer ultra petita, ils n'émettent qu'un simple avis, les débats ne sont pas publics et leurs membres ne peuvent être récusés* »[156].

---

152 *C.E.17 décembre 1990, Centre communal d'action sociale de Caen C/Guesdou, req.n°84371.*

153 *CCA n°270/A du 27 novembre 1953, EKONG Yves Adolphe C/ Administration du territoire ; voir dans le même sens CCA n°455/A du 25 févier 1956, BABA Youssoufa C/ Administration du territoire.*

154 Voir à ce propos les développements de Michel DE VILLIERS in DE VILLIERS (M.), (sous la dir.), *Droit Public Général, op.cit.*, p.409.

155 Voir à ce propos, MORTET-BAILLY (J.), « Discipline », in CADIET (L.),(Sous la dir.), *Dictionnaire de la justice*, op.cit., pp.332-337.

156 *CCA n°294/A du 27 mars 1954, MOUCHILI Isaac C/Administration du territoire.*

Il ressort de cette décision trois traits saillants à savoir l'interdiction formelle de récuser les membres du conseil, le caractère des débats qui n'est pas public, la nature juridique de leur avis, mais aussi et surtout la possibilité d'élargissement de leur compétence d'attribution. En effet, contrairement aux juridictions en général, les débats du conseil se font à huis clos[157] et le conseil n'émet qu'un avis qui ne lie pas l'autorité habilitée à prendre la sanction. Bien plus, les membres du conseil ne peuvent être récusés et ils peuvent statuer sur les points autres que ceux qui étaient préalablement prévus au dossier. On dit qu'ils statuent *ultra petita*. Ils ne peuvent enfin pas être récusés par l'intéressé ou par l'autorité habilitée à prendre la sanction. Dans leur office, les membres du conseil de discipline doivent prendre connaissance de l'intégralité du dossier afin de formuler leur avis en toute connaissance de cause[158].

CONCLUSION

En dernière analyse, il s'agissait dans cette étude de décrypter l'élaboration prétorienne du principe du respect des droits de la défense dans le champ du contentieux disciplinaire de la fonction publique. Le fil conducteur de notre analyse a été la manière dont le juge administratif appréhende le principe des droits de la défense. La figure juridique prise pour illustrer cette analyse a été le contentieux disciplinaire de la fonction publique.

Il ressort de cet examen que le juge a opté pour les méthodes de réception/internalisation et d'interprétation. Dans le premier cas, le juge administratif s'est contenté de reprendre les règles applicables au principe des droits de la défense et de convoquer les jurisprudences du Conseil d'État français afin de motiver ses décisions. Quant à l'interprétation faite par le juge, celui-ci en s'adossant sur la méthode de la réception/internalisation a contribué à créer des normes applicables au principe des droits de la défense par les moyens de clarification des dispositions textuelles et jurisprudentielles du Conseil d'État français. Cette méthode d'interprétation

---

157 *MORTET-BAILLY (J.), « Discipline », in CADIET (L.) (Sous la dir.), Dictionnaire de la justice, op.cit.*, p.336.

158 *CCA n°318/A du 3 septembre 1954, EBANGOM Benoît C/Administration du territoire.*

a également permis au juge de consolider le principe des droits de la défense, mais aussi et surtout d'étendre le champ d'action dudit principe et dans certains cas de le rétrécir. Ces exercices ont permis au juge de contribuer à la garantie de l'État de droit non pas seulement par la protection des droits du mis en cause, mais aussi et surtout par la consolidation de la régularité de la procédure. C'est dans ce sens que converge le juge béninois à travers son œuvre jurisprudentielle[159]. Reste alors à souhaiter la mise en œuvre effective de la justice constitutionnelle camerounaise afin que ce dernier emboîte le pas au juge administratif qui représente pour l'heure -à défaut de l'action du juge constitutionnel dans ce domaine [160]- le garant par défaut des droits fondamentaux.

[159] *DCC 00-024 du 10 mars 2000(*aff.SOVI, obs. DJOGBENOU(J.), pp.605-609, in Association Béninoise de Justice Constitutionnelle, Cotonou, PUB, I-2013, *Annuaire Béninois de Justice Constitutionnelle.*

[160] Abstraction faite du cadre électoral où la Cour suprême siégeant en lieu et place du Conseil constitutionnel œuvre en matière d'élections présidentielle, législatives et sénatoriales.

LES USAGES DU DROIT EN AFRIQUE À L'ÉPREUVE DE L'UNIVERSALITÉ DES DROITS FONDAMENTAUX

Serge François SOBZE[1]

•

Résumé

Les Africains croient-ils encore à la qualité du droit qu'ils produisent ?

L'inféodation de la culture occidentaliste des droits de l'Homme, l'impérialisme culturel flagrant, font douter non seulement de la capacité, voire de la lucidité des Africains à mettre en œuvre leurs propres droits, mais aussi à apporter leur intelligibilité pour la construction d'une véritable culture de l'universalité des droits de l'Homme.

Cette situation nous amène à nous interroger sur la compatibilité entre les notions universalité des droits de l'Homme usages pluriels et parfois contrastés que connaît l'ordre juridique africain.

Face aux nouveaux paradigmes du droit telle la liberté de disposer de son corps, la liberté sexuelle, en quoi l'usage du droit en Afrique pourrait-il servir de voie idéale pour l'universalité des droits de l'Homme ? Loin de prôner -par le canal des usages du droit en Afrique- l'émergence d'une chapelle de droit *made in Africa*, il est impérieux de favoriser une culture de l'universalité des droits de l'Homme axée sur des divergences culturelles et identitaires, sur le compromis donc sur la prise en compte de la marge nationale d'appréciation.

Mots clés : usage- Afrique- création- universalité- identité culturelle-valeurs- marge nationale d'appréciation.

---

[1] **Chargé de Cours, Université de Douala (Cameroun).**

Abstract

Africans still believe the quality of the law they produce?

The allegiance of Westernist culture of human rights, cultural imperialism blatant, not only cast doubt on the ability of lucidity or African to implement their own rights but also to bring their intelligibility for building a true culture of universal human rights.

This situation leads us to question the filiation between the universality of human rights and plurals uses and sometimes contrasting facing the African legal order. Faced with new paradigms of law as freedom of marriage, sexual freedom, how the use of law in Africa could it serve as ideational way to the universality of human rights? Far from advocating -by the channel of uses to which we are made right in Africa- the emergence of a right to chapel made in Africa, it is imperative to foster a culture of universal human rights focus on cultural and identity differences, so the compromise on the inclusion of the national margin of appreciation.

Keywords: use- Africa- creation- production- effectiveness- universality- cultural identity- values- national margin of appreciation.

INTRODUCTION

Les usages du droit en Afrique sont le prédicat par lequel les Africains s'efforcent de trouver à leurs problèmes des solutions qui tiennent compte des caractéristiques particulières du continent et des peuples qui l'habitent. L'Afrique, en usant de son droit, est désormais le maître de ses productions juridiques et son peuple, par ricochet, cesse d'être « les négatifs des colonisateurs »[2]. C'est dire combien il est judicieux que chaque société valorise sa culture juridique, c'est-à-dire un ensemble de valeurs, de représentations, de discours, de techniques et des institutions relatifs au droit.

Cependant, peut-on au nom de l'universalité admettre que certaines normes universelles ne soient pas transposables dans certains instruments

[2] L. S SENGHOR, *Pierre Teilhard de Chardin et la politique africaine*, Cahier n° 3, Éditions du Seuil, p. 17.

nationaux ou régionaux du fait de leur incompatibilité ? Ceci est vrai tant qu'il est vérifié que l'homme n'est pas le même partout et que la protection de sa dignité et de son épanouissement ne nécessite pas les mêmes règles partout sur la terre.

Confronter les usages du droit en Afrique au sacro-saint principe de l'universalité des droits fondamentaux peut sembler exagérément ambitieux, voire difficultueux. Peut-on aisément déplacer l'interrogation sur le droit vers ses usages et vers ses effets sociaux comme l'aurait voulu Danièle LOCHAK ?[3] Il s'agit d'une entreprise difficile. Notre propos consistera donc en une réflexion sur les termes de la rencontre entre les usages et l'universalité avec mise en exergue de ce que d'aucuns ont appelé « les valeurs africaines ». C'est l'une des difficultés de ce sujet qui met en présence une antinomie aux termes entre eux complexes : usages et universalité.

Todas las naciones del mundo son hombres[4]. Par cet aphorisme, Bartolomé de Las Casas, analysait la dimension universelle des droits de l'Homme comme le marqueur de l'émergence d'un Etat de droit[5]. C'est dire que comme l'État de droit[6], l'universalité des droits de l'Homme, ce *jus novum* est encore une idée-force, un projet, un programme aussi bien dans les continents développés que dans des continents en voie de développement comme l'Afrique.

---

[3] La promesse avait été tenue par l'auteure en 1989 lors de la publication de l'ouvrage sur *Les usages sociaux du droit* par le CURAPP. CURAPP, *Les usages sociaux du droit, Paris,* PUF, 1989.

[4] Littéralement, toutes les nations du monde sont des hommes.

[5] J. Y. MORIN, *L'Etat de droit : émergence d'un principe de droit international* ; Académie de droit international, Recueil des Cours, tome 254, 1995, 462p. « Toutes les nations du monde sont des hommes » ; J. CHEVALLIER, « L'Etat de droit », *RDP*, 1988, p. 317 ; L. DONFACK SOKENG, « L'Etat de droit en Afrique », Revue du CERDIP, Vol. 1, n° 2, juillet –décembre 2002, p. 87 et s. Ce dernier appréhende le constitutionnalisme ainsi que l'état de droit comme le critérium d'identification des " nations civilisées ".

[6] G. CONAC, « Le juge et la construction de l'Etat de droit en Afrique francophone », in *L'Etat de droit. Mélanges en l'honneur de G. Braibant*, Dalloz, 1996, p. 105 S. MILACIC, « L'Etat de droit, pour quoi faire ? L'Etat de droit comme logistique d'une bonne gouvernance démocratique », in *Le nouveau constitutionnalisme. Mélanges en l'honneur de Gérard Conac*, Economica, 2006, p. 375.

Les usages du droit recommandent de puiser dans l'extra ou la métajuridique, de puiser dans la sociologie du droit[7] ou mieux de sortir du tropisme exégétique pour s'intéresser à ce qui *est*, aux usages que se fait la société du droit produit. Parmi les différentes théories juridiques, c'est le *positivisme factualiste* qui permet de mieux cerner les usages du droit dans une société donnée[8]. Et parce que « le droit est plus petit que l'ensemble des relations entre les hommes » pour reprendre l'heureuse formule de Jean Carbonnier[9], il est par ricochet plus petit que l'usage qu'en font ces hommes.

L'étude fondée sur les « usages du droit » présente une double difficulté : il faut d'abord s'accorder sur la notion de droit et, ensuite, réfléchir au caractère adéquat de la métaphore « usage du droit ».

On peut éviter la première difficulté en se plaçant d'emblée à l'intérieur d'un système de droit particulier, tels les droits africains[10] avec un regard sur leur dynamique.

Quant à la métaphore « usage du droit », elle pose le problème de méthode. Faut-il se limiter à l'examen des usages formels du droit, c'est-à-dire l'usage du droit par les législateurs ou les juges, ou faut-il rechercher ce que fait la société du droit et partant établir une filiation entre usages et nécessités[11]? Le choix est porté sur la seconde hypothèse parce que le droit

---

[7]J. CARBONNIER, *Sociologie juridique*, 1ère éd., PUF, Paris, 415 p. Selon l'auteur, si la sociologie du droit se limite à ce qui constitue le droit lui-même, les règles et les institutions, la sociologie juridique engloberait tous les phénomènes plus ou moins teintés de droit.

[8] Le *positivisme factualiste* considère que c'est dans le milieu social qu'il convient, soit de découvrir les règles de droit (usages, coutumes, règles corporatives), soit enfin de vérifier l'effectivité de l'application du droit formel, et par là même son adéquation aux besoins de la société.

[9] J ; CARBONNIER, *Flexible droit*, 8ème édition, LGDJ, Paris, 1995, p. 22. *Le droit est une écume à la surface des rapports sociaux ou inter-individuels* renchérit l'auteur.

[10] P.-F. GONIDEC, *Les droits africains*, Paris, LGDJ, 1976 ; J.-M. BIPOUN WOUM, *Le droit international africain Problèmes généraux des conflits*, L.G.D.J., 1970, 289 p.

[11] On se rapproche de *l'utilitarisme juridique* défendu par Jeremy BENTHAM. L'auteur définit le principe d'utilité comme un principe qui exprime « la propriété ou la tendance qu'a une chose de prévenir un mal ou de procurer un bien ». Le droit a pour objet de : « rechercher le plaisir et éviter la souffrance ».

est avant tout un produit de société. Le droit n'existant que par la société, tous les phénomènes juridiques sont par ricochet des phénomènes sociaux[12]. Autrement dit et pour reprendre Léon Duguit, le droit se trouve dans la réalité sociale et non dans les formules de loi, quelque solennelles qu'elles soient[13].

Le terme usage se perçoit étymologiquement à partir de la racine *usus* qui, en droit, se rapporte à l'utilisation d'une chose en tant que propriétaire ou non. Dès lors, user d'un droit c'est l'exercer ou s'abstenir de l'exercer effectivement. On parle d'usage ou de non usage d'un droit. Matériellement, l'usage renvoie à l'action ou à la faculté d'user et s'utilise couramment dans la trilogie des attributs du droit de propriété *usus*, *fructus*, *abusus* ou dans la définition de l'usufruit pour désigner le droit d'usage. *Jus utendi* ! [14] C'est la meilleure façon d'exprimer sa propriété sur un bien. *Usus efficacissimus renum omnium magister* [15].

Pour François N. DJAME, l'usage que l'auteur rapproche à juste titre de la coutume, mais sans l'identifier à celle-ci, est un « *simple phénomène sociologique* » qui peut, tantôt être codifié, tantôt servir de comblement des lacunes légales[16] et de ce fait, permettre au juge de trancher le litige porté à sa connaissance. Le juge se chargera de « *révéler que, dans un groupe social donné, une règle de droit est née de la pratique, en sanctionnant toute violation de ladite règle* »[17]. L'usage crée le droit.

---

[12]Ceci n'est vrai qu'à sens unique, car tous les phénomènes sociaux ne sont pas des phénomènes juridiques. Il existe comme le relève le Doyen Carbonnier, un *social non juridique*, formé par ce que l'on nomme dans une première approche les phénomènes de mœurs. J. CARBONNIER, *Sociologie juridique*, 1ère éd., PUF, Paris, p. 13.

[13] L. DUGUIT, *Traité de Droit constitutionnel*, troisième édition, tome deuxième, Paris, 1928, p. 2.

[14]Vocabulaire juridique Gérard CORNU, 10ème édition mise à jour janvier 2014. pp.1054 et s.

[15] L'usage est en tout le meilleur maître.

[16] Lire G. CORNU, « Libre propos sur la jurisprudence », *in* G. Cornu, *L'art du droit en quête de sagesse,* PUF., 1998, p. 174, cité par A. AKAM AKAM, « Le juge entre la loi et sa conscience » in *Revue de la Faculté des sciences juridiques et politiques,* Université de Ngaoundéré, p. 18.

[17] F. N. DJAME, *Usages et coutume en droit administratif camerounais*, Dianoïa, Paris, 2009, pp. 15 et s. L'auteur s'interroge sur les usages en droit qu'il ne faut pas confondre avec les usages du droit.

Il faut comprendre le droit dans la présente étude comme un système de régulation des comportements sociaux qui, à tort ou à raison, a paru très ancré à un certain modèle d'organisation des sociétés humaines. La définition que propose Narcisse MOUELLE KOMBI s'inscrit dans cette logique. Selon l'auteur, « *le droit, ensemble de normes dont la finalité est de réglementer les activités des collectivités humaines, de régir les rapports entre les divers membres du corps social et de résoudre à l'amiable les dissensions inévitables entre ces membres, s'apparente avant tout comme l'aboutissement d'un phénomène de genèse* »[18].

De ceci, il apparaît que « *le droit est constitué de l'ensemble des règles adoptées par une collectivité humaine et qui organisent la vie des individus en société* »[19].

Rapproché à la notion d'usage, on dirait tout simplement qu'à chaque société son droit selon la célèbre maxime *ubi societas ibi jus*. Nier l'influence de cette règle sur les usages variés et variables du droit, c'est dire que les règles de droit ainsi que les solutions juridiques sont les mêmes dans toutes les sociétés. Et pour paraphraser un auteur, c'est soutenir que le traitement médical est le même pour toutes les maladies[20]. N'a-t-on pas coutume de dire aux grands maux les grands remèdes ? Que dire, « *pour peu de chose, peu de plaid* » pour reprendre cette belle formule d'Antoine Loysel[21].

L'universalité quant à elle, renvoie à ce qui est pratiqué ou est au service de tous. Par opposition au nationalisme ou au régionalisme, l'universalité réfère à cette doctrine qui se donne comme virtuellement applicable à tous les systèmes juridiques. Elle est au cœur de nombreuses disciplines juridiques. On parlera d'universalité de fait ou de droit pour marquer l'ensemble des biens et des dettes formant un tout ou dont les éléments actifs et passifs sont inséparablement liés comme le traduit la maxime *Bona*

---

[18]N. MOUELLE KOMBI, *La guerre préventive et le Droit International*, Dianoia, Paris, 2006, p. 18.

[19]F. Bouchet-Saulnier, *Dictionnaire pratique du Droit Humanitaire*, 3e éd., Éditions la Découverte, Paris, 2006, p. 192; voir également D. Carreau, *Droit International*, Pedone, Paris, 1997; A. Leibowicz, *Philosophie du Droit International*, PUF, Paris, 1999, 431 p.

[20] ROULAUD, *Anthropologie juridique*, PUF, Paris, 1988. pp. 22-33.

[21] A. LOYSEL, *Institutes coutumières*, Ed. Laboulaye ; n° 694. Par cette formule, l'auteur voulait dire qu'à des affaires mineures conviennent des procédures sommaires.

non sunt nisi deducto aere alieno. Les finances publiques lui consacreront tout un principe : c'est le principe de l'universalité budgétaire[22].

Cependant, c'est au juriste René Cassin que l'on doit la qualification d' « universelle » attribuée à la Déclaration universelle des droits de l'homme qui faillit n'être qu'internationale[23]. À ce titre, l'auteur fera de l'universalité des droits de l'Homme un principe non dérogeable. Aussi dira-t-il : les droits de l'Homme « *sont universels ou ne le sont pas … il y a quelque chose dans chaque homme qui est universel* » [24].

Il s'agit encore d'un universalisme discuté au nom d'un localisme réfractaire[25] et du caractère *programmatoire* des droits consacrés[26].

C'est Karel Vasak qui, s'inscrivant en faux contre le label « faux et vrais droits de l'homme »[27], donnera aux dits droits une connotation universaliste[28]. L'auteur, à la suite de René Cassin, perçoit l'universalité comme les diverses sonorités des instruments d'un orchestre qui s'accordent sur la même mélodie[29].

---

[22] Qui désigne une règle en vertu de laquelle toutes les dépenses et toutes les recettes d'une collectivité publique doivent figurer dans son budget sans aucune compensation ou contraction entre elles.

[23] L'auteur voulait ainsi souligner que les droits affirmés ne concernaient pas des citoyens, ressortissants d'Etats, mais des individus appartenant à une même fratrie. L'idée a prospérée.

[24] R. Cassin, « La Déclaration universelle et la mise en œuvre des droits de l'homme », *R.C.A.D.I.*, t. 79, n° II, 1951, pp. 241-367 (275).

[25]Cf. La déclaration universelle des droits de l'homme, texteS rassemblés par Mario BETTATI, Olivier DUHAMEL et Laurent GREILSAMER pour le Monde, éd., Gallimard, 1998, mise à jour et augmentée en 2008.

[26] En dépit du caractère non contraignant, l'universalité tant prônée par la DUDH n'est plus qu'un simple idéal. Le préambule souligne déjà que l'Assemblée générale proclame la Déclaration comme un idéal commun à atteindre par tous les peuples et toutes les nations… L'implantation de ces idéaux dans des constitutions notamment africaines montre que l'instrument est devenu une référence, un repère. Les pactes de 1966 relatifs à cette Déclaration ont contribué à le rendre contraignant.

[27] R. PELLOUX, « Vrais et faux droits de l'Homme, problème de définition et de classification », *Revue de Droit Public*, 1981.

[28] K. VASAK, « Les droits de l'homme et l'Afrique, Vers les institutions africaines pour la protection internationale des droits de l'homme ? », RBDI, 1967. 2, pp. 459-478*;* M.-Joëlle Redor-Fichot, « L'indivisibilité des droits de l'homme », C.R.D.F. n° 7, 2009, pp. 75- 86.

[29] K. VASAK, « Les droits de l'homme et l'Afrique… », *op. cit.* p. 459.

Au vu de toutes ces considérations, se pose une question centrale : les usages du droit en Afrique s'accommodent- ils à la théorie de l'universalité des droits de l'homme ? Autrement dit, ces usages ne sont-ils pas en contradiction avec la théorie de l'universalité des droits de l'Homme ? Il est question de savoir si l'universalité des droits de l'Homme telle que pratiquée en Afrique rend compte des valeurs africaines ou elle n'est que la transposition en Afrique des conceptions occidentales de l'universalité dont le reflet de leurs cultures. Peut-on concilier usages avec ce qu'ils emportent (relativisme culturel) et universalité ?

Une étude sur les usages du droit à l'aune de l'universalité des droits de l'Homme présente un intérêt à la fois historique et pratique.

D'un point de vue historique, elle retrace l'histoire selon laquelle les Africains, subjugués par les droits étrangers, ne croyaient pas véritablement en leurs propres droits. Le constat fait par Alain Bockel révélait que le droit applicable dans les États africains était, pour une part importante, moins l'émanation de la société profonde que l'exécution ou la transposition de recettes éprouvées en Occident[30]. Face à cette situation, l'universalité en Afrique ne peut être qu'un artefact ou mieux et en fonction du cliché choisi, un produit *importé*[31], *exporté*[32], *imité*[33] en tout cas, une universalité d'*emprunt*[34] ou venue *d'ailleurs*[35]. C'est paradoxalement le contraire du sens et de l'essence de la notion d'universalité.

---

[30] A. BOCKEL, *Droit administratif*, Dakar-Abidjan, Nouvelles Éditions africaines, 1978.

[31] B. BADIE, *L'Etat importé, l'occidentalisation de l'ordre politique*, Paris, Fayard, 1992.

[32] G. HERMET, *Exporter la démocratie ?* 2ème éd., Paris, Presse de Science Po., coll. « La bibliothèque du citoyen », 2008.

[33] J. RIVERO, « Les phénomènes d'imitation des modèles étrangers en droit administratif », *Mélanges W-J. GANSHOF VAN DER MEERSCH, Bruxelles, Bruylant, 1972, Tome 3.*

[34] Cette expres0sion est tirée de la formule « *emprunts étrangers* », employée par les auteurs A. MABILEAU et J. MEYRIAT, *Décolonisation et régimes politiques en Afrique noire,* (dir.), Paris, Armand Colin, 1967.

[35] L. SINDJOUN, *L'Etat ailleurs Entre noyau dur et case vide,* Ed., Economica 2002, 325p ; C. JAFFRELOT et ALII, *Démocraties d'ailleurs. Démocraties et démocratisation hors d'Occident,* Paris, Karthala, 2000.

De même, l'étude a cette particularité de contribuer à la consolidation de l'autonomie des droits africains[36] et de marquer la place de l'Afrique à la construction de l'universalisation des droits. En outre, les nouveaux paradigmes du droit, tel le mariage pour tous, qui constituent l'un des points d'actualité de cette réflexion nécessitent une appréciation des États africains parce que ne faisant pas partie des valeurs universelles. À ce titre, l'étude recommande, face à la pratique contrastée de l'universalité des droits fondamentaux, une vision nouvelle fondée sur le relativisme culturel et donc sur la prise en compte des valeurs africaines. Il convient donc d'examiner tour à tour l'existant (**I**) et le projeté (**II**).

I. **L'existant : le contraste entre usages et universalité des droits de l'Homme**

La géométrie variable de l'universalité des droits de l'homme est devenue flagrante[37] au point que l'on s'interroge sur la finalité même du principe. L'universalité n'est-elle pas que cet arbre qui cache la forêt ? Qu'est-ce qui fonde l'universalité des droits et quel est le but visé par le principe? Il est question de montrer le double visage de l'universalité des droits de l'Homme, sa preuve et ses épreuves, comment elle se pose ailleurs en s'imposant en Afrique, comment il existe un réel déphasage entre les objectifs assignés à ce principe et les résultats acquis (**A**) et, comment, du fait des spécificités, l'universalité cède progressivement la place à la *pluriversalité* (**B**).

---

[36]Voir M. ONDOA, *Introduction historique au droit camerounais : La formation initiale, éléments pour une théorie de l'autonomie des droits africains*. Les Éditions du Kilimandjaro, 2013, p.28; S. F. SOBZE, De « La création du droit en Afrique » à « Comment fabrique-t-on le droit en Afrique ? » Quelles innovations pour la sécurité juridique en Afrique ? in *La fabrique du droit en Afrique*, Symposium juridique Libreville, les 21 et 22 novembre 2013, pp. 45 et s.

[37] On peut citer certaines règles et pratiques qui au nom des normes internationales sont d'application dans certains ordres juridiques alors qu'elles sont prohibées ailleurs parce qu'elles se heurtent à leur façon d'être ou de vivre. La dépénalisation de l'homosexualité dans certains Etats et sa répression dans d'autres atteste de cette disparité. La libre circulation des biens et des personnes reste encore une « vache sacrée » pour certains Etats, et pourtant, une politique redoutable pour d'autres. Que reste-t-il du droit d'asile à l'ère de la politique d'immigration choisie ou sélective ? On n'est pas loin d'un « *chœur à deux voies* » selon la formule du professeur Jean RIVERO.

A. Un divorce entre les objectifs assignés et les résultats produits

L'universalité est un concept situé même si progressivement elle se trouve en situation. L'internationalisation de l'universalité et de l'indivisibilité des droits de l'homme est un échec pour le droit international des droits de l'homme comme le démontre Adama Kpodar. En effet, pour l'auteur, si le droit international des droits de l'homme a réussi à assurer aux droits de l'Homme une dimension mondiale dans leur identité, et hisser les droits de l'Homme, auprès des États, au rang des obligations de première catégorie, il faut dire que la persistance de l'argument du particularisme et la recrudescence des droits spécifiques sont ses principaux échecs. C'est d'ailleurs sur le fondement du particularisme que la doctrine a affirmé l'impossible internationalisation de l'universalité et l'indivisibilité des droits de l'Homme[38]. L'internationalisation de l'universalité du fait de la recrudescence de certaines réticences étatiques est progressivement perçue comme « l'angle mort » du droit international des droits de l'Homme.

La proclamation de l' « universalité et de l'indivisibilité des droits de l'Homme » a été consacrée lors de la conférence de Vienne de 1993, laquelle conférence a érigé la promotion et la protection des droits de l'Homme au rang « d'objectif prioritaire de l'ONU »[39].

Par la suite, cette universalité s'est souvent trouvée tantôt en liberté, tantôt sous contrainte parce qu'appelée à faire des concessions avec d'autres cultures sinon réfractaires, du moins peu ordinaires ou trop originales. Elle connaît une importante limitation du fait d'un ordre public international en plein essor autant que de la contestation de certains peuples au nom de la prise en considération de leurs cultures. C'est la manifestation de la *situationalité* de l'universalité.

Du fait de ce relativisme, l'universalité s'apparente plus à une « profession de foi » qu'à une réalité juridique tangible[40]. Faut-il conclure à l'introuvable

---

[38] A. KPODAR, « Les droits de l'homme saisis par le droit international », *Revue Togolaise des Sciences Juridiques*, Janvier-Juin 2012 n° 0002, p. 28.

[39] Cf. Conf. Déclaration et programme d'action de vienne, des 14- 25 juin 1993, Doc, A/ CONF. 157/ 23, p. 5.

[40] J. MOURGEON, « L'universalité des droits de l'homme entre foi et droit », pp. 1265-1282, *in Libertés, justice, tolérance, Mélanges en hommage au Doyen G. Cohen-Jonathan*, Bruxelles, Bruylant, 2003.

théorie de l'universalité ? Loin s'en faut! L'universalité, à l'instar d'autres concepts juridiques, connaît un fondement juridique[41]. Mireille Delmas-Marty le relevait en ce sens : « *à l'heure de la mondialisation économique, l'universalité des droits de l'homme est plus que jamais à l'ordre du jour. Elle montre la voie, si l'on veut éviter une mondialisation hégémonique, pour inventer un droit commun réellement pluraliste* »[42].

L'universalité rend compte de *l'opérationnalisation* à l'échelle mondiale des notions de globalisation ou de mondialisation telles que prônées par Marshall McLuhan dans son « village global » ou Harold Innis dans son « empire mondial », mais aussi, de l'effectivité d'un droit « *inter-civilisationnel* » selon la formule d'Onuma Yasuaki[43]. L'universalité est le marqueur de l'éclosion des particularités, ainsi que de l'émergence des spécificités qui fondent l'identité d'un peuple[44]. Autrement dit, les droits fondamentaux, droits conçus à partir de la rationalité de l'homme, sont inhérents à la nature de celui-ci, et donc marqués du sceau de l'universalité. Héritage des déclarations des droits du XVIIIe siècle, ils se rattachent au puissant courant jus naturaliste qui fut inspiré par la tradition judéo-chrétienne et imposé par l'Occident comme étant " la culture universelle " pour ne plus dire celle des " nations civilisées ". Cette puissante idéologie profondément enracinée depuis les lumières consiste à ériger la théorie des

---

[41] L. HAMON « L'Etat de droit et son essence », *RFDC*, 1990, n°4, p. 699.

[42] M. DELMAS-MARTY, « La méthodologie en droit comparé », propos liminaire à la première partie de la Table ronde consacrée à cette thématique, *in* : Jean du Bois De GAUDUSSON (dir.), *Le devenir du droit comparé en France,* Journée d'étude à l'institut de France, 23 juin 2004, Presse universitaire d'Aix Marseille (PUAM), 2005, pp. 21-23 (spéc. p. 21).

[43] Onuma YASUAKI, *A Transcivilizational Perspective on International Law, RCADI*, vol. 342, 2009, pp.77-418. (spéc. p. 101). L'auteur récuse toute « *internationalisation de type hégémonique* », expression empruntée à Mireille DELMAS-MARTY, « La méthodologie en droit comparé », *op cit. in* : Jean du Bois De GAUDUSSON (dir.), *Le devenir du droit comparé en France,* Journée d'étude à l'institut de France, 23 juin 2004, Presses universitaires d'Aix Marseille (PUAM), 2005, pp. 21-23 (spéc. p. 21).

[44] N. MOUELLE KOMBI, *La démocratie dans la réalité camerounaise, Libertés, légitimité, et modernité politique sous Paul BIYA*, Dianoïa, 2013, 361p. (spéc. p. 35) ; R.-G. NLEP, *L'administration publique camerounaise. Contribution à l'étude des systèmes africains d'administration publique*, Paris, LGDJ, 1986, pp. 127et s.

droits de l'Homme en une sorte de culture universelle à laquelle devrait se référer toute société politique qui se veut moderne ».

L'universalité des droits de l'Homme[45] tire sa source de la dignité humaine[46], notion qui atteste le fait que l'homme soit le même partout et son épanouissement exige que ses droits soient protégés. C'est ce fait qu'expriment les normes universelles, notamment la Déclaration universelle des droits de l'homme de 1948[47], les pactes de 1966 relatifs aux droits civils et politiques, économiques, sociaux et culturels, ainsi que les instruments nationaux et régionaux considérés comme des « ensembles normatifs inspirateurs »[48].

Elle s'appuie aussi sur divers instruments régionaux tels que les conventions européennes et interaméricaines des droits de l'Homme, la Charte africaine des droits de l'homme et des peuples[49], la Charte africaine de la démocratie, des élections et de la gouvernance et la Charte culturelle de l'Afrique[50]. Ces derniers instruments qui encadrent le cheminement de

---

[45] G. COHEN-JONATHAN, « Universalité et singularité des droits de l'homme », *Revue trimestrielle des droits de l'homme,* 2003, pp. 3-13.

[46] J. KIS, *L'égale dignité.* Essai sur les fondements des droits de l'homme, Paris, Seuil, coll. Esprit, 1989, p. 79.

[47] La Charte des Nations unies a l'avantage de consacrer l'universalité des droits de l'Homme, notamment quand elle dispose dans son article premier que les nations unies ont pour but de : « réaliser la coopération internationale (...) en développant et en encourageant le respect des droits de l'homme et des libertés fondamentales pour tous sans distinction de race, de sexe, de langue ou de religion ». Lire les auteurs C. VERSELLE, *La Déclaration universelle*, Paris, *Librio*, 2008, p. 9; Roger KOUDE, « La déclaration des droits de l'homme ou l'émergence progressive d'un nouvel ordre éthico-juridique mondial ». *Revue aspects, hors série* – 2008, pp. 59-82.

[48]Lire J. COMBACAU, « Chapitre VI : Sources internationales et européennes du droit constitutionnel », in M. Troper et D. Chagnollaud (dir.), *Traité international de droit constitutionnel*, Tome 1 : Théorie de la Constitution, Dalloz, 2012, p. 407.

[49] Dans le préambule, il est dit que les Etats africains ont pris l'engagement de favoriser la coopération internationale en tenant dûment compte de la Charte des Nations Unies et de la Déclaration universelle des droits de l'homme.

[50] Adoptée à la 13ème session ordinaire de la Conférence des Chefs d'Etat et de Gouvernement de l'OUA le 5 juillet 1976 à Port Louis, île Maurice, la Charte dit sans détour en son article 1(f) qu'elle a pour objectif de favoriser la coopération culturelle internationale pour une meilleure compréhension entre les peuples dans laquelle l'Afrique apportera à la culture humaine sa contribution originale et de qualité.

l'Afrique sur la voie de l'appropriation des valeurs universelles au rythme de ses réalités culturelles, sociologiques et selon les démarches objectives reflètent « *la volonté du continent d'appartenir à la civilisation de l'universel fondée sur des valeurs communes* »[51].

Les institutions juridictionnelles notamment la CIJ[52] ou la CPI sont des « garde-fous juridictionnels » de la théorie de l'universalité des droits de l'Homme. Et Kofi Ata Annan de dire : « *la création de la Cour Pénale Internationale est un gage d'espoir pour les générations à venir et un pas de géant sur la voie du respect universel des droits de l'homme et de l'État de droit* ».[53]

Le phénomène de constitutionnalisation de l'universalité des droits de l'Homme est pris en compte par les constitutions africaines[54], notamment celles ayant connu la trilogie du professeur Mélèdje à savoir « *faire, défaire et refaire* »[55] ou un « reflux constitutionnel »[56]. Par ailleurs, le préambule de la

[51] Voir, « Rapport du premier forum africain de dialogue », Délégation permanente, Union africaine, Genève, 2009, cité par M. JEUGUE DOUNGUE, « La gouvernance électorale en Afrique : l'appropriation des valeurs universelles au rythme des réalités culturelles africaines », in J.-Didier BOUKONGOU et L. TENGO (dir.), *Gouvernance et lutte anticorruption en Afrique*, presse de l'UCAC, juin 2015, pp. 125-149.

[52] V. art. 9 du statut de la Cour Internationale de Justice où on peut lire qu'il y existe dans chaque zone " des grandes formes de civilisation représentatives " des principaux systèmes juridiques du monde "

[53] Kofi ATA ANNAN, Secrétaire général des Nations unies, Campidoglio, Rome, 18 juillet 1998, à l'occasion de la signature du Statut de Rome de la Cour Pénale Internationale.

[54] Lire le préambule de la Constitution du Burkina Faso du 11 juin 1991, modifiée le 27 janvier 1997 et le 22 janvier 2002 : « Souscrivant à la Déclaration universelle des Droits de l'Homme de 1948 et aux instruments internationaux traitant des problèmes économiques, politiques, sociaux et culturels » ; Le Préambule de la Constitution de la République du Sénégal du 22 janvier 2001 : « Le peuple du Sénégal souverain affirme son adhésion aux instruments internationaux adoptés par l'Organisation des Nations Unies et l'Organisation de l'Unité africaine, notamment la Déclaration universelle des droits de l'homme du 10 décembre 1948, la Convention relative aux Droits de l'Enfant du 20 novembre 1989… ».

[55] F. D. MELEDJE, « Les révisions des constitutions dans les Etats francophones. Esquisse de Bilan, RDP, 1992 n°1, pp. 111-134 ; F. D. MELEDJE « Faire, défaire et refaire la constitution en Cote d'Ivoire : un exemple d'instabilité chronique », in Fombad (Ch.), Murray (Ch.), *Fostering constitutionalism in Africa, Pretoria University Law Press*, 2010, pp. 309-339 ; E. DONFACK, « La révision des constitutions en Afrique », RJPIC, 1989, n°1, pp. 45-71.

Constitution camerounaise du 18 janvier 1996 le confirme par son attachement aux principes fondamentaux de la Charte des Nations unies et de la Déclaration universelle des droits de l'homme. La Constitution marocaine reconnaît la souscription du Royaume aux principes, droits et obligations découlant des chartes des organismes internationaux et réaffirme son attachement aux droits de l'homme tels qu'ils sont universellement reconnus. Le « patrimoine constitutionnel »[57] africain est donc propice à l'universalité et se présente non seulement comme le gardien du bien-être de la population, mais aussi une adhésion aux principes consacrés par le droit international.

Cette évocation des textes universels et des principes fondamentaux est un *effet de label* qui vient témoigner l'engagement des États africains à apporter une garantie efficiente aux droits et principes consacrés de même qu'elle permet d'examiner le potentiel d'application et d'implication internationales des constitutions africaines[58].

C'est dire que l'universalité perçue sous l'angle des droits de l'Homme ne saurait être une nouvelle forme d'impérialisme. La finalité des droits de l'Homme n'étant pas, comme le souligne G. Soulier, « *de résoudre tous les problèmes posés en société, elle est d'empêcher que ces problèmes soient posés sans les hommes et résolus contre eux* »[59]. Et pour paraphraser Mirabeau, « *il est de l'essence de [l'universalité] d'appartenir à tous* ». C'est le début du consensus que pourrait connaître cette notion aux sens variés.

B. Une confusion entre universalité et *pluriversalité*

Doit-on aborder le concept universalité au pluriel ou au singulier? Un peuple a-t-il le privilège de l'universalité ? L'historien africain Ki-Zerbo semble proposer une appréhension la plus objective en ces termes :

---

[56]J. M. KOMBILA, « Peut-on parler d'un reflux du constitutionnalisme en Afrique et au Cameroun », *Recht in Afrika*, 2010, pp. 33-82.

[57]L'expression est empruntée à L. SINDJOUN, *Les grandes décisions de la justice constitutionnelle africaine*, p. 581.

58 N. MOUELLE KOMBI, « Les dispositions relatives aux conventions internationales dans les nouvelles Constitutions des États d'Afrique francophone », *RJPIC* 2003, n° 1, pp. 5-38.

[59]G. SOULIER, in *Rupture-Solidarité, L'Afrique (centrale) des Droits de l'Homme*, Ed., Karthala, Paris, nouvelle série n° 3, 2001, 286 p.

« l'universel *c'est ce qu'il y a de plus précieux dans tous les particuliers qui doivent se rencontrer comme les plans latéraux à la pointe d'une pyramide »*. L'universel, « *ce n'est pas le particulier des uns imposé à tous les autres. Ce n'est pas la juxtaposition stérile de tous les particuliers. C'est l'agrégation par inter-fécondation de ce qu'il y a de meilleur, de plus succulent et de plus grand dans tous les particuliers afin d'en faire une raison de vivre suffisamment puissante...* »[60].

Il ressort de cette sagesse africaine que personne ne détient le monopole de l'universalité.

Cependant, certains États, au nom de l'universalité ou d'un pseudo *ordre public international*, ont internationalisé[61] leurs usages au détriment de ceux des autres notamment africains. Par exemple, dans l'ordre public[62] français, la position des juridictions inférieures consiste à consacrer le mariage homosexuel comme partie intégrante d'un ensemble de « principes supérieurs d'un nouvel ordre public international » d'inspiration française »[63].

Dès lors, les effluves d'un *ordre public international français* se propagent dans la sphère internationale et influent sur tous les engagements politiques et diplomatiques de l'État.

Ce concept intrusif du juge français vise à véhiculer une certaine idée culturelle, juridique et morale de la France et fragilise les cultures africaines hostiles à l'homosexualité notamment, l'interdiction d'un mariage pour les

[60]J. KI-ZERBO, « Les droits de l'homme en Afrique: tradition et modernité », *in Foi et développement*, n° 237-238 - nov/déc 1995.

[61] C'est soustraire une notion ou un concept au droit interne qui le régissait jusqu'alors, et le placer sous l'empire du droit international, qui le régirait dorénavant. Voir L. DELBEZ, « Le concept d'internationalisation », *Rev. Gén. dr. int. publ.*, 1967, p. 6.

[62] Sur la notion d'ordre public, Voir Raymond POLIN (dir.), *L'ordre public*, 1ère éd., PUF, Paris, 1995, pp. 1-2; M. J. REDOT (dir.), *L'ordre public. Ordre public ou ordres publics*, Bruylant, Bruxelles, 2001, p. 56; R-J DUPUY, « L'ordre public en droit international », in R. POLIN *op. cit.* pp. 103-116.

[63] Cour de cassation, Première chambre civile, arrêt n° 96 du 28 janvier 2015, n° 13-50. 059, *affaire du mariage franco-marocain entre personnes de même sexe* ; v. MESA Rodolphe, « Le mariage franco-marocain entre personnes de même sexe validé », *Dalloz Actualité* édition du 3 février 2015 ; Cf. Figaro vox, 15 décembre 2015, La France imposera-t-elle le mariage homosexuel au Maroc ?

personnes de même sexe, tel que consacré par la Moudawana (code marocain de la famille en son article 4) ou la polygamie perçue comme une coutume ancestrale africaine.

Par ailleurs, l'appropriation par d'autres États de cette conception française de *l'ordre public international* est susceptible de mettre à mal l'institution du droit international privé censé concilier les intérêts divergents en cas de conflits de lois[64].

L'occidentalisation tendancielle du monde pour reprendre cette expression de Serge Latouche[65] semble donc se traduire en Afrique par une extraversion des cultures : les usages du droit en Afrique semblent plus dictés par l' « universalisme démocratique » que par le relativisme culturel[66].

En outre, la Charte arabe des droits de l'homme du 15 septembre 1994 adoptée par le Conseil de la ligue des États arabes[67] qu'on a toujours marginalisé lorsqu'il faut aborder les questions des droits de l'Homme en Afrique, mettait déjà l'accent sur la dignité humaine, sur la primauté du droit, sur le droit des peuples à disposer d'eux-mêmes « et de leurs richesses »[68]. Elle fait référence aux « principes éternels »[69] définis par le droit musulman, conception fortement religieuse qui nous invite à nous interroger une fois de plus sur l'universalité effective de l'instrument. Le relativisme qui y en découle vient confirmer que la théorie de l'universalité peut être remise en cause.

---

[64] Horatia MUIR WATT, « Les modèles familiaux à l'épreuve de la mondialisation », Arch. Phil. droit 45 (2001). Le droit international privé selon l'auteur se trouve progressivement privé des moyens d'exercer sa fonction proprement coordinatrice des systèmes de valeurs opposés. Lire B. D. CHATUE, *Les conflits de loi dans l'avant-projet de code camerounais des personnes et de la famille. Vers une réforme conséquente ?*, L'Harmattan, 2013. 265 p.

[65] S. Latouche, *L'occidentalisation du monde*, Paris, La Découverte, 1989.

[66]Voir L. SINDJOUN, « Les nouvelles constitutions africaines et la politique internationale : contribution à une économie internationale des biens politico-constitutionnels », *Etudes internationales*, vol. 26, n° 2, 1995, p. 333.

[67] Elle est la plus ancienne des organisations régionales et compte en son sein neuf Etats africains : Maroc, Égypte, Algérie, Djibouti, Soudan, Libye, Mauritanie, Somalie et Tunisie.

[68] Art. 1(a) de la Charte.

[69] Selon ces Etats, le *monde arabe* est considéré comme le « berceau des révélations divines ».

Il faut dire que la nouvelle Charte de 2008[70] a eu pour originalité de purifier le système arabe des droits de l'Homme en le privant de son « *venin religieux* », d'où sa forte tendance universaliste[71], malgré la subsistance de certaines controverses. On peut citer quelques-unes, notamment la controverse autour de la peine de mort appliquée aux enfants mineurs[72], la *discrimination positive introduite au profit de la femme par la Shari'a islamique et les autres lois divines*[73] et l'assimilation du sionisme au racisme[74]. Cette *déferlante* constitue la principale faiblesse de la Charte qui demeure hostile à l'universalité et conserve en son sein les vestiges d'un particularisme poussé.

À la suite de ces expériences, on peut conclure que l'universalité n'est plus à sens unique comme auraient prédit les pères créateurs du concept. Son unicité est, pour reprendre les formules de Gérard Fellous, sinon « contestée » du moins « menacée » en ce début du XXIe siècle. La conception unitariste des droits de l'homme quels que soient ses atouts et les libérations auxquelles elle a pu conduire les peuples opprimés ne constitue cependant pas un horizon indépassable, encore moins un axiome universel : elle peut et doit s'enrichir « des apports d'autres cultures ».

---

[70] La nouvelle Charte arabe des droits de l'Homme adoptée par le sommet de la Ligue des Etats arabes en mai 2004 est entrée en vigueur en 2008 et a déjà connu la ratification des Etats comme l'Algérie, le Bahreïn, les Émirats arabes unis, la Jordanie, la Libye, la Palestine et la Syrie.

[71] Il est d'ailleurs mentionné dans le préambule que les Etats réaffirment leur attachement à la DUDH, aux pactes internationaux relatifs aux droits de l'Homme et la déclaration du Caire sur les droits de l'Homme en islam.

[72] La Charte arabe de 1994 condamne sans détour en son article 12 la peine de mort appliquée contre des personnes âgées de moins de 18 ans. Cependant, l'article 7 de la version révisée de 2008 apporte une exception ainsi formulée : « ...sauf disposition contraire de la législation en vigueur au moment de l'infraction". Cette extension peut être perçue comme une boîte de pandore pour les oppresseurs. Lire les articles 6 (5) du PIDCP et 37 de la Convention sur les droits de l'enfant. Lire également la Charte africaine des droits et du bien-être de l'enfant en son article 5(3) « La peine de mort n'est pas prononcée pour les crimes commis par des enfants ».

[73] Article 3-C de la Charte.

[74] Le racisme et le sionisme y sont considérés comme les formes d'atteinte aux droits de l'Homme et de trouble à la paix mondiale. Art. 1(b) de la Charte.

Y a-t-il lieu de conclure à la crise de l'universalité ou de ressusciter le choc classique entre l'universalité des droits fondamentaux et le relativisme culturel s'il est avéré qu'à la faveur du mouvement de démocratisation qu' a connu le monde, et plus particulièrement le continent noir à la fin des années 80, l'adhésion de l'Afrique au standard universel de la démocratie libérale et des droits fondamentaux ne fait plus aucun doute?

Le système africain de protection des droits de l'Homme fait partie intégrale d'un ensemble planétaire qui, depuis la Charte des Nations unies et la Déclaration universelle des droits de l'homme, ne cesse de s'affirmer.

En clair, l'universalité n'est pas le produit d'une génération spontanée, encore moins une révélation prophétique. L'universalité est un *construit* destiné à la promotion des intérêts de tous.

Au demeurant, la question de l'universalité est aussi un problème de conscience, le sentiment d'appartenir à la même *famille universelle*[75]. On comprend que l'Union européenne soit fortement décriée comme le *laboratoire de la mondialisation*[76]. L'universalité doit donc être une construction de tous par tous et au service de tous. Les arbres de l'universalité ne doivent pas cacher aux Africains la forêt de l'usage de leurs droits, la nécessité de mettre en pratique leurs identités, de défendre leurs cultures. L'universalité c'est la juxtaposition des cultures comme le rappelle si bien François Terré ; les droits de l'Homme. Comme " c'est l'homme qui les constate ou les déclare : en tant que droits, ils sont des créations de son esprit, des fruits de sa culture. Mais en même temps, cette culture, résultat de l'action de l'esprit créateur, est nécessairement diverse et diversifiée "[77].

L'universalité même si elle se nourrit de la serve normative et institutionnelle, « *a horreur du pluriel* »[78]. L'ambiguïté[79] fondamentale entre

---

[75]J.- F. COLLANGE, « Les droits de l'homme, quelle universalité ? » in : *Autres temps, Les cahiers du christianisme social*, no 25, 1999, pp. 49-54 ; R. J. DUPUY, « Les droits de l'homme, valeur européenne ou valeur universelle ? », *RASMP*, 1989, pp. 425 et s.

[76] L'expression est de M. DELMAS-MARTY, *Trois défis pour un droit mondial*, Seuil, 1998. L'auteur qualifie l'Union européenne de laboratoire de la mondialisation.

[77] Cité par G. SOULIER, in *Rupture-Solidarité, L'Afrique (centrale) des Droits de l'Homme*, Karthala, Paris, nouvelle série n° 3, 2001, p. 179.

[78] M. D.- MARTY, « Le processus de mondialisation du droit », *Le droit saisi par la mondialisation*, Ch. A. MORAND (dir.), Bruylant, 2001, pp. 64-65.

usages et universalité est le fondement de « l'universalité de contiguïté » qui émerge progressivement dans l'ordre juridique africain.

II. Le souhaitable: l'avènement de *l'universalité de contiguïté*[80]

De plus en plus, on assiste à la crise de « l'universalité occidentale »[81] des droits de l'Homme au profit d'une « *universalité polyphonique* » qui prend en compte les particularités et les réalités culturelles des peuples y compris celles de l'Afrique. L'imposition du modèle occidental de l'universalité n'a plus le monopole qu'on lui prêtait.[82] La « *loi du monopole* »[83] pour reprendre cette formule de Norbert Elias ne joue plus en sa faveur. D'où l'universalisme relatif ou le relativisme tempéré[84], ou encore suivant la formule de Michael Walzer, « l'universalisme de la contiguïté »[85], c'est-à-dire l'universalisme qui prend en compte les particularismes culturels. L'enracinement de ce modèle d'universalisme calqué sur les particularités des sociétés passe par la prise en compte de leurs valeurs intrinsèques (**A**) ainsi que l'acception de la nouvelle pratique internationale qualifiée par les États de marge nationale d'appréciation (**B**).

A. L'urgence de la prise en compte des valeurs

Peut-on séparer sans toutefois les dénaturer les valeurs de la culture, de l'identité ? Si toutes les cultures sont des valeurs, toutes les valeurs ne sont pas des cultures même s'il existe une « valeur authentiquement culturelle ».

---

[79] Cette ambiguïté est résumée par Raymond Polin en ces termes : " l'homme, parce qu'il est homme, crée sa culture, mais que justement, cette culture est diversité, car l'homme est libre ".

[80] Il s'agit d'une universalité relative, celle qui prend en compte les valeurs, les particularismes culturels.

[81] E. HUSSERL, *La crise des sciences européennes et la phénoménologie transcendantale*, trad. fr. par G. Granel, paris, Gallimard, 1976.

[82] L. SINDJOUN, « L'Afrique dans les relations internationales », *African Sociological Rewieu*, n° 2, 1999.

[83] N. ELIAS, *La dynamique de l'Occident,* Paris, Calmann-Lévy, 1975, pp. 29-45.

[84] B. BADIE et G. HERMET, *Politique comparée*, Paris, Armand Colin, 2001, pp. 28-37. Lire L. SINDJOUN, *L'Etat ailleurs, Entre noyau dur et case vide*, éd., Economica, 2002, p. 16.

[85] Cette expression est reprise par L. SINDJOUN, *op. cit.* p. 16.

La culture est plus grande que la valeur[86]. Et les auteurs Badié et Smouts de dire, la culture au-delà des représentations, des valeurs et des modèles de comportement est un « système de signification communément partagée par les individus membres d'une même collectivité »[87].

Disons d'emblée que le concept valeur n'est pas éminemment juridique, il peut être emprunté à d'autres sciences telle l'économie (la valeur boursière ou pécuniaire, ce que vaut en argent une chose). Il a, par la suite, désigné une certaine prestation ou un certain bien d'où sa réception par le droit (valeur mobilière, mise en valeur d'un patrimoine, prise en compte de la valeur de l'objet endommagé en cas de réparation).

La notion de valeur a définitivement *révolutionné*[88] le droit en général et le droit des droits de l'Homme en particulier.

En droit international public, alors que les normes conventionnelles ne concernent, en vertu de l'effet relatif des Conventions, que les États parties et que les normes coutumières peuvent être récusées par un « objecteur persistant », la référence aux « *valeurs communes* » des Nations unies illumine le développement du droit international public, en traduisant une *opinion juris* collective.

En droits de l'Homme, on assiste, dans la pratique, à la contestation de certains droits liés aux valeurs, notamment le droit à la vie, l'interdiction dans certaines sociétés de l'interruption volontaire de la grossesse (IVG)[89], la

---

[86] En référence à cette formule de J. CARBONNIER suivant laquelle : « *le droit est plus grand que la règle de droit* », in *Flexible droit*, 10ème éd., p. 22.

[87] B. BADIE et Cl. SMOUTS, *Le retournement du monde*, Paris, Dalloz-FNSP, 1992.

[88] J.- PHILIPPE DEROSIER, « Qu'est-ce qu'une révolution juridique ? Le point de vue de la théorie générale du droit », *Revue française de droit constitutionnel,* 2015/ 2 n° 102, pp. 391-404. D. KOKOROKO, « Révolution et droit international », *Revue Togolaise des Sciences Juridiques*, Janvier-Juin 2012 n° 0002, pp. 7-21.

[89] V. Cour d'appel de Paris, *Arrêt perruche* du 17 décembre 1993. Interdite par certaines législations africaines à l'exception des cas jugés thérapeutiques, l'IVG est reconnue en France comme une liberté selon cet attendu célèbre du juge français « Attendu que dès lors que les fautes commises par le médecin et le laboratoire dans l'exécution des contrats formés avec Mme P... avaient empêché celle-ci d'exercer son choix d'interrompre sa grossesse afin d'éviter la naissance d'un enfant atteint d'un handicap, ce dernier peut demander la réparation du préjudice résultant de ce handicap et causé par les fautes retenues ».

reconnaissance de l'euthanasie[90], de la peine capitale, ou de l'homosexualité ici, l'interdiction là-bas. On est tenté de dire que le droit international des droits de l'Homme oscille entre *Valeurs* et *Droits*. S'il est une chose que recherche généralement le juriste, c'est la qualification d'un concept ou d'un acte et la détermination de sa valeur juridique. Le mot valeur n'a pas que fait le bonheur du droit, il est aussi vieux que la philosophie[91], que la République. On parlera d'une part des valeurs républicaines qui diffèrent en fonction de la forme de celle-ci (laïcité, égalité, indivisibilité, unité, citoyenneté) et d'autre part, des valeurs universelles tels la démocratie, l'État de droit, la bonne gouvernance, la sécurité juridique, etc. Mais qu'est-ce qu'une valeur ?

Pour Heinrich Rickert, « *la valeur elle-même n'est ni un bien, ni un objectif, ni une fin, non plus qu'un moyen* ». Selon lui, il faut faire une distinction fondamentale entre des valeurs qui sont en elles-mêmes des valeurs (des « valeurs en propres »), et des valeurs dont la validité dépend d'autres valeurs (des valeurs conditionnelles). La vie n'a de ce fait, de valeur que conditionnellement[92]. La valeur, c'est ce qui permet à une chose ou à une personne de s'affirmer ou d'être perçue en tant que tel, c'est aussi une *qualité*[93]. On parlerait d'une valeur inhérente pour magnifier une valeur réelle ou primitive et d'une valeur ajoutée ou artificielle.

À dire vrai, les droits africains brillent par une certaine hybridation prenant en compte à la fois les valeurs universelles et les valeurs authentiquement africaines. Parmi ces valeurs universelles, on peut citer celles liées à l'humanisme (le respect de la dignité humaine)- rien dans l'échelle des valeurs, disait Jean Rivero, ne se situe au-dessus du principe de

---

[90] V. Conseil d'Etat français, *affaire Vincent Lambert* rendue en juin 2014. Selon la haute juridiction française, « débrancher les fluides » de Vincent Lambert est bien un acte légal, conforme à la loi Léonetti qui confie au médecin la responsabilité de décider de l'arrêt d'un traitement qui témoignerait d'une « obstination déraisonnable ». La procédure collégiale a été bien respectée. Tout est fait dans la vertu républicaine.

[91] H. RICKERT, *Le système des valeurs et autres articles*, Paris, Librairie philosophique, J. VRIN, 2007, p. 30.

[92] H. RICKERT, *Le système des valeurs et autres articles*, Paris, Librairie philosophique, J. VRIN, 2007, 279 p.

[93] C'est nous qui le soulignons.

dignité de la personne humaine-)[94], celles liées à l'individualisme (reconnaissance de l'autonomie de l'individu), et celles liées au libéralisme (promotion du pluralisme politique, économique et social). Par ailleurs, ces droits baignent dans un contexte où règnent d'autres valeurs, d'autres visions des choses et du monde. Que dire, chaque société à ses valeurs d'où la considération à tort ou à raison des valeurs ethniques, religieuses et linguistiques, l'hospitalité, l'unité africaine, la solidarité comme des valeurs ancestrales africaines. C'est de ces valeurs qu'il s'agit ici, contrariées pour quelques-unes par le principe d'universalité. C'est aussi vrai que chaque peuple a ses valeurs de civilisation qui du reste ne sont jamais ni fermées ni figées et évoluent avec les mœurs et les mentalités[95].

Comment rendre compte de la pratique universaliste des droits dans une Afrique dont on sait que l'administration est plongée dans un contexte économique, socioculturel, et politico-institutionnel particulier, ce qui déteint sur la qualité du droit qu'elle produit. Ce contexte est dominé par la coexistence des structures sociales traditionnelles et de structures sociales modernes et induit un conflit de rationalité. C'est le syncrétisme qui caractérise les droits africains[96]. S'agit-il des valeurs sociales ou juridiques ?

Le concept valeur tire son assise juridique du préambule de la Déclaration universelle des droits de l'Homme qui souligne que : « *considérant que dans la charte les peuples des Nations Unies ont proclamé à nouveau leur foi dans les droits fondamentaux de l'homme, dans la dignité et la valeur de la personne humaine…* ».

Dans la même veine, la Charte africaine des droits de l'homme et des peuples dès son préambule rappelle que les Africains tiennent compte des vertus de leurs traditions historiques et des valeurs de civilisation africaine

---

[94] Lire M. FABRE-MAGNAN, « Le statut juridique de la dignité humaine », *Droits* 2013/2 (n° 58), p. 167-196; Vous trouverez chez l'auteur les éléments de réponse à la question de savoir si la dignité humaine est un « *droit* » ou une « *valeur* » ; V. également S. SOBZE, *La dignité humaine dans l'ordre juridique africain*, Thèse de doctorat en droit public, Université de Yaoundé II, avril 2013, 596 p.

[95] T. ATANGANA-MALONGUE, « Libres interrogations d'une civiliste sur l'homosexualité au Cameroun », *Revue de droit international et de droit comparé*, 2013, n° 4, p. 495.

[96] J. M. BRETON, *Droit public congolais*, P., Economica, 1987, p. 172.

qui doivent inspirer et caractériser leurs réflexions sur la conception des droits de l'Homme. Aussi impose-t-elle en son article 29(5) à l'individu le devoir :

> *« de veiller, dans ses relations avec la société, à la préservation et au renforcement des valeurs culturelles africaines positives, dans un esprit de tolérance, de dialogue et de concertation et d'une façon générale de contribuer à la promotion de la santé morale de la société ».*

La Charte culturelle de l'Afrique se veut un instrument de promotion des valeurs africaines. Elle dit dans son préambule qu'il est *urgent* d'édifier des systèmes éducatifs qui intègrent les *valeurs* africaines de civilisation, afin d'assurer l'enracinement de la jeunesse dans la culture africaine. Aussi entend-elle développer dans le patrimoine culturel africain toutes les valeurs dynamiques[97], notamment par l'introduction des valeurs culturelles africaines dans l'enseignement à travers l'organisation de festivals nationaux et panafricains[98]. La Charte africaine des droits et du bien-être de l'enfant promeut l'intégration des valeurs de la civilisation africaine dans toute réflexion relative à la protection des droits de l'enfant[99].

Il faut dire que les droits africains sont des droits d'inspiration libérale[100]. Ils reposent sur des valeurs issues de l'idéologie des droits de l'Homme. Leur légitimité est par conséquent conditionnée par la prise en compte des aspirations de la conscience collective.

Par ailleurs, les valeurs occidentales peuvent-elles constituer un *précédent* pour l'Afrique ?

Si la réponse affirmative à cette question ne fait plus de doute, il ne s'ensuit pas que leur modèle peut et doit être transporté *tel quel* en Afrique. Tant les raisons d'opportunité politique que l'état d'intégration moins avancé de l'Afrique militent en faveur d'un réexamen et même d'une

---

[97] Article 1(h) de la Charte culturelle de l'Afrique du 5 juillet 1976.

[98] Article 10 de la Charte culturelle de l'Afrique.

[99] V. Préambule de la Charte africaine des droits et du bien-être de l'enfant adoptée le 11 juillet 1990 et entrée en vigueur le 29 novembre 1999.

[100] Lire G. LEBRETON, *Droit administratif général*, Tome 1, L'action administrative, P. Armand Colin p. 18.

révision de ce modèle. Une valeur ne peut pas être déclarée arbitrairement universelle. Elle doit être reconnue comme telle par chaque personne.

Il n'est plus question d'un transfert sans inventaire préalable. L'interrogation savante de Pierre Legendre nous réconforte dans cette position : « *d'autres cultures sont déjà et seront productrices de modernité. Sera-t-elle la copie conforme de nos illusions d'Occidentaux ?* »[101] Répondre par la négative, c'est attester que les constitutions africaines qui allient tradition et modernité et qui par ailleurs sont favorables à l'internationalisation[102], sont le reflet des réalités africaines.

Les constitutions des États africains ont toujours, pour la plupart, servi de base de données de la liste des droits de l'Homme à garantir, servant ainsi de vade-mecum à ce que Luc Sindjoun a qualifié de « *contexte normatif stimulant, porteur pour les droits de l'homme* »[103].

Cependant, leur définition devra tenir compte des conditions particulières à l'Afrique, par exemple le droit de se marier qui doit être réglementé en fonction des impératifs religieux de plusieurs pays importants. Il en est de même de la protection de la vie familiale qui devra prendre en considération les caractères propres à la famille africaine. Le collectivisme demeure l'épine dorsale de l'identité africaine et l'évolution incessante de l'individualisme issue des cultures occidentales contribue à ruiner l'originalité des droits africains et, par-là, les structures sociales des pays[104]. Cette évolution n'est donc pas « inéluctable », car les sociétés africaines

---

101 P. LEGENDRE, *Ce que l'Occident ne voit pas de l'occident*, Conférences au Japon, éd., Mille et une nuits, mai 2004, 140 p.

102A. ONDOUA, « L'internationalisation des Constitutions en Afrique subsaharienne francophone et la protection des droits fondamentaux », *Rev. Trim. Dr. h.* (98/2014), pp. 437-45 ; A. SALL, « Le droit international dans les nouvelles Constitutions africaines », *RJPIC* 1997, n° 1, p. 352.

103L. SINDJOUN, « Les nouvelles Constitutions africaines et la politique internationale : contribution à une économie internationale des biens politico-constitutionnels », *op cit.*, p. 335.

104 Le constat avait déjà été fait par René-A. KOUASSIGAN, *L'homme et la terre*, Éditions Berger-Levrault, Paris, 1966, 291 p.

demeurent formées de cercles *concentriques* et bâties pour reprendre la formule de Léopold Sédar Senghor, sur *le type même de la famille*[105].

Pour ce qui est de la limitation des droits de l'Homme dans l'intérêt du maintien de l'ordre et de la sécurité publics, elle devra tenir compte du rôle essentiel de l'État dans les pays en voie de développement en lui reconnaissant, dans l'exercice de son pouvoir discrétionnaire, une marge d'appréciation plus importante[106].

B. La déférence à la marge nationale d'appréciation

L'on pensait la marge nationale d'appréciation enterrée par la mondialisation du droit au nom du sacro-saint principe de l'universalité des droits de l'Homme. Le XXIe siècle la ramène sous les feux de l'actualité rappelant ainsi le lien sacré qui existe encore entre le couple « relativisme culturel » et « universalisme »[107].

La marge nationale d'appréciation reconnaît aux États une sorte de « droit à la différence ». Le risque étant de se livrer à « pluriversalité » des droits de l'Homme. En quoi consiste cette pratique ?

Il y a marge d'appréciation quand la loi (ou la règle de droit) a utilisé une notion imprécise ou indéterminée. En utilisant une telle notion, le législateur, habilite l'Administration à apprécier elle-même la situation au regard de cette notion. La théorie de la marge nationale d'appréciation permet d'autoriser l'Administration à choisir entre plusieurs qualifications juridiques des faits et, par voie de conséquence, à choisir entre plusieurs décisions possibles. Par exemple, selon que la situation est qualifiée de très dangereuse ou non pour l'ordre public, la police peut prendre la décision de

---

[105] L. S SENGHOR, *Pierre Teilhard de Chardin et la politique africaine*, Cahier n° 3, Éditions du Seuil.

[106] Voir K. VASAK, *op. cit.* pp. 475 et s.

[107] Les dangers d'une exacerbation du relativisme culturel ont été suffisamment mis en exergue par le professeur Etienne LE ROY. En effet, dans une contribution au colloque international de Port-Louis sur « L'effectivité des droits fondamentaux dans les pays de la communauté francophone », contribution intitulée « Les droits de l'homme entre un universalisme hâtif et le ghetto des particularismes culturels », le professeur relève que la prise en compte des particularismes a conduit certains à préconiser un « droit à la différence » qui peut justifier un "droit à l'enfermement", un "droit à l'oppression" et un "droit à la mort".

restreindre plus ou moins l'exercice d'une liberté ou encore de ne pas intervenir du tout. La marge d'appréciation permet dans l'ordre interne à l'Administration de choisir entre plusieurs appréciations possibles de la situation et le juge respecte l'appréciation retenue par l'autorité administrative pourvu qu'elle soit plausible ; il censure donc seulement l'erreur manifeste[108].

Dans l'ordre juridique international, la pratique de la « marge nationale d'appréciation » est une véritable *déferlante* surtout à l'aune de la prise en compte par le droit international des catégories nouvelles[109], telles les minorités sexuelles.

Dans cet ordre, on parle de la marge nationale d'appréciation lorsqu'un État moins avancé sur une question de droit ou moins imprégné sur son évolution, exige qu'on ne lui en fasse pas rigueur dans l'application ou dans la mise en œuvre. Il prend à cet effet, une distance raisonnable pour apprécier les contours du droit en question et de son applicabilité dans son ordre juridique. En droit des droits de l'Homme, elle signifie que certaines sociétés ne sont pas encore prêtes à faire appliquer certaines conventions y relatives. C'est donc un argument juridique tiré des conventions internationales relatives aux droits de l'Homme.

La question de la marge nationale d'appréciation a été le point d'orgue de nombreuses réclamations touchant à la *sensibilité humaine* comme l'homosexualité et l'hétérosexualité. Sa consécration jurisprudentielle intervient à la suite d'une jurisprudence internationale incitative à la

---

[108] M. FROMONT, *Le pouvoir discrétionnaire et le juge administration*, in : Festschrift für Hermann Jahrrei, Cologne, 1974, p. 67. La marge d'appréciation est distincte du pouvoir discrétionnaire. Ce dernier permet à l'Administration, de choisir le contenu de sa décision entre plusieurs contenus possibles quand les conditions posées par la loi sont réunies pour son intervention tandis que la marge permet à l'Administration de choisir entre plusieurs appréciations possibles.

[109] Les minorités au sens classique étant contenues dans les dispositions de l'article 27 du PIDCP à savoir les minorités ethniques, religieuses et linguistiques.

dépénalisation de l'homosexualité. Il s'agit de l'affaire *Dudgeon* c. *Royaume-Uni* du 22 octobre 1981[110].

Par exemple, la dépénalisation des actes homosexuels est le fruit d'un processus en Europe. À ce titre, Thérèse Atangana Malongué rappelle que pendant longtemps, les juges de la Cour européenne déclaraient irrecevables les plaintes des homosexuels allemands contre les dispositions répressives du code pénal[111] aux motifs que la pénalisation de l'homosexualité entrait dans la marge d'appréciation de chaque État pour « protéger la santé de la population et d'éviter la perturbation des adolescents ». Il faut attendre 1981 pour que la première décision imposant la dépénalisation n'intervienne sur le continent[112]. La Cour européenne des droits de l'Homme dans les arrêts *Schalk* et *Kopf* et puis dans les arrêts *Gas* et *Dubois* souligne que la question du mariage hétérosexuel est une question politique pour laquelle « les États disposent d'une large marge d'appréciation ».[113]

Cependant, il faut souligner, pour le nuancer, que la marge d'appréciation des États en matière de mariage est en train de se réduire explicitement avec l'arrêt Oliari and Others v. Italy du 21 juillet 2015 où la Cour fait largement appel au droit comparé (§178) en citant les États-Unis et l'Australie et oubliant soigneusement l'Afrique[114].

La prise en compte des usages africains à l'aune de l'universalité des droits de l'Homme participe du système de *congruence* des droits ou, pour reprendre Fanny Malhière, du « système d'équivalence des droits

---

[110] La Cour dira pour droit que la sanction des rapports sexuels entre adultes consentants constitue une violation de la vie privée. Cour eur. D.H. arrêt du 22 octobre 1981, *Dudgeon c. Royaume-Uni,* série A n° 45.

[111] Art. 175 du Code pénal (Reich Strafgesetzbuch) : « La fornication contre-nature, pratiquée entre personne de sexe masculin ou entre gens et animaux, est punie de prison ». Le texte est resté en vigueur de 1871 à 1994 (Voir cep. RDA abrogation en 1988).

[112] La Cour eur. D. H. ira plus loin dans les arrêts L. et V. c. Autriche et SL. c. Autriche du 9 janvier 2003 en condamnant la pénalisation d'actes homosexuels entre adultes et adolescents consentants âgés de 14 à 18 ans. V. A. MALONGUE *op. cit.* p. 495.

[113] C.J.C.E., 24 juin 2010, arrêt *Schalk* et *Kopf* c. Autriche ; C.E.D.H., arrêt *Gas* et *Dubois* c. France du 15 mars 2012.

[114] cf Arrêt Oliari and Others v. Italy du 21 juillet 2015 (http://hudoc.echr.coe.int/sites/eng/pages/search.aspx?i=001-156265).

fondamentaux[115] ». Elle rend compte de l'évolution du monde et des choses, de la réalité du village planétaire et de l'existence des concepts tels que la communauté de valeurs, la communauté des États, qui commandent d'avoir un regard synoptique et une perception mondialisée des choses.

Le relativisme culturel qui permet ici et qui aurait permis dans les années 1960 et 1970 de remettre en question l'universalisme des droits fondamentaux n'est pas une fuite en avant, « un moyen commode pour les États africains de s'affranchir de l'obligation de respecter les droits fondamentaux » comme l'aurait prétendu le juge Kéba M'baye, mais un répondant idoine à la montée fulgurante de l'impérialisme culturel occidental-libéral ou socialiste au nom de l'universalité des droits fondamentaux. Le relativisme culturel que prône la présente réflexion, et au modèle tempéré, n'est pas péjoratif, il s'appréhende dans une certaine mesure comme une réponse aux contraintes de la société internationale, une façon pour l'Afrique de faire son « *marketing culturel* »[116].

L'idée d'une « *conception pluraliste des droits de l'homme* » telle que suggérée par les auteurs Mireille Delmas-Marty[117] et Gérard Cohen-Jonathan[118] paraît pertinente. Ces droits seraient « *conçus à partir de principes directeurs communs, appliqués avec une marge nationale d'appréciation qui reconnaîtrait aux États une sorte de droit à la différence, mais à condition de ne pas descendre au-dessous d'un certain seuil de compatibilité, qui peut d'ailleurs*

---

[115] F. MALHIERE, « Le contrôle de l'équivalence des protections des droits fondamentaux : les juges et les rapports de systèmes », *Revue du droit public et de la science politique en France et à l'Étranger*, 01 novembre 2013 n° 6, p. 1523.

[116] L. SINDJOUN, « Les nouvelles Constitutions africaines et la politique internationale : contribution à une économie internationale des biens politico-constitutionnels », op cit., p. 334. L'auteur instruit l'usage du « marketing constitutionnel » comme procédé permettant aux Etats africains d'éviter d'être rangés dans le « jurassic park » des sociétés politiques anachroniques ou dans un musée des curiosités et des monstruosités politiques.

[117] « De la juste dénomination des droits de l'homme », *Droits et Cultures*, 1998 / 1, pp. 105-116.

[118] « La conception des droits de l'homme chez René Cassin », *René Cassin : une pensée ouverte sur le monde moderne, Colloque au collège de France, Honoré Champion,* 2001, pp. 92 et s, cité par Adama KPODAR, « Les droits de l'homme saisis par le droit international », *Revue Togolaise des Sciences Juridiques*, Janvier-Juin 2012 n°0002, pp. 22-40.

varier selon qu'il s'agit d'une question plus consensuelle ou plus conflictuelle »[119]. Il faut, pour y croire, un organe régulateur compétent.

Conclusion

Que conclure de ces constats divers et même ondoyants relatifs aux usages du droit en Afrique face à l'universalité des droits de l'Homme ? On ne peut s'empêcher de penser que les valeurs africaines se trouvent en quelque sorte prises en otage par « *l'impérialisme blanc* » au nom de la pseudo-universalité des droits de l'Homme. Dès lors, aborder une thématique basée sur la recherche du compromis entre relativisme culturel et universalité n'est pas la marque d'une volonté de subtil balancement ou le fruit d'un artifice dialectique paisible[120].

Quel est le sort réservé aux valeurs africaines à l'aune de l'universalité des droits de l'Homme ? Faut-il se résoudre à rendre les armes et à conclure qu'elles ont été phagocytées par les valeurs supposées universelles ?

L'universalité des droits de l'Homme ne peut être effective que si elle prend en considération les réalités socioculturelles de chaque peuple, si elle participe à la dyade déstructuration-structuration des sociétés locales[121]. Il est bien possible de penser le droit à partir de ses usages.

Il n'est donc pas question pour l'Afrique de « sortir de la communauté » ou encore de devenir un obstacle à la mondialisation des droits de l'Homme. Il est question pour l'Afrique de s'inspirer des instruments universels de protection des droits de l'Homme, ce qui permettrait d'éviter des distorsions récurrentes entre les systèmes régionaux et le système universel. L'Afrique montrerait ainsi qu'en étant elle-même, elle rejoint par ses aspirations les plus profondes celle de l'humanité tout entière. C'est

---

[119] Cités par K. VASAK, « Les droits de l'homme et l'Afrique, Vers les institutions africaines pour la protection internationale des droits de l'homme ? », RBDI, 1967. 2.

[120] Cette formule est empruntée à Anne LEVADE, « La construction européenne et son incidence sur les compétences étatiques et la hiérarchie des normes », *Revue française de droit constitutionnel*, 2015 /2 (n°102), pp. 287-306.

[121] L. SINDJOUN, *L'Etat ailleurs, Entre noyau dur et case vide*, Economica, 2002, p. 25.

pourquoi l'idée d'une *sur-idéologisation*[122] des droits de l'Homme comme modèle impératif, fait *d'un ordre public à vocation internationale et à usage planétaire*[123] semble porteuse pour l'Afrique. Il est nécessaire pour l'Afrique de conserver les acquis, de sauvegarder les droits existants surtout ceux qui ne sont pas hostiles aux normes de la société reconnues et acceptées. Et pour paraphraser Portalis « *...il est utile de conserver tout ce qu'il n'est pas nécessaire de détruire : les lois doivent ménager les habitudes, quand ces habitudes ne sont pas des vices ».*[124] L'idée de l'universalité n'exclut ni la différenciation ni la singularité et ne conduit pas non plus à l'exigence de l'uniformité absolue[125].

BIBLIOGRAPHIE INDICATIVE

CASSIN (R.), « La Déclaration universelle et la mise en œuvre des droits de l'homme », *R.C.A.D.I.*, t. 79, n° II, 1951, pp. 241-367.

COHEN-JONATHAN (G.), « Universalité et singularité des droits de l'homme », *Revue trimestrielle des droits de l'homme,* 2003.

COLLANGE (J.-F.), « Les droits de l'homme, quelle universalité ? » in : *Autres temps, Les cahiers du christianisme social,* n° 25, 1999.

DUPUY (R.J.), « Les droits de l'homme, valeur européenne ou valeur universelle ? », *RASMP*, 1989.

GONIDEC (P.-F.), *Les droits africains,* Paris, LGDJ, 1976.

GUTMANN (D), « Les droits de l'homme sont-ils l'avenir du droit ? », in *l'avenir du droit, Mélanges en l'honneur de F. TERRE*, Dalloz, 1999.

J. MOURGEON, « L'universalité des droits de l'homme entre foi et droit », pp. 1265-1282, *in Libertés, justice, tolérance, Mélanges en hommage au Doyen G. Cohen-Jonathan*, Bruxelles, Bruylant, 2003.

---

[122] L'expression est empruntée à Horatia MUIR WATT, « Les modèles familiaux à l'épreuve de la mondialisation », Arch. Phil. droit 45 (2001).

[123] Lire D. GUTMANN, *Les droits de l'homme sont-ils l'avenir du droit ?* », in *L'avenir du droit, Mélanges en l'honneur de F. TERRE*, Dalloz, 1999, p.329.

[124] Voir J.-E.-M. PORTALIS, *Discours préliminaire au premier projet de Code civil* édité aux éditions confluences et paru le 22 décembre 1998 ; également *De l'usage et de l'abus de l'esprit philosophique durant le XVIIIème siècle* (2volumes, 1820).

[125] A. KPODAR, *op. cit*, p. 38.

KI-ZERBO (J.), « Les droits de l'homme en Afrique: tradition et modernité », *in Foi et développement*, n°237-238 - nov/déc 1995.

KOUASSIGAN (R.-A.), *L'homme et la terre*, Éditions Berger-Levrault, Paris, 1966, 291 p.

KPODAR (A), « Les droits de l'homme saisis par le droit international », *Revue Togolaise des Sciences Juridiques*, Janvier-Juin 2012 n°, 0002, pp. 22-40.

PELLOUX (R.), « Vrais et faux droits de l'Homme, problème de définition et de classification », *Revue de Droit Public*, 1981.

PORTALIS (J.-E.-M.), *De l'usage et de l'abus de l'esprit philosophique durant le XVIIIe siècle* (2volumes, 1820).

REDOR-FICHOT (M.-Joëlle), « L'indivisibilité des droits de l'homme », C.R.D.F. n° 7, 2009, pp. 75- 86.

RICKERT (H.), *Le système des valeurs et autres articles*, Paris, Librairie philosophique, J. VRIN, 2007, 279 p.

VASAK (K.), « Les droits de l'homme et l'Afrique, Vers les institutions africaines pour la protection internationale des droits de l'homme ?, RBDI, 1967. 2, pp. 459-478.

PROTOCOLE DE RÉDACTION DES ARTICLES

L'envoi des articles au Comité éditorial se fait exclusivement par courrier électronique à l'adresse suivante : rasj.soa@gmail.com. La Revue n'endosse aucune responsabilité pour tout article envoyé à une autre adresse.

Le comité éditorial de la revue attache un prix particulier au respect des normes et standards ci-dessous indiqués :

1. La taille des contributions ne doit pas excéder 20 pages au format de la revue pour les articles proprement dits et 15 pages pour toute autre contribution.

2. Tout article soumis pour publication doit être envoyé sous le format Word, interligne simple, police d'écriture Times New Roman, taille de police 12, paragraphe aligné, marges de 2,5 cm.

3. Les articles sont accompagnés d'une biographie succincte de l'auteur, incluant sa qualité (grade, responsabilité académique, ou statut professionnel), son adresse e-mail dans une première note de bas de page, et d'un résumé de dix lignes maximum en français et en anglais avec quatre à six mots-clés.

4. Les citations dans le corps du texte doivent être transcrites entre guillemets doubles, avec le même type et la même taille de la lettre du texte.

5. L'appel de note est continu et se place après le mot ou le groupe de mots auquel il se rapporte, séparé par un espace insécable.

6. Les références bibliographiques des articles sont citées comme suit :

a) Pour les articles des revues : Nom (intégral)et Prénom (initial) de l'auteur, Titre de l'article entre guillemets doubles, *Titre de la revue en italique*, Numéro du volume, Numéro du fascicule, Année de la publication, Pages initiale et finale de l'article ou Page (s) exacte (s) de la citation.

Exemple : LECA J., « Pour une analyse comparative des systèmes politiques méditerranéens », *Revue française de science politique ou RFSP*, vol. 27, n° 4, 1977, p. 557-581.

b) Pour les livres : Nom (intégral) et Prénom (initial) de l'auteur, *Titre du livre en italique,* Lieu de publication, Maison d'édition, Année de publication, Pages initiale et finale de l'article ou Page (s) exacte (s) de la citation.

Exemple : MBAYE K., *Les droits de l'homme en Afrique*, Paris, Pedone, 2002, p. 180.

c) Pour les ouvrages collectifs : Nom (intégral) et Prénom (initial) de l'auteur, Titre de l'article entre guillemets doubles, Mention « in » en italique, Nom du directeur de l'ouvrage, nom de l'ouvrage en italique, Lieu d'édition, Maison d'édition, Année d'édition, Pages initiale et finale de l'article ou Page (s) exacte (s) de la citation.

Exemple : MAZERES J.-A., « Qu'est-ce que la puissance publique ? », *in* Raimbault P. (dir.), *La puissance publique à l'heure européenne*, Paris, Dalloz, 2006, p. 9 à 20.

N.B. Les articles expertisés (selon le principe de *Peer Review)*, retenus et publiés dans la *RASJ* deviennent la propriété de celle-ci. Leur reproduction partielle ou intégrale est soumise à l'autorisation expresse de la direction de la Revue.

PROTOCOL FOR SUBMITTING ARTICLES

Contributions can only be submitted through electronic mailing to the following address : rasj.soa@gmail.com. The editorial board of AJL shall not be liable for any contribution which is not sent to above address. The editorial policy of the Journal requires strict adherence to the following guidelines and standards :

1. Articles must not exceed 20 pages and other contributions (Case Law, Legislation and Bibliographic Surveys) 15 pages.

2. All contributions must be sent in Word format (.doc or .docx), single line spacing, Times New Roman font, size - 12, aligned paragraphs, and margins of 2.5 cm.

3. All contributions must include a brief biography of the author in an opening footnote, their academic or professional status, email address and, for articles, a short abstract written in French and English of not more than 200 words each followed by four to six key words ;

4. Citations in the body of the paper should be in single smart quotes, with the same font as the text but smaller in size (10).

5. Footnoting should be continuous and must appear after the relevant word or group of words, separated by normal spacing.

6. Bibliographic references of articles should be quoted as follows :

a) For articles of a Journal : Author's name and surname, Title of the article in inverted commas, *Title of the Journal in italics*, Volume Number, Fascicle Number, Year of publication, first and last pages of the article or exact page(s) of the quotation.

Example : Flemming P., "The Justiciability of Socio-Economic Rights in Africa", *International Human Rights Law Review* or *IHLR*, vol.vol. 27, n° 4, 1977, pp. 557-581.

b) For books : Author's name and surname, *Title of the book in italics*, Place of publication, Publishing house, Year of publication, First and last pages of the article or Exact page(s) of the quotation.

Example : Raz J., *Authority of the Law*, London, Stevens, 2002, p.180.

c) For collective works : Author's name and surname, Title of the article in inverted commas, *"in"* in italics, Name of the director of the book, *Title of the book in italics*, Place of publication, Publishing house, Year of publication, First and last pages of the article or Exact page(s) of the quotation.

Example : IngelmanJ. "Foreign Direct Investments in Africa ?" *in* Craig P.(Ed.), *Foreign Capital Flows in Developing Countries : Incidence on Development*, Cincinnati, Butterworths, 2006, pp. 9 - 20.

N. B. Articles reviewed (following the Peer Review principle), validated and published by the AJOL become the property of the Journal. Any partial or complete reproduction is subject to the prior authorisation from the Editors of the Journal.

Questions juridiques aux éditions L'Harmattan

Dernières parutions

CONCILIATION ET MÉDIATION DEVANT LA JURIDICTION ADMINISTRATIVE
Actes du colloque du Conseil d'État du 17 juin 2015
Sous la direction de Jacques Biancarelli et Béatrice Blohorn-Brenneur
Voici près de 25 ans que le Conseil d'État, confronté à une judiciarisation croissante de la société, réfléchit aux modes alternatifs de règlement des différends afin de les pacifier et de rendre les justiciables davantage confiants en la justice administrative. Après avoir rappelé le contexte juridique et les enjeux d'une telle impulsion, un bilan comparatif des pratiques du juge administratif et du juge judiciaire a permis de mesurer combien il est nécessaire et urgent de compléter la boîte à outils dont dispose le premier. Voici une réflexion, les références et les outils nécessaires à la juridiction administrative.
(Coédition GEMME, 24.00 euros, 246 p.)
ISBN : 978-2-343-07270-8, ISBN EBOOK : 978-2-336-39774-0

L'ERREUR JUDICIAIRE
Apprendre à douter pour lutter contre les erreurs judiciaires
Sous la direction de Xavier Pin
L'erreur judiciaire hante autant qu'elle jalonne l'histoire de notre justice pénale. Nous avons tous en mémoire de retentissants procès ayant vu des individus accusés ou condamnés, avant d'être disculpés, graciés ou réhabilités. Le législateur y est sensible au point de réformer régulièrement la procédure pénale pour tenter d'éviter, de corriger ou de réparer, autant que possible, de telles erreurs. Une loi du 20 juin 2014 réforme les procédures de révision et de réexamen des condamnations pénales définitives : elle est l'occasion d'essayer de comprendre ces fiascos judiciaires.
(Coll. Droit privé et sciences criminelles, 15.00 euros, 126 p.)
ISBN : 978-2-343-07284-5, ISBN EBOOK : 978-2-336-39807-5

LE DROIT CONSTITUTIONNEL DE LA Ve RÉPUBLIQUE
(Treizième édition)
Lascombe Michel, Toulemonde Gilles
Cet ouvrage s'adresse aux étudiants en droit, aux élèves des instituts d'études politiques et aux candidats aux concours administratifs. Il couvre l'essentiel du programme de droit constitutionnel, c'est-à-dire aussi bien les constitutions françaises depuis 1789 que l'actuel texte constitutionnel. Cette nouvelle édition tient compte des derniers développements induits par les changements politiques, des dernières réformes des règlements des assemblées et de la jurisprudence la plus récente.
(Coll. Logiques Juridiques, 42.00 euros, 506 p.)
ISBN : 978-2-343-07916-5, ISBN EBOOK : 978-2-336-39877-8

LA PROXIMITÉ EN DROIT INTERNATIONAL PRIVÉ DE LA FAMILLE
Bouyahia Sabrine Maya - Préface de Lotfi Chedly et Marie Goré
Parmi les méthodes proposées pour trancher les litiges présentant un élément d'extranéité, figure celle reposant sur le principe de proximité. L'étude porte sur deux systèmes de droit international privé de la famille différents (droit français et droit tunisien) pour mettre en exergue d'une

part l'adaptation de cette méthode aux spécificités de chaque ordre étatique et d'autre part son adéquation avec tous les différents systèmes de droit.
(Coll. Logiques Juridiques, 54.00 euros, 618 p.)
ISBN : 978-2-343-05464-3, ISBN EBOOK : 978-2-336-39866-2

QUARTIER-FEMMES ÉCROU 10970
Boh-Petit Dominique
Cellule 24 : une femme dit toute sa souffrance d'être enfermée. Elle a tué. Son histoire est à la rubrique des faits divers. La Cour d'assises la jugera. Bien des années plus tard, elle est libérée. La vie doit reprendre. Ce récit est parfaitement conforme à la réalité. Tout a existé et existe encore.
(Coll. La justice au quotidien, 15.00 euros, 130 p.)
ISBN : 978-2-343-07436-8, ISBN EBOOK : 978-2-336-39812-9

GABELOUS ET CONTREBANDIERS
Histoire des fermiers généraux de Dijon (1760-1780)
Evrard Sébastien - Préface de Marc Fradet
En exhumant un registre du personnel de la direction des fermes de Dijon, l'auteur retrace, entre 1760 et 1780, la vie méconnue de centaines d'agents au service du doit et de l'impôt. Ces derniers servaient un système protecteur (la retraite fait son apparition dès 1768), parfois très rémunérateur, mais qui s'avère aussi, sous certains aspects, une machine à broyer les hommes : le régime des sanctions que met en place la Ferme est d'une efficacité redoutable. En définitive, la Ferme présente un aspect mitigé.
(Coll. Mémoires des Douanes, 28.50 euros, 278 p.)
ISBN : 978-2-343-06683-7, ISBN EBOOK : 978-2-336-39845-7

DICTIONNAIRE OHADA
(3e édition)
Bitsamana Hilarion Alain
Ce dictionnaire spécial du droit des affaires OHADA propose une définition claire et précise, avec tous les compléments nécessaires, des principaux termes utilisés tous les jours se rapportant à l'OHADA. Un ouvrage de référence permettant de décoder l'OHADA, accessible à toute personne s'intéressant au monde des affaires en Afrique comme à l'étranger.
(39.00 euros, 398 p.)
ISBN : 978-2-343-07656-0, ISBN EBOOK : 978-2-336-39786-3

LA DÉJUDICIARISATION ET LES PROCÉDURES NON CONTENTIEUSES EN AFRIQUE
Amboulou Hygin Didace
La déjudiciarisation comprend l'ensemble des mécanismes de gestion des différends en rationalisant les moyens matériels et humains de la justice, afin de pallier les déficiences du système judiciaire et de limiter les surcharges des juridictions. Les institutions de nombreux pays sont analysées et les déjudiciarisations en droit public et en droit privé sont abordées.
(Coll. Études africaines, 17.50 euros, 156 p.)
ISBN : 978-2-343-06928-9, ISBN EBOOK : 978-2-336-39805-1

COMMENT RENFORCER L'INDÉPENDANCE DE LA MAGISTRATURE AU SÉNÉGAL ?
Ngom Babacar
Préface de Amadou Mahtar Mbow
L'ouvrage présente dans une première partie les garanties légales d'indépendance de la justice, notamment la règle de la séparation des pouvoirs, le principe de la soumission des juges à l'autorité de la loi et celui de l'inamovibilité du magistrat du siège. Après une analyse critique de ces dispositions, l'auteur formule des propositions de renforcement de l'indépendance de la magistrature.
(13.50 euros, 124 p.)
ISBN : 978-2-343-05158-1, ISBN EBOOK : 978-2-336-39837-2

LE DROIT PÉNAL DES AFFAIRES AU CAMEROUN
Djila Kouayi Kemajou Rose
Préface de Victor-Emmanuel Bokalli
Dans le domaine des affaires, la liberté d'entreprendre et d'investir comporte de nombreux risques, au rang desquels le risque pénal. La délinquance en col blanc n'étant plus réservée aux grandes sociétés commerciales, les moyens de lutte et de sécurisation des investisseurs nécessitent un droit pénal des affaires dont l'objectif est la recherche d'une éthique dans ce domaine.
(Coll. Études africaines, 35.50 euros, 350 p.)
ISBN : 978-2-343-07840-3, ISBN EBOOK : 978-2-336-39777-1

50 ANS DE MARIAGE
Réflexions d'un notaire sur l'évolution du couple ces cinquante dernières années
Dauptain Pierre
De la pilule contraceptive jusqu'au mariage pour tous, l'auteur nous propose une réflexion sur les lois qui ont accompagné l'évolution du couple au cours des cinquante dernières années. Il analyse cette évolution pour aborder les problématiques juridiques et morales qui font tant débat de nos jours. Il s'appuie sur des travaux de juristes ou de sociologues, des articles de presse, mais aussi sur les chansons et les films qui ont marqué ces années et qui témoignent de façon si éclairante des changements de mentalités.
(Éditions Pepper, 16.50 euros, 148 p.)
ISBN : 978-2-343-07677-5, ISBN EBOOK : 978-2-336-39690-3

MÉTHODOLOGIE ET ASPECTS FORMELS DE LA RECHERCHE
Petit manuel à l'usage des juristes
Marain Gaëtan
L'ouvrage propose un véritable apprentissage du formalisme qui doit permettre aux étudiants et aux professionnels confrontés à la rédaction d'une thèse ou d'un mémoire juridique d'aborder ce travail avec sérénité. L'auteur donne une méthode de recherche pour définir le sujet, trouver et compulser les références utiles, échafauder un plan. Il aborde également les thèmes des citations d'auteur, notes de bas de page, mise en page. Il traite enfin du travail de relecture et de l'épreuve de soutenance.
(19.00 euros, 178 p.)
ISBN : 978-2-343-07638-6, ISBN EBOOK : 978-2-336-39556-2

RISQUES, ACCIDENTS ET CATASTROPHES
Liber amicorum
En l'honneur de Madame le professeur Marie-France Steinlé-Feuerbach
Sous la direction Hervé Arbousset, Caroline Lacroix et Benoît Steinmetz
L'étude et l'analyse des risques sont au cœur des réflexions du Professeur Steinlé-Feuerbach. Ses nombreux écrits de doctrine sur la thématique des accidents et des catastrophes ont amené à ce que ses collègues et amis lui dédient cet ouvrage. Ces mélanges donnent une vue d'ensemble d'une matière devenue une véritable discipline transcendant le clivage droit public-droit privé.
(Coll. Sciences criminelles, 34.00 euros, 334 p.)
ISBN : 978-2-343-07169-5, ISBN EBOOK : 978-2-336-39677-4

ÉTAT, COLLECTIVITÉS TERRITORIALES ET DROITS SOCIAUX
Étude du droit comparé
Sous la direction d'Olivier Lecucq
Comment, selon leur organisation territoriale respective, La France, l'Espagne et l'Italie œuvrent à la satisfaction des droits sociaux. Quels sont les rôles de l'État en ce domaine ? Quelles sont les actions qui en découlent et comment se coordonnent-elles ? Quelles en sont les implications en termes d'égalité des citoyens et des territoires ? L'ouvrage tente de répondre à ces questions en interpellant la réalisation de l'État social dans un contexte de crise, de réduction des déficits et de maîtrise des dépenses.
(Coll. Bibliothèques de droit, 22.50 euros, 221 p.)
ISBN : 978-2-343-07585-3, ISBN EBOOK : 978-2-336-39683-5

LE PRINCIPE DE PRÉCAUTION
Au carrefour de la philosophie, du droit et des sciences
Calderaro Norbert
La notion de principe de précaution, qui donne lieu à beaucoup de controverses, nécessite de la part d'un juriste une analyse objective pour écarter ce qu'elle n'est pas et définir son contenu véritable. Après un aperçu des sources philosophiques, l'auteur réalise une synthèse du principe de précaution en droit international, européen, en droit comparé et en droit interne. Il intègre notamment les tout derniers développements de la jurisprudence du Conseil d'État.
(18.50 euros, 180 p.)
ISBN : 978-2-343-05457-5, ISBN EBOOK : 978-2-336-39452-7

LES COLLECTIVITÉS TERRITORIALES ET LA SPÉCULATION
Goasdoué Mélissa - Avant-propos de Michel Verpeaux
Préface de Julien Martin
L'ancien dispositif empêchant la conclusion d'opérations financières spéculatives par les collectivités locales ayant échoué, un nouveau dispositif fonctionnant au cas par cas a été mis en place. Après une étude des imperfections de la notion de spéculation puis des liens unissant ces imperfections à l'échec du précédent dispositif dans la protection des collectivités contre les risques spéculatifs, le présent ouvrage s'attache à démontrer comment et dans quelle mesure cette protection est désormais rendue possible.
(Coll. Droit des collectivités territoriales, série Travaux, 15.00 euros, 140 p.)
ISBN : 978-2-343-07619-5, ISBN EBOOK : 978-2-336-39520-3

LE DROIT DE LA GUERRE
Traité sur l'emploi de la force armée en droit international (3 volumes)
Cumin David
Aussi ancien que la guerre et que le droit international dont il constitue le cœur historique, le droit de la guerre existe. Croisant droit et polémologie, portant sur les conflits armés internationaux et internes, ce traité expose, explique et reconstruit l'ensemble du droit international contemporain relatif à l'emploi de la force armée - auteurs et acteurs de la belligérance, ses buts, moyens, théâtres, régimes - et propose une analyse critique de la responsabilité réparatrice et punitive.
Volume 1 (Coll. Droit comparé, 46.00 euros, 458 p.)
ISBN : 978-2-343-06498-7, ISBN EBOOK : 978-2-336-39588-3
Volume 2 (Coll. Droit comparé, 60.00 euros, 760 p.)
ISBN : 978-2-343-07707-9, ISBN EBOOK : 978-2-336-39589-0
Volume 3 (Coll. Droit comparé, 48.00 euros, 468 p.)
ISBN : 978-2-343-07708-6, ISBN EBOOK : 978-2-336-39590-6

LA RESPONSABILITÉ DE PROTÉGER
Nouvelle approche du droit international
Gandou D'Isseret Crépin Gyscard
Le droit d'ingérence humanitaire se comprend comme une éthique de détresse, une obligation de protéger les personnes en danger de mort. La responsabilité de protéger traduit en acte la nécessité impérative de prendre soin de l'homme, ou de la collectivité humaine en général, quand les conditions de son existence connaissent une détérioration significative ou quand elles sont sur le point de le devenir.
(Coll. Harmattan Congo, 16.50 euros, 152 p.)
ISBN : 978-2-343-06724-7, ISBN EBOOK : 978-2-336-39575-3

L'HARMATTAN ITALIA
Via Degli Artisti 15; 10124 Torino
harmattan.italia@gmail.com

L'HARMATTAN HONGRIE
Könyvesbolt ; Kossuth L. u. 14-16
1053 Budapest

L'HARMATTAN KINSHASA
185, avenue Nyangwe
Commune de Lingwala
Kinshasa, R.D. Congo
(00243) 998697603 ou (00243) 999229662

L'HARMATTAN CONGO
67, av. E. P. Lumumba
Bât. – Congo Pharmacie (Bib. Nat.)
BP2874 Brazzaville
harmattan.congo@yahoo.fr

L'HARMATTAN GUINÉE
Almamya Rue KA 028, en face
du restaurant Le Cèdre
OKB agency BP 3470 Conakry
(00224) 657 20 85 08 / 664 28 91 96
harmattanguinee@yahoo.fr

L'HARMATTAN MALI
Rue 73, Porte 536, Niamakoro,
Cité Unicef, Bamako
Tél. 00 (223) 20205724 / +(223) 76378082
poudiougopaul@yahoo.fr
pp.harmattan@gmail.com

L'HARMATTAN CAMEROUN
BP 11486
Face à la SNI, immeuble Don Bosco
Yaoundé
(00237) 99 76 61 66
harmattancam@yahoo.fr

L'HARMATTAN CÔTE D'IVOIRE
Résidence Karl / cité des arts
Abidjan-Cocody 03 BP 1588 Abidjan 03
(00225) 05 77 87 31
etien_nda@yahoo.fr

L'HARMATTAN BURKINA
Penou Achille Some
Ouagadougou
(+226) 70 26 88 27

L'HARMATTAN SÉNÉGAL
10 VDN en face Mermoz, après le pont de Fann
BP 45034 Dakar Fann
33 825 98 58 / 33 860 9858
senharmattan@gmail.com / senlibraire@gmail.com
www.harmattansenegal.com

L'HARMATTAN BÉNIN
ISOR-BENIN
01 BP 359 COTONOU-RP
Quartier Gbèdjromèdè,
Rue Agbélenco, Lot 1247 I
Tél : 00 229 21 32 53 79
christian_dablaka123@yahoo.fr

Achevé d'imprimer par Corlet Numérique - 14110 Condé-sur-Noireau
N° d'Imprimeur : 133081 - Dépôt légal : octobre 2016 - *Imprimé en France*

www.ingramcontent.com/pod-product-compliance
Lightning Source LLC
LaVergne TN
LVHW011439061026
849535LV00004BA/868